EZRA POUND AND *GLOBE* MAGAZINE

Modernist Archives Series

Series Editors: Matthew Feldman (Teesside University, UK) and Erik Tonning (University of Bergen, Norway)

From letters, journals, and notebooks to unpublished or out of print works, unfamiliar but important writings in translation and forgotten articles, Bloomsbury's *Modernist Archives* series makes available to researchers at all levels historical archival material that can reconfigure received views of Modernist literature and culture.

Annotated throughout and supported by extensive contextual essays by leading scholars, the *Modernist Archives* series is an essential resource for anyone with a serious interest in 20th Century Literature and Culture.

Forthcoming titles

W.B. Yeats's Robartes-Aherne Writings
Wayne K. Chapman

The Correspondence of Ezra Pound and the Frobenius Institute, 1930–1959
Edited by Ronald Bush and Erik Tonning

Global Modernists on Modernism
Edited by Alys Moody and Stephen J. Ross

EZRA POUND AND *GLOBE* MAGAZINE: THE COMPLETE CORRESPONDENCE

Edited by Michael Thomas Davis and Cameron McWhirter

BLOOMSBURY ACADEMIC
LONDON • NEW YORK • OXFORD • NEW DELHI • SYDNEY

BLOOMSBURY ACADEMIC
Bloomsbury Publishing Plc
50 Bedford Square, London, WC1B 3DP, UK
1385 Broadway, New York, NY 10018, USA
29 Earlsfort Terrace, Dublin 2, Ireland

BLOOMSBURY, BLOOMSBURY ACADEMIC and the Diana logo
are trademarks of Bloomsbury Publishing Plc

First published in 2016
This paperback edition published in 2021

A catalogue record for this book is available from the British Library.

A catalog record for this book is available from the Library of Congress.

ISBN: HB: 978-1-4725-8959-0
PB: 978-1-3502-7347-4
ePDF: 978-1-4725-8961-3
eBook: 978-1-4725-8960-6

Series: Modernist Archives

To find out more about our authors and books visit
www.bloomsbury.com and sign up for our newsletters.

In Memory of James Taylor Dunn and Omar Shakespear Pound

CONTENTS

EDITORIAL PREFACE TO MODERNIST ARCHIVES

Archival excavation and thick contextualization is becoming increasingly central to scholarship on literary Modernism. Over the past generation the dissemination and increased accessibility of previously unpublished or little-known documents and texts has led to paradigm shifting scholarly interventions on a range of individual authors (Pound, Eliot, Joyce, Beckett, Woolf, *inter alia*), neglected topics (the occult, "primitivism", fascism, eugenics, modernist publishing, the writing process), and critical methodologies (genetic criticism, intertextuality, book and source history). This trend will only increase as large-scale digitization of various archives gathers pace, and existing copyright restrictions gradually lapse. *Modernist Archives* is a new book series that will channel, extend, and interrogate this trend by publishing hitherto unavailable or neglected primary materials for a wider readership. Each volume also provides supporting, contextualizing work by scholars, alongside a critical apparatus of notes and references.

The impetus for this new series emerges from the editors' well-established series *Historicizing Modernism*. The focus there is analytical, and here reproductive. The monographs and edited collections in that series have revealed the extent to which contemporary scholars are increasingly turning toward archival and/or unpublished materials in order to reconfigure academic understandings of Modernism, their working contexts, and broader historical rootedness, as well as authorial methodologies. Intrinsic to the diverse range of cutting-edge projects this successful series has presented is a shared interpretative approach: the use of an empirical methodology, engaging explicitly with unpublished materials and contextualizing these materials in relation to published writings and subsequent criticism vis-à-vis a given Modernist author or topic.

Understanding and defining "primary sources" as a broad category that includes letters, diaries, notes, drafts, marginalia, or other archival deposits of a contextualizing nature, the 'Modernist Archives' series will produce volumes that not only unearth significant unpublished materials and provide fresh scholarship on them, but also develop cutting-edge editorial presentation-techniques that preserve as much information as possible in an economical and accessible way. Also worth noting is the potential in moving beyond single-author studies to the dissemination of archives surrounding the relations of literary Modernism to other media (radio, television), or important cultural events or debates. The series thus seeks to be an enabling force within Modernist scholarship, encouraging work that might otherwise not easily find a home.

It is becoming ever more difficult to read this extraordinary period of literary experimentation in isolation from contextualizing archival materials, sometimes dubbed the "grey canon" of Modernist writing. The difficulty, we suggest, is something like a loss of innocence: once obviously relevant materials are actually accessible, they cannot be ignored. They may challenge received ideas about the limits or definition of "Modernism"; they may upend theoretical frameworks, or encourage fresh theoretical reflection; they may require new methodologies; they may textualize the self, or revise the very notion of "authorship"; they may require types of knowledge that we never knew we needed – but *there they are. Modernist Archives* in no way seeks to prejudice the results or approaches that scholars in this area will produce in the exciting times ahead for this burgeoning field. By commissioning a wide range of innovative and challenging editions, this series aims to once again "make strange" and "make new" our fundamental ideas about Modernism.

ACKNOWLEDGMENTS

This book took a long time to reach publication and it would not have done so without the unflagging help of many people. First and foremost are the late Omar Pound and the late James Dunn, who for years actively promoted and aided this project. Both men lived Pound's maxim sent in a letter to Dunn on February 13, 1938: "waaal itza gt/life if you don't weaken." They brought energy, enthusiasm, and expertise to this project. The *Globe* letters to Pound appear with the permission of the late James Taylor Dunn. An earlier version of this introduction appeared in EZRA POUND AND EDUCATION © 2012 National Poetry Foundation, reprinted with permission.

Others also provided help and support, including Elizabeth Pound, the late Maria Bach-Dunn, three librarians at Hamilton College: Frank Lorenz, Ralph Stenstrom, and Randall Ericson, Patricia Willis, curator (emerita) of the Yale Collection of American Literature at Yale University's Beinecke Rare Book and Manuscript Library, and librarians at Princeton University and the New York Public Library. Many thanks to Jean-Michel Rabaté and Ronald Bush for bringing this project to the attention of Bloomsbury Academic as well as to Declan Spring at New Directions, agent for the estate of Ezra Pound, for his support. We are grateful to Erik Tonning and Matthew Feldman, editors of Bloomsbury Academic's *Modernist Archives* series, for accepting this book. Much gratitude is due for the patience and support of Bloomsbury publisher David Avital and editorial assistant Mark Richardson. Special thanks to Robert E. Spoo for his input.

And thanks to Ramsay McWhirter for supporting her husband for years on this project. The knotty subject of Ezra Pound got the two strangers talking at a summer party in a stuffy Chicago apartment many years ago. Her husband and their progeny, Blythe and Finn, are forever grateful to the poet as a result.

EDITORIAL NOTE

Pound's letters to James Taylor Dunn, as well as the extant manuscripts of his contributions to *Globe*, are in the Special Collections and Archives at the Burke Library, Hamilton College. The letters of James Taylor Dunn to Ezra Pound as well as partial carbons of Pound's letters to Dunn are in the Ezra Pound Papers (YCAL MSS 43) in the Yale Collection of American Literature, housed in the Beinecke Rare Book and Manuscript Library at Yale University.

Pound's letters present a bit of a challenge to the editor. His idiocentric style of letter writing spreads the text of his letters over the pages, spacing and phrasing as if he were "scoring" them. Likewise, his spellings and punctuation can be eccentric, but in many cases deliberate and meant to carry his meaning.

Therefore, in this edition the spacing of Pound's text on the page has been retained wherever possible. Pound's idiosyncratic spellings, capitalizations, punctuation and other symbols have been retained in our transcriptions. Pound often gave non-standard or incorrect spellings for personal names and places. These have been retained in the letters and unpublished contributions, but have been corrected in the notes to the letters and contributions as well as in the Biographical Appendix. Names in bold in the notes to the letters appear as entries in the Biographical Appendix.

Parenthesis ( ) in the letters and unpublished contributions to *Globe* are Pound's. Editorial insertions in the text are indicated by square brackets [ ]. Pound's handwritten additions to the typewritten text are indicated by diamond brackets < >. Pound's strikeouts are indicated with a line through the deleted word: ~~word~~. Pound also strikes out words by typing over them with a repeated capital letter and these have been retained. Pound's underlining has been represented as such: Peter Fanning; tomb of Sallustio Bandini.

Pound's letters to *Globe* are presented in chronological order sequenced with those that he received from Dunn and the staff of *Globe*. For reference each of Pound's letters are designated **EP1**, **EP2**, etc. Likewise James Taylor Dunn's are **JD1**, **JD2**, etc. There are a few letters included from other *Globe* staff and they are also designated in this fashion: the initials of their name along with a number, both in bold, indicating the order in which the letter appears in the correspondence according to the correspondent. These letter designations are used in the Introduction, Afterword, notes and Biographical Appendix to reference a specific letter in the correspondence.

Pound's published contributions to *Globe* are reproduced as they appeared in publication. The unpublished contributions have been edited along the same lines as described for the letters above. Where published and unpublished materials overlap, notes to the text have been provided cross-referencing the overlap between published and unpublished text.

ABBREVIATIONS

HWL	handwritten letter
HWC	handwritten postcard
TSL	typed signed letter
TSC	typed signed postcard
PMK	postmark
P	plain stock paper
YCAL	Yale Collection of American Literature, Beinecke Rare Book and Manuscript Library, Yale University. Letters designated in this manner are in The Ezra Pound Papers (YCAL MSS 43) unless otherwise indicated.
BL	Burke Library, Hamilton College, Special Collections and Archives
GS	*Globe* stationery
TAX	Pound's stationery with Gaudier-Brzeska profile drawing on right-hand side and motto: "Tax is not a share[.] A nation need not and should not pay rent for its credit."
GBS	Pound's stationery with Gaudier-Brzeska profile drawing in the center at the top of the page.

Introduction

THE CONTEXT AND SIGNIFICANCE OF THE CORRESPONDENCE

On June 16, 1936, James Taylor Dunn, a recent alumnus of Hamilton College in upstate New York, wrote to a fellow alumnus, the well-known poet and critic Ezra Pound. Dunn invited him to contribute to a new journal Dunn and his brothers were creating. It was a travel magazine to be named *Globe: The International Magazine* and it was, as its subtitle would later read, an "Intimate Journal of Travel, Romance, Adventure and World Interest." Sent from Minnesota, where *Globe* was to be published, Dunn's letter outlined what they wanted from Pound:

> We are under the impression that *Globe* articles should have: (1) not more than 2,000 words, 1,000 preferred, meaning a firm practice of concision; (2) intimacy and lightness of touch, and (3) truth, authenticity and credulity.
>
> As for subject, it is unrestricted—provided only that your article show relation between people and place. In other words, setting (background) should impress as much local color as possible on the characters. **(JD1)**

After some initial haggling, Pound agreed to act as "European correspondent," providing *Globe* with a "letter" from Europe for each issue as well as other pieces. A flood of letters followed.

THE CONTEXT OF THE EXCHANGE WITHIN POUND'S CAREER

When James Dunn began his correspondence with Pound, the poet was fifty years old and had been living in Rapallo, Italy, for the previous eleven years. Pound was in a period that would prove to be the most controversial and complex of his career, a period that would determine the bizarre course of the rest of his life. To appreciate the significance of Pound's correspondence with *Globe*, it is necessary to examine where Pound's career was in the mid-1930s, how it got there, and what projects, concerns, and contacts Pound had when he made his mark on *Globe*.

Looking at Pound's career in the 1930s, an obvious question presents itself to the general reader, or even to the Pound scholar: Why, at this advanced point in his career, did Pound invest so much energy and effort in helping to launch a fledgling travel magazine edited by a group of young men in their twenties in the heart of the American Midwest? His efforts on the part of *Globe* were not very different from those on the part of literary journals like *The Little Review* or *The Dial*. *Globe* made no pretense to publishing literature, and James Dunn also made it clear from the outset that politics as such would not be a welcome subject in the magazine. What was the attraction to Pound?

The answer to that question is not simple. It lies in Pound's interests and activities during the first half of the 1930s and in the reception of his work during this period within literary and publishing circles in America—particularly in New York. The Dunn/Pound correspondence itself helps to cast light upon Pound's increasingly strained relations with the American literary scene throughout the decade.

THE ITALIAN VENUE—FAREWELL TO LONDON AND PARIS

The reasons for Pound's presence in Italy in the 1930s go back to his childhood, student years, and the early days of his expatriate life. While at the University of Pennsylvania and later at Hamilton College in upstate New York, Pound developed a lifelong interest in Romance languages and literature. He took a deep interest in Renaissance Spanish poetry and drama, and developed a fascination with the medieval Provençal troubadour poetry. This interest in Provençal reinforced and deepened Pound's appreciation of Dante, a poet who was steeped in this same southern European tradition. In fact, Dante took the troubadour poet Arnaut Daniel as his superior in the art. Pound also was drawn to the work of Dante's contemporary and friend Guido Cavalcanti. Pound would study Cavalcanti's work over the next few decades and translate the bulk of his poetry, and would use this translation work as the basis for the libretto of his second opera, *Cavalcanti* (1933). Pound's interest in both classical and Renaissance Latin poetry led him to consider Italy as essential to his mix of poetic and aesthetic traditions. Later, while in the thick of literary London in 1914, Pound came into contact with F. T. Marinetti, a central figure in the Italian Futurist movement, whom Pound saw as both rival and counterpart to his own London Vorticist circle. During the early 1920s, Pound's interest in Italian history and the contemporary Italian scene would deepen during archival work he pursued in various Italian cities to gather material for his Malatesta Cantos (Cantos VIII–XI).

Pound's earliest trip to Italy was in 1898, at the age of twelve, in the company of his Aunt Frank. After he left America in 1908 to take up residence in London, Pound frequently visited Italy from London and later, from Paris. He favored the Hotel Eden in the village of Sirmione, located on Lake Garda in the north, an area associated with the Roman poet Catullus. In 1924, after almost four years in Paris, Pound and his wife Dorothy looked for a home in Italy, ultimately deciding on the town of Rapallo. Except for a brief trip back to the United States in 1939, Pound stayed in Italy until November 1945, when he was flown back to the US to face an indictment for treason.

At the time Dunn contacted him in the mid-1930s, Pound had not visited the United States since 1910. He kept in touch with American literary and publishing circles through other expatriates showing up in London or Paris for various periods of time. Pound also served over almost two decades as foreign correspondent/editor for and/or contributor to the period's "little magazines," including *Poetry* (1912–present, but Pound most active 1912–17), *The Little Review* (1914–29, with Pound most active from 1917–19; 1921–3), and *The Dial* (1920–9, with Pound most active from 1920–6) as well as many lesser-known and ephemeral publications based in America.

Social and economic factors changed the ecology of publishing in the United States and the character of its literary elites after World War I until the onset of the Great Depression in 1929. Now on the western coast of northern Italy, and out of the range of the diminishing expatriate circles in London and Paris, the middle-aged poet found himself more and more out of touch with contemporary American culture. Literary circles in the United States, especially those in New York City, had begun to evolve far beyond what he had experienced briefly during the first decade of the century. It is telling that one of the first things that Pound requested from Dunn was a packet of American magazines that the editor considered diagnostic of the times and competition for *Globe*. When they arrived Pound responded:

> Thanks for the nasty magazines just come. …
>
> There is NO use in Minimizing the force of competition from the very able sons of bloody bitches collected in the three mags/ you have sent
>
> to buck this kind of crap; and NOT be able to pay high rates is no cinch. **(EP8)**

Pound had long relied upon such news and samples from the United States to keep him abreast of developments. His need now had increased substantially. A few years before, Gorham Munson, a literary editor with *The New York*

Sun and founder of the Social Credit magazine *The New Democracy*, wrote at least two extensive letters to Pound detailing the state of literary New York from its editors and critics to its publishing houses. Munson, like Dunn, also sent magazines to Pound.[1]

By the 1930s, the age of the peripatetic "little magazine" projecting the avant-garde upon an international stage was past. Never very economically viable, and often backed solely by private money from wealthy patrons, these periodicals were victims of the grim economic realities of the Depression era. Magazines that did survive, such as *Vanity Fair* (established 1914), *Vogue* (established 1892, acquired by *Vanity Fair* in 1936), *The New Republic* (established 1914), *The American Mercury* (1924–50), the *New Yorker* (established 1925), or later *Esquire* (established 1933), either had a long-established commercial (advertising) base and large subscription or were quick to develop such an economic anchor. Pound still harkened back to those days, despite his own failed attempt at publishing a "little magazine," *The Exile* (it ran only four issues during 1927 and 1928). In a letter to Munson, Pound lamented:

> The sales resistance, or printing resistance to any CONTEMPORARY mental activity has again reached a crisis, at no time since 1917 when just before the Little Review relieved the constriction, permitting a [*sic*] the prom[p]t and regular publication of "current prose writings of Joyce, Wyndham Lewis, Eliot and myself", have I felt so great a degree of annoyance at the inane obstructionism of contemporary writing.
>
> This is in no way a detraction from the excellent work of special publications, such as Blast,[2] and New Democracy[3], neither of these papers can attend to their own work and to the work which [I] indicate.
>
> The Little Review printed Cantleman, the beginning of Ulysses and Fenollosa's Essay on the ideograph[4].
>
> There is NO American publication now capable of concentrating W. C. Williams invaluable records of contemporary life as lived under the course of our filthy and degrading economic system,[5] along with Frobenius,[6] Cocteau[7], and myself ...
>
> (EP to Gorham Munson, late 1935–early 1936, but possibly earlier '30s [uncorrected carbon, YCAL])

While Pound was attempting to recreate the past, other authors of his generation and circles were adapting to the new demands of the publishing world, and thereby gaining legitimacy, authority, and fame that Pound would be denied.

T. S. Eliot, whose earliest poetry Pound placed in *Poetry* and whose first book *Prufrock and Other Observations* was subsidized by Dorothy Pound in 1917, by the mid-1930s was a strong presence in the Anglo-American literary establishment. He had joined the firm of Faber & Gwyer, later Faber & Faber, in 1925, and by the 1930s was an influential editor bringing a stable of prominent poets to the firm. In 1922, Eliot founded *The Criterion*, which he edited for most of the era between the world wars. Eliot established his journal with the financial support of an Lady Rothermere. During the 1930s *The Criterion* was a major literary arbiter on the international scene and was taken over by Faber & Faber. Eliot's own critical prose and poetry was published by Faber & Faber.

James Joyce's *Ulysses*, after years of censorship and confiscation, had found a home with the prestigious American publishing firm of Random House. Bennett Cerf at Random may have won the censorship issue in court in 1933, but it was Pound who had first placed Joyce's masterwork in *The Little Review* in 1918. He also had convinced *The Egoist* to serialize *Portrait of the Artist as a Young Man* in 1914.

Gertrude Stein, rarely published in the United States during her three-decade career despite her international reputation, had at last produced an American bestseller in 1933: *The Autobiography of Alice B. Toklas*. In 1934–5, on the strength of Stein's success, Gertrude and Alice undertook a successful and well-publicized lecture tour of the United States that not only confirmed their celebrity status, but also secured Stein publishing venues with major American publishing houses like Harcourt Brace and Random House.

Ernest Hemingway's first book, *in our time*, was published in 1924 under Pound's editorship by William Bird's small Three Mountains Press in Paris. But by the 1930s, Hemingway was an established novelist with Scribners as his publisher. He had considerable celebrity cachet, appearing in venues such as *Esquire* and *Life* magazine both as a subject and as an author of fiction and journalism. Pound had not achieved such fame. His past notoriety was such that it earned him mention in many literary venues, such as in Janet Flanner's "Paris Letter" for the *New Yorker,* but he was far from the active player he once was.

Some of his old friends tried to help. It appears to have been Hemingway who suggested to the editor of *Esquire*, Arnold Gingrich, to encourage Pound to contribute to that magazine. Ford Madox Ford, always nomadic and down at heel, was ensconced as an academic in the United States. He tried to persuade Pound to come back to America and join him in a professorship at Mount Olivet College in Michigan. Despite fundamental disagreements with T. S. Eliot on religious, political, and literary matters, Eliot provided Pound with a consistent publishing venue in London at Faber & Faber. Though Boni and Liveright published Pound in the 1920s, for most of the 1930s he did not have a consistent publisher in the United States. Farrar and Rinehart picked up major work—especially sections of *The Cantos*—initially published by Faber & Faber in England. This situation would be rectified only when James Laughlin

IV, a young Harvard graduate inspired by Pound during visits to Rapallo in the mid-1930s, established his publishing house, New Directions, in 1938. From then on New Directions would serve as Pound's publisher in America.

POUND'S MULTI-FACETED INTERESTS AND URGENT CONCERNS DURING THE 1930S

Though it is common to characterize the 1930s as a period in which Pound turned from poetry and aesthetics to propaganda, politics, and economics (a view shared by even a number of his contemporaries), this position often is overstated. Scholars of the American literary scene in the United States during the 1930s have characterized it as a decade in which many American writers became politically "committed" either to the left or the right. The notion that Pound's mid-life career involved a turn from poetry assumes a strict division between aesthetics and politics—a division that Pound, along with many other artists in the 1930s, would not have accepted. It also ignores the fact that since the beginning of the 1920s, Pound concentrated his poetic powers on *The Cantos*. In a letter to Delmore Schwartz in 1938, Pound responded vigorously to the idea that poetry now no longer concerned him:

> ...When the HELL or in what context did I ever say I had given up or was giving UP literature for economics?
>
> I know peePull SAID I had given up poesy fer muZIK etc/but WHEN? where? in what time or space did either of these giving's occur?
>
> (EP to Delmore Schwartz, March 20, 1938 [YCAL])

The poetry, for Pound, played a double function, both literary and pedagogical. As he wrote at a slightly earlier time in the decade:

> Cantos also base for econ/hist/, as the Kublai,[8] a good deal is NOT in pros[e] hists/of econ/ as e:g: Jeff Mark's Modern Idolatry.[9] And note again that in lecturing at the Universita Bocconi,[10] I used pages or passages as the briefest and cleanest exposition of data RE/money or banking.
>
> Also E/P/ not interested (1935) in verse of writers who are too "dumb" to peecive [*sic*] economic motivations, and distortions of LIFE due to econ/ pressure.
>
> (this follows on from remarks printed by E/P/ as early as 1910).[11]
>
> (EP to Gorham Munson, February 18, 1935 [YCAL])

Pound opened the decade of the 1930s with the publication of *A Draft of XXX Cantos* by Nancy Cunard's Hours Press (1930), subsequently published in America by Farrar & Rinehart, and Faber & Faber in England in 1933.

Throughout these years, Pound researched, composed, and published three other sections of *The Cantos*: *Eleven New Cantos: XXXI-XLI* ("Jefferson: Nuevo Mundo", 1934/5), *The Fifth Decad of Cantos* (Siena and the so-called "Leopoldine Reforms", 1937), and *Cantos LII-LXXI* (Chinese history—John Adams, 1940). Some of the most memorable poetry of *The Cantos* was written during this period: Canto XXX ("A Lady asks me ..."), Canto XLV (the "Usura" Canto), and Canto XLIX (the so-called "Seven Lakes Canto").

The character of this poetic output clearly indicates the political and economic interests that Pound had at the time, and how fused they had become with his aesthetics. *Eleven New Cantos: XXXI-XLI* opens with Thomas Jefferson writing to George Washington prefaced with a quotation from the Vulgate of Ecclesiastes: *Tempus loquendi,/Tempus tacendi*. That is, "A time to speak, a time to hold one's peace." The final Canto in the series opens with Mussolini commenting to Pound on his poetry during his one brief meeting with the dictator on January 30, 1933: "'Ma questo,'/ said the Boss, 'e divertente.'/ catching the point before the aesthetes had got there; ...'. (Canto 41)" Somehow Pound took this comment on a *A Draft of XXX Cantos* sent to Il Duce—which translates roughly as, "But this is entertaining"—as a profound insight into his work. It was a strained interpretation at best. Nevertheless, the opening passages of Cantos XXXI and XLI juxtapose the early American Republic and its founding fathers with the Italian fascist state and Mussolini. This forms a type of *inclusio*, an association that he further worked out in his book, *Jefferson and/or Mussolini* (1934).

As has been argued in recent scholarship, Pound's interest and eventual commitment to the Italian fascist movement probably developed during his work on the Malatesta Cantos in the early 1920s.[12] However, Pound's economic interests, which in the 1930s become entwined with his commitment to Italian fascism, are a much older concern. These can be traced back to his association with A. R. Orage and *The New Age* just before and during World War I in London.[13] Indeed, Pound himself wrote in 1949 in a preface to his *Selected Poems* that he in "... 1918 began investigation of the causes of war, to oppose same." Such an investigation turned upon a search for war's economic roots. During the course of his correspondence with Dunn these concerns not only took him into the American past and the Italian present, but into other historical directions as well.

As in the composition of the Malatesta Cantos in the early 1920s, in 1935–6 Pound incorporated historical materials into his poetry. These were housed in Siena at the Archivio di Stato, in the Palazzo Piccolomini, and related to the founding of the seventeenth-century Sienese bank Il Monte dei Paschi. This research formed the basis for the *The Fifth Decad of Cantos*, which Pound was finishing just as he began his correspondence with *Globe*. More importantly, after the publication of *The Fifth Decad of Cantos*, Pound again turned to

China. Pound's study of Chinese history, politics, and aesthetics went back to his years in London, but his interest in Confucian classics intensified in the mid- to late 1930s. During this decade Pound engaged in a concentrated study of the Chinese language and embarked upon translations of three other Confucian classics, *The Analects*, *Unwobbling Pivot*, and, in the 1940s after his arrest for treason, *The Odes*.

Another interest Pound pursued during this period was the work of the German anthropologist, ethnologist, and archaeologist Leo Frobenius. Frobenius' work dealt with the histories, cultural development, art, and folklore of a variety of indigenous African peoples. Pound must have learned of Frobenius and his work sometime around 1928, since this is when he begins his correspondence with Frobenius and his Forschungsinstitut für Kulturmorphologie at the Johann Wolfgang Goethe Universitat in Frankfurt am Main. Pound made Frobenius' personal acquaintance in 1929 when he traveled to Frankfurt to attend the premier of George Antheil's *Transatlantic*. In 1933, Pound found a partner in the promotion of Frobenius' work in a young American assistant at the Forschungsinstitut named Douglas C. Fox. Pound had Fox contribute material to *Globe* on the subject of African rock art and folklore. Pound also consulted Fox on lecturing and publishing opportunities in Germany, as well as on the subject of support for producing an English translation of Frobenius' multi-volume work, *Erlebte Erdteile*.

Pound also continued his intense involvement with music. This interest manifested itself on a number of fronts: composition, archival research, reviewing, and organizing concerts. In 1931, the BBC broadcast Pound's opera *Le Testament de Villon*, which had premiered in Paris in 1926. This successful broadcast motivated him to begin the composition in 1932 of another opera, *Calvacanti*. Between 1933 and 1939, Pound was the primary force in the organization of a series of concerts (the "Concerti Tigulliani") in Rapallo. Their innovative programs were designed to provide "specimens" of various music to draw out comparisons almost in the manner of a taxonomist or anatomist. The programs were rich and complex, including works by Mozart, Bach, Vivaldi, Franck, Bartók, Pergolesi, Stravinsky, Haydn, Debussy, Purcell, Chopin, Honegger, and Antheil. Pound undertook the publicity and review of these musical events, the reviews often appearing in the local paper *Il Mare*. Not only was Pound interested in his own scholarly work in the area of "old music," he also encouraged Olga Rudge in her archival studies of Vivaldi, which contributed significantly to Vivaldi's revival in the twentieth century. In relation to these scholarly activities, Pound was intensely interested in emerging photographic technologies that he recognized as being crucial to the preservation and reproduction of manuscript materials. In this he was an early advocate, urging the use of microfilm techniques to record and disseminate music manuscripts of the medieval and baroque periods for both scholarly and performance purposes. Like almost all of Pound's pursuits during the 1930s, these activities were directly connected to previous interests and activities going back over decades.

But Pound's alignment with fascist politics, his propaganda for monetary reform movements outside the mainstream, and his use of anti-Semitic rhetoric alienated him from the New York publishing world and emerging intellectual elites in the mid-1930s.

FACE OFF WITH A NEW LITERARY SCENE IN NEW YORK

The periodicals, publishing houses, and literary-cultural elites of New York City held enormous sway over both mainstream and avant-garde culture in the United States in the 1930s. Pound's involvement in the New York-based literary scene ten or fifteen years before that decade was extensive and in many ways crucial, but both he and the times had changed.

Pound had very little direct contact with American literary culture, or with American economic and political realities, despite his ruminations in *Patria Mia*. In fact, he formed his economic and political views in the context of Edwardian and Georgian London, not the contemporary American scene.

However, Pound's insinuation into the American literary scene before World War I took place on an apolitical basis. He was not simply a contributor to the "little magazines" springing up in the United States; he was a foreign editor/contact for any number of them, able to place European avant-garde writers in American-based journals. He was also able to keep expatriated American writers like himself before an American reading public in these same periodicals. Finally, in this unique position, he introduced American artists to a European audience. In this way Pound performed a crucial function, keeping readerships on two continents aware of writers and movements that might have otherwise escaped their notice. Such a role, at least during this period, transcended ideologies.

The situation among New York cultural elites was open, flexible, and varied enough for many individuals, including Pound, to have leading positions without a need to adhere to any clearly defined political ideology. Yet even during this early period, a type of political culture developed within the Greenwich Village avant-garde that would ultimately alienate Pound, as well as other modernists, from much of the American literary scene and publishing world in the 1930s.

Though Pound may have been only generally aware of and largely indifferent to it, there was a distinct leftist orientation within the avant-garde movements in New York. Yet in pre-World War I New York, leftist political associations among the literati were fluid and not directly involved in vetting the relevance of contemporary art or writing. These movements put forth general agendas for the arts, but created no rigid ideological "litmus test" for artistic production. Leftist movements of this period, despite their zeal, were not ideologically or institutionally well-defined or organized. While leftist politics and political movements entered the literary arena, they did not, as they would later, present themselves as the ideological arbiters of literary significance or merit. They existed along with emerging modernism often in a fragile symbiosis. The presence of the Industrial Workers of the World's "Big Bill" Haywood and leftist writer John Reed in Mabel Dodge's Fifth Avenue salon, Emma Goldman's friendship with *The Little Review*'s Margaret Anderson and Jane Heap, and the wide political and literary editorial net cast by Max Eastman and Floyd Dell in *The Masses*, are but a few of the most obvious examples of the tendency towards cross-fertilization of the radical left and emerging high modernist movements in America as well as in Europe. However, these political movements and their associations with the literary avant-garde, as well as the left's pre-World War I publications, would seem quaint and naive to the new left of the 1920s and 1930s.

World War I fundamentally changed how the radical left and radical right expressed themselves. It also changed how they related to the arts in general and the avant-garde in particular. In this new context these forces asserted themselves not as peripheral subversive movements on the edges of liberal democracies, monarchic or imperial states. The war propelled radical groups of both on the left and the right into new positions of national and international influence. The Bolshevik Revolution of 1917, the formation of the Soviet Union, the various thwarted revolutions in Germany, and Mussolini's seizure of power in 1922 in Italy all represented potent challenges to liberal democracy and already mortally wounded "old regimes."

To a new generation of intellectuals, "progressive" and "reactionary" forces became sharply defined and polarized in literary circles and in the world of the "little magazines." The Marxist-Communist left slowly shifted the orientation of contemporary literary journalism in New York circles in the 1920s. Though significant portions of the left cooperated with Moscow's leadership of the international communist movement in the late 1920s and early 1930s, the Marxist-Communist left was not ideologically monolithic, or always Soviet directed. The rise of Trotskyite factions, other anti-Stalinist groups, independent Marxist socialists, and other leftist thinkers led to the fragmentation of the left. Rancorous, violent disputes between various groups erupted. Yet, the fundamental Marxist-Communist inspiration of many of these movements is evident. A good example of this complex evolution is the archetypical Village journal *The Masses*.

Though Pound never contributed to *The Masses* or its subsequent incarnations, *The Liberator* or *The New Masses,* he was aware of these periodicals and carried on correspondence with their editorial staffs. In turn, *The Masses* and its successors were aware of Pound and his contribution to the promotion and development of modernism—though aesthetically, these periodicals may not have been in sympathy with the modernist movement. Their occasional interaction showed the contrasting positions they would take both in terms of aesthetics and politics.

The Masses was established in 1911 by a Dutch immigrant, Piet Vlag, but it was not until Max Eastman took over as editor in 1912 that it became well known as a radical socialist-labor journal with a strong commitment to promoting contemporary literature. *The Masses* saw social change in general as its mission, supporting such causes as women's rights and suffrage, birth control, labor organization and strikes, and various progressive movements. *The Masses* ceased publication in January of 1918 when editorial consensus, always a fragile thing at magazines, finally broke down over internal disputes concerning America's entrance into World War I. But before its disappearance, a group of seven editors and contributors involved with *The Masses* faced prosecution for publishing articles and cartoons with the alleged intent to obstruct the recruitment of soldiers and to subvert the draft.

Immediately after this unsuccessful prosecution of the defunct magazine's staff, Max Eastman and Floyd Dell, with the aid of Eastman's sister Crystal, founded the successor to *The Masses*, *The Liberator*. This new periodical did not have the broad "bohemian," rambunctious spirit of its *Masses* ancestor. The new periodical reflected a new sense of "seriousness," a "committed" left politics now informed by the Bolshevik Revolution and the Soviet experiment. Max Eastman would turn over the editorship of *The Liberator* to the African American poet Claude McKay and Mike Gold when he left the United States in 1922 to be a first-hand witness to the formation of the Soviet Union. Eastman would come to know both Lenin and Trotsky and become one of the first to question the legitimacy of Stalin's rise to power in 1924. But before he left for Europe, he decided that if *The Liberator* ran into financial or editorial problems it was to be turned over to the Worker's Party, which meant it would come under the direct control of the Communist Party. Even though *The Liberator* was one of the leading radical left journals in the United States with a circulation of about 60,000, editorial squabbles and financial problems eventually resulted in its transfer to the Worker's Party. It later merged with the *Labor Herald* and the *Soviet Russia Pictorial* to form the *Worker's Monthly*.

Mike Gold, born in 1893 as Itzok Isaac Granich, was out of an editorial position at *The Liberator* but had already by 1924 made his reputation as an aggressive, uncompromising exponent of communism in both politics and literature. Gold had been involved not only with *The Liberator*, but also with *The Masses*, which was sometimes characterized as his "schoolhouse." Converted to radical politics in 1914, he not only embraced communism, but also passionately believed in "proletarian literature." In fact, one of his frustrations with the direction of *The Liberator* was that, as it developed, less and less room was made for literature in its pages. So in 1928, when Gold came to exercise significant editorial influence over another of *The Masses*' spinoffs, *The New Masses*, he made sure that it provided space for proletarian literature.

Many today consider Gold's literary criticism and editorial judgments to be unsophisticated advocacy of politically charged "social realism." But Gold's work at the helm of leftist publications vividly illustrated the ideological barriers that crystalized in leftist literary circles after World War I. It was this editorial attitude that Pound would be forced to confront in the 1930s. Pound tangled with Gold in sporadic correspondence from 1930 to 1937. Though Pound was sufficiently impressed with Gold to recommend that James Dunn solicit a contribution from him for *Globe*, these few letters reveal these writers simply talking past each other—a situation to be repeated with others throughout this decade.

Gold's conception of the arts is well illustrated by his comments in "Towards Proletarian Art". In this essay he wrote:

> Masses are never pessimistic. Masses are never sterile. Masses are never far from the earth. Masses are never far from heaven. Masses go on—they are the eternal truth. Masses are simple, strong and sure. They are never lost long; they have a goal in each age ...

And further on:

> The Revolution, in its secular manifestations of strike, boycott, mass-meeting, imprisonment, sacrifice, agitation, martyrdom, organization, is thereby worthy of the religious devotion of the artist. If he records the humblest moment of that drama in poem, story or picture or symphony, he is realizing Life more profoundly than if he had concerned himself with some transient mood. The ocean is greater than the tiny streams that trickle down to be lost in its godhead.[14]

Pound, on the other hand, for once was more measured in his notions of art and socio-political activism. In 1928, he wrote in his short-lived journal *The Exile*:

> The young American writer (as apparent in mss. rejected by this office) suffers from a lack of perception. Concern with his own, often quite uninteresting interior, cd. be with advantage replaced by observation of his milieu, not merely its otiose factors but the members of it having organic social function...no undergrad need lack a subject matter while we still have

> congressmen. I strongly suggest our "fiction" writers occupy themselves with portraits of the *types* of humanity now permitted to govern America, congressmen, members of state assemblies, lobbyists, etc.
>
> As in Greek tragedy, the fate of kings was of more import than the fate of a slave, so now the type of critter whose stupidity or lucidity functions in the social organism to the benefit, but more usually the malefit of his milieu is better literary matter than affairs of a few tired bar-flies and bar flutter-boys.[15]

In stark contrast to Gold, Pound did not feel that art should involve the proletariat as either creator or subject. Rather he called for a literary focus on those who belong to the power elites ("... the fate of kings was of more import than the fate of a slave"). Stevedores, factory workers, and miners do not figure in Pound's aesthetic imagination, as much as, oddly enough, modern machinery and other forms of technology. Regardless of the merits of such a position, it would not be one that would endear Gold to Pound. The letters throw the tension between the two into high relief.

In his first extant letter Pound wrote to Gold:

> Do be historic. Fascism did not "preserve capitalism in a bad hour". Italy was bright and lively and had a revolution before any of the other limburger cheeses of Western Europe. You ought to know that. You ought to know that the workers seized the factories. That capitalism was bust. Just as the Russian govt. left the capital in a revolution years ago. The first Douma talked itself to death.
>
> The Italian workers seized the factories but they were to[o] damn "dumb", ignorant, stupid to know that credit has to be administered (whether by a communist committee or rampant individualist individual).
>
> Also get it into your head that one does not have to be a communist to be convinced that a four hour day; four days a week, for all male[s] between the ages of 20 and 40, is not only enough; but is all that is now possible for a social balanced order in a country possessing machinery.
>
> Call me a Manichean or something else that I ain't if it makes you happy.
>
> Reed's "Ten Days" is effective.[16] Your "[J]ews without Money"[17] is effective. You have yet to convince me that there is any danger of communism in America.
>
> Will you get someone on your staff to READ C. H. Douglas's work from beginning to end and present a clear analysis of it; showing where it is wrong and where it is right?
>
> That is the sort of thing I mean by looking questions in the face. Italy and Russia are the two countries that have made the most active experiments

since 1914. You obfuscate your editorials by assuming that Italy is BEHIND America and England.

Do you realize that during the five years of the N. Masses you have printed almost no clear statement of creed, or program? You have used the term "communist" but you have not made that term clear to your readers. Some of them who meet you out of office hours may know what you mean, but an editorial statement has been lacking.

We disagree? probably. But what is there about capitalism that you dislike that I don't also dislike?

Do I want a counter revolution in Russia?
(EP to MG, October 16, 1930 [YCAL])

Gold replied from Russia on December 7, 1930 (YCAL):

Your ideas are cockeyed. I think but—I'd better not argue 'em in a letter. Wish you'd make a trip here sometime & find out [with] your own two (two) (dva) (due) eyes what it's all about—reading is not enough & I have long despaired of ever convincing anyone by mere writing of buchstaben–

Your letters were forwarded me & I have quit trying to answer. Ezra you are a great man (maybe no one is) but your new manner is too stenographic & personal to answer anyway. You should be more patient in presenting your ideas in logical order. Pardon the insult. I am not too over strong on logic myself but have gotten an aura of a little discipline from my contact with certain realisms[sic], I hope.

There are no rich men in [the] USSR & one doesnt have to control them.

There are counterrevolutionaries & most of them get shot! Workers are important because they produce the means of life. Factories are universities for the masses—have libraries, orchestras, lectures, schools, kindergartens, laboratories, etc., etc. If you don't believe it come here and see.

Something greater than literature is being produced here—its so big, I for one, feel puzzled about describing it.

A new world! The words seem trite but when you track(?) down the clues yourself, bigger than any detective story.

Best wishes

Mike Gold

A sporadic correspondence continued for months. It most likely came to an end early in 1937. Pound proselytized to Gold arguing that the Russian communist experiment and the Italian fascist regime had much in common:

> [November 1933]
>
> Dear MOIKE
>
> If you ever read anything, or if American papers ever print anything except what they are asked to print by the Mellon, Insull, Kreuger, Wiggin interests, EVEN YOU must by now be beginning to see that I have had at least a trace of reason in telling you that Muss// was a good guy. In fact the only guy outside of Russia that can come up to Lennin.
> Incidentally, you might as well KNOW that Lennin bawled out the wop communists for not sticking with Muss/ or keeping with him [...]
>
> (EP to MG [YCAL])

But Gold, not used to being flexible in either dogma or associations, exploded over Pound's persistence in writing to him. Gold clearly thought that Pound should have considered anyone who was an editor of the *New Masses,* and now at *The Daily Worker,* an enemy:

> I am amazed that you write to people like myself. Personally I cannot feel friendly to anybody who is a Fascist and who spreads the confusion that you do. What in hell is it all about anyhow.
>
> How can you say that you had [Louis] Aragon's[18] poem printed in London when Aragon would like nothing better than to blow everyone of you Fascists off the face of the earth. Are there no principles in the world anymore[?].
>
> You say communists don't answer your questions. There are so many books that answer all your questions and you have read them all. What more can anyone do. You are a Fascist and to hell with Fascists.
>
> (MG to EP, January 30, 1934 [YCAL])

It was not only from lock-step communist quarters that Pound could expect censure at this point in his career. Though leaning distinctly to the left, and intensely interested in and sympathetic to the Soviet experiment, Edmund Wilson remained an independent thinker whose critical work was influential in New York literary circles and beyond. In 1931, Wilson delivered an eloquent, carefully nuanced, but nonetheless strikingly negative assessment of Pound and his work:

> Pound's work *has* been partially sunk by its cargo of erudition, whereas Eliot, in ten years time, has left upon English poetry a mark more unmistakable than of any poet writing in English. It is, in fact, probably true at the present time that Eliot is being praised too extravagantly and Pound, though he has deeply influenced a few, on the whole unfairly neglected. I should explain Eliot's greater popularity by the fact that, for all his fragmentary method, he possesses a complete literary personality in a way that Pound, for all his integrity, does not. Ezra Pound, fine poet though he is, does not dominate us like a master of imagination—he rather delights us like a miscellaneous collection of admirably chosen works of art. It is true that Pound, in spite of his inveterate translating, is a man of genuine originality—but his heterogeneous shorter poems, and the heterogeneous passages which go to make his longer ones, never seem to come together in a whole—as his general prose writing gives scrappy expression to a variety of ideas, a variety of enthusiasms and prejudices, some ridiculous and some valid, some learned and some half-baked, which, though valuable to his generation as polemic, as propaganda and as illuminating casual criticism, do not develop a distinct reasoned point of view as Eliot's prose-writings do.[19]

Wilson's assessment of Pound took on the tone of a post-mortem.[20] Wilson seems to have been using Pound as a foil to bring out Eliot's intrinsic superiority. In fact, Wilson only was reporting Eliot's position within the contemporary literary world. Wilson's appraisal of literary developments at the beginning of the 1930s was that high modernism—the work of such artists as Pound, Eliot, Yeats, Proust, Joyce, Stein and the like—had had its day. He argued that it had played its critical, revolutionary role and now must give way to another movement, one that would not be so removed from political, economic, or social realities; not so focused on the imagination of the individual. The new literature had to be more engaged in the realities of the world, he argued.[21]

The sense that Pound was out of touch with the American literary and political scene is evident in his correspondence with those who were sympathetic to him. Responding in 1931 to a submission which he had solicited from Pound for *The American Mercury*, H. L. Mencken bluntly wrote him:

> If I printed this it would disgrace you. There is not an idea in it that has not been hashed to death by ninth-rate editorial writers, and it is thrown together so carelessly that it is simply devoid of effect. You are talking of an imaginary United States. Come back and take a look and you will do the thing all over, and in an entirely different way.
>
> In God's name, what is the charm of the Italian dunghill?
>
> (HLM to EP, January 13, 1931, Redman, *Fascism* p. 90)

During the 1930s, Mencken tended to punctuate his correspondence to Pound with such "wake-up calls," climaxing in a letter penned in 1936, not long after Pound began his involvement with *Globe*.

> You made your great mistake when you abandoned the poetry business, and set up shop as a wizard in general practice. You wrote, in your day, some very good verse, and I had the pleasure, along with other literary buzzards, of calling attention to it at the time. But when you fell into the hands of those London log-rollers, and began to wander through pink fogs with them, all your native common sense oozed out of you, and you set up a caterwauling for all sorts of brummagem utopias, at first in the aesthetic region only but later in the regions of the political and aesthetic baloney. Thus a competent poet was spoiled to make a tin-horn politician.
>
> Your acquaintance with actual politics and especially with American politics, seems to be pathetically meager. You write as if you read nothing save *The New Masses*. Very little real news seems to penetrate to Rapallo. Why not remove those obscene and archaic whiskers shake off all the other stigmata of the Left Bank, come home to the Republic, and let me show you the greatest show on earth? If, after six months of it, you continue to believe in sorcery, whether poetical, political, or economic, I promise to have you put to death in some painless manner, and erect a bronze equestrian statue to your memory, along side the one I am setting up for Upton Sinclair.
>
> Meanwhile, please don't try to alarm a poor old man by yelling at him and making faces. It has been tried before.
>
> (HLM to EP, November 28, 1936, Mencken, *Letters*, p. 411)

In the late 1930s, Delmore Schwartz wrote to Pound after receiving a letter that showed, at least in Schwartz's opinion, how out of touch Pound was with the publishing world in the States:

> ... it [*Poetry*] is a dead thing which no one would think of attacking, like *The Atlantic Monthly*.
>
> And your unawareness of this fact makes me wish to tell you that you seem—seems, my lord!—to have slowed up—if you will forgive me for presuming to tell you where you stand. What I mean is this: in the old days when you were busy digging up Joyce and Lewis and Eliot, and even ten years ago when you printed those wonderful poems by Yeats next to Zukofsky in *Exile*, you were in the middle of everything and knew what was going on with exactitude, and as a result everybody benefitted. Now you seem to have

> your gaze trained on Jefferson and social credit and Harold Monro. and a phenomenon like Auden—to the author of "Lustra" and "Mauberly", the satirist of the British ought to be an item of some interest—does not seem to exist for you—I mean, as a critic ...
>
> Well: what one wishes is that you continue to be our contemporary in the fullest sense of the term.
>
> (DS to EP, Schwartz, *Letters*, p. 51)

Schwartz also strongly reacted to Pound's increasing anti-Semitic rhetoric. In his last letter to Pound, Schwartz confronted the poet about his anti-Semitism. Schwartz was associated with the *Partisan Review* and part of the "New York intellectual" scene during the 1930s. He wanted to maintain some connection with Pound but, like many writers and critics in the United States, he found himself repelled by his positions. Schwartz went so far as to write Pound a letter of "resignation" after reading his *Guide to Kulchur*.

> I have been reading your last book "Culture"[*sic*]—there I find numerous remarks about Semite or Jewish race, all of them damning, although in the course of the book you say:
>
> "Race prejudice is a red herring. the tool of a man defeated intellectually, and of the cheap politician."
>
> Which is a simple logical contradiction of your remarks about the Jewish people, and also a curious omen of a state of mind—one which can support both views, race prejudice and such a judgment of race prejudice, at the same time in the same book.
>
> A race cannot commit a moral act. Only an individual can be moral or immoral. No generalization from the sum of particulars is possible, which will render moral judgment ....
>
> Furthermore, this view of individual responsibility is implicit in the poetry for which you are justly famous.
>
> ... Without ceasing to distinguish between past activity and present irrationality, I should like you to consider this letter as a resignation: I want to resign as one of your most studious and faithful admirers.
>
> (DS to EP, March 5, 1939, Schwartz, *Letters*, p. 68)

Clearly, as far as his credibility in the United States was concerned, the 1930s were a difficult period for Pound.

When Dunn wrote to Pound inviting him to contribute to *Globe* in June 1936, the Great Depression still lingered on at the end of the first administration of Franklin Roosevelt; fascist Italy had invaded and conquered Ethiopia in March of 1935; Hitler had re-occupied the Rhineland in March of 1936; Stalin had recently begun the Moscow show trials of the old Bolsheviks; and the Spanish Civil War had just erupted. These events and others could be traced back to social, political, and economic developments following World War I. Such developments galvanized positions in terms of art and politics into polarized camps. Pound could not understand that these opposing groups could *not* be expected to communicate with each other. His failure to comprehend this fact was evidenced by his correspondence with Mike Gold, Mencken, Schwartz, and a bewildering array of others of all ideological stripes. Pound's "openness" to communication across all ideological lines might be in part admirable, but obviously naive—especially in the mid-1930s.

Another aspect of Pound's alienation was subtle but important. Events since World War I not only changed the politics of many literary circles but also changed the aesthetics of younger artists. Pound too embraced stronger political commitments, well to the right of the majority. But his artistic views remained unchanged from that of his early career in England. His aesthetics in the 1930s were simply the continuation of a sensibility found in works like *Spirit of Romance* and his early literary essays. Thus he became a fine target for Edmund Wilson's careful, dismissive criticism. Because of his deepening commitment to a foreign totalitarian regime, eccentric systems of economic reform, and his anti-Semitic rhetoric, Pound had little credit with old friends and colleagues. He found himself out of touch, out of the American literary conversation, and deprived of American outlets for publication.

Into the welter of Pound's activity, and the controversy surrounding him, came James Dunn's modest request for a contribution. Little did he suspect what he was in for; Pound was ready for any opportunity.

THE CONTEXT OF GLOBE

The headline on the February 7, 1937, story published in the *St. Paul Pioneer Press* was bold: "ST. PAULITE'S WORLD MAGAZINE TO MAKE DEBUT SOON, Sailor-Traveler Edits 'Globe'; Seeks 'Reality'." Sub-headlines of the article continued: "J.W.G. Dunn Has Ezra Pound as General European Correspondent; Saroyan and Jesse Stuart Contribute to First Issue, On Sale Week From Saturday."

The staff writer reported that "Young Mr. Dunn hatched a vast and vague idea" for a monthly magazine featuring essays from all over the world. The reporter described the magazine's goal as "catholic and all-embracing," with the only criterion being good writing. As stated in the headline, Pound was to have a prominent role in this unique magazine's brief life: "Ezra Pound, famed essayist, critic and scholar, at Rapallo, Italy, will be the general European correspondent with a monthly article interpreting the broad flow of events there."

In the summer of 1936, three Minnesota brothers had banded together to launch a sophisticated travel magazine from offices in their home city of St. Paul. John W. G. Dunn, Jr., known as "Jack," aided by his younger brother, Montfort and the youngest brother, James, hoped to gather an array of writers from around the world. Travel agencies and tourist bureaus would be the primary advertisers, with educated world travelers being the chief audience.

Despite the Depression and growing signs of world war, the brothers were optimistic about their commercial venture. Other magazines had started up during the decade and were doing well, including *Esquire*, founded in 1935, and *Life*, founded in 1936. The first issue of *Globe*, appearing on newsstands in March 1937, showcased writers including William Saroyan, Paul Morand, George Schuyler, Montague Summers, and Pound. On the inside cover, under the heading "SHARING THE WORLD," the editors stated the magazine's purpose. "With profound hope and pardonable trembling," they wrote, "we now offer a truly international magazine."

In the twelve issues that followed, the magazine highlighted writers including Sherwood Anderson, Hilaire Hiler, Henry Miller, Vardis Fisher, and Harrison Salisbury. James Taylor Dunn, the youngest brother, described his *Globe* duties in his private journal as that of "a glorified bus boy, book reviewer, 'Guardian of the Manuscripts' and editorial conference caller." Just graduated from Hamilton College, the youngest Dunn was given the difficult duty of lining writers up for the magazine. In the summer of 1936, James Dunn single-handedly contacted about 400 writers and artists.

Employing the connections of his alma mater, Dunn wrote to several well-known Hamilton graduates, including journalist Samuel Hopkins Adams, folklorist Harold W. Thompson, and *New Yorker* critic Alexander Woollcott. Woollcott ignored the letter. Adams politely declined. Thompson wrote that he was too ill. Only two Hamilton alumni responded positively to Dunn's paltry offer of one cent per word (by contrast, the *Saturday Evening Post* was offering ten cents a word). One reply came from the proletarian novelist Joseph Vogel, class of 1926, then struggling to write while also feeding his family. The other response came in handwritten scrawl from Siena, Italy: Ezra Pound was on board with the promise "I also try to get authors to write for us." Dunn wrote in his private journal: "I secured Ezra Pound/ Though I rather doubt whether or not that is a thing—an accomplishment—to brag about!"

James Dunn, Pound's junior by three decades, was put in charge of handling the poet, though others stepped in on occasion.

In contrast to Dunn's private caution in dealing with the eccentric poet, Pound embraced *Globe* and declared himself part of the project, just as he previously muscled himself onto the staff of *Poetry*, *The Little Review*, *The Dial* and other small magazines. By his eighth letter to *Globe*, Pound was using the pronoun "we."

Yet, despite the St. Paul's Pioneer Press' characterization of *Globe* as being "catholic and all-embracing," Dunn had at the outset written explicitly to Pound stating the journal was to be neither literary nor political in its focus. So how did Pound, both as writer and adviser/foreign correspondent, fit into the rather restricted venue of the travel-oriented *Globe*?

Pound showed a flair for the right type of idiom when he wrote to Louis Untermeyer in 1930, advising the anthologist on accommodations in Rapallo:

> Dear L.U.
>
> The Casino is better at twice the price, can't be done on licherchoor alone, but if you are representing the family banking house, by all means don't deprive etc ... .
>
> The Europa is, I think the worst placed hotel in Rap. Savoia much better (I usually send comfortable bourgeois there, cook not so good this year as two years ago). the Moderno was good enough for Vail-Guggenheims.[22] (No reports on the present cuisine available.)
>
> There are others at a few lire less per diem.
>
> Bristol has an aussicht and also the Verdi if you want to study English pathology, both comfortable. (save for the mentality of the denizens.)
>
> On the hole should suggest Savoia or Moderno unless you want eyetalyan ammosphere in which case the Marsala and Rosa Blanca are both on the sea front. but lack drawirn rooms. However; licherary gents have survived 'em and a front room in the Marsala gets all the sun there is.
>
> (EP to LU, January 2, 1930)

While adept at giving this type of advice (which puts one in mind of Gertrude Stein's wicked remark pegging Pound as a "village explainer"), Pound wished to disseminate information relating to his own agenda through the medium of the *Globe*. Pound saw in the magazine an opportunity to bring his own political and economic agenda (stamp-script, corporatism, etc.) to the American public. In writing to Jean Barral, a French right-wing writer based in Nice, Pound makes his agenda and strategy clear:

> I zaccpting [sic] low pay,
>
> on the chance we MIGHT (say one chance in 20) build up a strong center

> of information in the U.S.A. and give them proper view of Europe. What they want is color and detail.
>
> Describe Nice electionism café awnings etc. with Henessy in the foreground or his cook, or chauffeur, or whatever[.] The message wd. have to be clothed. I am probably doing all the sheer political economy the mag. will stand.
> To save time you might send them an trial article, or send it to me, and I will give you an opinion as to whether I think they are free YUP to the limit of what the public will buy. I mean IF they don't bring out a magazine that will crash in six months.
> NOT an ideological or literary publication. A news and adventure publication. with stress on travel.
> Write 'em about the bouche du Rhone. as well as trying to educate 'em.
> (EP to JB, September 24, 1936)

Dunn found himself barraged with letters, an instant student of the "Ezuversity" correspondence course. "I will take on European end of the mag .. .for 6 months BECAUSE there is such Thundering need of SOME communication to U.S.A. + no paper covering it."

> Thank heaven you are NOT trying to start a "literary magazine". Literature in the sense implied in the phrase "a literary magazine" is having a vacation. All the men with enough intelligence to write a good story or novel are concentrated on problem of monetary and credit issue, the nature of money. (EP4)

Pound looked to *Globe* to bolster his credibility as a journalist. From the beginning, his career often intersected with newspaper and magazine journalism. After he moved to Paris in the early 1920s, he became associated with Ernest Hemingway, then a reporter for the *Toronto Star*. Through him Pound became familiar with other journalists based in Paris, among them the Canadian Morley Callaghan, Lincoln Steffens, Guy Hickok, and Sisley Huddleston—all of whom, with the exception of Hemingway (because of his high fees), Pound recommended to Dunn as possible contributors to *Globe*.

It is not surprising that Pound was keen on getting an official press card and letter from *Globe*. Dunn obliged Pound by sending him a letter stating his official relationship to *Globe*:

> To the Gentlemen of the Press and Parties Interested: This is to certify that Mr. Ezra Pound is an authorized general European correspondent of GLOBE, the International Magazine. [Signature] J. W. G. Dunn, Jr. Editor and Publisher.

In his cover letter Dunn promised a press card as soon as possible: "We are getting out a real carte d'identité. If you want to send us a photo-mat picture we can stamp it with a seal, etc. However, don't bother if you find the enclosed letter sufficient." **(JD9)** To which Pound responded with: "Thanks for authorization letter. I enclose photo/an official card might come in handy/can't do any harm." On the back of the passport photo Pound then playfully typed: "E.P. wif his/glasses on/and trying to/look journalist/ic taken years ago/when he/ looked older" **(EP9** [photo enclosed]). Pound entered the fray for *Globe* not as a reporter, but as a talent scout for the magazine.

Pound's name and efforts lent credibility to the struggling magazine. But he was not responsible for all well-known names that appeared in the pages of *Globe*. By the time James Dunn had written his first letter to Pound, he and his brothers had been astute enough to line up a number of writers associated with Pound or his crowd. Dunn's second letter to Pound (August 26, 1936) mentioned authors that had already sent material to *Globe*. They included William Carlos Williams, Joseph Vogel, Upton Sinclair, and the Parisian artist, editor, and art critic/historian Amédé Ozenfant. Nevertheless, Pound proved a rich source for recruiting writers. His suggestions often bore fruit and significantly expanded the range of *Globe*'s offerings.

Already in his second letter to Dunn, Pound let loose a deluge of suggestions. Pound began with Erskine Caldwell, and moved on to Basil Bunting, Gorham Munson, James Laughlin, and a reporter, Harold Franklin, for a Chicago-based journal *The Delphian Quarterly*. Later suggestions included Lincoln Kirstein, E. E. Cummings, Joe Gould, H. L. Mencken, Ford Madox Ford, Morley Callahan, as well as lesser-known people and even family members such as Pound's daughter, Mary Rudge. Pound's suggestions provide a unique window upon his contacts and projects during the second half of the 1930s. In fact, the Dunn/Pound correspondence almost takes on the character of a census of Pound's associations in the middle to late 1930s and provides the reader with insights into his activities and interests at the time.

For example, one of Pound's early suggestions was Langston Hughes, who contributed two pieces to *Globe*, "Just Traveling" (May, 1937) and "Samarkand the New" (July, 1937). Pound's connection with Hughes stemmed from an exchange of letters which began with Pound's request for the poet's support in trying to get Leo Frobenius' multi-volume *Erlebte Erdteile* translated into English (EP to LH, December 26, 1931). The work dealt encyclopedically with African art, anthropology, archaeology, and folklore. Pound had written to Tuskegee and other African American universities and colleges thinking that they would be the logical academic supporters of such an enterprise. Hughes was enthusiastic about Pound's project:

> I am sorry to have been so long about answering your letter but I have been

> on a lecture tour of the south all winter. I was certainly very much interested in what you had to say about Frobenius. Certainly I agree with you about the desirability of his being translated into English and I have written to both Howard and Fisk Universities concerning what you say, and sending them each a copy of your letter that was sent to Tuskegee. (LH to EP, April 22, 1932, Roussel, *Letters*, p. 213–14)

Though support for the translation did not materialize, Pound kept up a sporadic correspondence with Hughes until 1935. In the course of this exchange, Pound commented to Hughes:

> I think it very important to have a chair of africanology in at least one of the Amer. univs./same place where there is not and cannot be an inferiority complex//subject much more alive now than mere repetition of greek and latin classics AS they have been taught for four centuries. (EP to LH, July 25, 1932)

Pound thought highly of Hughes' poetry and prose and was anxious to propose him as a *Globe* contributor. When Hughes' "Just Traveling" appeared, Pound wrote to Dunn: "Langston Hughes is GOOD. So much more easy than Hem's laborious squeezing it out. ... I am for as much Langston Hughes as you can get." **(EP26)**

Pursuing another Frobenius front, Pound recommended that Dunn get in touch with Douglas C. Fox. Fox, as noted above, was a young American journalist who became a research assistant at Frobenius' Forschungsinstitüt für Kulturmorphologie in Frankfurt. Fox did not hide his enthusiasm for Frobenius' or Pound's interest in gaining a wider audience for the anthropologist's work. After Fox's first letter to him from Frankfurt, Pound wrote:

> Dear Mr. Fox:
>
> CHEERS! You are obviously what I want. I have been booming and battling and cursing for 5 years at least re/Am/edtn/Frobenius Langston Hughes and I even had a go at the black universities. Hughes is a civilized man, and a damn good one to judge by his letters ... (EP to DCF, December 17, 1933 [YCAL])

In his next letter, Fox floated a plan for generating interest in Frobenius' work:

> Seems that the logical introduction to Frobenius would be through the Felsbilder [rock drawings and/or pictographs] which, in recent years, have been much more in the public eye. Did you see the exhibition in Rome, or

> the one in Paris which lasted more than a month and ended a week ago? I think he is known to the English speaking world only through very dull but beautifully illustrated articles on the Felsbilder which appeared after recent excavations in the Illustrated London News. And then people only know that he found them, have no idea of how he tied them up with ancient cultures (that still live, how through them he brought new light to bear on past and present, etc.) how his intuitive methods solved problems which the practical men had only the faintest conception of etc.
>
> The whole thing retrospectively, is simple, can be put into 1500 words,...and stated so plainly that it will slide down the murkin throat. I already know what to say but will spend next week at the institute checking up on fact.
> (DCF to EP, December 25, 1933 [YCAL])

When Pound recommended Fox to Dunn as a contributor, Fox had the chance to write just the type of article he described in this letter to Pound. Fox's "Cultures in the Rock" appeared in the May 1937 issue of *Globe* in conjunction with an exhibition of African rock art organized by Frobenius' institute at the fledgling Museum of Modern Art in New York.[23] In fact, at the time of the article's publication, Fox was in New York supervising the exhibition. This *Globe* article had a great deal of influence on Pound's own treatment of Frobenius in *Guide to Kulchur.*

Pound suggested W. H. D. Rouse, the noted classicist and translator of Homer, to *Globe*. Pound was involved in an extensive exchange of letters dealing with Rouse's translation of the *Odyssey* when he not only recommended him as a contributor to Dunn but took the initiative to write Rouse himself: [24]

> Dear W. H. R. D.
>
> These Globe people want adventure—low pay, but they do pay.
> cd. you do
> think you cd. do reminisce a bit more fully about hunting Homer by sail boat in the Aegean?
> That might arouse interest. and you cd. tell the immature denizens of Minnesota the great adventure in simple language
> (EP to WHDR, September 1936 [YCAL])

A bit confused as to geography, Rouse initially responded:

> Re Iowa—let me see specimen. My own adventures are so simple and uncinematic, no thrill in the blood, only memories and human nature—they wouldn't work much in print, though I can do something with them in

> speaking, with a friendly audience. Not like the America of staid Baptists who saw lantern slides of the Holy Land and Thrace (?) and took all my jokes literally.
>
> (WHDR to EP, October 2, 1936 [YCAL])

However, having given it some thought, Rouse did come up with a contribution, "Greek Skipper," which ran in the June 1937 issue of *Globe*.

The fruit of Pound's efforts on behalf of *Globe* was evident in Dunn's letter of October 6, 1936 giving Pound a report on the progress of the first issue of the magazine:

> Dear Mr. Pound:
>
> Just a note about *Globe* and how it is coming along. At your suggestion we wrote to Hilaire Hiler and have received an excellent article called "Cuisine in Bohemia" which will appear in our first issue. We also sent a follow up letter to Erskine Caldwell, and in return got a very encouraging letter, a copy of which I enclose. As I see it now, the first issue will contain the following:
>
> "Emigrants" by L. A. G. Strong
> "Woman Slayer" by George Schyler
> "Merry Reno" by William Saroyan
> "The Tragic Land of Spain" by Sisley Huddleston
> "No Country" by H. E. Bates
> "Cuisine in Bohemia" by Hilaire Hiler
> "A Chinese Man of Letters" by Vincent Starrett
> "Marseille" by Paul Morand
> "Just Traveling" by Langston Hughes
> "Kangaroo" by Alfred Richard Wetjen
> "Bar-Eyed Wolfs' Boy" by Jesse Stuart
> "The Sugar Beet Country" by Hope Williams Sykes
>
> Plus your own "Europe 1936." The letter part of the magazine is the only thing incomplete.
>
> James Laughlin has been written to, but as yet no reply has been received. **(JD6)**

Huddleston, Morand, Hughes, Laughlin, Caldwell, and Hiler were all, of course, Pound suggestions. Yet Pound's political and economic agendas did not recede into the background.

This is demonstrated by the fact that Pound took the opportunity to send off a copy of the first issue of *Globe* to Il Duce himself :

15 May 1937

Al Capo del Governo

Eccellenza e Duce

Valendomi dal invito esteso dal S. E. Polverelli quattro anii fa, mando a S. V. una copia del GLOBE finalmente uscita col mio articolo sul IMPERO. Articolo scritto in Settembre scorso ma l[']indigugio dovuto ai preparativi per una grande diffusione.

La revista non P politica sono il loro correspondete per l[']Europa ma non posso garantiregli opinioni d[']altri scrittori. Posso solamente assicurare S. E. che mandara notizie sinceri aproposido l[']Italia.

Dal ufficio mi scrivono: Prejudice is much against Nazi and Fascism.[25]

Nel GLOBE non ch'e pressione di publicita commerciate. Qundi una certa liberta. Ma nessum direttore di una revista gran' traggio [*sic*] puo resistere alle opinione de suoi lettori.

Il pericolo d'avvelenenamento dal Inghilterra essiste in America. commune linguaggio, abitudini. [26]

[To the Head of the Government

Excellency and Duce

Taking advantage of an invitation extended to me four years ago by His Excellency Polverelli, I am sending to Your Excellency a copy of the finally released GLOBE with my article on the EMPIRE. Article written in September, but held up due to preparations for a mass mailing.

The magazine is not political. I am its European correspondent–but cannot guarantee the opinions of other writers. I can only assure Your Excellency that I shall send along the real news concerning Italy.

They [the *Globe* editors] write me from the office: Prejudice is much against Nazi and Fascism.

Commercial advertisers not exerting pressure upon GLOBE. Hence, a certain freedom. But no editor of a magazine with a wide distribution [?] is able to resist the opinions of its readers.

Danger of British poisoning exists in America. Common language, habits.]

Economics and politics were not what the *Globe* creators had in mind. They wanted a successful magazine that had a wide readership, and plenty of advertising money. Labyrinthine discussions of the theory of Social Credit or early American history—let alone Italian fascism—would not accomplish this objective. Pound's arch-conservative leanings, including his recommendation that *Globe* go after "Coughlin's public," meaning the supporters of Father Charles Coughlin, made them uneasy.[27] Pound's own contributions to the magazine often concerned the editorial staff.

An article Pound wrote about the abdication of Edward VIII was well received by reviewers of *Globe*'s first issue. Later essays, however, lost focus. His articles were often fragmented, jumping from economics to history to contemporary politics to personal remembrances with little transition. It was not normal fare for a mainstream magazine. To Pound, these intellectual leaps were a way to illustrate the connectedness of events.

"The only way to understand Europe (or any other continent) is by a collection of details, though most of them will appear irrelevant and unconnected," Pound wrote in "Deflation Benefit." For most *Globe* readers, it was just confusing.

"Your first article, 'Abdication,' definitely met the approval of many of our readers. Later letters, however, have been called 'obscure'," Dunn wrote on April 27, 1938 **(JD22)**. On February 20, 1937, J. W. G. Dunn wrote to Pound: "We are sending to you 'That League in Calvin's Home City' which is too serious for GLOBE. Many of the people and situations dealt with are beyond most of us here. Perhaps a politico-economic piece of this nature would be acceptable elsewhere" **(JWGD1)**. Pound himself labeled his articles "a mixed lot of snippets" in a letter to Dunn on March 18, 1937 **(EP21)**.

Another problem was Pound's anti-Semitism. In his letters and articles, he made ugly references to "kike choinalism" and the month of "jewlie". Dunn ignored them and such references in his articles never saw publication. In correspondence, Dunn's chief tactic in dealing with Pound's prejudice was simply not to respond to his remarks. Pound seemed to realize the tension with Dunn, and made efforts to explain himself. These "explanations" were by no means successful, but they provide insight into the prejudice with which Pound wrestled. Such is the case in a letter dated March 18, 1937, Here Pound argued:

r.s.v.p.re/this

New Testament is the strongest anti-semitic propaganda ever published/ BUT of course it is so wrapped in the pink cotton wool of familiarity that that ASPECT is NOT and it has become UTTERLY innocuous/ whereas Ben Franklin's feelings of the subject have not.[28] Even in Eng/ and Italy people are being forced into ant-semitism by jewish folly. I mean people who never thought of it before and who ON PRINCIPLE are opposed to race prejudice and race discrimination.
This I take it is UNFAMILIAR ground in St. Paul.
Damn hard to handle/ heaven knows I don't particularly want to tackle it.. BUT the office ought to KNOW a lot the Globe don't print. I don't think it wd/ be wise editing to do very much with it until Globe has run at least a year ...

You will probably get a lot of jewish sob stuff ... more picturesque than any analysis of jew influence can be.
AND, damn it! it is not bad because it is jew. All that line of talk wd. talk distracts from the MAIN issue.

IF jews wd. take any sort of part in econ/ reform as distinct from communistic obscurantism and financial obscurantism
there wd. be no need of any anti-semitic stuff at all.

I know of only ONE jew (alleged to be jew) in ALL the monetary reform aggitation. And one other riding with Prof. F. who wobbles.

They are destroying France and England ... Don't think me merely nutty for saying this. Ben Franklin was a practical man ... It is hard as hell to do justice. A minority race can NOT fight in the open. Not if it has any sense at all. The small jew suffers for the sins of the big gombeen men. The fight ought NOT to have to be fought on lines of race prejudice.[29] Only way to avoid that is by spread and acceleration of spread of economic light. Hope this isn't too heavy for the OFFICE ear. **(EP21)**

Such ideas were embedded in a passage of the Cantos written during this period:

... poor yitts paying ...
... for a few big jews' vendetta on goyim
I think wrote Miss Bell[30] to her mama
that when not against the interests of Empire

we shd/keep our pledges to Arabs.
Thus we lived on through sanctions, through Stalin
Litvinoff,[31] gold brokers made profit
rocked the exchange against gold
Before which entrefaites remarked Johnnie Adams (the elder)
IGNORANCE, sheer ignorance ov the natr ov money
sheer ignorance of credit and circulation.
Remarked Ben: better keep out the jews
or yr/ grand children will curse you,[32]
jew, real jews, chazims,[33] and *neschek*[34]
also super-neschek or international racket...
(Canto LII)

Globe editors could not let Pound's vitriolic harangues make it to print. One blast by Pound against the Daladier administration in France was censored by the business manager. "Our financial condition is such that we find it impossible to publish invective material concerning a country that is advertising in GLOBE," Dunn wrote on March 31, 1938. Pound wrote back in a conciliatory tone, perhaps fearing he might lose his last significant access to the American public. "When I am Not writing CANTOS/ I do not care a hoot how much I am EDITED."

The letter, however, also conveyed Pound's growing sense of alienation from America. The term "invective" had stung him, and he returned to the phrase with sarcasm throughout his letters to *Globe*. "What you and All others ever heard of Americans DONT GET is that it is utterly impossible FROM HERE to know what is considered detrimental by bizniz managers."

* * *

In the end, Pound's success as a writer for *Globe* was limited. Only half the articles that he wrote for the magazine were ever published. Several were judged offensive. Others were considered confusing. Some were never published because of *Globe*'s untimely demise.

With war threatening to engulf the world, recent college graduates in Minnesota had little chance of establishing a national travel magazine. As Dunn recorded in his personal journal, "We were all untested amateurs with enthusiasm and good ideas but destined to fail especially since the magazine was born in the Midwest (St. Paul) at the depth of the Depression when Hitler was coming to power."

Despite family loans, *Globe* was constantly short of money. Writers balked when checks were delayed. Distribution was poor. They had hoped *Globe* would reach a circulation of 50,000 copies a month sold in America and Europe. At its peak, *Globe* sold 20,000. Louis Zukofsky wrote to Pound on December 7, 1937, after *Globe*'s last issue had come out, that "the day of the little magazine is definitely over. Nobuddy sees even a commercial venture like Globe anywhere around ..." Dunn summed up the three brothers' shortcomings: "No training or experience in the world of business or with the possible pitfalls in publishing a magazine from scratch." (*Pound/Zukofsky*, p. 182)

Financial woes interrupted production in 1938, and the magazine started to come out once every two months. Advertisers left the magazine, and it finally died at the close of the year. The sale of the last issue was negligible. The end was anti-climactic for Jim Dunn, who paraphrased Eliot: "Definitely with a whimper—How I wish it had been with a bang."

The editors' correspondence with Pound also ended with a whimper. Jim Dunn wrote his last letter to Pound in April 1938. Across the Atlantic, Pound had heard warnings from friends that *Globe* was in trouble. He wrote two final desperate letters in December 1938. On December 18, he outlined a plan to keep the magazine afloat by transforming it into an archconservative political journal. He offered to help by cutting his price: "If you are hard up and want to try THIS kind of Mag/ and can give me as much liberty as I now have in "ACTION" and the British Union Quarterly, and dare use a monthly letter from me, I will cut my rate from 20 bucks to 5 bucks for a series of 12 articles."

On December 23, he received his final epistle from *Globe*. It was a one-paragraph letter from Montfort Dunn, the magazine's art director. Montfort enclosed a check for Pound's last article, and gave no indication of the magazine's financial troubles. Pound urged the Dunns to keep going. His sense of isolation is conveyed in the last lines of his essay published in the final *Globe* (November–December, 1938), "United States of Europe?": "I sometimes wonder why GLOBE readers don't write and TELL one what they want to hear about Europe," he complained. "The old place is still here." (See Contribution #8)

Below the end of the article, the editors offered their address for any American interested in contacting Pound. No one wrote before *Globe* ceased publication. Pound's work for *Globe* was finished. After two years, he had been paid a total of $185. Ahead lay war, radio broadcasts, prison camp, treason charges, and years in a government psychiatric hospital.

The correspondence was revived once, in 1959, a year after Pound was released from St. Elizabeths. Pound wrote to James Taylor Dunn, but he never received the letter, having moved back to Minnesota after serving as a librarian in Cooperstown, NY. Pound ended his letter referring to *Globe*. "A noble effort," he wrote. (See EP51 and "Coda" to the letters below)

NOTES

1. See unpublished letters to Pound from Gorham Munson (YCAL) February 28, March 4, and March 11, 1932.
2. *Blast* was a New York-based literary magazine edited by Fred R. Miller and his wife Betty. It was billed as "A Magazine of Proletarian Short Stories" and ran only for five issues from September 1933 until November 1934. The Millers were friends of William Carlos Williams, who probably informed Pound of the journal's existence. Williams found *Blast* a brief but welcome outlet for the prose he was producing at the time; each of the five issues of *Blast* carried a short story by Williams.
3. *The New Democracy*, edited by Gorham Munson, was published in New York from 1933 to 1936. Initially it was a fortnightly, and later, a monthly review. *The New Democracy* dealt primarily with Social Credit economics, but also found room for the publication of literature, including contributions from T. S. Eliot, Marianne Moore, E. E. Cummings, Henry Miller, and Pound. In 1937, after *The New Democracy* had folded, James Laughlin took the title of its literary section "New Directions" as the name of his newly established publishing house.
4. "Cantleman's Spring-Mate" by Wyndham Lewis appeared in the *The Little Review*, IV 6 (October, 1917), pp. 8–14. However, it was suppressed in the United States by the Postmaster General for obscenity. *The Little Review* published episodes I–XIV of James Joyce's *Ulysses* from March 1918 to December 1920 until the magazine was again suppressed and its editors, Margaret Anderson and Jane Heap, tried for publishing obscene material. "The Chinese Written Character as a Medium for Poetry" by Ernest Fenollosa and Ezra Pound appeared in *The Little Review*, VI 5 (September 1919), pp. 62–4.
5. During the first half of the 1930s, William Carlos Williams was working regularly in prose and produced a number of short stories, some of which appeared in the collection *The Knife of the Times and Other Stories* (Ithaca, NY: Dragon Press 1932). Others short stories appeared in various literary periodicals such as *Blast* (see footnote 2 above). He was also engaged in writing his long-standing project, the novel *The White Mule*, which was finally published in 1937 by James Laughlin's New Directions.
6. Leo Frobenius (1873–1938), German anthropologist and archaeologist. Pound had been interested in Frobenius' work in the archaeology, anthropology, art, and folklore of indigenous African peoples since the late 1920s. Pound was to place an article by one of Frobenius' assistants, the American, Douglas Fox, on African rock art in the *Globe*.
7. Jean Cocteau (1889–1963), French writer and artist. Pound probably met Cocteau in April of 1921 and since that time considered him one of the best writers in contemporary French literature.
8. Probably a reference to the Mongol emperor Kublai Khan (1215–94), who figures in the opening of Canto XVII (first published in a limited edition, *A Draft of the Cantos 17–27* by John Rodker in London in 1928). Kublai Khan also appears in the course of *Cantos LII–LXXI* (the so-called Chinese–Adams Cantos), which Pound worked on from 1937 to 1939 and which appeared in its first edition with Faber & Faber, London in 1940.

9. Pound is referring to Jeffrey Mark's *The Modern Idolatry, Being an Analysis of Usury and the Pathology of Debt* (London: Chatto & Windus, 1934).
10. During March 21–31, 1933, Pound gave a series of lectures at the Bocconi University in Milan at the invitation of its rector Ulisse Gobbi. The series was entitled "An Historical Background for Economics."
11. It is not clear what Pound was referencing here, although it was about this date that he began his association with A. R. Orage and his journal *The New Age*. It is during his association with Orage and his journal that Pound began to take an interest in economic issues and gained exposure to the work of C. H. Douglas on Social Credit (cf. Redman, *Ezra Pound and Italian Fascism*, pp. 17; 51–2). Pound's first contribution to *The New Age* dates to November 1911.
12. See Chapter 4, "From the Patron to *il Duce*: Ezra Pound's Odyssey," in Lawrence Rainey's *Institutions of Modernism* (New Haven: Yale University Press, 1998).
13. See Chapter 1, "A. R. Orage and the Education of a Poet," in Tim Redman's *Ezra Pound and Italian Fascism* (Cambridge University Press, 1991).
14. Originally published in *The Liberator* (February 1921), quoted here from *Mike Gold: A Literary Anthology*, edited by Michael Folsom (New York: International Publishers), pp. 66–7.
15. *The Exile* 4 (1928), pp. 116–17.
16. John Reed's *Ten Days that Shook the World* (New York: Boni & Liveright, 1919) was his eyewitness account of the October Revolution in Russia.
17. Pound was referring to Mike Gold's autobiographical novel about life in the New York City slums, *Jews without Money* (New York: Boni & Liveright, 1930).
18. Louis Aragon (1897–1982), French poet, sometime communist, and co-founder along with André Breton and Philippe Soupault of the Dadaist/surrealist movement. Pound had included one of Aragon's most noted poems, "The Red Line," a paean to the Soviet Union, in his *Active Anthology*, which had just been published by Faber & Faber in October 1933. It appeared in a translation made by E. E. Cummings. Pound had been promoting Aragon's work as early as 1920 while foreign editor with *The Dial*.
19. *Axel's Castle: A Study in the Imaginative Literature of 1870–1930* (New York: Collier Books, 1991 [first edition 1931]), pp. 111–12.
20. Pound's diminishing presence in the American media in the mid- to late 1930s was striking. In 1918, according to Gallup, Pound published 116 contributions to periodicals. None dealt with economics or politics. Forty-five of these articles were published in American journals and newspapers. In 1936, the number had dropped to ten American articles out of 107. By 1938, Pound contributed only nine articles to American publications out of a total of fifty-eight articles, and five of those articles were either political or economic in nature. His "National Culture: A Manifesto," written that year for American readers, was never published because his Boston publisher ran out of money. He complained that it took him a year and a half to get a blurb about the Thomas Jefferson–John Adams correspondence published in the *North American Review*. In desperation to reach American readers he privately published "An Introductory Textbook," which was a pamphlet on American history.

21. In his conclusion to *Axel's Castle*, Wilson wrote of the end of this formative phase of high modernism:

    > The writers with whom I have here been concerned have not only, then, given us works of literature which, for intensity, brilliance and boldness as well as for an architectural genius, an intellectual mastery of their materials, rare among their Romantic predecessors, are probably comparable to the work of any them. Though it is true that they have tended to overemphasize the importance of the individual, that they have been preoccupied with introspection sometimes almost to the point of insanity, that they have endeavored to discourage their readers, not only with politics, but with action of any kind–they have yet succeeded in effecting in literature a revolution analogous to that which has taken place in science and philosophy: they have broken out of the old mechanistic routine, they have disintegrated the old materialism, and they have revealed to the imagination a new flexibility and freedom. And though we are aware in them of things that are dying—the whole belle-lettristic tradition of the Renaissance culture perhaps, compelled to specialize more and more, more and more driven in on itself, as industrialism and democratic education have come to press it closer and closer—they none the less break down the walls of the present and wake us to the hope and exaltation of the untried, unsuspected possibilities of human thought and art. (op. cit., pp. 288–9)

22. Pound must have been referring to a trip to Rapallo made by patron and art collector Peggy Guggenheim (1889–1977) and her husband the writer/artist Laurence Vail (1891–1968). However, it probably had not been a recent trip—Peggy Guggenheim's relations with her husband were strained in the last years of the 1920s and her divorce from Vail became final in the summer of 1930.
23. The exhibition opened on April 28, 1937.
24. Rouse's friendship with Pound was a long and significant one, even though it was conducted by letter. After Pound returned to Italy following his release from St. Elizabeths in 1958, he seems to have gone through his old correspondence, annotating it and bringing some organization to the vast collection. In the margin of a carbon of one of Pound's letters to Rouse from the 1930s, thc poet wrote in longhand: "8 Jan 59/Rouse saved my/life. i.e. he sent me the text of the/ Odes that saved/ my mind in the/ hell hole." Apparently Rouse had sent Pound a copy of the Confucian *Odes* to Pound soon after he arrived in Washington, D.C. under indictment in 1945. Pound often referred to Howard Hall at St. Elizabeths (where he was initially held from December 21, 1945 to early 1947) as the "hell hole."
25. Pound quotes here from Dunn's letter to him of April 22, 1937.
26. Italian text taken from carbon of Pound's letter to Mussolini in the correspondence files at the Beinecke Rare Book & Manuscript Library at Yale University. An English version appears in C. David Heymann, *Ezra Pound: The Last Rower* (New York: Viking Press, 1976), pp. 324–5. Heymann identifies Polverelli as Gaetano Polverelli, who "succeeded Alessandro Pavolini as Minister of Popular Culture on February 5, 1943. Prior to this, Polverelli had been head of Mussolini's Press Office (1931–3) and was Undersecretary of the Ministry of Popular Culture until his appointment as minister. The invitation in question is a letter that Polverelli had sent to Pound in response to the latter's epistle of

February 8, 1933; on that occasion Polverelli suggested to Pound that any articles deemed important enough to be seen by the Duce be sent to Mussolini directly" (Heymann, p. 325).

27. EP to JTD, May 5, 1937. Correspondence files at the Beinecke reveal carbons of at least seven letters Pound wrote to Coughlin, who was broadcasting from the National Shrine of the Little Flower Church in Royal Oak, Michigan. Pound was apparently able to hear Coughlin on radio. At the end of January 1935, Pound wrote to Coughlin: "These Four Jan/broadcasts are magnificent ..." Pound's letters, dating from November 1933 to December 1936, were never answered by Coughlin himself, or even his staff. Pound seems to have received only a series of form letters briefly acknowledging receipt of his letters.

28. Pound was referring to a spurious remark attributed to Benjamin Franklin. Pound quotes it in Canto LII: "... better keep out the jews/or yr/grand children will curse you ..." The comment was allegedly made by Franklin at the Constitutional Convention and has been repeated often in anti-Semitic propaganda, including Nazi propaganda from the '30s. However, there appears to be no documentary evidence from the convention that Franklin ever made this comment. The source usually cited for it, Charles Cotesworth Pinckney's diary, upon examination does not record any such remark. (Cf. Earle Davis, *Vision Fugitive: Ezra Pound and Economics* [Lawrence, KS: University of Kansas], pp. 179–80.)

29. As Delmore Schwartz noted in his "letter of resignation" quoted above, Pound's attitude toward anti-Semitism was bifurcated. Though he engaged in anti-Semitic rhetoric, Pound was capable of denying its relevance. He made this point in his *American Notes* for November 21, 1935, in the British journal the *New English Weekly*:

    > Usurers have no race. How long the whole Jewish people is to be sacrificial goat for the usurer, I know not ....Whenever a usurer is spotted he scuttles down under the ghetto and leaves the plain man Jew to take the bullets and the beatings. All hostilities are grist to the usurer, all racial hates wear down sales resistance on cannon. (*The New English Weekly* [VIII:6], p. 105, also quoted in *Ezra Pound: Selected Prose 1909–1965* [New York: New Directions, 1973], 300n.)

30. Gertrude Bell (1868–1926), author, explorer, cartographer, and amateur ethnographer. Bell was considered an expert on the Arab Near East and was recruited by British intelligence. She became involved, as did T. E. Lawrence, in fomenting the Arab revolt against the Ottoman Empire during World War I. Bell also attended the peace conference in Paris and Versailles which in large part decided British policy towards the Near East after the war.

31. M. M. Litvinof (1876–1951), Russian revolutionary and major political figure in the Soviet regime, especially the Ministry for Foreign Affairs during the Stalin era.

32. See note 29 above.

33. What Pound referred to here is not entirely clear. *A Companion to the Cantos of Ezra Pound*, edited C. F. Terrell (Berkeley: University of California Press, 1980) suggests that Pound means *chaseirim*, Yiddish/Hebrew for "pigs."

34. Hebrew term in the Old Testament for "interest" on loans, or "usury."
See Exodus 22:24, Deuteronomy 23:30, and Leviticus 25:36.

PART ONE

The Letters: 1936–1938

JD1

TSL on GS (YCAL)

[June 16, 1936]

Ezra Pound
Via Marsala 12, int. 5,
Rapallo, Italy

Dear Mr. Pound:

Hamilton College being our mutual Alma Mater,[1] I'm taking this liberty of approaching you myself rather than having my brother write a letter that might be casually cast into the waste basket.

Late this fall or early in the winter we are publishing the first issue of *Globe*,[2] a travel magazine. In all ventures of this sort the public's first impression is always the most lasting. We want the best kind of magazine possible, and are well-enough financed to get out 6 issues of *Globe* in a traveler's size (5 by 8), 64 pages, colored illustrations and art work. Will you help us make the magazine a success?

We are under the impression that *Globe* articles should have: (1) not more than 2,000 words, 1,000 preferred, meaning a firm practice of concision; (2) intimacy and lightness of touch, and (3) truth, authenticity and credulity.

As for subject, it is unrestricted—provided only that your article show relation between people and place. In other words, setting (background) should impress as much local color as possible on the characters.

Would you be kind enough to write for us or find something that seems to fit our editorial requirements and send it immediately for us to look over and report on within 2 weeks? The rates are 1¢ a word—payment on acceptance.

Cordially yours,

(Signed: James Taylor Dunn/ '36)

James Taylor Dunn, Associate Editor of *Globe*

(In Pound's handwriting in the left margin: "Globe./1033 Lincoln Ave/St Paul/ Minn.")

[1] James Dunn had just graduated from Hamilton College in the Spring of 1936. Pound was a member of the class of 1905. Dunn later wrote that he did not know much about Pound at the time that he wrote soliciting a contribution. But after his correspondence with the poet began, Dunn began to read Pound's work. "I started reading EP after he submitted material for publication. I didn't get into his poetry except for some of his earlier works and translations. What interested me most was his prose, especially his essays" (Dunn to McWhirter, December 4, 1991).
[2] The first issue of *Globe* appeared in March, 1937.

EP1

HWL P (BL)

On the back of the envelope: For "color" 2000th anniversary of Horace. Vide the postage stamp.

Siena ~~ans~~ address for reply.
13 Aug 310 San Gregorio
Venice

Dear Dunn:

Current Rates? meaning of Harpers'? or of what.

Economic life? as I wd. write it or tempered to supposed prejudice of local opinion ?
Cd. do progress of architecture (modernist) in Italy. with photos.[1] more important the direction and cumulative meaning of Italian Bank reform[,] new wheat law[,] raise of pay of 2,000,000 workmen.[2] I use a typewriter. but am now in vacation.[3] don't think you will get any more letters in this cat scrawl. = I take it serious history: say of the Leopoldine reforms,[4] contemporary american revolution is OUT side globe intentions

---

Naturally I can't tell what you want.—with not even sample copy of globe or list of contributors. what about monthly letter. 1000–1500 words. on contemporary Italy?// all depends whether you want it full, or with flowers and gloves on. "colorful"—horse race here on sunday[5] but I should think that had been done to death//

"Esquire" lay down when ging. started to print for England[6]—and was afraid Italian news ʕ wd. displease the Brits. (last autumn) It DID.
Your program O.K.—I have always been for decentralization and getting some U.S. stuff printed outside Noo Yok and Baaaston.—at least enough to break strangle hold.

//
For american art. suggest you get in touch with Hilaire Hiler.[7] (~~address~~ you cd. reach him co. M. Hiler 200 W. 57 New York

but H. H. is in Cal. or was when I last heard.

Yrs

Ezra Pound

On the back of the final page: Who directs yr. European services in <u>general</u>? Any idea of correlation & elimination of duplications?

[1] The only evidence that Pound followed up on this suggestion is a short article submitted to *Globe* accompanied by three photos entitled "Railway Station SIENA" (Contribution #17). Exactly when it was submitted or written is not clear.

[2] The Italian bank reforms Pound mentions probably related to the creation of two agencies, the Instituto Mobilare Italiano (1931) and the Institute for Industrial Reconstruction (1933). These agencies initially discouraged and ultimately forbade bank loans to industry. They bought up bad industrial debt, thereby stabilizing the banking system and protecting the savings and investments of the middle class. This strategy was an effort to minimize of the impact of the effects the Depression of 1929–33 in Italy. This program restructured the Italian financial system. In effect, the program nationalized Italian industry, eliminating much of the Italian private debt, thus shielding banks, industry, and small investors from financial ruin due to default on large private sector loans to industry. Likewise, a mainstay of Mussolini's agricultural program was the so-called "War for Wheat" which emphasized the expansion of domestic wheat production and consumption. This required the government assistance in the introduction of modern agricultural techniques, the stabilization of market prices, and land reclamation. These steps were coupled with a protectionist tariff to minimize the import of foreign wheat. In 1936, around the time Pound was writing for Dunn, the Fascist government introduced new laws requiring farmers to sell their wheat to national marketing agencies which then set the retail prices of the grain.

[3] During the 1930s, Dorothy Pound regularly left Italy for the summer months, often from mid-June to mid-August, to visit her mother Olivia Shakespear and her son Omar in London. For these months Pound would generally be in residence in Venice and Siena with the violinist Olga Rudge. While in Siena, Pound researched the practices of the seventeenth-century Sienese bank, Il Monte dei Paschi at the Archivio di Stato, in the Palazzo Piccolomini. This archival research formed the basis for Cantos XLII–LI (*The Fifth Decad of Cantos*). Pound's musical interests also played a part in his choice of Siena.

During the 1930s, his musical attentions turned toward the task of recovering and reviving the work of certain Baroque period composers, especially Vivaldi. In 1936, at Pound's instigation, Olga Rudge catalogued the Vivaldi manuscripts in Turin. Over the next few years, Pound's interest and Rudge's work would play a part in the founding of Accademia Musicale Chigiana which was created under the patronage and guidance of the Sienese Count Guido Chigi Saracini. The Accademia would help in re-establishing not only Vivaldi, but also other such neglected composers as Bach. Olga Rudge later served as secretary to the Accademia in Siena.

[4] These economic reforms took place under Grand Duke Leopold I of Tuscany (1747–92) who was later Holy Roman Emperor (1790–2). His activities, as well as those of his son and successor as Grand Duke, Fernando III (1769–1824), are related in Canto XLIV.

[5] This traditional Sienese horse race known as "Il Palio." It was inaugurated in 1310 and still is held annually in the Piazza del Campo.

[6] **Arnold Gingrich**

[7] **Hilaire Hiler**

JD2

TSL GS (YCAL)

August 26, 1936

Mr. Ezra Pound,
310 San Gregorio,
Venice, Italy.

Dear Mr. Pound:

Thank you for your letter of August 13th.

I suppose by this time you have already received our letter to you concerning our rates: "The rates are 1¢ a word and up...the longer, the higher. This means that the longer GLOBE, the intimate journal of travel, romance, adventure and world excitement stays in business, the higher rates it will be able to pay." Due to the present (unfortunate) exchange rates will make a proportionate alteration in your case.

As we are now at work on GLOBE's first number we could only give you as an indication of its needs the names of some of those who have sent material: William Carlos Williams,[1] Adele de Leeuw,[2] Joseph Vogel,[3] George Schuyler,[4] Upton Sinclair,[5] Willy Ley,[6] Ozenfant,[7] Micum M. Pavilcevic (in translation).[8] Except for the second (an article on a Bali Cremation) these are informal accounts of; a fight on a cattle boat, a man and woman in a bedroom, conjugal revenge in Montenegro, etc. this may sound on the story side, but others will fill the gap: Café songs of Belgrade (with music), night life in Bucharest, Hollywood monsters, etc.

Anything on travel will be without neck-craning and all the paraphernalia of the picturesque. (In re Siena: an uncle, large and loud, did for me once the "colorful" race in the Piazza del Campo, miming the horses and riders, to the alarm of a small crowd of kids. As an article on this pageant will be in some magazine again it does seem pointless).

Our first interest is authenticity; nothing that would make the natives laugh, nothing about the place being O.K. if it weren't for the people. The matter of wearing gloves is up to you; certainly no roses. We do not suppose any preference on the part of the reader.

A monthly letter might lead to some space complication, even if we omitted other sources outside the seasonal flux of visitors (Tel-Aviv, Tokio, Rio, etc).

Contemporary architecture in Italy (with photos) also sounds good. Perhaps a *series* of photos with provocative phrase identification (the ornamentation of ideas).

The cumulative meaning of the various economic reaction in Italy would I think receive attention here, where the water is thin from much filtering. Articles of this sort (and the definitely political or tendancieux are "out"), must have punch and be within the word limit.

I hope after this letter you will send something. Perhaps you can understand the value of your suggestions while GLOBE is *still* (after two years contacting some 7,000 people) in a formative stage. We have no general European Director.

Sincerely yours,

James Taylor Dunn (signed)

[1] **William Carlos Williams** apparently had been solicited for a contribution to *Globe* by the Dunn brothers before they had contacted Pound in Rapallo. Williams' contribution was the short story "To Fall Asleep." It appeared in the third issue of *Globe* (June 1937, pp. 33–7).
[2] **Adele de Leeuw**
[3] **Joseph Vogel**
[4] **George Samuel Schuyler**
[5] **Upton Sinclair**

[6] **Willy Ley** (1906–69), German-born American science and technology writer dealing primarily with aerospace technology and natural history.
[7] **Amédée Ozenfant**
[8] **Micun M. Pavicevic.** His short story "A Breach of Family Honor" appeared in the first issue of *Globe* (March 1937, pp. 119–23).

EP2

HWL P (BL)

address for reply
Siena presso Scarpa
29 Ag. 310 San gregorio
Saturday Venezia, Italy.

Dear Dunn,

re/ yr. 17the Ten per thousand is NOT my current rate. Esquire.[1] pay $175 for a short article. & the current rate of lousy London weeklies is £5/5 or £6/6. $25 to $20. per thou. HOWEVER if you want to run a decent mag. will take a chance under certain conditions.—monthly letter on what is most alive in Europe 1000 to 1500 words.= I can't be bothered to count. I go by rough estimate of typed pages. & am usually supposed to practice laconism.= I get to a typewriter next Wednesday (bar accident.).

I will take on European ~~and~~ end of the mag. @ $10 to $15 monthly for six months BECAUSE there is such a Thundering need of SOME communication to U.S.A. & no paper covering it.

I note you want people and place—you <yourself> say frankly a travel mag. yr. brothers ad was not so specific <nor is stationary of the Globe>.

Take it as start that travel for the moment is not Spanish tho' world excitement is.[2] & that Italy is the most interesting country in Europe 1936 let ~~also~~ alone giving (as it always did) the highest return per milage covered, to any traveler who has to consider his expenses at all.

I can't be bothered to do the kind of travel article that I did in 1906.[3]

And I am an authority on current European affairs—though I don't expect people to believe it YET. That is apart from a few people.

Any how I know a d/m sight more about 'em than Morganthau (Jr.)[4], Izzy Strauss.[5] etc. & more than anyone you can get to write for ten or 15 bucks a shot.

Let us say the intelligent traveler ought to know what is going on.= & if he hasn't seen a place Before & after he ought to be told what has intervened.

AZ you are in a hurry I will send an article from Venice next week. That can serve as a starter. Specification of what a new 64 <page> mag. can be. & why it is needed. My view of your opportunity. & summary of state of Europe. ~~Spet.~~ Sept 3rd 1936.[6]

Letters to the Dial. 1923 .paid $50.[7] and I was dealing with frog literature. I know a damn sight more now that I did then.

I think colour illustrations a waste of money. usually horrible any how. has Manuldruck[8] process got to U.S. or are you partially financed by coulour printer?? otherwise shd. think you better hold down to coloured frontpiece & and use finance to ameliorate quality of TEXT.

Unless yr/ brother is twice yr/ age you may both be inexperienced.—even were your rates 5 cents a word NO European author of any standing "submits" work for approval. = that is part of civilization. Mind not shit on and strapped down under the business manager. WHEN the author has a mind, the edition discovers the fact and invites a contribution under certain circs. (usually liklihood of being let in for libel action.) he asks permission to delete a few expressions, or asks the author to modify for a given reason.

NO magazine can succede as a means of communication between intelligent men. or any other system. the editor has got to have impersonality & exhibit the minds of his contributors. otherwise his mag ends by being a mere lie and sham. I shd. not be helping you if I left this unsaid. Every mag. that has ever cut a NOTCH has started with the conviction that at least 3 or 4 writers were worth printing. They don't need to agree on any mortal. If I write on current events, I shall NOT be sending what you already BELIEVE. I don't care how much the editors attack it, or how much other contributors attack it.— but consider it a waste of print if attacks are based on mere ignorance, & fixed ~~ica~~ ideas dating from 1918, 1890, or whatever. SOMETIME that fact that I have been absolutely right so often will begin to count. Plenty of people have thought me crazy but nobody thinks me crazy because of things I said ~~15~~ 20 or 15 years ago . & I am now just as aware of econ. & european politics, & situation as I was of literary situation & values in 1910-1917-1920.

may as well put the dots on the iiii s.

Yours,

E Pound

Have you any idea who else you think shd. be =included= Naturally as you are not a literary effort. you are not out for newly experimental writers.—Are you asking Caldwell?[9] over

I imagine his rates are higher by now. but you have got to have a few writers at the start if only once . & most of the good ones are out of reach at anything near yr. rate. Bunting [10] is just back from the Canaries. & cd. provide more___ Spanish stuff not literature, but London is accustomed to £5/5 rate. minimum.

Harold Franklin does Travel for the Delphian.[11] but not at yr. rate. I don't see how you can get much good stuff so cheap. save by interesting at least a few people to do regular monthly job.// and then it depends on WHOM you get. Do you want me to write to g. Munson[12] & young Jas. Laughlin ??[13]

[1] **Arnold Gingrich**'s magazine *Esquire*.
[2] By the time Dunn had written his first letters to Pound, the Spanish parliament had collapsed (June 1936) and Spanish Civil War broke out. The Battle of Barcelona had taken place in mid-July and, by the end of that month, battle lines were drawn throughout Spain.
[3] This early article was probably "Burgos, A Dream City of Old Castile" (*Book News Weekly* [25:2] October 1906, pp. 91–4). Pound wrote the piece after his return from his first solo trip to Europe in the summer of 1906. The article was a review of an eccentric book, *Le secret des troubadours* by Josephin Péladan.
[4] **Henry Morganthau Jr.**
[5] **Jesse Isidor Straus**
[6] This article appeared as "Europe MCMXXXVI: Reflections on the Eve of a New Era" in the second issue of *Globe* (May 1937, pp. 106–10; see Contribution #2).
[7] In a letter to Pound dated March 8, 1920, Scofield Thayer offered Pound the position of "foreign editor or English Agent" for *The Dial* and offered him $750 per year (see Sutton, *The Dial,* p. 13). This would amount to $62.60 per month.
[8] Manuldruck was an offset printing process developed in Switzerland that improved print quality while reducing costs. Pound was interested in innovations and techniques in printing, photography and microfilming which provided ways of preserving and publishing manuscript materials.
[9] **Erskine Caldwell**
[10] **Basil Bunting**
[11] **Harold Franklin**
[12] **Gorham Munson**
[13] **James Laughlin IV**

JD3

September 11, 1936

TSL GS (YCAL)
Mr. Ezra Pound,
310 San Georgio (presso Scarpa),
Venezia, Italy.

Dear Mr. Pound:

Thank you for your letter of August 29. Your conditions are okay, also the suggested introductory article. You can understand the type of pressure that makes us in a hurry and the good reasons that may account for a delay in getting out our first number. We were going to wire you but thought better of it, so you get the difference. Our usual cheque to you will be $20.

We are enclosing our original draft for page allotment of material. You will notice that "Foreign Correspondence" gets 20 pages (average page content 500 words); a possibility of half a dozen regular contributors with another half a dozen rotating for two or three places on the list, (countries of minor importance). Of course this estimate can be cut to three or four men covering the whole of Europe, maintaining topical division by countries. The return to the individual would thus be higher. Do you think some decent men *could* be obtained under the same temporary conditions that you are willing to accept? If not, this section tones down to the quality of Andre de Fouquieres[1] and Pierre Audiat[2] or the New Yorker (we have contacts for this type of rubrique).

You will also note that the general attention of the magazine is directed at the constraints in people and place. As material come in the angle seems even sharper. Of course in the "reportages"there is an opportunity to suggest what is *happening* to them collectively, but again it is more likely the social side would be treated as a *condition*, with no direction of opinion.

We assume that monthly letters survey the whole social side and not present complete analysis of isolated problems, unless the actual situation is in itself a preoccupation (Spain and Portugal). We know personally enough about the obsessions of European news, peddling a war scare daily for the past four years. During that time Americans have discovered a new field of sensation-interest, though with no attempt at making head or tale of a muddle of facts that are fast confusing and annoying them. There is also the point of establishing a direct and immediate contact with the cultural side.

Our method in getting contributors has been largely inclusive. Our response return has been about 10%. In the case of promises or some indication that an author sees the point, in spite of the vagueness of our ad, we follow up.

Some are willing to take the chance. Except for yourself, no one has used much imagination.

We have written Caldwell (July 31) but his reply isn't in yet. It would be a big help if you can put us in contact with others. Is Laughlin still in Harvard?[3]

The question of colour work is too obscure to go into. If our schemes pan out we will be convincing people that four colour process plates *are* a waste of money. According to our present plans leaving out illustrations wouldn't advance our text prices much.

Yours,

James Taylor Dunn (signed)

[1] **André de Fouquières**
[2] **Pierre Audiat**
[3] **James Laughlin IV** had graduated from Harvard in the spring of 1936.

JD4

TSL GS (YCAL)

September 12, 1936

Mr. Ezra W. Pound,
310 San Geogorio (presso Scarpa),
Venezia, Italy.

Dear Mr. Pound:

Evidently I made no direct mention of a check in my last letter.

Yours,

James Taylor Dunn (signed)

[1] Dunn would have found Pound listed in alumni records at Hamilton as "Ezra Weston Pound." Pound used this form of his name during his undergraduate years instead of the later "Ezra Loomis Pound".

JD5

TSL GS (YCAL)

September 16, 1936

Mr. Ezra Pound,
310 San Gregorio,
presso Scarpa,
Venezia, Italy.

Dear Mr. Pound:

This is to report receipt of your manuscript "Europe, 1936".[1] It will go in as is unless we put in footnotes and go completely OBVIOUS. However, the moment isn't very near and the idea that we aren't trying to get out a literary magazine as an interior decoration for the skulls of our readers is not so easy to get across. Or that we are avant garde privately. Thank you for having understood this from the beginning.

Meanwhile, a question not bearing on your article but on yourself, if you have any special personal comment on what you're doing and how you feel or can we quote from a letter.

Yours,

(Signed) James Taylor Dunn

for J.W.G. Dunn

[1] Contribution #2.

EP3

TLS P (BL)

310 San Gregorio VENEZIA . 24 Sept. [1936]

Dear Dunn.

NOTE, I find awful slip in carbon of my article.
Europe 1936. <Page ONE> Para/ <ONE> III. line 2. Sallustio BANDINI[1] not Bandello. (I may have corrected it in yr/ copy.) if not, correct it NOW.
tomb of Sallustio Bandini.
I got a shock in looking over it last eve. As I wrote you from Siena in ink, I have no record of what I said.[2]
I take it you can't afford to have me put time in<t>o organizing European end. I ~~will~~, <have> pro bono publico, writ~~e~~ <ten> to (to save TIME)

Jean Barral,[3]

6 Place Garibaldi, Nice.

Basil Bunting [4] 6 South Hill Park Mansions, Hampstead

London N.W.3.

But you shd. write <to them>on receipt of this. They COULD do the job if the pay satisfy<s> em. Barral might even be able to write direct in English. esp. if you were prepared to correct small slips of expression. That wd. be quicker than having him send stuff in French. IF he will take the trouble for the price. I shd. suggest Bunting be asked how MUCH of the London and Eng/ stuff he wants to do,

(slow bloke) and whether he wants

Bridson[5] to help. and or Angold.[6]

Butch.[7] Is too busy. and would only do econ. pure.

Your best card with the people I now name is that I am doing a monthly letter. as a trial. to see if the mag. CAN rise enough. <be a good enough mag.>

You wd. be lucky IF Guy Hickok of Brooklyn Daily Eagle[8] wd. touch the Paris news. <as distinct from Barral's all france> IF he has gone back to Paris etc. He never answers letters. and as regular old guard journalist I doubt if you can pay for him. but TRY.

address Brooklyn Eag<le.> Brooklyn. or N.Y.

Harold Franklin,[9] 320 W. 76th St. New York does just the kind of travel etc. stuff that your contents list looks as if you wanted.

Jas Laughlin,[10] present address, Robin Hill, Norfolk, Conn.

D. C. Fox, Forschungs Institut.[11] 26 Gr Eshenheimer str.

Frankfurt am Main, Germany.

<*EP has written in the margin*: am speaking to Izzo and Camerino here in Venice./ Try e.e. cummings and Joe Gould>[12]

for Frobenius african exploration (archeological, but with adventure and legends collected.[13]

All these people could do what you want. It is now up to you to persuade 'em. and to make CLEAR WHAT you want them to do.

With low pay, all you can do is persuade. you cant expect any GOOD writers to accommodate himself very much. Certainly no one will go out for 15 or 20 bucks as they do for 150, 175 from Esquire, (Hem gets 450 I hear)[14]

AND most of the stuff you seem to want cd. be done by college boys, so long as you have some strong stuff and don't let crude ideology mess into foreground.

As TIMING is very important. <L>et me know when first issue is to come out and how far ahead you go to press.

Must be SURE my monthly guide letter goes in, but want to hold second one as long as possible, so as to catch events as near printing date as possible. WHEN it happens to matter.

Most of my items will be necessary, I mean they'd have to get printed in Globe some time.

Best play wd. be <for me.> to send BODY of article in ample time, and a couple of sheets supplementary, to go in IF they catch the printing, and if not to precede the next article.

Thus.

<A> body for say ~~OCT**~~ Nov

<B> couple of pages for Nov, IF they get there
or to start the DEC.

<C> body for DEC.

and so on, in this matter.

I mean whe~~m~~<n> ~~thre~~ <there> are pretty details, like Krassin's daughter.[15] sometimes I will, or may send the Stop Press, just as items. one line <each> and take 'em up as subject matter in the following article.

And HELL YESSS. You ought to run Joe Gould's Oral History.[16]

e,e, cummings, 4 Patchen Place. New York

Joe Gould care cummings, or last known address, Box 484 Central Islip N.Y.[17] you have a chance of getting cummings if he knows I'm in and that you are ASKING Gould. That oral hist. has been waiting for you for 15 years. other editors too god damn dumb to see it. You may have to cut and select the Gould. but it is a Feature. I cited it in Dial artcl. on "Dr. Williams position <1928>"[18] This essay is in Polite Essays,[19] which is now in press FABER, London. assuming that Cambridge <Univ.> Press is printing for Faber, simultaneous with "Collected Poems" of Ford Madox Ford, being pubd. by Ox<f>ord Univ. Press.[20]

you can use those items in page of author's bio. blurbs.

My recent books. Nott and Co. London. new editn. TA HIO, of Confucius, done into American Language.[21]

<*Vertical handwritten note in right margin*: "|14| Memories of the West. try Bulah Patterson, Big Timber. Mont.">[22]

Fenollosa "Chinese Written Character" (Nott and Co. with notes by E.P.)[23] "Polite Essays", Faber. in press, will prob. be out when your first issue appears. also try

<1.> H. W. Hawk, [24]Rancho Kwen Channo, S. Christobal. N. Mex.

he might do a local skitch no use sending him a circular.

Am trying to keep off the god damn lierary blokes.

<2.> I doubt whether Fack, Hugo Fack,[25] 309 Madison St. San Antonio, Tex can do anything but economics

<3.)> F. M. Ford, Guarantee Trust. 4 Place de la Concorde. you can't pay rates of a man [26] in Harpers and American Murk.[27]

<4> Possibly Peter Fanning, [28] 12 York Street Newcastle England cd. provide remembrances.
<3. [sic] > Hilaire Hiler,[29] for ART, Rodin Studios, 200 W. 57th N.Y. or Paris local colour.

(Initialed in the margin) EZ
P

[1] **Sallustio Bandini**
[2] See EP1.
[3] **Jean Barral**
[4] **Basil Bunting**
[5] **D.G. Bridson**
[6] **John Penrose Angold**
[7] **Montgomery Butchart**
[8] **Guy Carlton Hickok**
[9] **Harold Franklin**
[10] **James Laughlin IV**
[11] **Douglas Claughton Fox**
[12] **Leo Frobenius**
[12] **Carlo Izzo**
[13] Between 1904 and 1935, **Leo Frobenius** made fourteen expeditions to Africa to gather ethnographic, folkloristic, and art historical material relating to a wide range of African peoples living in many areas of the continent. A popular book in English, *African Genesis* (1937), prepared by Frobenius with the assistance of **Douglas Clayton Fox**, presented a selection of these African tales. Frobenius held that it was important to recognize that the rock art found in many regions of Africa had a direct relationship to the folklore that still made up the oral literature of these same regions.
[14] Pound's fee for *Esquire* contributions was $150 for 1,500 words. Pound had slightly underestimated **Ernest Hemingway**'s fees. By 1936, Arnold Gingrich, *Esquire*'s editor, was paying Hemingway $500 per 1,500 words. These fees allowed Hemingway to purchase his famous fishing boat the *Pilar*.
[15] This appears to be **Leonid Borisovich Krasin.**
[16] **Joseph Ferdinand Gould**
[17] **Edward Estlin Cummings**
[18] Pound's essay, "Dr. Williams' Position" (1928) appeared in the November 1928 issue of *The Dial*. Pound comments here:

> "Williams has written: 'All I do is try to understand something in its natural colours and shapes.'....But the concrete example of this literary process, whether by Williams or by that still more unreceived and uncomprehended native hickory, Mr Joseph Gould, seems an unrelated and inexplicable

incident to our populace and to our 'monde—or whatever it is—littéraire'. We have, of course, distinctly American authors, Mr Frost for example, but there is an infinite gulf between Mr Frost on New England customs, and Mr. Gould on race prejudice; Mr Frost having simply taken on, without any apparent self-questioning, a definite type and set of ideas and sensibilities, known and established in his ancestral demesne. That is to say he is 'typical New England'. Gould is no less New England, but parts of his writing could have proceeded equally well from a Russian, a German, or an exceptional Frenchman—the difference between regionalism, or regionalist art and art that has its root in a given locality."

[19] *Polite Essays* was issued February 11, 1937 by Faber & Faber.
[20] **Ford Madox Ford**'s *Collected Poems* appeared in 1936, issued by Oxford University Press, New York, with an introduction by **William Rose Benét**. It is not clear why Pound thought of this publication as being simultaneous with his *Polite Essays*—though there was an essay dealing with Ford in this volume ("The Prose Tradition in Verse")—especially since Pound's book of essays appeared in 1937.
[21] This was the first British edition of Pound's *Ta Hio, The Great Learning: Newly Rendered into the American Language* published in May 1936 at the Kynoch Press for Stanley Nott Ltd. It was issued as the second volume in the "Ideogramatic Series, Edited by Ezra Pound." This edition of the *Ta Hio* was essentially a reprint of the "translation" that Pound brought out with the University of Washington Book Store in April 1928. Pound attached great significance to the *Ta Hio*. Commenting in an essay of 1934 entitled "Dateline," he asserts: "As to what I believe: I believe the *Ta Hio*. When a dozen people have convinced me that they understand that so lucid work, I may see reason for accepting a more elaborate exposition."
[22] **Beulah (neé Busha) Patterson** (1886–1979), Pound's cousin on the Pound side of the family. Mrs. Patterson kept up an occasional and entertaining correspondence with Dorothy Pound and this exchange may have spurred Pound to recommend her to Dunn.
[23] As **Ernest Fenellosa**'s literary executor, Pound edited and annotated his essay "The Chinese Written Character as a Medium for Poetry." It first appeared in Pound's 1920 collection of essays *Instigations*. The edition mentioned here, issued by Kynoch Press for Stanley Nott Ltd in March 1936, was the essay's first independent appearance (see previous note).
[24] **Harold W. Hawk**
[25] **Hugo Robert Fack**
[26] Dunn contacted Ford directly. However, Pound's comment about low rates was on the mark. Ford shot back to Dunn: "The Globe appears to be a very spirited undertaking...your terms are low and my expenses...are very high.

Moreover, as a writer I am remarkably voluminous and I can sçarcely write anything worth saying in less than six or seven thousand words" (FMF to JWGD jr., Jan 16, 1937).

[27] In the 1930s, Ford was regularly publishing articles in the well-established American magazine *Harper's* as well as in H. L. Mencken's *American Mercury.* The series of articles Ford published in the *American Mercury* during this period was issued in book form under the title *Portraits from Life* (1937).

[28] **Peter Fanning**

[29] **Hilaire Hiler**

EP4

TSL P (BL)

Venice, [September 29, 1936]

Dear Dunn

Not my place to comment on what I am doing. Got enough to do doing it.

If you want comment on what you are doing: Thank heaven you are NOT trying to start a "literary magazine". Literature in the sense implied in the phrase "a literary magazine" is having a vacation. All the men with enough intelligence to write a good story or novel are concentrated on the problem of monetary and credit issue, the nature of money (not the tricks used in getting it out of others, but the way it gets into existence at all).

This is to be distinguished vigorously from social studies as conceived in carrot=fed generation of Shaws, Webbs, Welles, Fabians,[1] and their still lower derivatives in America. verbal expression of psychological fiction went out when Max Ernst did two books of engravings: "Woman with a Hundred Heads", and "Dream of a Young Girl in Convent."[2]

E. P.

you can print any of this you like,
next pages are private.

Dear Dunn

Private.

Herewith a note you may quote from if you like. ~~this~~ <these 3 pages> page ~~is~~ <are> private.

I THINK yr/ difficulty is that you WANT a kind of work for which there IS a large market. The best men who have trad<e> s~~h~~<k>ill in this upper bracket

<of> journalism aren't looking for new mags. they are already being paid elsewhere.
Only an ideal or a sense of mission of some kind causes men to write for no <,> or low<,> no pay.
You don<'>t or shouldn't want foreign news sifted through what <B>ritish <S>ecret <S>ervice or some oil company thinks the americ/ peepul ought to know. That rules out a number of snappy well connected correspondents.
You CAN <,> with time get very young men. But unless you follow system of o~~y~~<t>her mags/ of information, either anonymous writing and/or same blokes writing over two or three pseudonyms, you don<'>t offer a living full wage to your European staff. Nor cd/ you pay traveling expenses.
Were I 20 or 25 years younger I might see the fun in filling the stage with a few new writers. Men<c>ken used to write a good deal of Owen Hatteras in the S.Set. etc.[3]
An office name used by several people prevents identification of it with any of the staff. They try to live up to the talented character of Josephus Jones/ Hildebrand Brown or whoever.

Am willing to pinch hit in an emergency.

But you ought to get some clever guy IN St Paul.
I mean it is younger men's job.

<320 W.76. N.Y.>

Franklin might do a good deal.[4] Laughlin[5] is interested in his own writing. But also versatile. He and ~~Sloo~~ Slocum,[6] might come on.
I have written <J.> Cournos[7] co/Criterion,[8] as haven't his address here. He c<d.> do Russian stuff. reads it as easy as english.
I suggest you write to Peter Fanning[9]

12 York St. Newcastle England.

SAY that for your purpose it don<'>t matter about his using new material. <H>eaven knows he has seen enough. All you want is that the adventures or thing seen shall not have been printed in the U.S.A. and not in England in the past few months. <or out of print.>
I should say GET cummings [10] and keep off...oh well...no use my prejudicing you against anyone. But get the BEST of the avant guard, in e,e,c[ummings], and you keep the rest in order, and can be as conservative as you like throughout the other 94 pages.

[*vertically written in the right-hand margin:* <?? Marianne Moore on events.[11] 260 Cumberland St. Brooklyn N.Y.>]

[*vertically written in the left hand margin:* < W. D. H. Rouse[12] Histon Manor Cambs. England. "Trailing 'by sail boat.".]

You probably know the Northwester<n>[13] and other regional mags.

You can invite theire[sic] dozen best writers.
Ask G. S. Hutchison,[14] Inkford House, Aylesbury Eng.
and
J. Hargrave,[15] Wayside, Kings Langley, Herts. Eng.
for adventure stories, not politics
I don<'>t see how people like Ion Munro[16] and Fodor[17] cd. write at yr. rates. AND I don't kno<w> what the ethics is for correspondents of particular papers, spilling it elsewhere.
Sir Leo Chiozza L. Money.[18] Old Quarry, Bramley, N. Guilford
Surry
might reminisce <ask him what its like, being a cabinet minister.> on the other hand he might lamm in a sonnet and you<'>d be did.
The Fanning and the Cournos <& Rouse> are the two best bets in this lot.
Let me know WHEN you want my NEXT "Europe". Is it going to be 1937 ??
WHEN a partocular thing was needed for the Little Review,[19] I often found it easier to invent an author and write it for him than to get it out of some half baked ass/pyrant .
am in fact at the moment or rather for the fortnight and STILL <struggling> with a writer who has an ORDER for an article. needs an opening paragraph which I cd. do in eight minutes.

Will take a week to get it written. so that the ed/ can use it.

Of course IF I do it <,> my style will stick out from the rest.

//

As to the pinch hitting, I can if needed in emergency do an article on a particular topic, more elaborate than the Europe notes and explaining the topic, rather than giving it as item of news <using pseudonym.>

BUT demme, I don<'>t want to turn dray horse. I ought not to do ha~~n~~<c>k. <O>r if so, it ought to be VERY LITTLE, and so well paid that I wdn<'>t have to worry about any other income.

per year

I cant be the whole European staff for less then DeKruif gets for a single Home Choinul article.[20]
and you aren't looking for phantom army ANYhow.
B.M.G. Adams [21] 4 Grantchester Rd. Cambridge. Eng. (hasn't so far as I know written anything for ten years.)
Try ~~Bridson, 20 Dayne Ave. Prestwyn~~ Manchester
~~D.G.~~
D.G. Bridson [22]59 Lansdowne Rd. — West Didsbury <Eng.>
Hell, wot about <J.> Farrel. always the same damn <Studs> Lonnigan ???[23]
a bit dull by now. cd. he do a different

[*Handwritten vertically in the right hand margin*: also Langston Hughes.[24] (once at) 837 E. 24th St. Los Angeles or his pubs.]

[*Handwritten vertically in the left hand margin*: Charlotte Hirsch,[25] 68 Rue Brancion, 7 Vauginard Paris]

Now there is a ex member of the ex russian general staff that might just, or his wife might, reminsce. try. Gen Golijewsky[26]
7 rue Felix Faure, Paris XV <France>
saying I said so.
[*Signed in the upper right margin*:] <Yrs EP>

[1] These are various political-economic reform movements associated with the Irish playwright, essayist, and critic George Bernard Shaw (1856–1950), the English socialists Beatrice (1858–1943) and Sidney (1859–1947) Webb, and the English historian, essayist, novelist, and science fiction writer **H. G. Wells** (1866–1946). The socialist Fabian Society was formed in England in 1884. The Society took a gradualist approach to political, economic, and social change. It also advocated political action through legal means and existing political institutions to achieve the political-economic transformation of society. Pound came in contact with these movements as well as individuals such as Shaw and Wells during his stay in England between 1908 through 1919. These associations came through his friendships with **Yeats, Ford Madox Ford**, and Violet Hunt.
[2] Pound admired **Max Ernst**'s *La Femme 100 têtes* (1929) and *Rêve d'une petite fille qui voulut entrer au Carmel* (1930).
[3] *Smart Set* was a New York-based periodical founded in March 1900. From 1914 until 1923 it was edited by **H. L. Mencken** and George Jean Nathan. Owen Hatteras was a pseudonym Mencken frequently used in the pages of *Smart Set*.
[4] **Harold Franklin**
[5] **James Laughlin IV**
[6] **John Jermain Slocum**
[7] **John Cournos**
[8] The *Criterion* was founded in 1922 by T. S. Eliot with the financial backing of Mary Lilian, Lady Rothermere, wife of Harold Sidney Hainsworth, the Viscount Rothermere, owner of the *Daily Mail*. It was initially published by R. Cobden-Sanderson, London and later taken over by Faber & Faber. The first issue appeared in October 1922 and the journal ran until 1939.
[9] **Peter Fanning**
[10] **Edward Estlin Cummings**
[11] **Marianne Craig Moore**
[12] **William Henry Denham Rouse**

[13] This may be the *Northwestern Chronicle* edited in St. Paul, Minnesota, and printed in Milwaukee, Wisconsin, as was *Globe*. However, the *Northwestern Chronicle* appears to have ceased publication in the late 1920s and no evidence exists that Pound ever contributed to the paper.

[14] **Lt. Colonel Graham Seton Hutchison**

[15] **John Hargrave**

[16] Probably **Ion Smeaton Munro**

[17] **Marcel William Fodor**

[18] **Sir Leo George Chiozza Money**

[19] *The Little Review* was one of the most influential of the "little magazines" active in the first decades of the twentieth century. Founded in 1914 in Chicago by Margaret Anderson and Jane Heap, *The Little Review* went on to live a peripatetic life, edited from the shores of Lake Michigan, in California, and finally in New York and Paris. Pound acted as foreign correspondent for *The Little Review* from 1917–19 and was again involved in 1921–3. Pound's own work frequently appeared in *The Little Review*.

[20] According to a letter to Pound, **Paul Henry De Kruif** mentions a number of his articles in *The Ladies' Home Journal*: "Forgotten Children," "Dollars for Childern," "If We Get Rain," and "Heartbroken Children" (PDK to EP, August 18, 1934 [YCAL]). Pound wrote to De Kruif about the articles: "Sorry not not have [sic] seen yr/Home Chional articles. Paper not on sale here (thank god) and you don't xpect me to subscribe??" (EP to PDK, carbon, no date [YCAL]).

[21] **B. M. G. Adams (Mrs. Evelyn St. Bride Scratton)**

[22] **G. D. Bridson**

[23] **James T. Farrell**

[24] **(James Mercer) Langston Hughes**

[25] **Charlotte Teller Hirsch**

[26] **Honor Goleyevsky**

JD6

TSL on GS (YCAL)

October 6, 1936

Mr. Ezra W. Pound,[1]
310 San Gregorio,
presso Scarpa,
Venezia, Italy

Dear Mr. Pound:

Just a note about *Globe* and how it is coming along. At your suggestion we wrote to Hilaire Hiler and have received an excellent article called "Cuisine in Bohemia"[2] which will appear in our first issue. We also sent a follow up letter to Erskine Caldwell,[3] and in return got a very encouraging letter, a copy of which I enclose. As I see it now, the first issue will contain the following:

"Emigrants" by L.A.G. Strong[4]
"Woman Slayer" by George Schuyler[5]
"Merry Reno" by William Saroyan[6]
"The Tragic Land of Spain" by Sisley Huddleston[7]
"No Country" by H. E. Bates[8]
"Cusine in Bohemia" By Hilaire Hiler
"A Chinese Man of Letters" by Vincent Starrett[9]
"Marseille" by Paul Morand[10]
"Just Traveling" by Langston Hughes[11]
"Kangaroo" by Alfred [sic *Albert*] Richard Wetjen[12]
"Bar-Eyed Wolfs' Boy" by Jesse Stuart[13]
"The Sugar Beet Country" by Hope Williams Sykes[14]

Plus your own "Europe 1936"[15] The letter part of the magazine is the only thing incomplete.

James Laughlin has been written to,[16] but as yet no reply has been received.

Sincerely,

James Taylor Dunn (signed)

encl.

[1] For the address "Mr. Ezra W. Pound" see **JD4** note 1.
[2] **Hilaire Hiler**'s article, about recipes from artists, did run in the first issue of *Globe* (March, 1937, pp. 74–6).
[3] **Erskine Caldwell**

[4] **Leonard Alfred George Strong**
[5] **George Schuyler**
[6] **William Saroyan**
[7] **Sisley Huddleston**
[8] **Herbert Ernest Bates**
[9] **Charles Vincent Emerson Starrett**
[10] **Paul Morand**
[11] **Langston Hughes**' story "Just Traveling," about his visit to Paris, was the lead article of the second issue of *Globe* (May 1937, pp. 4–7).
[12] **Albert Richard Wetjen**'s "Kangaroo," the story mentioned above, never appeared in *Globe*. Wetjen published three articles in *Globe*. His first, "Glow-worms in Glory," about visiting a cave in New Zealand, was published in the first issue of *Globe* (March 1937, pp. 114–18).
[13] **Jesse Hilton Stuart**
[14] **Hope Williams Sykes**
[15] See Contribution #2 and **EP2** note 5. This article actually ran in the second issue (May 1937) of *Globe*.
[16] **James Laughlin IV**

JD7

October 12, 1936

TSL GS (YCAL)

Mr. Ezra Pound
Via Marsala 12/5
Rapallo, Italy.

Dear Mr. Pound:

Thanks for the photos, suggestions and names.[1] I have written, following your indications, to 14 of them (Oct. 5th). Later I realized you meant by "come on" for Laughlin and Slocum to come out there to St. Paul.[2] There is room for one at the office (a transformed apartment). I will talk with my brothers.

John Cournos writes (evidently as soon as he got your letter)[2] he would be willing; wants to know exactly what our slant is, and also enclosed a piece (about meeting someone in a pub, England).

We are bringing out our prospectus in another week. (Copies for advertisers and subscribers and general follow-up). We have made initial contacts with publishers' representatives east of here. I will let you know how fast things move on this line and give you date of release of first number approximately a month in advance, also regular date of month when GLOBE will be put to bed. Your scheme of time delay in sending on material, Stop Press line ought to keep things warm.

Your check for October is enclosed. What exchange do you get? I referred to your "biog. blurb" when I wrote for "Comments". So the question was answered anyway.

Sincerely,
[Signed]
James Taylor Dunn

[1] Dunn is referring to **EP4** in which Pound apparently enclosed photos—though Pound does not mention them in the letter.
[2] **John Cournos**' piece, which Dunn describes as being "about meeting someone in a pub, England," never ran. *Globe* did publish a number Cournos' articles on the Soviet Union and leftists in New York City.

EP5

TSL TAX (BL)

October 23, 1936

Dear Dunn

NO. I didn't mean you to give office job to Slocum or Laughlin[1]. S. is rich and <J>as/ <L.> don't need a job and ought not to be in office.
Cournos[2] out to be very serviceable office man. (even Zukofsky[3] might. but wd. be too intent on literary experiment and possibly incapable of taking orders.
Cournos is old enough to bend to common sense and needs of a magazine.
practical needs etc. <Turn hard
to this & that>
I am suggesting to L[aughlin]/ that he stop off in St. Paul. to see you.
lire
Chq. mentioned was not in envelope of <yr.> letter mailed on Oct 12 I got 10.95 for dollar this a.mn[sic] another transaction.
Expect D.C.Fox[4] here is a week or so.
<yrs. EP>

[1] **John Slocum**
[2] **John Cournos**
[3] **Louis Zukofsky**
[4] **Douglas Clayton Fox** had written Pound on October 21, 1936 (DCF to EP [YCAL]) that there was a possibility that he would be in Florence sometime

between October 30 and November 10 and wanted to know if he could travel to Rapallo to visit Pound.

JD8

TSL GS (YCAL)

October 13, 1936

Mr. Ezra Pound,
Via Marsala 12/5
Rapallo, Italy.

Dear Mr. Pound:

It happens again!

Here's the check left out of yesterday's letter.

Sincerely,

[Signed]

James Taylor Dunn

EP6

TSC (BL)

[pmk: 25.10.36 Rapallo/Genova]
Via Marsala 12-5
24 Oct. 24 [1936]

J.T. Dunn esq
GLOBE
1033 Lincoln Ave
St Paul
Minn.
U.S.America

chq/ recd. Do make it CLEAR (gently for he is elderly) to Peter Fanning[1] that what you want from him is FACTS; first hand facts; things he has seen <or IS seeing> and KNOWN in North England.
He cant get continental news in Newcastle.
His job ought to be North England the Clyde ; British labour etc. that is what he KNOWS; plus some american xxperience years ago.

When possible TELL writer what YOU want from them. It always helps both writer and edtr. eases relations when they propose something worse and/ no harm IF they (in 1% of possible cases) have something better or [*in the left hand margin*] a brain wave.

<yrs E.P.> [*signed by hand in upper left of the card*]

[1] **Peter Fanning**

EP7

TSC (BL)

[pmk: 27.10.36 Rapallo/Genova]
Oct. 27, [1936]

J.T.Dunn esq
GLOBE
1033 Lincoln Ave
St Paul
Minn.
U.S.America

what become of Morley Callaghan.??[1]
I turned up a vol of Exile yester/ and found him readable.[2]
If insuffcient new fiction/what price second serial rights on stuff utterly unknown and buried in mags/ of under 1000 circ. 0f 1920; 1923 etc. there are even a few of my trans/ of P.Morand; unpubd/ because brit swine of pubr/ went bankrupt. series whereof Dial had some.[3] Morand MUCH better at the time than since. dunno what the copyright etc. ~~pp~~ position is. I believe they were good reading by time I got thru with 'em fer my own instruction you might tell me who IS
[*continues vertically on left side, obverse of the card*] is now read/ and/or still read in the U.S.A. and whom you would LIKE to print. and/or among europeans. expect Fox here in ten days or so.[4] did I say send notice of mag to Bulah Patterson; Big Timber Montana?[5]

<E.P.>

[1] **Morley Callaghan**
[2] **Morley Callaghan**'s story, "Ancient Lineage" appeared in *The Exile* 3: 79–89
[3] Pound is not accurate in his account. In 1922, Pound and the London publishers Chapman and Dodd agreed to Pound making a translation of **Paul Morand**'s *Ouvert la nuit*. However, when Pound submitted the manuscript of the translation, the publisher Guy Chapman suspected that the translation was

inferior. His fears were confirmed by an independent reader. Chapman then rejected the translation as unsuitable for publication. Chapman's firm, then Chapman & Hall, did go bankrupt a few years afterwards, but their collapse had nothing to do with the failure of Pound's translation to appear (for details see Gallup E6d, pp. 448–9). In 1920 Pound already had been pushing *The Dial* when he was *The Dial*'s correspondent in Paris. Pound suggested translations from Morand's new book of poetry, *Feuilles de temperature*, which Pound referred to as "Fever Chart." He recommended two other pieces, "Hungarian Night" and "Turkish Night," which were Pound's early translations from Morand's *Ouvert la nuit*. Only one of these pieces saw print in The Dial: "Turkish Night" (LXXI 3 [September 1921]).

[4] **Douglas Clayton Fox**

[5] **Beulah Patterson**

EP8

TSL TAX (BL)

3 Nov. [1936]

Dear Dunn et frere

Thanks for the nasty magazines just come. I notice one was open at ARTHUR P/[1]

If you want to git a rise out of my old man mention Arthur.

Reply is

"NO relation."

Cuthbert[2] (deceased)<,> Roscoe[3] ; yes, but where the shit Arthur come from I don't know.

BUT he is NOT among the ~~knowl~~ known products of any of my Gt/ Grandfathers 12 brothers[4].

He is the hired yes man fer General Motors.

There is NO use in Minimizing the force of compitition from the very able sons of bloody bitches collected in the three mags/ you have sent.

To buck this kind of crap; and NOT be able to pay high rates is no sinch.

God damn it/ a country that stands Lippmann!![5]

accepts Lippmann and Marcossen[6] and Sokolsky[7]...

The baccillus is as hard to isolate as syphillis worm. colourless.

The sign of hope is in diminished bulk of Americ. MURKury.[8]

Damned if I see how to buck this line up<,> as far as eastern circ. is concerned. I mean ON a small capital.

Sugar in the urine. That is my first diagnosis. But it is vague/ it is metaphorical. INVITE editorial confidence/ private:

WHICH populace are you aiming at. ?

Wouldn't it be better to try for a paying circulation among Coughlin's[9] public than among those already fed to the gills by the N. York slop ?
Good GAWD/ Madox Ford with a Preface by Benet. !![10]
Waaal; thaaar she blows. If a man has weaknesses
The damn TROUBLE about getting BETTER stuff than the Atlantic etc. is that it takes TIME.
<I mean for a man to write ~~after~~ & collect the facts.>

That means PAY that will cover board bill of blokes that do the work. This no<t> beefing. But the clearer we see what we are up against...the better we go.
Globe rates really cover over time work of men who have <other> jobs paying a living wage.
as I see it/ a couple of damn hard workers in the office doing DIGEST racket/ clipping indefatigably.[11]
and as large a circle of special workers...by the way; do you ever see the LISTENER; B.B.C.[12] weekly said to have the largest circulation in England?? and Eng/ is NOT the U.S.
Other side of the question is how much BETTER can Globe be and get away with it?
Oh well/ I spoze I can get to go blind at my next article. But let me know WHICH of the various brands of American mugg's zeen; we have got to sell against. I mean mOSTLY as distinct from against 'em all.

4th. Nov.

Judging from the first reports of election I take it practical editing will INCLUDE a tolerant (at least) attitude toward the Nude Eel?[13] An optimistic search for the merits of the President, if not of Mr. Farley ??[14]

DO be specific on these points.
Either we build up a paper which moves with the ship of state
(trying to act as a small part of the rudder)
or we bust.
If fragments of the american form of govt. can be saved /so much the better... or is even this angle taboo in St. Paul?
At any rate the election proves that the BOUGHT stink of the Atlantic Monthly does NOT represent the gt/ heaRRRT ov the peepul.

<yrs
EP>

[1] **Arthur Pound**
[2] **Cuthbert W. Pound**
[3] Receiving a misaddressed book in 1935, **Nathan Roscoe Pound** forwarded it to its intended recipient in Rapallo. Pound responded to Roscoe's cordial note with the following: "Respected DEAN, and estimable cousin (at least Dad says you are of the line of the eleven brothers of Joel and Elisha, along with the late Cuthbert (who seems to have been a good scout, or at least by his obits..." (EP to NRP, December 16, 1935 [YCAL]). Homer Pound was correct about Roscoe Pound's connection to his family, though his knowledge of the exact connection was vague. Their common ancestors seem to be John Pound II (1685–1756), his son Elijah Pound I (1712–80), and Elijah I's son, Elijah Pound II (1756–1839). Joel L. Pound was the grandson of Elijah II. All were Quakers living in the Pennsylvania-New Jersey and New York state area, except for Joel who died in Medford, Minnesota, perhaps in the mid-nineteenth century. (See Sayre, *The Life of Roscoe Pound*, pp. 16–17; compare genealogical chart after p. 110 with Pound and Litz, *EP/DS*, "Pound Ancestry Chart," p. 353.)
[4] Pound likely was referring to Elijah Pound III (1802–91), the father of Ezra's grandfather Thaddeus Coleman Pound. (See Pound and Litz, *EP/DS*, "Pound Ancestry Chart" and discussion pp. 353–4.)
[5] During **Walter Lippmann**'s rise as journalist and political pundit, Pound was very aware of Lippmann's influence and that of his journal *The New Republic.* By 1917, Pound's complete revulsion is evident when he writes to Margaret Anderson at the *The Little Review* about the distribution of copies of an issue of the journal: "...Also find Charlotte Hirsch...A letter sent in care of that Pig Lippmann, on the New Republic, might reach her..." (Scott et al., *Pound/The Little Review*, May 5, 1917, p. 30, also see notes 33–34).
[6] **Isaac Frederick Marcosson**
[7] **George Ephraim Sokolsky**
[8] **H. L. Mencken's** *The American Mercury*
[9] **Charles E. Coughlin**
[10] Pound was referring to **Ford Madox Ford's** *Collected Poems,* with a Preface by **William Rose Benét** (New York: Oxford University Press, 1936).
[11] Pound was antagonistic towards **William Rose Benét.** Typical of this attitude was Pound's response in 1933 to Benét's repeated invitation to the poet to contribute to an anthology in which poets were to choose their own poems and then comment upon them:

> ...I appreciate your kindness in cabling but I am afraid I shall have to be even more explicit in my answer. I think you have done too much harm, as asst. edtr. of the *Sat. Rev. Lit.*, from year to year pouring poison into or onto the enfeebled or adolescent Amurkn mind; or at any rate doing yr. and [Henry Seidel] Canby's damndest to preserve mildew [H. S. Canby

was an influential editor and critic also served as the chair of the Book of the Month Club] ...That may be Greek to you. I have no proof that you or C. EVER make the faintest effort to understand anything whatever outside yr. own set of fixed ideas and conveniences. Yr. weekly never opens up to what I consider decent opinion or sound criticism....Yr. proposed anth. is merely another effort (however delicate) to shove over more god damn'd stuff, personal touch, anything, absolutely anything to shield yr. booblik from fact, what is printed on the page" (Page, *Letters*, EP to WRB, January 23, 1933, pp. 243–4).

[12] *The Reader's Digest* was founded in Greenwich Village by DeWitt Wallace and his wife Lila Acheson. It collected and republished versions of articles which had already run elsewhere, or ran serializations of recently published books. The *Digest* grew rapidly and by the 1930s was one of the most widely read journals in the United States.
[13] *The Listener*, established 1929, is the official broadcast magazine of the BBC. In June 1936, D. F. Aitken, an editor for *The Listener*, solicited an article from Pound on the subject of medieval music for the journal's July issue. Pound responded with "Mediaeval Music and Yves Tinayre," which appeared in its July 22 issue. Pound contributed two more items to *The Listener* in 1936.
[14] The "Nude Eel" was Pound's punning reference to the Roosevelt administration's "New Deal" programs and policies. Pound may have picked up this pun from **E. E. Cummings**' poem on **Joe Gould**:

little joe gould has lost his teeth and doesn't know where
to find them(and found a secondhand set which click)little
gould used to amputate his appetite with bad brittle
candy but just(nude eel)now little joe lives on air
(#27, *No Thanks* [1935])

[15] **James Aloysius Farley**

JD9

[November 7, 1936]

TSL GS (YCAL)

Mr. Ezra Pound
Via Marsala 12/5
Rapallo, Italy.

Dear Mr. Pound:

Your typescript came two days ago.[1] Sorry this delay about going to press. GLOBE will be on the stands December 1st, or on the outside the 15th, and dated January 1. The prospectus will be sent you by next Wednesday and give you some idea of what we already have.

Is it all right to re-arrange the paragraph order of "That League in Calvin's City"?[2]

We are looking up Krassin's daughter and will probably find out who she is.[3] I suppose Neimeyer is the same class with de Wendel.[4]

The MID-WEST turned out to be more communist that expected. Nobody seems to know how long it will survive.[5]

Did your publisher who went bankrupt have American rights to your translations of Morand?[6] The unpublished ones sound interesting. We have been more general and specific, with the exception of some East European writers—Eugene Relgis, Zsolt Bela, etc.[7] Many have gone completely political and practically off the market unless they think they are associating themselves with the Cause.

Second rights on things buried in magazines could be used, but this is largely a matter of choice and related to their timeliness.

Morely Callahan [sic][8] was written to on September 2nd but we have had no answer as yet. Naturally a lot of people may come in when they see the magazine printed. We wrote Bulah Patterson about two weeks ago.[9] We heard from Fox and he is sending some stuff[10]. Peter Fanning has already sent in something on Hitler,[11] his idea being to write a series covering key men in Europe. There seems to be nothing new in what he wrote and we will try to get back to him on something closer to his own experiences. Cournos is sending in a monthly Russian letter and relaying material.[12]

We can't take up the matter just now of getting people around here. It is too damn confusing as it is. Our printer is 150 miles away, which will be ice-bound half the winter.[13]

The second issue should go to press by the 1st to the 5th of January, and all material be in by then, still keeping open a few stop lines.

Laughlin seems to be quite busy editing a new magazine devoted to American Sur-Realism.[14] I don't know if his case is going to be that of Erskine Caldwell who is doing a mid-weekly story and informed us some time back that his writing for us depended on whether that went through.[15]

We are getting out a real carte d'identité. If you want to send us a photo-mat picture we can stamp it with a seal, etc. However don't bother if you find the enclosed letter sufficient.[16]

Yours,
[Signature]
James Taylor Dunn

[1] This was probably the typescript of "That League in Calvin's Home City" (see Contribution #10) which was dated by Pound in the manuscript as being completed October 18, 1936.
[2] See note 1 above.
[3] For **Krasin**'s daughter Ludmila Mathias see **EP3**.
[4] **Otto Ernst Niemeyer**
[5] According to J. T. Dunn's notes, *The Mid-West*, lasted only for one tabloid "pre-issue" (August 1935, with a welcoming letter from Malcolm Cowley) and three subsequent regular issues (November 1936–January 1937). Dunn characterized the journal as "Stalinist-oriented." *The Mid-West* was published in Minneapolis, Minnesota, a contributors and artists associated with the journal contributed to *Globe* after it folded [Dunn Notebook].
[6] **Paul Morand**
[7] **Eugen Relgis** and **Zsolt Bela**
[8] **Morley Callaghan**
[9] **Beulah Patterson**
[10] The material **Douglas Clayton Fox** sent appeared as "Cultures in the Rock" in the May 1937 issue of *Globe* (pp. 11–16).
[11] *Globe* never published any of these proposed articles by **Peter Fanning.**
[12] **John Cournos**
[13] *Globe*'s printer, Cuneo Press, was about 325 miles away in Milwaukee, Wisconsin.
[14] **James Laughlin IV** was one of the founders of *View* along with Charles Henri Ford and Parker Tyler, but was with the magazine briefly before starting his publishing house, New Directions. *View* published a number of avant-garde American writers in the 1930s and 1940s.
[15] **Erskine Caldwell**
[16] Dunn enclosed a note on *Globe* stationery that read: "To the Gentlemen

of the Press and Parties Interested: This is to certify that Mr. Ezra Pound is an authorized general European correspondent of GLOBE, the International Magazine. [Signature] J. W. G. Dunn, Jr. Editor and Publisher"

JD10

TSL GS (YCAL)

November 10, 1936

Mr. Ezra Pound,
Via Marsala 12/5
Rapallo, Italy.

Dear Mr. Pound:

We have been working out deadlines, etc. and the 18th of the second month preceding the issue is very close. GLOBE will be on the stands simultaneously over the country on the 20th of the month, dated the 1st. With this arrangement it seems unwise to come out with the January 1st issue on the 20th of January, dated February 1st—deadline the 18th of December.

If you want to send in something especially timely, either to begin or conclude the main body of "Europe, 1936"[1] you have the above dates to go by. You can wait until the 18th and cable us the additional release. Naturally with the lapse of time between the deadline and the appearance on the stands such communications might be inside stuff and news only what you feel sure would not get out (if ever) before GLOBE.

The beginning of "Europe, 1936" is appearing in the prospectus.

Yours
[signed]
James Taylor Dunn

[1] Pound's article "Europe MCXXXVI" ran in the second issue of *Globe* (May 1937, pp. 106–10; see Contribution #2).

EP9

TSL GBS (BL)

<24 Nov>[ember 1936]

[stamped received] Dec 7 1936

Dear J.T.D.

Yes; quite all right to re=arrange the paragraph order in league in Calvin's City.[1]

General idea is that I send the stuff and you decant it/
judging the local scene and the possibilities of reception.
So long as you don't alter my meaning; its O.K. with me.
Thanks for the authorization letter, I enclose photo/ [2] an official card might come in handy/ can't do any harm to have it.
//
I shan't hustle for the deadline Dec. 18/
In fact events have caught up with the first article/
You might put an edt. note to THAT effect.
That wd. strengthen my remark on Jugoslavia.[3]
I shall let those two articles stand/ I want the more recent items for a third article that will be more solid ~~tHHHHHHHHHHH~~ as a survey than if I use up little<r> bits as stray items
Will note the I8TH . regular date. That roughly means Ist to 4th. <from> here ; I imagine.
es// An edt/ note on date I wrote you from Venice
which was Sept. 3.
and the Jugoslav Italian rapproachment in Nov. might be worth noting.[4]

<(2.>

esp/ if you measure it against the damn BUNK of the A.P.[5] and some of the Brit. papers
Not matter of news "scoop" but of having ~~just~~ enough HORSE SENSE to understand what is.

Let the articles stand/ date 'em and then I will do the March article so that that will get my account of Europe up to the minute. The first two can perfectly well be a sort of preface and the March article will leave here sometime between Xmas and I. Jan.

<introduction
for [?] your readers to
contemporary europe [sic].>

the poin<t> of view and comprehension is enough ahead of Gunther[6] and co/ to keep stuff fresh west of the Mississippi and ON the Boston east shore, until

March. (there is 20 years time lage in parts and 5 in others/) three months not too much to take up that slack.

stop press can start in third issue.

EP [signed]

[1] See **JD10** and Contribution #10.
[2] Pound enclosed a small photograph of himself with a typewritten inscription on the back reading: "E.P. wif his glasses on and trying to look journalistic/ taken years ago when he looked older."
[3] See also "Europe MCMXXXVI" (Contribution #2) note 14. Pound mentions Yugoslavia in the opening of an undated submission, "A Continent Or" (Contribution #15), which *Globe* did not run. Internal references indicate that this piece was sent to *Globe* in 1937. Since *Globe* received "Europe MCMXXXVI" on September 18, 1936 (see **JD5**) it is clear that Pound is referring to his comments in this contribution.
[4] Negotiations between Italy and Yugoslavia were underway in late 1936 to resolve a number of long-standing disputes between the two countries. On March 26, 1937, Mussolini's son-in-law Count Galeazzo Ciano, Italy's Foreign Minister, and Yugoslavia's Premier Stoyadinovitch signed a treaty in Belgrade. It guaranteed the existing borders between the two countries, defined the terms of sea trade in the Adriatic, and included a non-aggression pact.
[5] The Associated Press.
[6] **John Gunther**

EP10

TSC (BL)

<26 Nov[ember 1936]>

Oh yes/ lemme have 40 copies of that prospectu
prospectus/
I take it you have already sent it to all
names I have mentioned in letters to you
Please send exchange subscription of Globe
to Katue Kitasono[1]
I649 Nishi 1 chome Magome machi
Omori, Tokio Japan.
he edits a live mag/ and has translated <EP>
chunk of my Cavalcanti study.
<Good contact>

[1] In his initial letter to Pound dated April 1936, **Katue Kitasono** informed

Pound that he was considered a major influence within his circle of associates in Japan. Kitasono wrote that they had formed an association of twenty-one artists called "VOU Club" and that the group had launched a journal likewise called *VOU* . Kitasono wrote Pound that he had forwarded two copies of the latest issue of the journal to him in Rapallo for the his review and comment. Pound responded enthusiastically to Kitasono's letter and forwarded to him a copy of his translation/edition of *Guido Cavalcanti Rime* (Genoa, Italy: Edizioni Marsano, 1932). In his next letter to Pound, Kitasono informed him that he had taken the essay "Mediaevalism" from Pound's book, translated it into Japanese, and published it in a recent issue of *VOU* (the translation appeared, according to Gallup, in two parts in *VOU* 13 (October 1936) and *VOU* 14 (November/December 1936—see Gallup nos. D177–8). It is interesting to note that Gallup indicates that this is not the first time Pound has appeared in *VOU.* Though Pound's extant correspondence with Kitasono reveals no indication that he was aware of it, translations of the poems "Ts'ai Chi'h," "Alba," and "Heather" made by Kitasono seem to have appeared in *VOU* 11 (August 1936). Similarly, a translation of an abridged version of a chapter of *ABC of Reading* by Shoko Ema, apparently unbeknown to Pound, appeared in *VOU* 12 (September 1936)—see Gallup nos. D175–6.

JD11

TSL GS (YCAL)

December 3, 1936

Mr. Ezra Pound,

Via Marsala 12/5,
Rapallo, Italy.

Dear Mr. Pound:

As far as the advertisers go, our competitors are: Town and Country, Asia, National Geographic, Travel, etc. in the same field. As a general mag. it would be the American Mercury, the new Scribners, Reader's Digest and the new Coronet (see the enclosure), which may be discontinued as Gingrich is now planing another one. In any case the present one looks thrown together and does touch on some of our intentions as expressed in various mailing pieces we have been sending out for the past months.

We checked our contents for the first issue against the Atlantic, Reader's Digest, Esquire for duplication of type material to our own satisfaction. Of all it duplicated least for “Travel” 24 out of 28 articles would not have been printed by them.

The big illustrateds, new “Life”, “Mid-Week” etc. are not in our line. We are catching up, by the way, on Erskine Caldwell[1] as his regular story has not appeared in the last two issues. The magazine is so nasty now it can’t possibly keep it up.

We will know fairly soon about increasing our rates to writers. Of those you wrote we report:

W. H. D. Rouse—(excellent).[2]
Leo Chiozza Money—(article en route).[3]
B.G.M. Adams—(ones he sent were not very good;
satire of English woman of 40, but we asked for more).[4]
General Golijewsky’s letter was returned (inconnu à cette addresse).[5]
Charlotte Hirsch wrote us and is sending on something soon.[6]
Jean Barral—(heard from, will send something on Nice).[7]
Douglas Fox—(Frobenius translation—miles away from E.Jolas—and his own on archeological experiences).[8]
Harold Hawk is revising article on Taos at our suggestion[9]
Peter Fanning sent us an article on Jarrow—good but in need of cutting.[10]
Bridson—(a good one on Rhodes).[11]
Others I have already mentioned.

You are right about F.R. and with the ship of state.[12] At least as far as his foreign policy is concerned. Did you see his speech in extension in Buenos Aires?[13] Understand he is going to cut another 40% on the intellectuals in W.P.A. (artists, musicians, etc.) What is back of the propaganda against Ed. VIII (going fair for three years now), even to the new suits and collars a la Duke of York. How has he stood politically with Eden, for example.[14]

We enclose our check.

[signed]
James T. Dunn

Here are a few names:

Kurt Lubinski (reporter)[15]
Herman Hesse[16]
Jocob [sic] Schaffner[17]
Annette Kolb[18]
Bruno Frank[19]
Ernst Slaeser[20]
Klaus Mann[21]

<Your card received eight days
after mailing—The copies will be

sent you immediately after
are off the press.

Lina Ciao’s Unknown Sicily [22]the

Henrich Hauser[23]
Heinrich Mann[24]
de Monfried[25]
Marcel Griaule[26]
Carco[27]
Bizet[28]
Cendrars[29]
Kessel (?)[30]

best yet. The prospectus
seems a bit thrown together. We
hope you like it, but invite
severe criticism, J.T.D>.

encl: $20

[1] **Erskine Caldwell**
[2] **W. H. D. Rouse**
[3] **Sir Leo Chiozza Money**
[4] **B. G. M. Adams**
[5] **Honore Golijewsky**
[6] **Charlotte Hirsch**
[7] **Jean Barral**
[8] **Douglas Clayton Fox, Leo Frobenius,** and **Eugene Jolas.** In 1936 Jolas made a translation of Frobenius' article "Birth of a Fable" for *transition.* It ran in *transition* 26 (1936), pp. 191–2.
[9] **Harold Hawk**
[10] **Peter Fanning**
[11] **D. G. Bridson**
[12] See Pound's comments on the Roosevelt Administration in **EP8.**
[13] On December 1, 1936, President Franklin Roosevelt pledged non-intervention in a European conflict, and urged other American nations to do the same. He said in part: "The madness of a great war in another part of the world would affect us and threaten our good in a hundred ways. And the economic collapse of any nation or nations must of necessity harm our own prosperity. Can we, the Republics of the New World, help the Old World to avert the catastrophe which impends? Yes, I am confident that we can."
[14] **Sir Anthony Eden**
[15] **Kurt Lubinski**
[16] **Hermann Hesse**
[17] **Jakob Schaffner**
[18] **Annette Kolb**
[19] **Bruno Frank**
[20] **Ernst Slaeser:** unidentified
[21] **Klaus Mann**
[22] **Lina Caico**
[23] **Henrich Hauser**
[24] **Heinrich Mann**

[25] Henri de Monfried
[26] Marcel Griaule
[27] Francis Carco
[28] Bizet: unidentified
[29] Blaise Cendrars
[30] Joseph Elie Kessel

JD12

TSL GS (YCAL)

December 7, 1936

Mr. Ezra Pound,
Via Marsala 12/5,
Rapallo, Italy.

Dear Mr. Pound:

We sent you a first copy of the prospectus; the others will be along in a short time from the printers.

Note on misleading appearances:

1. Articles are not continued in rear advertising section (or continued at all).
2. Paper stock will be divided:
   (a) Enamel, 32 pages for black and white, photo reproductions, etc.
   (b) Heavy book stock, 64 page form with 2 combinations of 2 colors each.
   (c) Cover in 4 colors (if we get back cover ad).

Total size of GLOBE: 128 pages.

3. Prospectus is in collapsed form.

(a) Any illustrations will accompany the article.
   (b) Your arch (from Taragona) was overprinted for obvious reasons; an experiment.[1]

Received your photos and the letter dated and mailed the 24th, which arrived 2 days after your Nov. 27th card.[2]

Cordially,
[signed]
James T. Dunn

[1] *Globe* editors had been planning to run Pound's essay "Europe MCMXXXVI" in their first issue, but actually published it in their second issue. The main

art introducing Pound's essay was an etching of a Roman arch like one in Tarragona, Spain.
[2] See **EP9** and **EP10**.

EP11

TSL TAX (BL)

<13 Dec> 193~~7~~ <6>

Dear Dunn: and at once[1]

I trust you can use the enclosed ANONYMOUSLY/
folk poetry is anonymous, AND I want to treat the British darce with more constructivity, I cant catch yr/ Feb. issue now, AND whole press so full of fuzz that my job shd/ be to try to find out a bit MORE. which will take time.

I have
just writ to a cousin of the R's where Ed/ is now said to be.[2] BUT I [d]on't imagine that said cousin is on speaking terms with 'em since the Credit Anstalt swash[3]...however stick that under yr. hat.
Letter~~s~~ from Bill Woodward <just come> (Image and Man, Meet Gen. Grant. bloke)[4]
W.E.Woodward 340 E. 57 th <st.> New York.
He has finished his History of the U.S. why don't you get him to do a monthly letter on Washington/

tell him to S[ ]ILL it/
give him chance to write in print as he writes me.
Of course he is no longer a kid/ and can get higher rates but see if he won't try it for the fun/ plus the little sweetener. You can use my name.
Other thing he cd/ <d>o swell wd/ be vignettes of Washington figures/

I shd/ like to read him on
Tinkham[5]/Lemke[6]/Landon[7] after the slosh/ Bankhead (senator)[8]
He cd afford to do it cheap as is wd. serve as a book later.
He is at loose end/ that is yr/ chance. N O W NOW.
Let me pick the figures, so as to get out side the Sat. Eve Post selection.[9]

Might call 'em CARDS. if that narth Eng/ term has been addomesticated in the U.S.

My wife who has never seen the U.S. seconds this suggestion/ she havin seen Bill's letters during the past three years.

<Yrs
E.>

[Enclosure]

GOING AWAY

(anonymous folk song in the
making)

King Edward left 'em flat.
He said : I've parked my gat,
But they pinned a dukedumb on his britches[10]
as he left 'em.
As the car pulled out of Windsor
He said : I've saved my skin, Sir.
But they pinned a dukedumb on his britches
as he left 'em.
Oh ! Here's to our ex=king !
I hope he'll never swing.
But they've pinned a dukedumb on his britches
as he left 'um.
Young Davie[11] wuz a card
But ladies were debarred
From the precincts of the Castle
so he left 'em.
Baldy said[12] : Bigod !! I'll frame him,
For the high life will never tame him.
And they pinned a dukedumb on his britches
AS he left 'um

[1] Pound enclosed a bit of his own doggerel entitled "Going Away" as faux anonymous "folk poetry" on the abdication of **Edward VIII** (enclosure to this letter above).
[2] After abdicating, **Edward VIII**, now the Duke of Windsor, departed on December 12, 1936, for Austria to stay at an estate belonging to Baron Eugene de Rothschild.
[3] In May 1931, Austria's central bank, the Credit-Anstalt, failed. The collapse caused a diplomatic and economic crisis throughout Central Europe.
[4] **William E. Woodward**
[5] **George Holden Tinkham**
[6] **William Lemke**
[7] **Alfred ("Alf") Mossman Landon**
[8] **John Hollis Bankhead II**
[9] *The Saturday Evening Post.*
[10] After abdicating, **Edward VIII** took the title of the Duke of Windsor.
[11] **Edward VIII** was christened Edward Albert Christian George Andrew Patrick David. However, from his birth the royal family always called him David.
[12] **Stanley Baldwin**

EP12

TSL TAX (BL)

. 17 Dec. [stationery date 1937 corrected to 1936 by hand]

Dear Dunn

I am holding the English stuff in order to put together as much of a puzzle as possible.

The inside stuff just started arriving yesterday.

Italian correspondents the best and the most thorough but not INSIDE.

I figure your printing date makes it useless for me to try to catch the number now going to press.. so

better say MORE; and be coherent.

<"anonymous">

Print the vulgar ballad/ the ballad will continue/ and has the main balance of truth in it.

The manner in which the stunt was to be pulled was known considerably in advance.

Oh well/ I am, naturally holding back all the other
stuff/ and my next mss/ will be on Edwardus.[1]

Recd/ 20 dollars. thanks.

A crime has been committed but the number of suspects
present is so LARGE...
and the roots of it going BACK.....

etc.

yr/

Prospectus has evidently been lost en route.

Sure CUT the Fanning.[2] He won't fuss. Glad the Caico[3] satisfactory.

Not clear re/yr/ list of names. Do you mean you have 'em. <?>
or want my opinion about getting them ??

Yr/ other question. My opinion of Eden is that he is narsty piece of work/ and CERTAINLY anti Edward[4]. HHHHHH Beckett<'s> "Yorkshire Post"[5] was cog in the framing.

But Eden I think merely the pimp not the Pornoboskos[6] or big shot running the whore house.

Eden's bitch[7] didn't approve of Wallie/[8] and Wallie NOT exactly a pixchoor pos' card of Victoria's successor BUT lorrr luvv yew dearie, thet aint th arf ov it.

yrs
<EP>

[1] Pound often used "Edwardus" in referring to **Edward VIII.**

[2] **Peter Fanning**

[3] **Lina Caico**
[4] **Sir Anthony Eden**
[5] **Rupert Evelyn Beckett**
[6] Greek term (πορνοβοσκός) for a "brothel keeper."
[7] **Anthony Eden**'s wife was Beatrice Helen Beckett, daughter of Sir William Gervase Beckett, Director of the Westminster Bank, the older brother of Rupert Evelyn Beckett.
[8] **Wallis Warfield Simpson**

EP13

TSL TAX (BL)

< 10
- Jan>

Dear Dunn

Find Stancioff<'s> gone back to Bulgaria[1], but have written after 'em.
Also trying to find Golijewsky,[2] via consulate in Paris.
What about Guy Hickok of Brooklyn Eagle[3] . Can YOU find him?
...Am <w>ondering if Jacqueline Maury [4]I22 rue d Assas, Paris vi
wd/ be of use. Stuff so DAMNED over civilized I don't know that it wd. be comprehensible. Ten years ago it appeared to me she had got to age of thirty and never met anyone but Remy de Gourmont[5], a few females and finally Ez. / and world entierly formed in some sphere utterl<y> unknown.
There also is or was Brigit Patmore/ ??[6]
I may as well keep on remembering people who might have somethin
Do try to git ole F.M.Ford, via his N. York pubrs.[7] I think he is in N.Y.
///
Nother point on which I am NOT AT ALL sure.. wd. the traffic CARRY one column/not whole page, of literary NOTICES. I mean the maximum high brow stuff. With that amount of space there cd. be NO attempt at puffing the usual best selling crap. It wd be meaningless unless devoted exclusively to stuff that EITHER I, Bill [W]illiams,[8] Eliot,[9] M.Moore[10] wd. swear was the real thing.
I am not the least sure it wd. belong in the Globe.
BUT... I made a list of nine or / ten writers whom I think ARE.
I submitted it to Eliot/ he says first "It's pretty complete"[11]
Then he offers TWO alternatives. one, I think, cause he had just read it.
Then he don't want to be committed on Pirandello,[12] and hasn't heard of Crevel[12] (both now dead).
Am also writing to Bob McAlmon...[13] I dunno if he has drunk himself into writer's cramp yet. He wd. have been damn useful if you had started in 1920.

<over>

am not urging any of these points/ merely raising 'em.
what about Prorok ?[14] that is my queery to yr/ tabl[e] contents ... and I have no serious basis.. am merely asking what you know of him..

if the copy is lively thaZatt...

Matsumiyo [15] has a good book on Japanese poetry (so far as I cd. judge from hasty glance. He is sending me t[y]pescript sometime/

but it may be too gentle and leisurely...

not Globe pace and snap.

<y
E
P>

<prospecti
recd>

[1] **Dimitri Stancioff**
[2] **Honore Golijewsky**
[3] **Guy Hickok**
[4] **Jacqueline Maury**
[5] **Remy de Gourmont**
[6] **Brigit Patmore**
[7] **Ford Madox Ford**
[8] **William Carlos Williams**
[9] **T. S. Eliot**
[10] **Marianne Craig Moore**
[11] On December 6, 1936, Pound wrote to T. S. Eliot: "As an intellectual exercise/whom do you OMIT or ADD to this brief list of authors or derivatives?..." (YCAL). Pound then gave a list which included James Joyce, Eliot himself, Wyndham Lewis, Pound himself, Jean Cocteau, Frobenius, René Crevel, W. C. Williams, Pirandello, Katue Kitasono, Ford Madox Ford, and E. E. Cummings. Eliot wrote back on December 8, 1936, saying that he thought that Pound's list was fairly complete (TSE to EP, [YCAL]).
[12] **Luigi Pirandello**
[12] **René Crevel**
[13] **Robert McAlmon**
[14] **Baron Byron Khun de Prorok**

JD13

TSL GS (YCAL)

February 5, 1937

Mr. Ezra Pound,
Via Marsala 12/5,
Rapallo, Italy.

Dear Mr. Pound:

Received yours of the 15th and 17th of December and the 10th of January.

Reaction here to prospectus has been more than favorable; we are still busy getting out the 20,000 of these. Meanwhile, as representatives are being appointed. GLOBE will be distributed nationally, 55,000 for the first issue. Publication date had to be set off on acc't. of printer (we changed). It will be on the stands February 20th. Milwaukee Cuneo Press is trying to rush the magazine through so as to meet the agreed-on dates. As it is we will probably be a day or so late off the press.

Your Edward article[1] is being run in the first issue in place of "Europe 1936." Perhaps the latter can be revised a bit for the April issue, on which we are now working. A caricature of Edward by Walter Molino of Milan[2] will run with your article.

The $20 check will be sent as soon as my brother returns from Chicago. Please pardon the delay.

Sisley Huddleston writes a Geneva letter for the second issue.[3] Guy Hickok is silent[4] in spite of two letters. I am trying to contact the additional people mentioned by you (Woodward, Maury, McAlmon (also recommended by Mr. Williams).[5] The whole staff is still in doubt about Prorok, though we are running an installment. The copy <u>is</u> lively and he has a definite following. Ford Madox Ford wrote my brother and then answered his letter saying the rates were too low and that he rarely if ever writes anything under the 8,000 word count.[6] He seemed decidedly interested, however, though that doesn't help us much. W. E. Woodward regrets, et cetera.

What should we do about third (May) issue? Deadline on editorial material for that number is the 25th of March. Should we run the League article,[7] or would you care to revise it. Someday soon I hope we will be on schedule—the whole thing is so abnormal now.

First proof for "Abdication" included.

Yours,

[signed]
James Taylor Dunn

[1] Dunn was referring to Pound's article "Abdication" which concerned the recent abdication of Edward VIII (see **EP11** and **EP12**). It ran in the first issue of *Globe* (March 1937, pp. 82–7).
[2] **Walter Molino**
[3] **Sisley Huddleston**'s piece "That League" (*Globe*, May 1937, pp. 98–101).
[4]**Guy Hickok, W. E. Woodward, Jacqueline Maury,** and **Robert McAlmon.**
[5] **William Carlos Williams** had known **Robert McAlmon** since 1920 when McAlmon arrived in New York from Los Angles via Chicago. The two collaborated on a literary magazine called *Contact* which ran for five issues from December 1920 to June 1923. In its mimeographed pages appeared the work of Pound, H. D., Glenway Wescott, Kay Boyle and other writers that McAlmon would come to know in Paris in the later 1920s. In the early 1930s Williams and McAlmon tried to revive the magazine, but only managed to issue the first number of *Contact* II in February 1932.
[6] **Baron Byron Khun de Prorok.** *Globe* ran a three-part article by Prorok, "Untamed Ethiopia" (March 1937, pp. 124–8; May 1937, pp. 114–20, and June 1937, pp. 80–3).
[7] **Ford Madox Ford**

EP14

TSC (BL)

<26 Jan>

Will you guarantee to print the article
I can get on the Tel Aviv orchestra?

Huberman, Toscanini etc//[1] evidently GOOD ~~news~~
news/
but I don't want to get a repeat of
something already printed in the U.S.A.

timing important/ for eg/ Article of Por's
that Living Age SAID they wanted[2], turns out
to have been secreted somewhere in the
U.S.A. two years ago.
When you c'mon OUT ?

<EP>

[1] **Bronislaw Huberman**
[2] **Odon Por**

EP15

TSC (BL)

<12 Feb>
[stamped received] FEB 24 1937

12th. Feb. No Globe. recd here YET.

I am holding back next article until I
know whether you have been held up by FLOODS

or whatever ?????
In any case as <parcel & book> post is erratic
you better send me word when the first
issue is actually ~~HH~~ sent out.

Packet from England has taken I3 days and
not arrived yet. Things git LOST.
Letter<s> so far as I know always arrive
and time seems ro be regular. I may find
referring to pub/ctn date says you are to be
out of 20 Jan/ dated I Feb

[no signature]

JWGD1

TSL GS (YCAL)

February 20, 1937

Mr. Ezra Pound
Via Marsalla, 12/5
Rapallo, Italy

Dear Mr. Pound:

GLOBE is out at last (on the stands today and selling like hot-cakes in some spots we know of). We will send you a copy as soon as it is possible, but there seems to be some agreement that keeps is from mailing it immediately. Hachette is handling out European distribution.

Your "Abdication" appears in this issue, illustrated by a cartoon done by a young student I met in Milano.[1] He does most of the drawings for "Libro e Moschetto", the weekly paper of GRUPPO UNIVERSITARIA FASCISTI. "Abdication" pleases us very much. (No rose carrying with gloved hands).

Now about GLOBE and our distinguished general European correspondent. GLOBE has been late all along the line. A majority of the people who knew about the "vast plans" doubted even up to the moment the first issue went to press that it would ever appear. But now that it has started rolling and must appear once a month, our arrangements with you commence on a more clock-like basis.

We are sending to you "That League in Calvin's Home City" which is too serious for GLOBE.[2] Many of the people and situations dealt with are beyond most of us here. Perhaps a politico-economic piece of this nature would be acceptable elsewhere. We send you carbon copies to do with what you will. The enclosed check pays for the month of April in which we are using "Europe 1937". [3] To date we have sent you (including $20 we enclose) $85. We have two of your articles to publish; "Abdication" in March issue, and "Europe 1937" in April issue. Your next letter will go into the May issue. In other words, $40 of the $80 was for articles, and $45 for the delay and your invaluable service in working up our world contacts and in masterful advice to the editors of GLOBE. In April, we will pay you $20 for May. I hope this economical discussion of money straightens us out.

Do you have translations of foreign verse we might look at; poetry showing human character and local color of fascinating spots in the world. Also, we are anxious to get our hands on stories by good Italian authors (living). Anything further you can do along this line will be appreciated.

Several clippings are enclosed which may prove of interested. A letter is on hand from your cousin, Earle Bailey[4] of Chippewa Falls Wisconsin; plus a cordial invitation to visit him.

Via Sweden we received a very nice article on GLOBE[5] and Montague Summer's "London Goes to Satan",[6] written by D. B. Wyndham Lewis [sic].[7] It appeared in THE BYSTANDER for January 13th. Mr. McAlmon answered our letter (and yours).[8] He's sending us some articles.

Cordially,

The Editors of GLOBE

[Signed]
J.W.G. Dunn, Jr. Editor

[1] **Walter Molino**

[2] See Contribution #10.

[3] See Contribution #2.

[4] Earle Bailey was Pound's cousin living in Chippewa Falls, Wisconsin.

Chippewa Falls was the home of Pound's grandfather Thaddeus Coleman Pound and the site of his lumber company.

[5] Apparently this is **Rodger L. Simons**' letter "Stockholm" which appeared in the March 7, 1937 issue of *Globe*. Simons contributed three other letters: "Scandinavia," "Danish Trivia," and "Too Many Olsons" (in issues for May, July, and September 1937 respectively).

[6] **Montague Summers**' "London Goes to Satan," the first of several articles for *Globe*, appeared in the first issue (March 1937, pp. 39–44).

[7] **Dominic Bevan Wyndham Lewis**

[8] **Robert McAlmon**

EP16

TSL TAX (BL)

2I Feb [stamped received] Mar 5 1937

Dear [J. T.] Dunn[1]

Good. Glad you snapped the Edward into first number.[2] That wd. have gone out of date.
No use in my trying to correct proofs NOW, as it is supposed to have been on the stands yesterday.
a that for those/ pornoboskos,[3] not prono/
and it wasn't Sammy in Dyrham but Swabey///[4] but it don't matter.
//
The Europe could ~~can~~ be labled I937 .[5] BUT I think you better leave it I936.
Put in an editorial note to the effect that both the Europe and the League article[6] are necessary introduction. <to my stuff>
Say Frankly when I wrote 'em/ and let that carry if possible the idea that events have lived up to 'em.
People are now reading Arnold Wilson[7]/<much more retrospective.>
I shall keep my Hitler article[8] hanging on the hook here until the last minute.
That is to say, YOU shd/ have it on April 25th. for June issue ??
Using Eng/Italy/then Germany, I shall have
set down the main stakes.

As I remember the articles I need those two pretty much as they stand as INTRODUCTION and to make what I shall go on saying clear to the readers. Anything really out of date you can cut better in office than I cd. here.
I enc/ a list of people to whom the Globe shd be sent as introductory measure/ exchange copies

<vide p.s.>

<y. E P>

<21
Feb >

Don't worry over my saying "Hitler article" it wont cut into anything you are getting direct from Germany.
I am giving Italian view of Germany.
Incidentally Bib Ibbotson[9] has just been here for a week/
married a german, and has losts of nephews inside and in constructive organizations/
Am afraid he is aiming at N.Y.Times or something Tried to get him for Globe..
ANYHOW he was full up with Eng/ and U.S. press misrepresentation, also a lot of clear data re French IDIOCY in Metz and Coblenz in 1933.[10]
Permanent address
J.D.Ibbotson,[11] Hamilton College Clinton, N.Y. <as you may know>
Send LIBRARIAN a Globe circular ;
(Library has all my stuff)
also sent one to
Prof. Harold W.Thompson[12]
State College, Albany, N. Y.
(he might also WRITE for Globe)
Sorry about Woodward/[13] I doubt if Claude Bowers[14] is lively enough.
What about Lloyd Stryker ? was his book on Andy Johnson[15] lively enough ? and does he DO anything more?
I dont suppose the Beards[16] wd. write at Globe rate ?
There is also Sam Adams [17] OUT of reach.. but perhaps worth higher rate to the paper..

<EP>

[separate sheet]

Odon Por [18](new address) 54 via Angelo Masina, Roma Italy

J. A. Macnab 28 Fawcett St. London S.W. I0
(with note saying you wd. like Brit. Union
(better than his office) Quarterly[19] in exchange
with back numbers to Oct 1936.

Kitasono Katue [20], I649 Nishi 1 Chome
Magomemachi, Tokio, Japan.

Sung Hsien Zong,[21] Hon. Sec. 862 Boone Rd. Shanghai, China
optional/
Hon. Hajime Matsumiya [22], Japanese Embassy, Rome
Hon. Yanagisawa [23], Japanese Embasy, Brussles, Belgium

certainly to George Holden Tinkham[24]
House of Representatives, Washington D.C.

YES leave that League article.

If you get G[eorge].H[olden] .T[inkham].'s attention it would be useful to the paper.

Mongomery Butchart,[25] 48 Bloomsbury St. London W.C.I.

F. V. Morley,[26] Fabers, 24 Russell Sq. London W.C.I.
(mark, offered in exchange for the Criterion[27])

(I am giving individuals, rather than simply saying "editor" but you can also send to edt. office if you like.

Action,[28] Sanctuary Buildings ; Gt Smith St. London S.W.I. New English Weekly[29], 7 Rolls passage, London E.C.4

[Written on the back of the envelope]

P.S. send globe also to
D. C Fox[30]
26 gr. Eschenheimer
58,
Frankfurt
g/M

[1] Pound wrote this letter in response to James Taylor Dunn's letter of February 5, 1937 (**JD13**).
[2] Pound's article "Abdication" (see Contribution #1) ran in the first issue of *Globe* (March 1937, pp. 82–7).
[3] A spelling error in his article "Abdication." See **EP12** and Contribution #1.
[4] **Reverend Henry S. Swabey**
[5] "Europe MCXXXVI" ran in the second issue of *Globe* (May 1937, pp. 106–10). See Contribution #2.
[6] This was Pound's essay "That League in Calvin's Home City" (see Contribution #10). This article was never run in *Globe*.
[7] **Sir Arnold Talbot Wilson**
[8] Probably Pound's article "...And Excursions" which, in part, discusses Hitler's economic policies as reported in the Italian press (see Contribution # 12). *Globe* paid for the piece (see **JD15**) but never ran it.
[9] **Joseph Darling Ibbotson**
[10] Probably a reference to the French opposition to Nazi calls for a return of the Saar valley to complete German control.
[11] See note 8 to this letter.

[12] **Harold William Thompson**
[13] **W. E. Woodward**
[14] **Claude Gernade Bowers**
[15] **Lloyd Paul Stryker**
[16] **Charles Austin Beard** and **Mary Ritter Beard**
[17] **Samuel Hopkins Adams**
[18] **Odon Por**
[19] **John Angus McNab**
[20] **Katue Kitasono**
[21] **Sung Hsien Zong**: unidentified
[22] **Hon. Hajime Matsumiya**
[23] **Ken Yanagisawa**
[24] **George Holden Tinkham**
[25] **Montgomery Butchart**
[26] **Frank Vigor Morley**
[27] For *The Criterion* see **EP4** note 8.
[28] *Action* was the British weekly newspaper created as an organ of the "New Party" under the leadership of British Fascist leader **Sir Oswald Mosley**. The paper first appeared on October 8, 1931 under the editorial direction of Harold Nicolson. Mosley did not directly influence the editorial policy or choice of articles, which was largely left to Nicolson. Robert Skidelsky, in his biography of Oswald Mosley, characterized *Action* in the following manner: "It was the organ of a party whose own profile and as yet not been defined—suspended between vestigial socialism and an incipient fascism.... As a result it suffered from precisely that vague and eclectic modernism which was the bane of the New Party itself. It was trendy without being coherent" (*Oswald Mosley*, p. 281).
[29] After leaving *The New Age* in 1922, **A. R. Orage**, due in part to his association with I. A. Gurdjeff and his movement, left Britain and traveled for some years in America and France. In 1932, Orage returned to London and there started a new periodical, *The New English Weekly*. This journal was to survive Orage's death in 1934, ceasing publication in 1949. As in the case of *The New Age*, Pound was a frequent contributor to this new periodical.
[30] **Douglas Clayton Fox**

EP17

TSL TAX (BL)

[March 7]

J.W.G.D.

Dear Dunn

I/

Re/ AbderKashun.[1] My ole PAW he sure will be pleased an my ole Maw she cert/ will sniff an fusss erbout <u>our</u> lack of kulchur and refinement.

2.

I want that OFFICIAL rain cheque, name plate, dawg license, WITH stamped photo, sayin I am the EARTH and the fulness thereof My OFFICIAL GLOBE brass chek to hang on my collar and pass the police cordons about fires and assassinations. A OFFICIAL choinulist
not to be highatted by s/o/b who lie in the N.Y.Herald etc.

3.

Bright lad named R (no relation of Raymond, Isadora or other) DUNCAN on way from India/ 10 hours Rapallo. I told him to send you FIRST hand about SNAKES and Gandi and Leopards in CooshBahar.[2]

BRIGHT lad.

4.

Will suggest Bunting plus Caico TRANSLATE Italian stories.[3] WHO is to pick 'em?
Riccardo Marchi[4] sketched on port of Liverno, and on cheese wagon OUGHT to be wot you want.
Me wife sez May Daniel[5] can do you flowers by English Wayside +
mebbe S. Alpine
the first tomtits in Suffolk etc.
Will git off NEW blast tomorrow. re/ Brit Labour/ Red Ellen
and Hitler's economics.[6] news. League stuff dead[7]
as the pewk hole sinks lower daily. Yaas, yaaas
news in that a bit old. BUT I must say the same things
sometime. will try to NEWS 'em
Eleven Japanese poets are sending me PoEMS sometime, BUT I dont know if they will be LOCAL colour/
One of the blokes was murmuring
about Ford Cars and east african ornament/[8]
reckon thy may be HIGH
brows with human interest.

7.[sic]

Am glad to hear ANYTHING good of D/B/Wyndham Lewis.[9]
The RIGHT Lewis is P. Wyndham Lewis[10], but he signs without the P cause he dont like hia ma called him PERCY.

Whether he can git
down to Globe level I dunno.
Who selects the EYETALYAN stories. The Lousing Age ordered a translation of Por and then didnt like the PORticulars[11]
If I tell Bunt/ to traduce some Marchi an you dont like it?
WOP happens?

Modus vivendi/ do YOU read the wop originals
and order the translations??

WHAT is rate of payment for
translations/ what % to author and to traductor??
I mean do YOU read Italian and pick the stuff to be done? Have I got to buy wop books and send them to you?? or do I tell Bunt to do a sample and you pay him five dollars whether accepted or not, and more if it suits??
Only way I see of getting QUICK action. Puts it up to him to pick the snappiest story in a vol/ of shorts/ taken from author I choose.

I think Criterion[12] once used a Marino Moretti[13]
GOOD, and not known in St Paul.
Tozzi[14] perhaps too serious?

to get quick action you cd/ send me set of PROOFS
of whole Globe, not waiting for issue. also I need
[typed in margin] I0 or I5 copies each issue for publicity
work. getting people to know it exists. yr E Z P.

[1] "AbderKashun" is Pound's punning reference to his article "Abdication" (Contribution #1) in *Globe,* March 1937.
[2] **Ronald Frederick Henry Duncan**
[3] **Basil Bunting** and **Lina Caico**
[4] **Riccardo Marchi**
[5] **May Daniel**: unidentified
[6] **(Cecily) Ellen Wilkinson**
[7] "That League in Calvin's Home City" was submitted to *Globe* October 18, 1936, but remained unpublished. See Contribution #10.
[8] Since April 1936, Pound had been in correspondence with the Japanese poet **Katue Kitasono** who, in 1935, had founded the poet's club VOU. In a letter dated February 26, 1937, Kitasono mentioned that he has sent Pound translations of some poems by a number of the VOU Club's members. (See also **EP10**, **EP20**.)
[9] **Dominic Bevan Wyndham Lewis**
[10] **Percy Wyndham Lewis**

[11] The "Lousing Age" is a punning reference to the journal *The Living Age* edited at this time by **Varian Fry**. *The Living Age* was a well-established New York-based journal which ran from 1844 to 1941. Pound had written to Fry and had interested him in running an article by Odon Por. Pound volunteered to translate it from Italian. Fry made it clear that he had little funds at hand for such a translation, but if it ran he would be able to come up with something. He added that he was sure that there was very little chance that he wouldn't run it since he was interested in running something by an Italian fascist and that Pound's connection with the piece made it even more attractive (VF to EP, November 30, 1936 [YCAL]).

When Pound submitted the piece, Fry responded that he had read it over and could not publish it since it dealt with the Milhaud Plan—which Fry felt had been done to death in the American media. Pound's annoyance was reflected in his scrawl at the top of Fry's rejection letter: "Waaal: my dear RIP von Christoper WINKLombus this izza joke on us for NOT discoverin' America yrs EZ"

Pound's translation of Por's article, entitled "Systems of Compensation," eventually appeared in the *British Union Quarterly* (vol. I:3 1937, pp. 31–48) with an introductory note probably written by Pound.

[12] For *The Criterion* and **John Cournos** see **EP4.**

[13] **Marino Moretti**

[14] **Federigo Tozzi**

EP18

TSL TAX (BL)

<8
March>

[stamped received] MAR 10 1937

Dear [J. W. G.] Dunn[1]

Yaaas/ I think I forgot to mention the chq/ came. My hurried of yester/ : Bloke here 8 hours re/ New English (not New England)

real licherary mag/ to be started.[2]

Waaal; re yr/ financial arrangements. "WE" are in this thing at LEAST as much fer the fun of it as for lucre.

and thaZZ O.KAY by EZ.

The Geneva mss/ being OUT. and it new the 8th.[3] You will have to stand a little seriousness in the enclosed.

I will start the next one on MUSIC[4], so'z not to be too specialized and too far from the reader.

IF you hadda sent me proofs of the WHOLE issue etc/ etc/ Until <I> see the whole mag/ I can NOT get a very full idea of the TONE required of yr/ central and by program heaviest and sereeyusest component.
As I see it/ the <G>eneva stuff was MORE out of date and off the days news, then TOO SERIOUS.
When you have time to be explicit in this corresponden<t> [sic]
PLEASE do.
It takes a damn sight longer to be explicit than a busy man usually has when rushing off letters.
If you mean I am NOT to MENTION America at all and for OBvious (to you) reasons I shd/ net even allude to the Western Hemisphere.
SPIT it out.
I think editing is a technical feat/ don't be afraid that I will think we are just pickin dayeseyes.
That R. Duncan kid n just back from Ghandi[5], etc. OUGHT to be useful

<got eyes.>

Am doing new book for Faber/ 70,000 due Sept. 30.[6]
what else ??
I think I will risk offering Bunting a quid (5 dollars)
to do a Marchi story.[7] otherwise wont get started
for a month. and he be SLOW.
It is local color stuff down by Livorno and the bloke is real. I know him. In fact will dig up a foto of him, me and Gino Saviotti.[8] <together.>
on Russia
Oh yes/ BEST caricature was in Guerin Meschino[9]
mis/cited in News Week. Mebbe you cd. do new drawing.
(they got lables [sic] and letter press wrong; mixed with another drawing and paper.
Scene Stalin, jailers firing squad and prisoners
Stalin/ Why the hell aint youse guys shot 'em?
Jailers :
Sorry, boss, we can't remember whevver youse told us to shoot them, or THEM to shoot US.

<ys EZ>

[1] This was Pound's response to J. W. G. Dunn's letter of February 20, 1937 **(JWGD1)**.

[2] **Ronald Duncan** visited Pound in the first part of 1937 in Rapallo on his way back from India. During this visit, Pound and Duncan discussed plans for a literary magazine. Duncan eventually published the journal, which was dubbed *The Townsman*, as a result of these discussions.

[2] **Ronald Duncan**
[3] "That League in Calvin's Home City" (see Contribution #10).
[4] Probably Pound's article "Deflation Benefit," which appeared in *Globe* (August 1937, pp. 66–71; see Contribution #5). The article opens with a discussion of the New Hungarian Quartet. Pound was very enthusiastic about the Quartet, having "discovered" them at the 1936 Venice Biennial. At Pound's invitation, the New Hungarian Quartet performed a Bartok/Haydn concert in Rapallo on February 18, 1937. Pound wrote an article for the Italian paper *Il Mare* announcing the performance and praising the Quartet. (For translation of the article see Schafer, *Pound and Music*, pp. 420–1. Also see **JD15** note 3.)
[5] **Ronald Duncan** contributed a piece on his visit to Mohandas Gandhi in *Globe*, "Visit to Gandhi" (August 1937), pp. 72–4.
[6] It most likely that this is the first edition of his *Guide to Kulchur*, published by Faber & Faber on July 21, 1938. This does not seem to be *The Fifth Decad of Cantos* since Faber & Faber brought this volume out in June of 1937—obviously before the submission date Pound seems to indicate.
[7] **Basil Bunting** Pound was referring to the possibility of Bunting translating a story by **Riccardo Marchi** for *Globe*.
[8] **Gino Saviotti**
[9] *Guerin Meschino* was a Milanese newspaper Pound regularly read during these years.

EP19

TSL TAX (BL)

<9
March>

[stamped received] MAR 20 1937

Dear Dunn, and Dunns in plural

I have now read my "League at Geneva" article over carefully.[1]
I AGREE I00% that it is good editing not to use it in Globe.
Seems to me to have gone stale from waiting six months.
I DON'T understand it's being TOO serious or beyond comprehension of Globe readers /
specially since Grey picked out my quote of Remy[2]
I am going ahead with Fourth article,
cause I don't like HURRY.

_______ I like to git the chores done EARLY. _______________

Sat BO, if you can git my pa's cousin Ida (aged 79)
onto the page..that wd. enliven somfn.

Ida Busha, Big Timber, Montana.[3]

Dare say Chippewa is nearer at hand. Don't know if Earle <Bailey>[4] has ever met the old lady.
Of course she couldn't WRITE it. Just bits come <out> now and then. Some of her last letter ehich dad gave me this morning is going STRAING into them Cantos.[5]

//

I am also contactin' Cap. Goldeni. First into somewhere or other Harrar, I think. Bloke I quote in Polecat Essays [6].

Trust hiz american lady friend will be able to make it suitable. Simple hearted lad, same fambly as the Venetian comediograph.

You can't have an Edward Abdication for every issue/ not unless I gotter write fiction.

<If> That bloke in Stockholm[7] cd. be useful getting my books into bookshops there. Be more use <to me> than a slight raise in pay rate. We got to use what we've got.
I mean your agent or whatever there.

<yr E.P.>

[On separate sheet—handwritten]

<Article III
went off yesterday
registered.
Hitler. & a few etceras [sic]
as seen from Rome>

[1] See Contribution #10.
[2] Pound was referring to a closing comment made by James Gray in his review of the first issue of *Globe,* sent to him by James Dunn, which appeared in the *St. Paul Dispatch* (Friday, February 19, 1937):

> In a little note on his article Pound quotes Remy de Gourmont's declaration that "To write what one thinks is a writer's sole pleasure". If Globe will stick to that motto it will continue to be as admirable as this first issue indicates that it intends to be.

> I have followed the de Gourmont principle in writing frankly what I think of Globe and it has been a great pleasure.

[3] Ida Busha (1865–?), cousin of Homer Pound, Ezra Pound's father.
[4] For Earle Bailey see **JWGD1** note 4.
[5] What the nature of this material was, and where and if it was used in *The Cantos*, is not clear. This letter from Ida Busha does not seem to have survived.
[6] "Polecat Essays" was Pound's punning reference to his *Polite Essays* (1937). Pound probably referred to Arrigo Goldoni, one of a group of government-sanctioned journalists who accompanied Italian troops as they invaded Ethiopia. Pound entitled the second essay in the book "We Have Had No Battles But We Have All Joined In And Made Roads" (p. 49). Pound commented in this essay: "I take this line from a letter of Capt. Goldoni to indicate the new *forma mentis* with the date line 1935." Harrar is an ancient walled city in eastern Ethiopia.
[7] **Rodger L. Simons**

EP20

TSL TAX (BL)

<11 March>

[stamped received] MAR 25. 1937

WHOOPS

AbsoLOOT scoop. EIGHT of the VOU club in Tokio have sent in translations of their stuff.[1] A page each.

Knocked me endways.

The ALERTNESS there in Japan. Nothin' like it here.
I asked them to do rough translation/ with original explanation, saying I wd. retouch. but no need of it.

I mean it for some high brow paper, but it is too good not to use in GLOBE. Average reader will just have to take trouble to read it twice.

Will send <it> along tomorrow for next day/ as soon as I can do a 200 word introduction[2], to clear up one or two points, make sure reader will know WHAT it is.
Good letters from Hank Mencken,[3] and Forschungs Institute[4] by sHHHH morning post.
Local colour, human interst/ this VOU stuff is the mind of NEW JAPAN. and some going. shown up by lightning flash.
<yr EP>

They have made one or two typing slips

I am asking Kitasono
to write you direct IF I have erred in any of my corrections. I have only corrected single letters in words.

[1] The manuscript Pound mentioned was sent by **Katue Kitasono,** Japanese poet and founder of the VOU Poetry Club (see **EP10, EP17**). It included poetry from Takeshi Fuji, Minoru Yasoshima, Toshio Sasajima, Tio Nakamura, Takeshi Koike, Koichi Kihara, Jyun Higashi, and Kitasono himself. The packet also contained a VOU Club manifesto by Kitasono. Pound wrote to Kitasono on the same day as this letter to Dunn: "The poems are splendid, and the first clear lighting for me of what is going on in Japan. The NEW Japan...."
[2] Pound wrote a brief essay for *Globe*, "The New Mind of Japan Laid Open Suddenly," as a preface to Kitasono's manifesto and the VOU Club members' poetry. When Pound submitted this essay and other material to *Globe* he added a note:

> "P/S not for print.
> I think it wd. be enormous loss to Globe not to take this opportunity to be FIRST in introducing the VOU/
> Further notices can be left to literary magazines. But this IS news item.
> If you don't SEE it, I shall be disappointed. In any case, please send SOON either proofs, or the mss/ for print or reprint in England. Where Globe is unlikely to be on sale.
> Little Review made a record, I think in ten years time GLOBE ought to be able to "point with pride."

[3] **H. L. Mencken**
[4] For Forschungsinstitut für Kulturmorphologie, see **EP3** note 11.

JD14

TSL GS (BL)

March 16, 1937

Mr. Ezra Pound,
Via Marsala 12/5
Rapallo, Italy.

Dear Mr. Pound:

Many thanks for your letter and the many names.[1] Harold Thompson[2] was written to last August and he responded immediately, saying he would like to write for us; but he has been quite ill. I write to him again today. His stories remind me very much of Carl Carmer's books[3] which are still best sellers in this country. I don't quite understand what Bibsie can do;[4] any suggestions on this will be appreciated. Robert McAlmon[5] has sent in many things, only one of which is even possible. The Library subscribed to GLOBE about a month ago.[6]

Was reading your QUI PAUPER AMAVI[7] when Christopher Hollis[8] telephoned two nights ago. Has lunch with him yesterday; agreeable arrangements were made, and he is sending an article frome Notre-Dame University in the very near future.

The Europe article will be labeled 1936, and an editorial note has been included. Will try Claude Bowers;[9] and Adams[10] is certainly worth higher rates. Mary Howell[11] has written us and sent in two articles, one of which we think can be used. Is she authentic? Her "Three Sisters" manuscript reads a bit like the atrocities reported during the Great War.

The six copies have been sent to you. Please write us your HONEST criticism; that's what we need if we are going to keep improving.

Your "Abdication" has been mentioned favorably in every review so far received. Enclosed is one of the best, from the St. Louis "Globe-Democrat".[12]

Mr. Ezra Pound -2-

What do you think of printing translated stories and articles that have already been published in foreign countries? There seems to be a definite reaction against the so -called "Digest Magazines" in this country. Will the inclusion of three or four of these in each issue place us in their class? We say on the cover Original Features From All Over the World."

Enjoyed your article on music reprinted in a recent number of "Living Age."[13]

Cordially,

The Editors of GLOBE

[signed]

James Taylor Dunn
Associate Editor

JDT/dt
Enc.

[1] J. T. Dunn wrote this letter in response to Pound's letter of February 21, 1937 (**EP16**).

[2] In fact, **Harold Thompson**'s first wife, Jean Alma Saunders, was the one who was ill.
[3] **Carl Carmer**
[4] **Joseph Darling "Bibb" Ibbotson**
[5] **Robert McAlmon** *Globe* never published anything submitted by McAlmon.
[6] Hamilton College Library.
[7] *Quia Pauper Amavi* London: The Egoist Ltd., 1919. Dunn purchased many first editions of Pound's work during their correspondence. Dunn later donated the books to Hamilton College.
[8] **Maurice Christopher Hollis**
[9] **Claude Gernade Bowers**
[10] **Samuel Hopkins Adams**
[11] **Mary Howell**
[12] In her "Here and There" column in the St. Louis *Globe-Democrat* of February 19, 1937, Katherine Darst reviewed the first issue of *Globe*. She wrote: "In the letter department comes the inevitable discussion of Edward VIII, but even those who have long ago stopped up their ears with cotton at the mention of Mrs. Simpson's Mr. Windsor will feel an awakening interest in Ezra Pound's statements that 'Edward Windsor is today in a position more powerful than when on the throne. He has but to whisper to some cub reporter: 'Let the TEN MILLION EAT,' and the mass corruption in Britain has dithers. Dave Windsor on his own feet can do more than he ever could have done on a throne surrounded by flummydiddles and gold braid and flunkies.' Any magazine that can breathe new life in the now frayed Windsor story is, for that feat alone, worth a bow."
[13] Pound's article was "Mostly Quartets," which appeared in the January 1937 issue of *Living Age*. This article is a reprint of the article as it appeared in *Listener*, XVI. 405 (October 14, 1936). For a "Mostly Quartets" now see Schafer, *Pound and Music*, pp. 401–6.

EP21

TSL TAX (BL)

18 March

[stamped received] APR 1 1937

Dear Dunn

As no copy of Globe has yet come/ I have to go it blind.
I don't THINK any contract really can keep you from sending copy of mag. to yr/ own staff either correspondents or agents/ as which I shd/ figure (technically).

I am sending you a mixed lot of snippets <(Delfation Benefit>[1]/ NOT yet knowing which public you are after.
There exists a religious pubk/ a catholic public/ a musical public/ etc.
Do you want BITS, say in every article or so/designed to catch any of these segments ?
Slash the article to suit and when I see the cuts, I will get an idea how "serious" etc/etc/ and how general a lot of interests I can aim at.
About caricatures/ If you want me to collect 'em, I can do so or send haphazard what I happen to see. I don't take the comics regularly.
I believe the Lit/Digest[2]/ and various papers have found that reprod/ of caricatures is useful...
I don't want to overlap/ waste to have two people covering the same ground.
The real NEWS is news of ideas/ in the sense that EVENT depends on the rate of speed at which certain ideas are penetrating Germany and Italy. Brook's Adam's diagnosis / 30 years
war)[3].

mebbe I better tack that on end of article.

One thing, about only one I am convinced of, is that I oughtn't to send what you are getting from someone else.
Until I know what the staff work is, and who is covering what/ that is a bit difficult [to] gauge.
I count ALL Italian and German stuff being unpopular UNLESS it is simple anti fascist and anti Nazi CRAP.

<r.s.v.p. re/ this.>

New Testament is the strongest anti-semitic propaganda ever published? BUT of course it is <so> wrapped in the pink cotton wool of familiarity that that ASPECT is NOT [sic] and it has become UTTERLY innocuous/ whereas Ben Franklin's feelings on the subject have not.[4]
Even in Eng/ and Italy people are being forced into anti=semtism by jewish folly. I mean people who never thought of it before and who ON PRINCIPLE are opposed to race prejudice and race discrimination.

This I take it is UNFAMILIAR ground in St Paul.

Damnd hard to handle/ heaven knows I don't particularly want to tackle it.. BUT the office ought to KNOW a lot the GLOBE don't print.
I don't think it would be wise editing to do very much with it until Globe has run at least a year...
You will probably get a lot of jewish sob stuff... more picturesque than HHH any analysis of jewish influence can be.

AND, damn it! it is not bad because it is jew. All that line of talk distracts from the MAIN issue.

IF the jews wd. take any sort of part in econ/ reform as distinct from

communistic obscurantism and financial obscurantism there wd. be no need of any anti-semitic stuff at all.
I know of only ONE jew (alleged to be jew) in ALL the monetary reform aggitation.[5] And one other riding with Prof. F. who wobbles.[6]
They are destroying France and England.. Don't think me merely nutty for saying this. Ben Franklin was a practical man.
AND the first Rothschild [7] was a sporting character, who put up no end of a fight. It is hard as hell to do justice. A minority race can NOT fight in the open. Not if it has any sense at all. The small jew suffers for the sins of the gombeen man.[8] The fight ought NOT to have been fought on lines of race prejudice. Only way to avoid that is by spread and acceleration of spread of economic light.
Hope this isn't to heavy for OFFICE ear.

<yr E.P.>

[1] "Deflation Benefit," Contribution #5.
[2] *Literary Digest* was established in 1890 by Funk and Wagnalls and was absorbed by *Time* in 1938. In the late 1920s it had a circulation of more than a million.
[3] **Brooks Adams**
[4] For Benjamin Franklin's alleged anti-Semitic remarks, see Introduction, p. 35 and note 28.
[5] Cf. Pound's letter of December 2, 1938, to Louis Zukofsky: "...so far as known, only ONE Jew, Ernst Loeb is working for monetary decency. He is in Holland and I suppose will get about as much 'hand' from the local sanhedrin as Spinoza had" (YCAL and Ahern, *Pound/Zukofsky*, p. 199).
[6] **Irving Fisher**
[7] It is not clear here whether Pound was referring to Mayer Amschel Rothschild (1744–1812) or his son Nathan Rothschild (1777–1836). Mayer Amschel built the family fortune from a trade in antiques into one profiting from his position as a financial agent to the court of the Elector William IX of Hesse-Kassel. Meanwhile his son Nathan in the early nineteenth century was a very successful textile exporter based in London. In fact, Nathan would become the head of the London branch of the family, marrying a daughter of a London merchant in 1906. Both father and son, working in tandem, laid the financial foundations of the Rothschild's international financial empire.
[8] Irish slang term. Pound defined it in **EP44** as "gombeen man, irish [sic] term for extortionate mortgage holders."

EP22

TSL TAX (BL)

23

March

<quite

clear

in carbon>

Dear Dunn

BLAST and damn it all you HAVE bitched ~~and~~ my third paragraph. I wrote/ can see passion in print if UNimportant.[1]

U N important. You can always print the unimportant. a mass of pewk like Brisbane or Lippmann[2] can <be> print<ed> at once.

When a thing hits on the jaw or has any real meaning it takes time to get it t<h>ru the barrage erected by filth and corruption and universal inertia.

<I mean if you can without

more fuss than it is worth

(over>

Please attempt a correction of that sentence.

The expansion of H. to Hoare[3] in final pp/ matters less. I couldn't think what had caused that, in the galley proofs but was then too late to correct it.

One copy of Globe; very little use. I mean I have to keep one copy for ref/

Do get it as a universal principle that the more there is in a bit of writing the harder it si to get it printed. May hell take Neimeyer and Morgan.[4]

'ever

<vide PS>

<EP>

[Typed vertically in left margin] As per earlier whoops/ I cd/ distribute, I think as cheapest form as advertising 20 copies of First and second numbers, and ten a dozen thereafter.

I don't know how you feel about printing errata

some edtrs/ think it useless. United front against public/ and author stands the racket.

Sentence as it stands looks conceited to me

I want the office at least to know that that is NOT what I wrote, but the opposite.

[1] See "Abdication," Contribution #1 note 2.

[2] **Arthur Brisbane** and **Walter Lippmann**

[3] **Sir Samuel John Gurney Hoare.** While editing "Abdication" (Contribution

#1), *Globe* took Pound's reference to "H." as indicating "Hoare." This was not Pound's intention. However, Hoare's policies as British foreign secretary were favorable to the regimes of Italy and Germany, and would have obviously been to Pound's liking.

[4] **Sir Otto Niemeyer** and **John Pierpont Morgan Jr.**

EP23

TSL TAX (BL)

28-31 March

Dear Dunn

What angle do you want me to crit/ FROM <?> I read a good deal of the Globe without effort.

Weak spots in some of the letters.

As the first rev/ you sent, observed. ole Huddle[1]/ wasn't giving away anything rough.

After all he wrote for the Times, and the Monitor, and he aint in the rough stuff tradition.

Whether he cd. EVER start writing the "dirt" I don't know. I haven't YET read thru <his Spain note.>

Never having edited a large circulation paper I do NOT
set up myself as a teacher of others.

My "reaction was favourable"

I will answer specific queeries if you have time to make 'em.

But I DO NOT know how to git the man in the street.

OR at any rate I have never been ALLOWED to go on when I thought I was about to do so.

It is less what I wd. like than : How strong will the public take it...

the only public worth a god damn WANTS it full strength.

What about George Tinkham[2]. He is better material ~~than~~ <than>

the gnu successor to Mr Bullet in Moscu[3].

Glad about Hollis[4].

Mary Howell is all too human[5]. I spose she means what she writes and that that is the way she see<s> it. <lot of fluff.>

basis in fact/ she won't MEAN to lie, she sees in them there scarlets and purples...

I won't sign any blank cheques save in ref/ to particular circumstances. And I really don't KNOW

what AUTHENTICITY for female journalists consists in.

Mary CAN'T be any further from right than that ASS Dorothy Thompson[5]

who worth the try to be wise guy <manner>, told the world Hitler wd/ never get on.
Mary got something at the time of the March Rome/[6] I believe a lot of CLEVER and austure and prudent journalists thought there was nothing in it.
Whether Mary has lived on the rep? of that ever since, I don't know.
I think I have sent, or have in my notes for next time a quote from Spanish Society girl// she wdn't have been shocked if the reds had murdered the rich/ she was shocked at their killing off the baker and drug=store proprietor.
village
The Prorok and Mont Summers got by.[7] Those were the items that <I>
was doubtful about before seeing 'em.
Wonder what the Liv. Age was lifting. They ordered a translation of Por/ and then refused to print it..[8]

waaaal; sech is like.

have
Two brit/ eds resigned and a sub/ed/ idem.[9] letters from two of 'em in last 24 hours.
I don't think " Original Features" on cover need mean NOTHING BUT O.F.
You have Or/Fea/, and for the rest I think quality (livliness) [sic]ought to outweigh any question of the whether it has been printed abroad.
I shd/ say 3 or 4 an issue was plenty <of reprint>
AND that it wd. give a much wider range/ I mean lot more good stuff available at LOW rates.
If you can BUY the most expensive copy/
WHEN you can buy it/ might consider strict rule against use of what has appeared elsewhere/ But 97 countries have papers that NEVER reached the U.S.
of mine
<in1911> Menken even printed poems in Smart Set that had already been collected in volume in London.[10]
Lets see what I can remember of Globe/ Saroyan. O.K.[11]
Kentucky trail[12], excellent. Morand weak [13], couple of letters in typescript rather flabby. and did give local condition of mind.

Nothing up to Por's level ? BUT can Odon P/ write with the necessary lightness. I wonder.
Wonder if Joe Bard wdn't be of use.[14] A bad man in many ways but might be useful.
What about ~~HHHHH~~ Mike Gold (Jews without Money, stuff)
Mike's write me "You are a fascist . God dman all fascists".[15]

O.KAY

And Joe Gould ? heard from ?[16]
Soryy about Bob Mc A//[17]

drink at last // it gits 'em.

Woman

Next Day/ Schuyler Palaver[18] /good stuff.

Looking thru GLOBE I find a good deal that did NOT catch my attention/ just slid over it, and forgot it was there.

Main reaction : Good

<Sugar Beet. OK.>[17]

<yr EZ>

[1] **Sisley Huddleston**

[2] **George Holden Tinkham**

[3] **William Christian Bullitt** and **Joseph Edward Davies**

[4] Pound wrote directly to **(Maurice) Christopher Hollis** urging him to write for *Globe*. He eventually wrote three articles for the magazine. Hollis' short piece "Roman Eagles Hatch Again!" appeared in the July 1937 issue of *Globe*.

[5] **Mary Howell**

[5] Through Hitler's press agent Ernst Hanfstaengl, **Dorothy Thompson** was able to arrange an interview with Hitler which took place in December 1931. When the interview was published, she wrote: "When I finally walked into Adolf Hitler's salon in the Kaiserhof Hotel, I was convinced that I was meeting the future dictator of Germany. In something less than fifty seconds I was quite sure I was not. It took just about that time to measure the startling insignificance of this man who has set the world agog." Other columnists expressed dismay at Thompson's conclusions. In later years Thompson acknowledged that the article was her greatest journalistic blunder. (The interview originally appeared in the April 1932 issue of *Cosmopolitan*, and quoted in part in Kurth, *American Cassandra*, pp. 161–2; for details of the interview and reactions see pp. 160–4).

[6] The Fascist "March on Rome" in 1922 marked the beginning of Mussolini's regime. Mary Howell apparently covered the events surrounding *Il Duce*'s rise to power, though exactly what published account Pound was referring to is unclear.

[7] *Globe* ran a three-part series by **Baron Byron Khun de Prorok**, "Untamed Ethiopia," beginning with the first issue of *Globe* (March 1937, pp. 124–8). These three articles were later incorporated into his book *Dead Men Do Tell Tales* (1942), an account of his expedition from Egypt into Ethiopia. **Montague Summers**' "London Goes to Satan" appeared in the first issue of *Globe* (March 1937, pp. 39–44).

[8] See **EP14**.

[9] **John McNab** was associate editor of *The Fascist Quarterly*; William Joyce was Director of Propaganda for the British Union of Fascists (BUF); and **John Beckett** was the current editor of the weekly newspaper *Action*, a publication of the BUF. On March 23, 1937, McNab wrote to Pound describing what

he considered a purge of the BUF by its leader **Oswald Mosley**. Joyce and Beckett were fired due to what Mosley described as a financial crisis—though McNab complained that no options such as pay cuts or working for no pay were considered. McNab resigned in protest and reports that not only was his resignation accepted but that he was "pitched out" of his office and led from BUF headquarters under guard.

[10] Pound was mistaken here; his first poem in *Smart Set* was "Silet," published in May 1912 (cf. Gallup C46). This poem was later included in *Ripostes* (October 1912). See also **EP28**.

[11] "Merry Reno," **William Saroyan**'s piece on the Nevada city, was the lead article of the first issue, pp. 6–7. Saroyan, despite his bitter complaints about *Globe*'s slow payment for his work, went on to write several more articles for the magazine.

[12] Pound was referring to **Jesse Stuart**'s story "Kentucky Constables" which appeared in the first issue of *Globe* (March 1937, pp. 49–52).

[13] **Paul Morand**'s article "Marseille," a sketch of the city's underworld, appeared in the first issue of *Globe* (March 1937, pp. 30–2).

[14] **Joseph Bard**

[15] **Michael Gold**

[16] **Joseph Ferdinand Gould**

[17] **Robert McAlmon**

[18] Schuyler's "Women Palaver," about sexual machinations in a small village in Liberia, was published in the first issue of *Globe* (March 1937, pp. 56–60).

[19] Pound was referring to "Sugar Beet Country," an article by **Hope Williams Sykes**, which appeared in the first issue of *Globe* (March 1937, pp. 33–8) about migrant workers in Colorado.

EP24

TSL TAX (BL)

3 April<-5>

Dear Dunn

re/ Critisizing Globe. continuing my last. I think my best line is to CONSTRUCT. Let me keep hammering ~~HH~~ on what is NOT in it, rather than trying to get out of my own skin to crab what gets IN.

I think you have a certain proportion of college graduates among yr/ readers.

I think they deserve ONE page out of the I28.

I think you can GET German interest if you have ONE serious page. It will keep the paper QUITE different from all other american periodicals (except the deadly dull a<n>d blind special journals)

I can dig up a letter of Dr Breasted's (Chic<a>go Archeologist. Assyrian Bulls ; Mexican expeditions etc.)[1]
The Germans have a whole mag/ for such correlations. We cd/ do a lot with one page.

I suggest that you print the enclosed from Dr. Besseler of the Staatliches Institut für X
Deutsche Musicforschung in Heidelberg.[2]
it seems to me good GLOBE publicity.
serious
Small print, quite enough. NO serious university prof. expects WORK to get headlines.
You might even do a tiny microfoto reprod of ~~his~~ <Besseler's> original. say 2 inches by one. nobody READ<s> photos of typed documents when they accompany text, but they like to see 'em.
NONE of these suggestions need be taken as imperatives. YOU are the edt/ dept. My job is to turn in stuff. ANY damnd idea practicable or not...
TAKING me as Methuselah/ to the Dunn brothers. I have seen a lot of mags/ stop and a lot more waste money by Exclusive attention so what they thought the public liked, I mean Exclusive in the sense that they didn't aim at building up a staff and in exciting the enthusiam of KNOWN individuals.
The OTHER or opposite ~~HHHHHH~~ fault (comes of excess) ~~i, e,~~ ends in being a house organd or trying to run on clique snobism.
I leave the pupular appeal to YOU. I think ONE page per issue cd/ be advantageously devoted to the serious public.
I mean to GETTING the absolutely top notch and/or most serious and heavy=weight fellows with us.
That don't mean it need be DULL.
After all your readers will have as many profs/ as ~~thHHHH HH~~ beetfarmers amongst 'em.
Give the profs. a hope. Let 'em feel they COULD get two lines of notice IF they were human enough to do something interesting.
I suggest using the Besseler letter because it shows interest in GLOBE.
It wdnt be a thing to use next year or in a mag/ that had been running a long time. git me?
I think Philology is NEWS when it is interesting to non=specialists.
A biologist gets printed on half page after 3 years work. I>E> when he isolates something that has a bearing on medicine etc.
30 years of Bill Shep[3], may yield two pages of GENERAL interest. IF they do, he ought to get two pages.
That emphatically does NOT mean that he ought to get MORE than two pages.

It DON'T mean that philology or literary research is interesting IN ITSELF.
It is only interesting when it digs out something.
you found for certain
If Shakespear had twins out of Queen Elizabeth that wd. take the matter out of the philological journals.
IF Elizabeth wrote Macbeth (as well as translating Ovid) ~~HH~~ the proof of it wd. be news.
list of
Such items can not be extended INdefinately. But a good news=hound can still find a few.
Dad is 78/ so pardon his enthusiasm for my work.[4] It is on right side? BUT don't think of reprinting that stuff of mine from Biosophic Rev[5] When said it is possible for Globe to reprint stuff I mean<t> from FOREIGN and inaccessible sources ONLY. vide verso.

[Back of page two]

A GLOBAL weekly has just come out in Italy. called Omnibus. first issue out on Saturday.
I wont start singing about it until I see whether it can keep pace.
Dunno if our circulars had any effect on starting 'em
It's a weekly/ AND several of us have been yelling against suburbanism and 1895 pt/ of view, for some time.
ALSO I don't KNOW whether or how soon these people will flop.
<EP>

[1] **James Henry Breasted**
[2] **Heinrich Besseler**
[3] **William Pierce Shepard**
[4] Pound's parents, Homer and Isabel, had moved from Wyncote, a suburb of Philadelphia, to Rapallo in 1928 after Homer had retired from the Philadelphia Mint. Like Pound, his parents found the cost of living in Italy attractive, and the closeness to their son would also have appealed to them. Homer's letter to Dunn has not survived, but he was always a staunch defender of his son's work and could have easily fired off a letter critical of *Globe* for rejecting a contribution from Pound. Pound's involvement with *Globe* was an inspiration for his own memoir which has been edited as *Small Boy: The Wisconsin Childhood of Homer*, by Homer L. Pound, Alec Marsh (ed.), with a foreword by Mary de Rachewiltz (The Ezra Pound Association: 2003).
[5] Pound seems to have been referring to an article "The Acid Test" which he published in *Biosophical Review*, New York, IV. 2 (Winter 1934/35), pp. 22–30.

JD15

TSL GS (YCAL)

April 22, 1937

Mr. Ezra Pound,
Via Marsala 12/5,
Rapallo, Italy.

Mr. Ezra Pound:

Much can happen in one month (the date of our last letter), GLOBE seems to be going over. We expected 20% sale on first number and got 60% with very little money put for advertising promotion. Curiosity sale accounts for a good deal of this, of course, but even discounting that, we can't help but feel encouraged.

Referring back to yours of March 17th. The Italian material received direct from the authors has been damn poor. Our translator here has done the best she could with mediocre stuff. Carlo Linati, (the best of the lot), Marcello Gallian, Orio Vergani, Nino Saverese, Filippo Burzio, Ciro Alvi[1] have been the only ones to send things in. This is the way we work with our translators; we send material received to, say, our German man in Omaha. He reads the manuscripts (understanding that we want short stories, reportages showing people against a background, etc., and those he thinks at all possible he reports on, giving us a detailed account of the article and his own reactions to it. We then write back yes or no.

When the translation is received; it is put into an envelope and passed on to our readers. If they don't like it, it's out. We, however, have to pay the translator our regular rates for the trouble he has taken; (at the present time, $1.00 per thousand words with bonus id printed). You might ask Bunting to do a sample.[2] We will agree to pay him what you say the first time. If it is good further arrangements can be made; if not, then we're out that much. Perhaps, however, you have suggestions as to how this translation business can be systematized.

The excellent music, et cetera, manuscript has been received.[3] It's one of the best and will go in the July issue, on the stands 15th. The deadline for August will be around the middle of

Mr. Ezra Pound -2-

June. Perhaps England has been hit on the nose enough.

No word from Duncan.[4] Manuscript from Hollis called "On Italians"[5] goes in July issue. Excellent stuff. Simons has been written to.[6]

Brother Jack gave him your address, so he will doubtless communicate direct with you.

Yes, prejudice is much against Nazi and Fascism. Whatever is said will have to be simple, direct, fair, emphatic, and not simply one person's viewpoint.

Our saying we sincerely regret the slip-up in your third paragraph (Unimportant) won't help much. We don't see where errata can be squeezed in.[7] We'll try, anyway.

Thanks for the O.K. stamp on first issue. The second one is now on its way to Rapallo. Caico's first article is to appear in June.[8] Jane Soames[9] sent in an excellent article on the Sultan of Morocco which is out being read; enjoyed reading her ENGLISH PRESS. The Mary Howell[10] manuscript was decided AGAINST by the editorial board. Hope she can send in more things, though. The reprint question has been decided—we publish only good, and only the best translations from the least known sources. Will try Gold again.[11]

The article in LIVING AGE was on Hindemith[,] Bartok, et cetera, called "Mostly Quartets," a radio talk of yours printed in the Listener.[12] Do you happen to know of any foreign book shop that might have your earlier books. Sylvia Beach?[13] I have built up quite a collection of your firsts.[14]

The enclosed check, much delayed, pays for "...And Excursions." Check covering July issues's "Deflation Benefit" will be sent as soon as the June issue is out of the way, which will be very soon.[15]

The extra six numbers of the first issue were sent long ago; word from your father says they arrived. One copy of the second issue went off first class several weeks ago as did the additional ones. Hope they reach Rapallo safely.

Bob Brown of Pleasant Plains Staten Island,[16] sent in several manuscripts that look promising. Now to see what the editorial board says. He mentioned both you and Hilaire Hiler. The latter recently sent in a photo taken a few years back which includes you Cocteau, Copeland, Man Ray, and others.[17] We plan to use it in GLOBE soon.

Concerning the VOU club poetry.[18] It has come up for much discussion and has been held over for two editorial conferences. Several of us are very much in favor of publishing the two intro-

Mr. Ezra Pound -3-

ductions together with three or four of the poems, but, being in the minority, there is nothing much we can do about it. The others feel that the subject's appeal is too limited. Do you want me to try placing them elsewhere? Just say yes or not (if the former, where) and I'll do my damnedest. They will be held until hearing from you.

Thanks again, Mr. Pound, for your interests and cooperation.

Cordially

The Editors of GLOBE

[signed]

James Taylor Dunn
Associate Editor

[1] A group of Italian writers who were loosely connected with Pound primarily through **Carlo Linati** (1878–1949), Italian modernist writer and friend of Pound and James Joyce. Marcello Gallian (1902–68) was a novelist. Orio Vergani (1899–1960) was a playwright, theater director, short story writer, novelist, and journalist. Nino Saverese (1882–1945) was a Sicilian novelist who co-founded the literary review *Il Sicialian Lunario*, which focused on Sicilian folklore. Filippo Burzio (1891–1948) was a philosophical writer, teacher, and journalist. Ciro Alvi (?–?) wrote a biography of St. Francis.
[2] **Basil Bunting**
[3] Dunn was referring to "Deflation Benefit" (Contribution #5), which was in part about the New Hungarian Quartet.
[4] **Ronald Duncan**
[5] **Christopher Hollis**
[6] **Rodger L. Simons** Pound hoped Simons would be able to place some of Pound's work in Sweden, where Simons was based.
[7] See **EP22** as well as Pound's published essay "Abdication" (Contribution #1). *Globe* editors ran errata on the error at the end of Pound's essay "Revolution by Radio" in the June issue.
[8] **Lina Caico**
[9] **Jane Soames Nickerson**
[10] **Mary Howell**
[11] **Michael Gold**
[12] For Pound's article "Mostly Quartets" see **JD14**.
[13] **Sylvia (neé Nancy Woodbridge) Beach**
[14] Dunn purchased many first editions of Pound's work during their correspondence. Dunn later donated the books to Hamilton College.
[15] "Deflation Benefit" (Contribution #5) appeared in *Globe* August, 1937 issue, pp. 66–71. "...And Excursions" (Contribution #12) was paid for as mentioned in this letter, but it never appeared in *Globe*.
[16] **Robert Carlton Brown**

[17] The photograph was taken outside **Hilaire Hiler**'s Jockey Club on the Boulevard du Montparnasse in 1923. It includes Man Ray, Hilaire Hiler, Kiki of Montparnasse, Tristan Tzara, Margaret Anderson, Walter Miller, Lew Copeland, Jane Heap, Jean Cocteau, Pound, Mina Loy and others. The photo was never published in *Globe*.
[18] See especially **EP20**; also see **EP10** and **EP17**.

EP25

TSC (BL)

2 May. VIA MARSALA 12 . 5

EZRA POUND [Stamped received] MAY 13.1937 RAPALLO

Drummond[1] has got his May GLOBE, mine not
here yet.
And you didn't send me an adjusted
date line. I am sending off my next
article by first post on Monday (tomorrow)
<registered>
Please let me know date of arrival.
The new article is aimed at July Globe

but not use my sending copy too early, if
there is a closer timing without to[o] much
chance of missing the issue.

cordially <E.P>.

[In left hand margin typed vertically] Fanning[2] enthusiastic over first number.

[1] **John Drummond**
[2] **Peter Fanning**

EP26

TL TAX (BL)

3 May

[stamped received] MAY 13.1937

Dear Dunn

GLOBE <for> May, MUCH better then March issue.

Old Hud quite ~~H~~ sensible re/Geneva/ TELL him you want the DIRT on Paris[1], if he is there. Whether he KNOWS or is capable of getting the real stuff, heaven alone knows.

NO editor will have asked him for it before.

He may NOT have the slightest idea what it is

OR having been born English he may be too prudent to risk his jobs with other papers by spilling the real stuff.

In any c[a]se it will take time AND REPETITION to make him understand that you want it.

Hughes //
Langston ~~HHHHHH~~ is GOOD.[2] So much more easy than Hem's laborious squeezing it out.[3]

//

I am doing this on Drummond's [4]copy/ mine not here yet.

///

Of course the Fox interests ME [5] and the people here are likely to see Globe.

designs excellently reproduced.

Photo Reportage EXCELLENT id[e]as.

that ass Linc. Kirstein, Hound and Horn[6] bloke had some good <photo> once/

don't know that it was ever used.

He was chasing New England tombstones[7]. I got a lot of photos when Putnam had New Review[8] Paris/

But he was part stupid and partly hadn't the money for reprods.

I will have a look-see if any edits left.

In any case Kirstein might be useful for that sort of stuff. NOT fer his canned licherary opinions.

Mangione : O.K. Sicilia cop.[9]

And I read the hill billy without difficulty. (Ed Bell)[10]

I suspect one of the <character> names was emeneded to pass the police cordon ??

Can Mont Schuler[11] do anthing or Globe ? Address I spose Brookings Institute/ heaven knows he did some work on Loeb chart of plenty/[12]

BUT that AINT the side of Mont. that you want.

I wonce baptized him with fire (off a rum omlet) an it nacherly stimulated my interest in his subsequent kay/reer.

ASK Fox about Weischoff and the other Forschung's bloke one who did

trading customs in the South Seas/ pubd/ it as science [13], but IF he can sort out individual stories it ought to ne USEFUL, IF he can do it.
there is a whole gang of 'em Globe shd/ get 'em before the National Geographic wakes up to it.

I will try again to find Golijewsky.

I miss Mike Harrison, or some equivalent.[14]
Whether Pitt Rivers [15] know anything more that already in print, I dunno.
e; e; cummings COULD[16] <vide
if you get him on the right clear
angle copy>
I am for as much Langston Hughes
as you can get.
SENTENCE to be added to yesterday's article/ or inserted if and where you see fit.
Even the patient John Donkey (né Bull) is showing peevishness at having Mont Norman's[17] boko

pound

in the watermark on English notes, the King's head having been taken off 'em. [typewritten and hand-written in right margin] <Coronation visitors invited to.>
<H>ave a squint at the helmet of <B>ritania or Minerva or whoever the lady is in the watermark.

[No signature]

[1] **Sisley Huddleston** contributed an article on the League of Nations, which was based in Geneva, entitled "That League" in the May 1937 issue of *Globe* (pp. 98–101).
[2] **(James Mercer) Langston Hughes'** story "Just Traveling," about his visit to Paris, was the lead article of the second issue of *Globe* (May 1937, pp. 4–7).
[3] **Ernest Hemingway**
[4] **John Drummond**
[5] **Douglas Clayton Fox**'s article in *Globe* "Cultures in the Rock" (May 1937, pp. 11–16).
[6] **Lincoln Kirstein**
[7] Pound wrote to **Lincoln Kirstein** on March 1, 1930, asking for any photos that he might have "...UNUSUAL photos of America and american life that you can't use in H[ound]. and H[orn]. (YCAL)" Pound had been asked by P-G Van Hecke to help in putting together a collection of photo images for a number of his magazine *Variétés: Revue mensuelle illustrée de l'esprit contemporain* (see Ahern, *Pound/Cummings*, p. 17). Kirstein sent Pound a group of photos, and in an undated letter (April 1930?) Pound gratefully responded and itemized

the images sent. Among the shots was a photo of “12 tombstones, some of my presumed family.”

[8] **Samuel Putnam**

[9] **Jerre Mangione**’s “Sicilian Policemen” appeared in the May 1937 issue of *Globe.*

[10] **Ed Bell**

[11] **Montgomery Schuyler**

[12] **Harold Loeb** was head of the Technocracy movement’s “National Survey of Potential Product Capacity” project. It brought out its findings as *The Chart of Plenty: A Study of America’s Product Capacity Based on the Findings of the National Survey of Potential Product Capacity* (1935).

[13] **Heinrich Albert Wieschhoff** and **Helmut Petri**

[14] Pseudonym of **Harrison Salisbury**

[15] Probably **George Henry Lane Fox Pitt-Rivers**

[16] **Edward Estlin Cummings**

[17] **Baron Montagu Collet Norman**

EP27

TSL TAX (BL)

4 May.

[stamped received] MAY 17.1937

<J.T.D>

Waal BEE/LEEVE you ME, Young Dunn
It ZA ERROR !
It za ERROR not to print that Jap stuff.
You may run up to 500,000 circ/ but if you cut the BEST kind of reader, you’ll end on the shit pile with Lorimer and the Shat. Eve Pust.[1]
//
All very well, to “appeal” but there is also the matter of RECORD. Worth ANY mag’s while to HAVE BEEN the first to print New Japan.
///
No I don’t want it cut. I offered it as WHOLE. And I don’t want you to hawk it around.
I’ve got places for it, but I let GLOBE have the first shot.
I. because GLOBE is worth building UP
(but not worth letting slide DOWN)
2. Chance of larger audience to Kit/Kat<ue>. and co//
<Waal> tell the great Elder Brother he is on the WRONG for onct.

///

Letter to him and new notes, went yeserday.
No. 2. much better than No. I..

<I spose
only make
Aug. not July
?>

The crit/here (foreign) is apart from me and Fox,
there is nothing TO it <(may.globe.)>
DON'T say so~~/~~ & for God's sake go on printing him, and lets hope he don't know he is doing it.
The way to INTRODUCE Hiler is to reprod/ some of his PAINTINGS
of tough types, lascars etc/
there is a great one of 3 or four sailors half nigger, lascar etc/ at table. All the GLOBE drive ; for
types and humans/ <Restaurant rue Torte.> <quick lunch & some harbours>
Particularly APT/, I am distinguishing this phase, from his architectures, houses etc/ but also one damn fine PORT.
Don't matter that it has been in catalog/ Human and literary interest.
<B>etter than even the photoreprotage/ though that is a damn good feature.
<Waal>
~~HHHHH~~ git clear about them JAP poems. ALL or NONE ; and please return 'em AT ONCE if you can't SEE it.

But count on rejection
lowering my moral.
Oh, yes; thanks Chq/ recd/
The wops you mention as bad, are NO USE to me. Linati[2] the only one I can have mentioned., as you say, the best, but not good enough.
<ond>
I putt Drumm~~ond~~ onto R.Marchi[3]. but his first draft <of trans.> was too slow.
not up to American stuff; or the Sicilian cop: ~~HH~~
by Mangione ???[4] an americo=wop ??
The intelligence in Italy is IN THE GOVERNMENT, blokes
like ~~HHHHHH~~ Monotti[5] get grabbed for office jobs
and good by free lancing.
the litterati are DUMB as hell ; font know there IS a new Italy or an empire.
I mean the old line pre I922 blighters.
and pseudo frogs.
Tozzi is dead [6]/ serious but too long and slow for Globe.
various other goodish blokes are dead (physically) I mean etat civil. dead. not merely mentally.
Of the living there LIGHT be a chance from
Notari (sky high prices.)[7] .
Marino Moretti[8]... once was good on Romagna ; but then git

to the sea shore, and summer life.

Marchi ; prob. too slow.

Longanesi, journalist running a near Gringoire, Candide.[9]

called OMNIBUS[10], <has> run four numbers, once a week. but don't seem to be able to find any live journalists even for that.

Had a blurb about me in third issue, by Praz !!!! half dead italian professor of wop in Liverpool university. full of Bloomsbury bug juice.[11]

re/ P/ 2. The ONLY Englishmen who will read GLOBE, will think Eng aint been hit on the nose HARD enough.

March

General McG/ [12] sent off copy to Viennese Parson who had Eddie read the service/

Old General (age 70 plus) hopes it will git to Mr. Windsor.

I don't think Miss S. Bitch[13] is likely to WANT to sell my works I suggest what's his names <in>

<(Blackwell)> [14]

Oxford. <Eng. F.B.> or Neumayer 70 Charing Cross Rd London. <w.c. 1.>

//

Re LIMITED appeal/ If you cut off the TOP class of reader, you limit the sales. The mag/ ought to be able to carry ONE item at least per issue, that has permanent value ? I mean that can force respect for the paper UP at the 100% level.

within 128 pages, there is bound to be enough chaff and fine cut.

nobody will STOP buying the paper because of ONE article that is too good for 'em.

It is worth having a paper for sake of the Fox on rocks.[15]

Hughes, Fox and Frobenius ~~can~~ <could> all read that Jap stuff with respect.

<R>emember you are getting your best stuff at rates far below Harper's pewk.

an exprit de corps among the writers is an ASSET.

No mag can run on cash alone.

<thanks for certified name plate> [16]

<yr

EZP>

[1] George Lewis Lorimer

[2] Carlo Linati

[3] John Drummond and Riccardo Marchi

[4] Jerre Mangione

[5] Francesco Monotti

[6] Federigo Tozzi

[7] Probably **Notari Umberto**
[8] **Marino Moretti**
[9] These were the French journals *Gringoire: le grand hebdomadaire parisien, politique, littéraire* and *Candide,* which, along with the *Je Suis Partout*, constituted the core of far right/fascist journalism in France in the 1930s.
[10] In 1936, **Leo Longanesi** launched Italy's first cheap "glossy" weekly magazine *Omnibus.* The initial run of the journal was 100,000 copies and it seemed destined for success. Unfortunately, the magazine was shut down by the Fascist regime in 1939.
[11] **Mario Praz**
[12] Possibly Colonel Henry King McGeorge (1865–1940). He retired from the Indian Army in 1921 and settled in Rapallo, where he met the Pounds. He was mentioned by Dorothy Pound in a letter to Ibbotson dated December 7, 1937.
[13] **Sylvia Beach** lent and sold Pound's work until her shop closed in 1941. The remark may be related to Pound's feeling slighted by Beach's staunch support of James Joyce as well as jealousy of Joyce's solid success as a writer in the 1930s (see also **EP28**).
[14] The English publishing house and booksellers Basil Blackwell, now Blackwell's Ltd.
[15] **Douglas Clayton Fox** published "Cultures in the Rock" in the May 1937 issue of *Globe.* The article introduced the reader to **Leo Frobenius**' work on prehistoric rock art and drew attention to an exhibition at the Museum of Modern Art of rock art from the Institut für Kulturmorphologie collections. Fox was sent to New York by the Institut to oversee the installation of the exhibition.
[16] Pound was referring to the arrival of his *Globe* press card.

EP28

TSL TAX (BL)

5 May

[stamped received] MAY 17.1937

My Dear Jheezus Wm/ Gor' D. .N

Before you JUDGE me a IDIOT. I wanna putt in the evidence.

On your side IZ Hank Mencken who wrut me 20 year ago that he had evidence that if he pit into the Am/Murk

"anything having the faintest trace of literary merit"

it knocked the sales.

waaaal Hank iz a joker.[1]

Now Reese (Holystone Holysmoke rubber ball kikie Reese)[2] is the slickes<t> jew publisher in YourUp. exuberant OIL.

And he has putt over the Alba<t>ross, and jew as he is has now got the Tauchnitz,[3] both together.

IN Germany and the MONOpoly on as you might say all continental pub/ing

Now printing nothing worth a fried fahrt except

in Engl<ish> reprints of British Crime Club detective stuff.

AND he started the series with Joyce's Ulysses.[4]

As a p<ra>ctical stunt to GET the german book buyer.

Notes that Wynd Lewis Tarr and Joyce's "Portrait" were already in Tauchnitz[5].

Now that Jap stuff is NEWS,[6] and as to "limited interest" there are gor knowz how many colledge boys in amurika and others TRYING to write poesy. and ONLY ONE live group of poets in the bleeding WORLD at this time.

Trust papa fer onct.

That Jap stuff can be held up as testimony to Globe's bein<'>

"wise" to the TOP:; for the next three years, if you never touch anything near it.

Not that there is likely to be another such item during the next three years.

Don't think it is going to snow live groups in the orient.

///

Secondly.

I .

I wrote to Haldie EDIB, yesterday. lady wot went thru Turk revol

ution with Kemal.[7]

said to be or have been in U.S.

good gal/ and writes nicely to[o] (or has it done for <her>.)

2. Sent out another search for Gen. Golijewsky.[8]

3.Helmut Petri is the name of the South Sea bloke I was trying to

remember/

address via ~~HHHHH~~ Fox of the Rocks (D. C.)[9]

//

I don't spose a MILITIRARY criticiam of Tukhachevsky wd/ be of general interest ??

Is Parry doing it intentionally ?[10]

After all ther is allus Ike Marcosson[11]...

AND Sokolosky[12]

whom I hope we ~~sahn~~ shan't include .

What I mean is, does Globe WANT hooey ?? Of course this kind of thing can ONLY be done by the naive... and it is interesting as a display of what the naive will take. It shows the original scene better than smart handling.

I can see editorial reasons for USING Parry ;

but NONE for taking him at his own ~~valua~~
valuation.
It WOULD be the psychoanalytic Quarterly and Vanity Fair.[13]
Vogel and Saroyan can both of 'em do better than in May number.[14]
Mangione and Hughes got 'em licked by ten kilometers.[15]
(this is confidential, yer kd bro sez you (?? or he) me to speak wot I think.
What edt/ pol/ re printing really BAD poetry ?
Menken in I910 REPRINTED a lot of mine, ~~i, e,~~ that had come out in volume in London, but was unknown in U.S.A.[16]
There are TWO poems of Buntings that belong to GLOBE.
Morpethshire
~~HHHHHHHHH~~ Farmer, and Gin the Gude Wife Stint.[17]
Better reprint real stuff like that, tnan use filler
sez me//
Other items I haven't yet got myse<l>f to read/ this list
continues from letter of a few days ago.
What you feel re/ Cougnlin's public?[18]
The Roda Roda is useful.;[19] perhaps 3 times a year that kind of thing ?

<yr EP>

[1] Though Pound provided a direct quote from **H. L. Mencken**, the Pound correspondence files preserved at in the Bienecke Library (YCAL) do not include a letter from Mencken with such a comment. Pound's memory also seems faulty; Mencken was editing *Smart Set* in 1917. *The American Mercury* first appeared in 1924.

[2] **John Holroyd-Reece**

[3] In 1932 **John Holroyd-Reece**, along with Max Christian Wegner and Kurt Enoch, launched the Albatross Press, based in Hamburg, Germany. It was to be a reprint paperback publishing house to rival the well-established house of Bernard Tauchnitz, based in Leipzig, Germany, and founded in 1837. Tauchnitz's series of British and, later, American authors were immensely successful and well-known. However, the success of Holroyd-Reece's Albatross Press was such that he was able to buy out and absorb his Leipzig rival.

Holroyd-Reece contacted Pound in 1932 with a request to include the "Ballad of the Goodly Fere" in Albatross' *Albatross Book of Living Verse*. Judging from his letters to the poet, Pound seemed to have responded to Holroyd-Reece making it clear that while he was happy to take Albatross' £5 for the right to reprint the poem, he was less than impressed with their choice of material. There followed an exchange in which Holroyd-Reece tried to keep up a cordial correspondence with Pound, but Pound seems to have bombarded him with criticism and fishes for a paid position as a reader for Albatross.

[4] Pound seems to have been referring to a contract that Joyce signed in 1931

with Albatross Press. This edition of *Ulysses* (revised by Stuart Gilbert) appeared in 1932 under the imprint of the Odyssey Press (see R. Ellmann, *James Joyce* [revised edn], pp. 652–3). Albatross also brought out its edition of *Dubliners* in 1932. Pound seemed to have considered such a commercialization of Joyce's work a "sell-out." Pound's pique at Joyce's reputation and marketability is already evident in an article he wrote for *The English Journal* in May of 1933.

> *The Portrait* and *Ulysses* were serialized by small honest magazines created to aid communication of living work; after the lapse of years, these vols. arrived at such a state of acceptance that parasitic publishers issued them. The Tauchnitz which cares only for money but pretends to other aims, issued *The Portrait* and the Albatross issued *Dubliners* and *Ulysses* in continental cheap editions, indicating that the books had passed out of the exclusive circle of people who think and want to know what is being thought, and into the general mass of people who read because an author has a "name", etc. (See reprint of the article in Read, *Pound/Joyce*, p. 247.)

This attitude was probably not unrelated to his cutting remark made about Sylvia Beach in **EP27**.

[5] **Wyndham Lewis**' novel *Tarr* (1918) was put under contract with Bernard Tauchnitz, Leipzig in 1930 and appeared under their imprint in 1931. Tauchnitz issued its edition of *Portrait of the Artist as a Young Man* in 1930.

[6] **Katue Kitasono** and the VOU group, see **EP10, EP17**, and **EP20**.

[7] **Halide Edip Adivar**

[8] **Honore Golijewsky**

[9] **Helmut Petri**

[10] **Mikhail Nikolayevich Tukhachvesky** and **Albert Parry**

[11] **Isaac Marcosson**

[12] **George Sokolsky**

[13] These two periodicals appeared in a list of credits in a "bio blurb" for **Albert Parry** in the May 1937 issue of *Globe*.

[14] **William Saroyan** and **Joseph Vogel**'s "Notes From a Cattleboat: Fight!", excerpts from his diary while a deckhand sailing from Naples to Malta in the early 1930s, was published in the May 1937 issue of *Globe* (pp. 30–3).

[15] **Jerre Mangione** and **(James Mercer) Langston Hughes**

[16] Once again Pound's memory was slightly off. His first contribution to *Smart Set* (XXXVII.1, May 1912) appeared to be the first publication of the poem "Silet" which reappeared in October 1912 in the first edition of *Ripostes*. The poem then appeared in the American editions of *Lustra* (1917), *Umbra* (1920), and finally in *Personae* (1926), where it still appears today. However, beginning in 1913, Pound did reprint a number of poems in *Smart Set* which first appeared in *Ripostes*.

[17] **Basil Bunting**'s "Gin the Good Wife Stin" and "The Compliant of the Morpethshire Farmer" were first published in Pound's *Active Anthology* (1933).
[18] **Reverend Charles E. Coughlin**
[19] **Alexander Friedrich Ladislaus Roda Roda**

EP29

TSL TAX (BL)

14 June

Dear Dunn
<T>rboule with Huddy is tht he aint HAPPY (not enough).[1] <P> erfectly easy to know one is analyzing
and when one is playing safe by sending the bits of surface the ploots WANT printed.
Waaal, I am sending you the GREAT human story. with a few photos of Wörgel/
Untergugenberger's death, quite young, brings it into news <June> again.[2]
GOOD cover/[3] complments of contrast in coulor to the last one AttaBhoy !!
<guidance.>
// Of course you send me NO ~~uidance/~~.
Now what about Kirstein's photos/ what about all the photos I have accumulated for years/
machines, U.S. feature stuff etc.[4]
do I ship the LOT to be held for me in Globe
archives, or do you wanna disKuss 'em ?? first .
I think at least some of 'em are funnier than this months churches.
(personally glad to se <H>amilton etc. but...am talkin as prophane membr of pubk/)[5]
Man Ray and Cocteau and Leger have all done FILM stuff that is still news after Io or !4 years. film mags haven't touched it at least not with any comprehension.
Mebbe I better try Leger [6] <?>
he is a dull writer, but might spot up the stills or something.
I am still sure I am right re/ NEWS value of those jap poets.
Say we aim at ONE high brow stunt every three months.
There CAN NOT be more than three good ones a year because there never have been, <never> Existed more than four good high brow stunts in any one year. That is a maximun, cause the production don't ever pass that.
I nominate <J>erre mangione again [7] <I miss him in June.>

Also sent on note showing my attempt to reach <H>alide Edidb/ hadn't reached her.[8] spose YOU try...

People ask how many copies of Globe are getting into USE .

<I> shd/ like to know/ either publically or privately/ I mean for boast or concealment.

LATER/

Coronos[9] good// the Turk[10]/ good and FRANK MA[11] !!!!

izza joye/ lez have more MA, man! that is the stuff fer this reader.

Damn Huddleston/ isn't even factual/ just stall/

either he is too god DAMNED lazy to get any Paris nooz or he is afraid it send it [sic].

Give him a friendly hint that you WANT some real personal stuff on Blum/<T>ardieu/ Herriot and <D>aladier[12]/ and if he don't send it give him the boot.

Cournos and the Turk are full of meat/ stuff people dont know, and equally interesting for high and low foreheads. or rather the more intelligent a man is, there more interest he minds.

also the canibal story[13]/ very olde but ever young/

thazz O.KAY

Am genuinely annoyed with ~~HHHHH H~~ Hud/ it is as if

any contact with the Times (or any other Brit. daily) leaves a man leporous for life.

I know that <P>aris press gang/ the good ones think the rest are morons, and the worse they are the more they blurr and purr.

O course Gunther [14] is an ASS, a bloody ass.

Prorok[15] whom you know I mistrusted, seems to be making good.

Man I wrote you know for Messageries address hasn't answered. but I will get it soon/

<H>achette is NOT disturbing you in Italy.

Of course Hachette is rotten ; like Smith and son in England. but we cant help THAT. <h>e has all France in his dirty pocket.

If you havent any <B>rit<ish> circulation/ send a few copies to F. B. Neumayer,[16] 70 Charing Cross Rd/

tell him my connection and he will at least start selling Globe in a private way.

I mean a dept where Englishmen cd/ break in with a shilling and get a copy.

<yr
EP>

<my V
mss.
starts
tomorrow>

[1] **Sisley Huddleston**
[2] Michael Unterguggenberger (1884–1936), was Burgermeister of Wörgl, a small town in the Austrian Tyrol that experimented with Silvio Gesell's stamp scrip briefly in the 1930s. Pound mentioned this innovation in Canto LXXIV. Pound published an interview with Unterguggenberger's widow in *Globe*, "Interview with Mrs. Unterguggenberger" (see Contribution #6).
[3] Pound was referring to the cover of the June 1937 issue of *Globe*, which featured a woodcut as cover-art entitled "Fish Venders in Portugal."
[4] For **Lincoln Kirstein** and his photographs see **EP26**. Pound made a collection of photographs that are now in the Pound Archive in Beinecke Library (see description in Ardizzone, *Machine Art*, pp. 167–70). These photographs were collected to illustrate an essay entitled "Machine Art" (ca. 1927–30). The essay and selection of the photographs are published in Ardizzone, *Machine Art*, pp. 57–83.
[5] Pound was referring to a photograph of Hamilton College's chapel that ran in the *Photo Reportage* section entitled "The Wedding Bells Ring" in the June 1937 issue of *Globe*.
[6] **Fernand Léger, Jean Cocteau,** and **Man Ray** experimented with film in the 1920s and early 1930s. When Pound moved to Paris in the early 1920s he came in contact with each of these artists. Pound was likely familiar with Man Ray's first effort in film which was entitled *Le retour à la raison*. This film "sort" was created especially for an evening of Dada productions organized by Tristan Tzara and held on July 6, 1923. May Ray used cut film stock and worked directly upon the film to produce his images as well as incorporating stills and other images in more conventional ways. *Emak-Bakia* (1926) appears to be Man Ray's second film. This film, which incorporated sections of his previous film *Le retour à la raison*, was more ambitious, but just as plotless. It could be described as an animated collage of images—which Man Ray felt allowed the film to achieve the state of poetry. The film concluded with a famous image of his mistress Kiki looking into the camera and closing her eyes, only to reveal upon each of her eyelids a painted and open eye. (See Baldwin, *Man Ray* pp. 121–45 for a detailed discussion of the genesis and nature of these films.)

In November 1924 **Fernand Léger** and Dudley Murphy created (perhaps with the help of Man Ray) a film called *Ballet Mécanique*. Another short film—it runs about 15 minutes—is again a non-narrative collage of various fleeting images and features the ever-present Kiki. The film was, as the title indicates, to be accompanied by George Antheil's notorious composition of the same name.

Pound was familiar with Jean Cocteau's first film, *The Blood of a Poet* (1930). Cocteau wrote the scenario, edited the film, and acted as its producer. The musical score was composed by Georges Auric.
[9] **John Cournos**
[10] **Falik Rifki Atay**

[11] **Frank Ma**
[12] **Léon Blum, André Pierre Gabriel Amédée Tardieu, Édouard Herriot**, and **Édouard Daladier**
[13] **George Schuyler**'s "The Lord's Work," an article about a secret society of cannibals in Liberia, appeared in the June 1937 issue of *Globe*.
[14] **John Gunther**
[15] **Baron Byron Khun de Prorok**'s third article appeared in the June 1937 issue of *Globe* (pp. 80–3), "Valley of the Vampires."
[16] F. B. Neumayer was a bookseller whom Pound knew from his London days and stayed in touch with up to the beginning of World War II.

EP30

TSL TAX (BL)

Shd. I write to S. paul
OR Millwawkee ???

<15 June>

<Dear JD>

CONTINUING

While waiting fer that Damn photographer, who like s pyanny playing to get on wiff the fotografts.

//

I miss snappy stuff about WASHINGTON. whazza matter ? cost too much ?
all the good guys writing it for too many other American papers ??
why not try e;cummings, 4 Patchin Place or is that too risky and "special" ???[1]
I dunno that Fr Frost is very good.[2]
what about Lin Yutang ??[3] posssible to get him ??
Frank Ma is O.KAY cheer by me.[4]
Kisch[5] very far below what Morand WAS in I92I. <H>eaven knows how far Morand has sunk by now. Anyhow my Morand is in a box in Paris, and can't be got in a hurry.[6]
AND I am not anxious at this date to have my name connected with his.
Mr Tukachevsky is OUT.[7] I never liked his fyce. And the Stakhalov sweating system was pewk. nasty man, Stakhalov[8].
and you NEVER will get civilization by a lot of mess=headed savages?

Can you get any stuff from the EDGES of Russia, Harbin or even Poland on this side.

I SEE that a lot of neg/ is going into the make up, and appearance of the mag/
but if you wd. let me know what you are SHORT of, I might have a few waves of brain re/ reinforcing.

NO.3 not a let down, but not an argument over No. 2.

??

For biob/ brevs/ you can note.

E.P. present years output.[9]

Books.

Polite Essays

Fifth ///// of Cantos

Decad

Digest of the Analects (brief except from Confucius).

Contributions to: British Union Quarterly, Criterion, etc.

(there are a couple of other important articles accepted; but better wait till they are out.)

The above hangs onto letter I sent yr/ bro/ yester. correlate if the family is still on speaking terms with eachother.

<yrs E.P.>

[1] **Edward Estlin Cummings**

[2] **Frances Mary Frost**

[3] **Lin Yutang**

[4] **Frank Ma**

[5] **Egon Erwin Kisch**'s article "Scum of the Revolution," which dealt with White Russians exiled in China, appeared in the June 1937 issue of *Globe*.

[6] In the early 1920s, Pound had translated **Paul Morand**'s *Tendres Stocks* with a preface by Marcel Proust. But when the Pounds moved to Rapallo, the manuscript was left behind unpublished in Paris. New Directions published Pound's translation along with Proust's preface in 1984 *as Fancy Goods; Open All Night / Stories by Paul Morand* edited with an introduction by Breon Mitchell.

[7] Around May 26, 1937, Stalin gave the arrest order for Marshal **Mikhail Nikolayevich Tukhachevsky** and removed him from his command. On June 11, 1937, Tukhachevsky and other military leaders were convicted of spying for Germany. Shortly after his conviction, Tukhachevsky and most of his family were executed.

[8] **Aleksei Grigorievich Stakhanov**

[9] The Faber & Faber edition of *Polite Essays* was issued in February 1937. Faber & Faber issued *The Fifth Decad of Cantos* on June 3, 1937; the American

edition of *The Fifth Decad* was issued by Farrar & Rinehart in November 1937. *Confucius, Digest of the Analects* was issued by Pound's Italian publisher Giovanni Scheiwiller, of Milan, in June 1937. Between January and June 1937, Gallup lists around twenty-two contributions to various periodicals, most frequently in the *British Union Quarterly*, *The New English Weekly*, *Criterion*, and *Rassegna Monetaria* (see Gallup, C1387–C1409, pp. 313–14).

JD16

TSL GS (YCAL)

June 14, 1937

Mr. Ezra Pound,
Via Marsala 12/5,
Rapallo, Italy.

Dear Mr. Pound:

Returned about a week ago from three weeks trip to New York, hence the silence. The Board, I find, is still insistent re the Japanese poetry.[1] Your help and encouragement has meant a great deal to us, and the contacts you have made have met with much favor; Fox, Caico, Rouse, Duff, Hollis, et cetera. We sincerely hope that the returning of these poems will not lower your "mora" too much.[2]

"Net Result", being more timely, was put in the July issue which is now about off the press. "Deflation Benefit" will appear in the August number.[3]

Many thanks for the comment on the magazine. We wrote to Hughes,[4] received a manuscript (excellent), rushed it through to appear in the July number. Mangione[5] was in Saint Paul the other day. He gave us several good Italian contacts. Am trying to get in touch with Silone's[6] translators in London, David and Mosbacher.[7] Silone lives in Zurich, doesn't he?

The check for July article is delayed, but we'll try to get it off to you as soon as possible.

Cordially,
GLOBE MAGAZINES, Inc.
[signed]
James Taylor Dunn
Assistant Editor

Vera Lawson's ms. received;[8] shall we send you check for letter from Chansa Hunan?[9]

JTD/dt
Poems returned under separate cover

[1] Dunn returned the VOU Club poets' manuscript to Pound along with his introductions to the collection. Pound sent them to **Ronald Duncan** and he published them in his new journal *The Townsman.*

[2] **Douglas Clayton Fox, Lina Caico, W. H. D. Rouse, Christopher Hollis,** and **Charles Duff.**

[3] For "Net Result" see Contribution #4 and "Deflation Benefit" see Contribution #5.

[4] In the article "Samarkand the New" (*Globe*, July 1937, pp. 40–4), **Langston Hughes** recounted his trip to this Central Asian city when he visited in the Soviet Union in 1932 and 1933.

[5] From 1937 to 1939, Jerre Mangione was a Coordinating Editor for the Federal Writers Project. It is likely that his visit to St. Paul was related to this work.

[6] **Ignazio Silone**

[7] **Gwenda David [Mosbacher]** and **Eric Mosbacher**

[8] Vera Lawson, an American poet living in Italy, married Pound's friend, the German composer Gerhart Münch in Naples in 1937. The manuscript was never published.

[9] In the July 1937 issue, pp. 99–100, *Globe* published an anonymous article entitled "China Wedding." The article was in fact excerpts from a letter to Pound from Edith Madge, an English missionary in Chansa, Hunan province, China. Madge, who taught music in China and India, corresponded with Pound for years. In a letter to Madge dated July 5, 1937, Pound wrote, in part:

> "Dear Edith, I sent some extracts from one of yr/ letters to GLOBE, anonymous, they now ask if they are to send me a small cheque/ I am telling 'em to send it to you. I removed names from yr/ account/ in fact I don't think any harm can be done. And it shd/ lead to yr:/ making small amount if you care to go on sending 'em simple descriptions of what you see in Hunan or put yr/ friends onto doing so." (This letter is in the personal collection of the late Omar S. Pound, now at the Burke Library, Hamilton College.)

JWGD2

TSL GS (YCAL)

June 21, 1937

Mr. Ezra Pound,
Via Marsala 12/5,
Rapallo, Italy.

Dear Mr. Pound:

Enclosed is your monthly $20.00. How far do you figure this carries you? On your index in front of me, I notice you have been paid including the enclosed for six months. This includes our fourth issue July. Do you consider that this makes us square to date including the July issue or including the August issue, which? We rely entirely on how you feel about it. I realize that your activity for GLOBE has been more than the letters alone and having you with us is of incalculable value. This is the zero hour for GLOBE: the inertia of summertime must be passed before hoped for autumn advertising.

Has GLOBE been brought to the attention of Mr. Mussolini?[1] I hope so or that it will. Would he write an intimate letter for GLOBE sometime? Mary Howell[2] sent us an article written by Marshal de Bono,[3] but there was nothing new in it so we had to send it back. The idea of getting world notables to write for GLOBE protagonizing certain ideas still holds good. Could you send us reviews on GLOBE published in Italian papers and magazines?

Now I wonder if we can turn southward, eastward, or westward a while in your general European letters. England has come in for more attention than it deserves and people are getting somewhat fed up on the Island's own trails and tribulations. How about Abyssinia, Rodi, Pantellaria, The Heel and Toe, Malta, and the route to the Indies, the Mediterranean basin, Iberian peninsula, and the communistic colossus? We still itch to receive native Italian authors.

Sincerely,

GLOBE MAGAZINES, Inc.

[signed]

J. W. G. Dunn, Jr. Editor

JWGD/dt
encl. $20.00

[1] Pound forwarded a copy of *Globe* (May 1937) to Mussolini on May 15, 1937. See introduction pp. 27–8 and **EP32**, note 2, below.

[2] **Mary Howell**
[3] **Emilio De Bono**

EP31

TSL TAX (BL)

[July 5, 1937]

Dear J. Taylor D/

Sorry about the Japs/ Hope it gets here in time f for

Duncan's first issue.[1]

Please send chq/ for chinese letter to

Edith Madge[2]

I FANG school

American Church Mission

Changsha Hunan / China

tell her you want more chinese impressions and stuff from Chinese.

Say I sent

in the extract, anonymously,
and that you were pleased to accept it. all resposibility mine.

<Please>
Print it anonymously/ as I sent it.

The I FANG is not ONE FANG, pronounce <u>ee</u> fang.

yE

I dont know HOW to expalin to yr/bro/how LITERARY some
people are/ for ex/ if a bloke that has pubd/ the
official summary of Benedetto Crose's phylosophy starts
trying to do a sketch of real life !!!!![3]

[1] Pound was responding to **JD16** where Dunn announced that he was sending back the Japanese VOU poets' manuscript along with Pound's introductions.
[2] For Edith Madge and her "article" see **JD16** note 8.
[3] **Emilio De Bono**

EP32

<5 July>

J/W/G/D
Globe.

20 bucks recd/

Dear Dunn:

Call it July, I thought I started work some time last year. Globe has been SENT to the private secretary in the approved manner, but can NOT expect the EXCLUSIVE attention of the First European.

He has other subjects which call for attention.[1]

Until I have yr/ certified sales for a given month, it is impossible to make ANY practical moves.

As you went to Hachette and not the Messageries, Globe has not got <on to stands> into this country, ans so far as I make out only a few copies are on sale in London.

NO possible chance of exclusive stuff from High personalities until prices approach Colliers and the circulation that of Sat/Post.[2]

The state of MIND of the serious characters wd/ be utterly incomprehensible to yr/ readers without a years technical study.

If you get the <next issue> British Union Quarterly with say 20 pages of the Milhaud Plan, you will get a faint idea of the way the serious european goes at things.[3]

Neither that kind of article, nor brief note from the point of view of men who have digested it / NOR fourt<h> of July oration wd/ be much use.

There are two men in Italy who review English and American books. neither of 'em likely to review a magazine.

The Italians who matter are mostly in executive positions and NO spare time whatever.

A digest of Rossoni's speech on amassi wd/ ~~present~~ Italy.[4]
<represent>

The half wits who try to write american magazine articles a la 1887 wont be of use. AND the question of RATES of pay arises in other cases. I believe Marinetti [5] gets 3000 lire
for a lecture.

You will see that I have moved onto Austria in the last note I sent you.[6]

Malta is out of the news/ Abyssinia is being colonized, roads built, blokes buying camions etc.[7]

will now switch to yr/ brother's letter.

Oh yes. P.S. Abyssinia is in the Italian Empire, but hasn't yet been moved into Europe.[8]

Even when I had the Dial's purese behind me[9], men like ~~HHHHH~~

Abel Hermant[10] didn't care a damn/ They are getting paid for their own kind of thing, why shift <and> stick it (from their point of view) out of sight, and try to accommodate themselves to some sort of standard they KNOW they don't know a damn thing about.

It is only people who are TOO intelligent for their circle who are interested in foreign contacts.

IN reason why European periodicals are often WEAK is the higher status of writers as such/ If a man of ANY standing is invited, he gets printed, whether the edtr/ likes the stuff or not. Hence danger of inviting/ etc. hence mass of unreadable papers. BUT greater amenity in the writer's life, and ultimately better literature/ I mean some stuff of durable interest, not simply the machine made swill that remaining in Harper's mortuary or the Shat Eve Pust of yester year.[11] It is a different life.

I will have a try at old VanDer PYL.[12] But he will prob. send you to hell and say Le Petit Parisien pays more ' (whether it does or not)

<yr E.>

[Handwritten in the lefthand margin] I will try Rampert: Zaffa[13] & a bloke whose name I forget but can find.

[1] For text and translation of Pound's cover letter sent to Mussolini along with the May 1937 issue of *Globe*, see Introduction, pp. 27–8.

[2] Mussolini's autobiography was serialized in 1928 in the pages of the *Saturday Evening Post*. The agreement between Mussolini and the *Post* for his autobiographical work was negotiated through Richard Washburn Child, a former ambassador to Italy. John P. Diggins wrote in his work, *Mussolini and Fascism: The View From America* (Princeton, 1972): "Under the direction of Cyrus Curtis, this vast weekly, with subscribers numbering almost three million in 1930, effectively created a respectable image of Mussolini." Among the *Post*'s writers was **Isaac F. Marcosson,** who described Mussolini as a political savior who had "turned red terror into white fear" and an economic genius who had engineered a "commercial revolution" (ibid., p. 27).

[3] Pound succeeded in placing his translation of **Odon Por**'s article entitled "Systems of Compensation" in the July–September issue of *The British Union Quarterly*. The eighteen-page article discussed proposals of French economist Edgard Milhaud. The Milhaud Plan called for a new form of payment for goods in international trade. Por wrote in this article: "This Plan, without modifying the energizing and monetary aims now functioning, proposes to guarantee the equilibrium of economic balances and the stability of monetary units with a systematic policy of reciprocity and compensation of exchanges by means of a new kind of currency (or bill), the 'compensatory bill'." Also see **EP14.**

[4] **Edmondo Rossoni**

[5] **Filippo Tommaso (christened Emilio Angelo Carlo) Marinetti**
[6] Pound's " Interview with Mrs. Unterguggenberger" appeared in the October 1937 issue of *Globe* (see Contribution #6). This piece dealt with the introduction of Gesellite stamp scrip in the Austrian town of Wörgl.
[7] Malta returned to full colonial rule by Britain in 1936. Malta had been under British rule since the Napoleonic Wars and had been granted limited self-rule in 1921. This was revoked in 1936. The British made this decision due to the threat of war during the Czechoslovakian crisis of 1936, the fact that Italy had laid claims to Malta, and the island's obvious strategic importance—especially for the defense of Egypt and the Suez Canal. See also "On Pleasing" (Contribution #11).
[8] In 1935, Italian troops invaded Ethiopia (Abyssinia), as a push to expand the Italian colonial empire. As Pound parrots in this letter, the Italian government made pretense to modernizing the "primitive" Ethiopian political, cultural, and social systems. In reality, to hold on to power in the region, it employed racial segregation and draconian measures to put down local revolts.
[9] In the 1920s, Pound worked as "foreign correspondent" for *The Dial.* The journal was backed by Schofield Thayer and James Sibley Watson. (For *The Dial*'s finances, see Rainey, "The Price of Modernism," pp. 77–106; especially pp. 92–100, in *Institutions of Modernism*).
[10] **Abel Hermant**
[11] *The Saturday Evening Post*
[12] **Fritz-René Vanderpyl**
[13] Probably **Marco Ramperti** and **Paolo Zappa**

EP33

TSL TAX (BL)

[stamped received] JUL 23.1937
12 July

Dear Dunn/s

July Globe a definite advance/< in the letters section> much more dynamism. Hollis and Roudybush good.[1] Huddy better, but hope for more, when my correspondence has got under his hide.[2]

I have writ to Antheil, to see what he can do on Hollywood.[3]

Talked with tourist guy/ who promised to speak S.I.R.T.[4] re/ news stands/ he says racket is to GIVE certain number of copies of first issue outright to stand people. We thought for here that if you had any back numbers you might use 'em in this way to get an opening. <dates don't so much matter this also for South America?>

Of course a promise to speak TO, by a bloke merely acting in friendship may take yheerz or may tayke for ever to function.

He meant it when he said it.

The younger Dunn, who wished to print Japs; might write to

Kitasono Katue ,

I649 Nishi 1 chome

magome machi

Omori, Tokio[5]

saying the HE wanted to print 'em, and as much interested but his big DAD brother thought they would better break in a licherary magerzeen/ <did Not belong in the globe>
whereto EZ haz now sent 'em. <send sample copy>

BUT THAT if any of their group wd/ care to send intimate letters, not special interest but of interest to plain simple americans, telling about what Japan is like you wd. be pleased to see 'em.

State rates of payment. Thee are a dozen of those chaps and a few of 'em ought to be able to contact.

Believe young Jarge, might do a sketch of Miriam Hopkins.[6] Is that GENERAL interest ? or Hollywood hunches.

What about actual congresman. Try young Voorhis on why Patman bill don't git on the CALENDER.[7]

<yr EP>

<over>[8]

[1] **Christopher Hollis** and **Franklin Roudybush**'s "Diplomacy the Greatest Game" appeared in the July 1937 issue of *Globe*.
[2] A carbon, which seems to date to May 1937, preserves a letter to **Sisley Huddleston**:

> My Dear Huddleston:
>
> Having a natural affection for you, I am definitely disappointed in the stuff you are sending GLOBE.
> I know you are an Englishman and that England is 94% pure shit, and that you once wrote for the Times which is the worlds great bleeding arse hole, with the Telegraph a protruding ulcer.

But you had the decency or luck to get out of that pissery/ and on the Monitor you had to be chaste and polite.
But the GLOBE dont ask for punk. If you know anything God knows the pimps and kike are good material.
Mabbe the terror is such that you dasn't portray 'em. But the SURFACE of Jouhaux and Blum and Hoch is perfect SURFACE for your journalism.
Either you have NO FRENCH news or what??
anyhow I was pleased to see yr/name on the original announcement of the Globe, and I wish to hell that you wd. send 'em something real
all too candidly yours.
Damn it, the GLOBE is an american paper; you arre NOT writing fr/suet faced compatriots who PREFER a smug lie to the real dope or SURFACE of the facts.
My Christ England and the English are a mess/

cordially yours,

EP

[3] **S.I.R.T.** Apparently this was a European publication distributor.
[4] **George Antheil**
[5] **Katue Kitasono**
[6] Pound was suggesting that *Globe* might be interested in running a piece by **George Antheil** on the Hollywood actress **Miriam Hopkins.**
[7] **Horace Jeremiah Voorhis.** In 1934, Representative **John William Wright Patman** and Senator Bronson Cutting introduced legislation that would have nationalized the Federal Reserve System. Antagonism between Franklin Roosevelt and Cutting made the bill even more difficult to consider than would have been normally the case. Bronson Cutting's death in an airplane crash soon after the bill was introduced in the Senate put an end to any possibility of it receiving the attention of Congress.
[8] On the back of this page Pound had the hand-written note: "Have you sent/ copies of globe to g. H. Tinkham?/ if not try[?] the/ whole/ set with my <u>compliments</u> [?]"

EP34

TSL TAX (BL)

13 July
[stamped received] JUL 26 1937

Dear Dunn

I cant splurge any more till I get a few CLEAR and definate answers/

I. no. of copies SOLD.
2. do you accept ads/ and if so at what rate ?
3. rates of payment.

Note. Not the faintest reason why M/ shd write "intimate letter" for you[1]. Nobody in Europe sees thru a fake quicker/ no use trying to invent a reason.
(will give you past history of WHY if you need it.)

4. Interviews ? Globe attitude toward same ? I can ASK interviews unless appearance absolutely guaranteed.

It might be possible to get brief letters or notes from Rossoni, or Bottai, or Delcroix or Farinacci[2] if one ran a series of brief summaries of day what these mean MEAN by the corporate state, or why they are in it. But two of 'em are cabinet ministers and all of 'em have means of putting in 24 hours a day. I don't see that one cd/ offer less than 500 lire per article/ but in any case let me know IF you want the notes/ whether you can pay or not.

Other men I suggest are Gen Fuller[3], Salazar of Portugal[4], who is GOOD. I don't KNOW that I can reach him.

HAVE you tried Pete Larranage. (P.J.M.)[5]
Kew Gardens Inn, Kew Gardens, Long Island.

ask him how it WORKS, and what it is LIKE economically to build roads over gorr knowz wot. (say I said so). I did pursuade him into N.E.Wkly/ but that was straight econ// [6]

5 (repeat) WOT about my photo collection ?[7]
wot about Hiler's ART ? sailors restaurants etc.[8]

Of course six copies IZ just NOTHING, if you expect me to shove the mag about.

In FORMING nucleus/ if immediate cash is difficult/ instead of raising pay rates, you might occ/ hand out shares in company. that wd/ stimulate push. Hollis/Couronos/Langston Hughes wd/[9] be my nominees for this statement. it would be just [typewritten in right margin:] I00/ dollar shares first coupons for

1938. BUT basic, not too many issued that they might conceivably bear 30% by 1941. <yr EP>

[typewritten in left margin:] really trying to help you build up something NOT shares at FIXED interest, but varying div. on profits

[1] Benito Mussolini, see **EP32.**

[2] **Edmondo Rossoni, Giuseppi Bottai, Carlo Delcroix,** and **Roberto Farinacci**

[3] **General John Frederick Charles Fuller**

[4] **Antonio de Oliveira Salazar**

[5] **P. J. M. Larrañaga**

[6] *The New English Weekly* see **EP16.**

[7] For Pound's photographs see **EP26** and **EP29.**

[8] **Hilaire Hiler**

[9] **Christopher Hollis, John Cournos, (James Mercer) Langston Hughes**

EP35

TSC (BL)

[stamped received] AUG 4 1937 <24 July>

Goin away from typewriter on Tuesday/ mebbe
look fer a bit of yokel colour/ therefor
sending letter "On Pleasing"[1] a bit before
necessary. Also letter from Swabey.[2] I have
INDIVIDUAL figures, when describing the local local
scene ; but his note is clear, and sound enough.
so you may as well keep it in case you
need it/ or have a hole. shdn't bother to
return it to him might be useful/ or
not. <sometime>
E.C. Lindeman <author of>(bk/ on Wealth and Culture)[3]
care Harcourt Brace/ might be useful to Globe.
And what about Louis Berman 993 Park An.[4]
N.York. you can use my name with Don Louis.

[typewritten in left margin:] I heard of Lindeman yesterday from Doc. Kast. [5] my name on good with Lin/

[typewritten on the left front of the card:] Wonder if J. Beach,[6] once of
Asolo, Veneto, Italy. cd. give
useful impressions, re music or wha[sic]
whatever.

? again/ Morley Callaghan,[7] once
35 Woolfrey Ave. Toronto.
did I suggest Sadakichi Hartman[8]
P.O.bx/ 372 Beaumont. Calif. ?
<E>

[1] See Contribution #11.
[2] **Reverend Henry S. Swabey**
[3] **Eduard Christian Lindeman**
[4] **Louis Berman**
[5] **Dr. Ludwig Kast**
[6] **J. Beach**: unknown
[7] **Morley Callaghan**
[8] **Sadakichi Hartmann**

JD17

TSL GS (YCAL)

July 28, 1937

Mr. Ezra Pound
Via Marsala 12/5
Rapallo, Italy

Dear Mr. Pound:

Have been waiting for the enclosed check to go through the mill and be signed before writing you. It pays for the August letter "Deflation Benefit."[1]

You, having seen all the GLOBES, have a good idea what we are seeking in our photo-reportage section. If you think Kirstein's and your photographs should fit in,[2] then send them on. And discussion will move much faster after we have studied them. Granted the church section was lousy, but the August is more our type—Mexican market. The Monte Carlo ballet, though the photos weren't too excellent, is also more our type.[3]

We miss Mangione[4] in GLOBE, too, but hope he will send on more material, at least for September. We're hounding him anyway.

Our letter to Halidé Edibe also returned. "Asia" publishers [sic] her,[5] but knows nothing of her whereabouts.

GLOBE'S first issue sold around 19,000—second issue very poor, only 13,000 (but May was a bad month for all magazines, even the steady ones).

June promises to be around 20,000 and July 25,000. We are seeking a steady 40,000 newsstand sale by the first of the year.

Antheil had a good article in that new super—"Cinema Arts."[6] We will follow up your letter immediately. We are exchanging with Katue[7] but as yet have lined up no Japanese translator in St. Paul. Will write again and ask that manuscripts be translated there, as was your poetry.

Mr. Ezra Pound -2- July 28, 1937

The magazines go off immediately to G. H. Tinkham,[8] in Washington.

The enclosed may interest you and your father.

How about Max Beerbohm.[9] Does he do anything these days?

Cordially,

GLOBE MAGAZINES, Inc.

[signed]
James Taylor Dunn
Assistant Editor

JDT/dl

encl: $20.00
Clipping

P.S. Suggestions were made at our last editorial conference that we would prefer more news, written in the spirit of "Abdication" or "Deflation Benefit" rather than monetary subjects and so forth. How about Mussolini's statement to the press that Russian Dictatorship was nearing an end?

[1] "Deflation Benefit" (Contribution #5) appeared in *Globe*, August 1937 issue, pp. 66–71.
[2] **Lincoln Kirstein**. For the photographs mentioned, see **EP26** note 4 and **EP29** note 8.
[3] See Pound's remarks in **EP29**. *Globe* ran a photo essay entitled "The Wedding Bells Ring" (June 1937, pp. 49–53). The July 1937 issue ran the photo essay "Ballets Russes of Monte Carlo" (pp. 49–55) and "Mexican Market" ran in the August 1938 issue (pp. 55–64).
[4] **Jerre Mangione**
[5] **Halide Edip Adivar**
[6] **George Antheil**
[7] **Katue Kitasono**
[8] **George Holden Tinkham**
[9] **Sir Maximilian Beerbohm**

JK1

TSL GS (YCAL)

Aug. 6, 1937

Mr. Ezra Pound
Via Marsala 12/5
Rapallo, Italy

Dear Mr. Pound:

This is a brief note from the business department of GLOBE Magazine. We are sending you herewith twenty copies of our advertising rate card showing the prices, mechanical requirements, etc., for advertising in GLOBE. These advertising rates are based on a guarantee of 20,000 circulation. We will show audited statements from the International Circulation Company as proof of our actual circulation on any given issue, and we will make proportional rebates to the advertiser for any number of copies under 20,000 sold. As a matter of fact, however, we expect to deliver "an extra bonus circulation" to our advertisers; that is, more than 20,000 copies.

The commission paid for advertising is 20% on the net amount collected by us — that is, after advertising agency discount and any other necessary discounts are taken.

If any European advertising is placed, the advertising copy and the illustrations must be in our hands on the 20th of the second month preceding date of issue; that is, advertising copy for the October issue of GLOBE must be in our hands August 20th at the very latest. We can not guarantee to show proof to European advertisers if copy is received as late as the 20th of the second month preceding the date of issue. If they desire to see proofs, we must have another month for carriage back and forth.

Incidentally it is not always possible to get certain European type faces here in America, so we will have to set the items as close to American typography as we can obtain. However, we can always be sure of a fairly good job of composition.

The matter for payment of the advertising must be worked out very clearly in advance with any European firms that care to advertise, since we have no machinery set up here for checking the credit of European advertisers. The way of receiving payment is obviously in advance, and in some accounts certain American publications require this type of payment. We are, of course, willing to give a 5% discount for cash in advance. Of course, we do not want to run the risk of insulting any creditable firms, by asking for cash in advance.

The only point is that this type of payment simplifies things a great deal, and perhaps the firms will see it our way. Of course, the firms will get within their rights in asking for "checking copies" of the magazine carrying their advertisement before making payment. If any advertising is sold in Europe, we hope that the credit risks can be carefully watched.

As you probably realize, GLOBE reaches and audience of people who travel and through whose interest of things foreign, it can be inferred that they are "prospects for luxury products abroad". In America today, the principal advertised luxury produce from a foreign country is liquor — wine, champagne, etc. These represent a good class of accounts for GLOBE. The transportation and steamship companies with headquarters in Europe are also good prospects.

This letter represents just a brief outline of the business details necessary to know in obtaining advertising for GLOBE.

We presume that you wish to pass the job of actually soliciting the advertising on to some person with whom you have business connections. We suggest that you offer them 15% commission and take a 5% override for yourself, but you can, of course, work out any arrangement with them that seems most feasible.

May I say in closing that I have thoroughly enjoyed the intimate letters (really informative articles) which have appeared in GLOBE, and I think that they have enjoyed the wide acceptance among our readers. Of course, the question about Italy which most Americans want answered is, "What's Mussolini going to do next, and how, if any way, is it going to affect us in the United States." You know, Mr. Pound, I'd like to hear your answer on that question myself.

Sincerely and respectfully yours,

GLOBE MAGAZINES, Inc.

[Signature]

Business Manager

James M. Keith/dt

encl.

EP36

HWL P (BL)

21 Aug.
SIENA .
postal address
Rapallo
as usual. [stamped received] SEP 1937

Dear J.T.D.

yrs. 28 July to hand. but no August globe yet recd. =

Trust typescript sent by this post. is gossipy enough.

Have added P.S. re Palermo speech in case dailies havent exhausted it. Often the sindicate news pic/as a detail. & OMITS the vital points.

re. Russia & Shanghai you ought to have direct stuff. not what I can get from papers. IF I get anything real I will send it.

Beerbohm[1] does nothing on & on rare occasions his PRICE.

but you needn't weep = plenty of RICH papers have offered PRICE, & nothing gets done.

Yes. 28. contained chg. whereof this may serve as receipt with thanks.

Handwritin' aint in the contrakk. =

The p.s. may be too simple. =
effort to get 'em to understand the simple.

yr E.P.

[1] **Sir Henry Maximilian Beerbohm**

EP37

HWL P (BL)

2 Sept as from Rapallo

[stamped received] SEP 13 1937

Dear Dunn

As it aint edt. job to belittle contributors..you might in Biog. Brev.[1] note that the publication ofmy article on Economic Orthology in current
RASSENA MONETARIA[2]
definately puts me on the map as an ECONOMIST = I don't mean I wasn't one before. but the opposition could until today have said it was a dilettantism or a poet's whim, or propaganda of a sect. =
The R.M. very old review

(2

editors a deputy. & the prof of Econ in Univ. of Rome (Fr. Spinedi.)[3] . – Yr readers may know me as poet +/or critic but these items might add.

———

Debut some years ago series of lectures at Universita Bocconi Milan[4]
might have been due to mere curiosity as to what a poet wd. say on the subject.
ABC of Econ., Impact, during Abyssinia war series of articles in British Italian Bulletin. = series of basic articles in British Union Quarterly of which the most important early this year "Intellectual Money"[5]

(3

The Volitionist questionnaire[6] four years ago appeared in various countries.//

The facts can be used. but not as a personal letter from me. you may as well have 'em. BIOG BREVS. seems right use & the continental recognition shd. in time correct parrochial

———

twaddle of the Keynes'[7] ~~& Cole's~~[8] Stamfs[9], etc. That shit Salter.[10] whom American Univs. still hire to bamboozel poor little stew/dents. god damn them and him.

Yr EZ

[1] Pound was referring to *Globe*'s "Biographical Brevities of Globe's Contributors" section, which usually appeared at the end of each issue. These were short sketches of the authors appearing in the current issue.
[2] Pound was referring to his three-part series, "Verso un'economia ortologica," "L'economia ortologica. Il problema centrale," and "Economica ortologica. Le basi etiche" which appeared in *Rassengna Monetaria*, XXXIV 5/6–9/10 (May/June, July/August, and September/October 1937). *Rassengna Monetaria* was established in 1904 and ceased publication in 1943.
[3] **Francesco Spinedi**
[4] At the invitation of the rector, Ulisse Gobbi, Pound gave a lecture series at the Bocconi University in Milan (March 21–31, 1933) entitled "An Historical Background for Economics."
[5] Pound was referring to several of his recent and not so recent publications that would support his claim to competence as an economist: *ABC of Economics* (1933), *Social Credit: An Impact* (1935), and "Intellectual Money" which appeared in the *British Union Quarterly* I:2 (April/June) pp. 24–34.
[6] In 1934, Pound printed a small broadside of eight dicta on economics under the heading "Volitionist Economics." He then sent it out as a questionnaire to most of his friends and acquaintances. It read as follows:

WHICH of the following statements do you agree with?

I. It is an outrage that they shd. run into debt to individuals by the act and in the act of creating real wealth.

2. Several nations recognize the necessity of distributing purchasing power. They do actually distribute it. The question is whether it shd. be distributed as favor to corporations; as a reward for not having a job; or impartiality and per capita.

3. A country CAN have one currency for internal use, and another, good both for home and foreign use.

4. If money is regarded as a certificate of work done, taxes are no longer necessary.

5. It is possible to concentrate all taxation into the actual paper money of a country (or on to one sort of its money).

6. You can issue valid paper money against any commodity UP TO the amount if that commodity that people WANT.

7. Some of the commonest failures of clarity among economists are due to using one word to signify two or more different concepts: Such as DEMAND, meaning sometimes WANT and sometimes power to buy; authoritative, meaning also responsible.

8. It is an outrage that the owner of one commodity cannot exchange it with someone possessing another, without being impeded or taxed by a third party holding a monopoly over some third substance or controlling some connection regardless of what it be called.

Answer to E. Pound
Via Marsala 12/5. Rapallo. Italy

[7] **John Maynard Keynes**

[8] **George D. H. Cole**

[9] **Stamfs**: unknown.

[10] **Baron James Arthur Salter**

EP38

HWL P (BL)

as from Rapallo [stamped received] SEP 15 1937
6 Sept.
Dear D. Here is an absoloot MUST. get in touch will F. Tweedell M.D. [1]
TWEDDEL

Plandone N.J. PLANDON
& get his report on his tuberculosis cure. SINCE his article in Medical World Jan 1931.
Calcium cure.

Yr EZ. P.

[1] **Dr. Francis Tweddell**

EP39

TSL P (BL)

Rapallo 25 Oct [1937] [stamped received] NOV 4 [1937]

GLB/

Oct/ a relief after sad falling leaves of Sept.

AGENDA.

I have belatedly read W. Lewis "Hitler"/ CONsider that it was pubd/ in I93I [1]
AND measure distance from W.L. to the Dottyt Thompson CRAP[2] handed out by whore journals in the U.S.
then send W.L> (as distinct from SINK L/[3]
a sample copy of GLOBE (Oct issue) and a polite invite; saying you know you cant pay his usual rates but you hope to CONtinue and persist into a time when GLOBE can
and that any rate you want him to know you want him.
GET the fact t<h>at in I93I he SAW Hitler coming//

That needed more foresight than my perception of Mussolini, even tho I did start saying M/ was RISING years before my Jeff/M was printed.[4]
address
Wyndham Lewis
I2I Gloucester Terrace
<L>ancaster Gate, London W.2

///
I have asked Butch[5] to get in touch with <u>Feia STARK.</u>[6]
you might also try.
///
Why not ask Irving Fisher[7] for something. he is a plausible writer. Good for 40 pages usually and then his books become mere lecturing, filing professorial time.

But good journalese style

///
~~HHHHHHHHHHHHHHHHHHHHHHHHHH~~
Duff an Dunc/ doing nicely.[8]
I think I Sept. was GLOBE's low (not merely because of my

<u>2</u>

illustrious abscence).
//
Waal naow EF you are doing AHT/ why the HELL not print some HILER [9]

<HILER> <.I mean pitchoor not cook bks.>

///
And another matter; why not try to gett HESS.[10] There is the most sympathetic figure in Germany/
I mean if you want to get WHY Germany is on the up/
apart from the Fuhrer .
Try an invitation to

edtr. Germany and You
Wikingverlag, Eichhornstrasse I0
Berlin W.9

say, if you like I suggested it.
(with his titles)
with HESS for you Ask IF they can get an interview
in a form you can print. That
we sympathize with Hess constructive effort, BUT that yr/ readers
etc/
that the interview shd/ be by someone who knows America
Am sending a light one that I wrote some weeks ago/
prepare fer a more seereeyus nex month.
also Browik .[11] O.K.
To Hell/ aint Horgan[12] ever heard of Sadakicki ??[13] chuck 'im out
Sadakicki is suitable TOPIC for Globe, even if you can't get anything from him.

<Yr EPound>

[1] Pound did not read **Wyndham Lewis**' book *Hitler* (1931) until the fall of 1937. Lewis would soon, in 1939, reverse his own evaluation of Hitler in his books *The Jews, are they Human?* and *The Hitler Cult* (both 1939). For a convenient summary of Lewis' and Pound's views of Hitler as they began to diverge in 1939, see Flory, *The American*, pp. 119–23.
[2] **Dorothy Thompson**
[3] **Sinclair Lewis**
[4] *Jefferson and/or Mussolini* (1934).
[5] **Montgomery Butchart**
[6] **Freyia Madeleine Stark**
[7] **Irving Fisher**
[8] **Charles Duff** and **Ronald Duncan**
[9] Pound mentions "cook books" because **Hilaire Hiler**'s contribution to the first and second issues of *Globe* was a two-part article on recipes entitled "Cuisine in Bohemia" (March 1937, pp. 74–6 and May 1937, pp. 88–91).
[10] **Rudolf Heß**
[11] **Jozef Borowik**
[12] **William Horgan**
[13] **Sadakichi Hartmann**

JWGD3

TSL GS (YCAL)

Jan. 26, 1938

Mr. Ezra Pound
Via Marsala 12/5
Rapallo, Italy

Dear Mr. Pound:

Here is your check for $20.00 to pay for your last letter, "Responsibility? Shucks!" which appears in the February-March issue of GLOBE.[1] GLOBE is now a bimonthly, instead of a monthly magazine. We are putting out 132 pages every month, giving a better quarter's worth and also a chance for the book to remain on sale longer and allow extra time for publicity and solicitation of advertising. As you may note, we have some advertising this month, and the Italians, bless their hearts, were the first people to advertise in GLOBE.[2]

We are starting an Italian Tour of the Month in this issue and you will note in it a casual mention of yourself, which we hope will not displease you.[3]

Instead of regular monthly letters now, perhaps you would like to write some general letters, showing the Italians as they really are now, and how the Italian mind really works. Perhaps you could do an article on the new Bohemia, or is there any Bohemia any more? In other words, what are the intellectuals doing these days?

How about Abyssinia?[4] The press has dropped it like a hot cake. The new empire in Tripolitania would be a good subject.[5]

An article on the lining up of world forces should also be very interesting; Communism versus Fascism versus Cooperating Nationalism versus spiteful doctrinism, etc. This should be as good as the Windsor-Simpson article. Explode some of the fatuous ideas that are flitting about. In spite of the New York city hissing of Mussolini in the movies, there are more Americans than ever visiting Italy this year.

Incidentally, what American magazines do you recommend as being the most worthwhile? There are so many American magazines it is hard to choose. If you care to receive some magazines we would be more than glad to place them on our exchange list and send to you for review purposes and help you to keep in contact with the American scene. Don't hesitate to ask for as many as you wish. This does not go for weekly publications. You probably got all the Italian magazines that you want, although if there are some Italian ones you would like to receive we can save you from buying them by placing them on our exchange list and having them sent directly to you.

Occasionally perhaps you would like to send in little fillers or jottings that you glean from the press and that we could publish with small stars between, along with your letters.

The next time you go to Genoa you might say something about it. I think it is one of the most interesting cities in the world, and one of the most maligned. Tourists seem to think Genoa is only the place where one waits for a train or boat, and gets away from it as quickly as possible.

Of all the suggestions that occur to us, the money question seems to be the farthest beyond the pale of general understanding or interest for the American public, and is, moreover, usually for a special magazine rather than for GLOBE.

When you write again, I hope that you will just look at the map of the Italian Tour, and if anything occurs to you that should not remain unmentioned along this itinerary, please jot it down. I wouldn't care to plagiarize your ideas in the tour but occasionally one thinks of something that should be broadcast. Anything along the line of general advice would be appreciated.

During the month of February I will be in New York city so if there is any hurry-up correspondence to communicate, I can be reached at our New York city office, 509 Fifth Avenue.

Again, dear Mr. Pound, we thank you for all the good work you have done for us and for your good will toward our international magazine.

Cordially yours,

GLOBE

MAGAZINES, Inc.

[Signature]
J. W. G. Dunn, Jr.,

Editor

JWGD/dl
encl: # 1659 $20

[1] See Contribution #7.
[2] The February/March 1938 issue of *Globe* carried nine pages of advertisements, including a full-page ad on page 3 for Italian Line ships and an ad on the back inside cover for the Italian Tourist Information Bureau.
[3] The February/March 1938 issue of *Globe* ran "Tour of the Month: Genova–Napoli (Part I)," pp. 86–91. Page 89 carried cartoon sketches of the various cities by an unknown artist. The Rapallo sketch showed two monocled, beret-wearing men with Vandyke beards talking over wine in a café. The description of Rapallo, which ran on page 90, read in part:

> RAPALLO: a larger edition of Santa Margherita. Here, on the café terrace, sits GLOBE's correspondent Ezra Pound, thinking of mean things to say about the money moguls. The large beret and discreet Vandyke of this keen-minded bohemian point him out as a familiar water front character. Here also is **Max Beerbohm**, resting on laurels received twenty to thirty years ago. In all, Rapallo has more than its quota of interesting people we all would like to know but never do....

[4] See **EP32** note 7 and **EP44** note 9.
[5] From Roman times the region now known as Libya was called Tripolitania because of the three important cities, Sabratha, Oea, and Lepcis Magna, located on this stretch of North African coast. Italy seized Libya from Turkey in 1911 and, in 1937–8, against several international agreements, Italy began to incorporate the Libyan region into the Italian Empire. The area was formerly declared part of the empire in 1939.

EP40

TSL GBS (BL)

I3 Feb
or St. Valentine's Day
tomorrow mornink.

Dear Dunn

Dogged as does it. Glad you haven't passed out. Gingrich offering I000 dollars class A. 500 bucks class b; down to I50 ultimate for the DOPE.
Have you seen his KEN letters ? How many <other> authors is he HHHH asking at those rates?
Hemingway and DeKruif on his board.[1] I have sent 'em three lines on a post card. but doubt if they touch.
waaal itza gt/life if you don't weaken. Funny I was about to write you re/ Corny Vanderbilt//[2] them you get him (and a dam poor bit of copy at that)
the it looks like as if Corny didn't like EZ or the rest is silence.
Jan/Feb not here yet/ but I am lining up the ~~HHHHH~~ forces. everything pointing to what I SAID months ago, only more so.
what about Cournos?[3] I have been rather general ; because IF I go into particulars it has got to be MONEY MONEY MONEY ALL THE WAY.
There is NO inside story until you get to WHO profits by it ?
Look at the peaceways stuff.[4]
did you get my puff of GLOBE in New English Weakly ?[5]
Wonder if Peaceway<s> or Pissways wd/ run an ad/
not saving War COST 25 grand per cadaver but WHO GETS the 25 grand ?
IF you are still in N.Y. why don't you ask 'em. ??
Have just corrected proofs of KULCH, but afraid Faber will spoil the title and soften it to the shorn british sheep.[6]
AND therby ruin my chances of getting the book printed in Amurikuh.
We have just had one GRAND music week in RAPallo/[7] give us time we will take the Applesass out of Salzbug.[8] A little good better than a whole lot of Bruno.[9]

Re/ Italian mind how it works. This is TOO DAMN SERIOUS for Globe. the mind is working on technical stuff, like the grain centers. Hell, any ape can make a KEN story out of some bloke like Kreuger forging a few bonds for a million[10]
but how the HELL are you going to write up some bit of dull honesty, like seeing that a peasant gets paid for his crop ?
I got about a dozen SEEREEYUS mags a month.
Rassegna Monetraia for example.[11] Globe can't carry that. And the questions

of statal organization are FAR further removed from anything any american has yet heard of.
Decrees on rate of "family cheque" allowance in different trades extension of this social dividend ; etc. ALL technical.
Re/ American Magazines. Can you send me KEN, Esquire, Coronet ; any magazines the SIZE of Globe, there are variuos digests.
In fact let me see your COMPETITORS

<ad

interim

EP>

Let me see what is getting GLOBE'S petential market or being bought where Globe isn't.
I know what the OLD line crap is. Takes year and a half to get a quotation of Jefferson into Nart Amurkin Recview.[12]
What I MIGHT do after the LINE UP/ has been printed is a set of Vignettes/ dsay half dozen Italians/ as individuals showing what Italians are like. Beginning with Rossoni[13] and trying a few letters of an old naval captain etc.

<EP>

<Halide Edib
has got a book
out on
India>[14]

[1] Pound seems to have been referring to either announcements of the first issue of **Arnold Gingrich**'s new magazine *Ken*, or a letter soliciting contributions to the magazine. *Ken, The Insider's World* was a magazine to be published by David Smart, the owner of *Esquire* and under the editorial direction of Arnold Gingrich from Chicago. George Seldes was solicited to act as editor in New York. Seldes was led to believe that **Ernest Hemingway** and **Paul de Kruif** were also to be on the editorial board—and the publicity that Gingrich put out on the magazine seems to have led Pound to believe the same. However, they were in reality only contributors to *Ken*. The magazine was to be a hard-hitting, left-leaning publication with stories about current events, politics, and investigative reporting. The first issue appeared on April 7, 1938 and ran an essay by Hemingway entitled "The Time Now, The Place Spain." However, as Seldes relates in his *Never Tire of Protesting*, *Ken*'s leftist orientation, reflected in his own articles for the magazine about the American Legion and its leadership, helped to make it an advertising pariah. Even with the financial backing of the successful *Esquire*, the advertiser-less *Ken* became a financial failure and folded soon after its launching.
[2] **Cornelius Vanderbilt**

[3] **John Cournos**

[4] World Peaceways was a non-profit pacifist group founded in 1931. Many mainstream American magazines ran its anti-war ads free of charge. *Globe* ran a full-page Peaceways advertisement on the reverse of the cover of its June 1937 issue.

[5] *The New English Weekly*.

[6] According to Donald Gallup, the original title for *Guide to Kulchur* (1938), specified in Pound's contract with Faber, was *"Kulch," or Ez' Guide to Kulchur* [sic]. Apparently, Faber suggested the change to simply *Guide to Kulchur.* There were also many changes in the text due to what the publisher considered potentially libelous material. In fact, the book was already printed and bound when it was decided to reprint, razor out and replace the offending material. This held up publication for about a month. For this and other details, see Gallup, A45, pp. 61–2.

[7] Pound sent Dunn a copy of the *Il Mare* announcement and program for a week of concerts (February 1–5, 1938) sponsored by the Stagione Musicale del Tiguilio to be held in Rapallo. The program included works of Vivaldi, C. P. E. Bach, J. S. Bach, Debussy, Purcell, Hindemith, Galuppi, Wilhelm Rust, and Mozart. **Olga Rudge**, Luigi Sansoni, Marco Ottone, and Renata Borgatti were the performers.

[8] The Salzburg festivals developed out of the Mozart-Stiftung concerts held in the city beginning in 1877. In the 1930s the festival's musical range broadened and it entered its "golden age." At this time its leading conductors included Bruno Walter, Krause, Fürtwangler, and Toscanini. During this decade Pound attended several of the Salzburg festivals. His reaction to them was decidedly cool. He was especially piqued by the 1936 festival and wrote critically of it in several venues.

[9] **Bruno Walter**

[10] As part of a scam to cover his financial empire's disastrous loss of cash, **Ivar Kreuger** forged Italian Treasury bills using Mussolini's letterhead as a template. This might be what Pound is referring to in this letter when he mentioned "... Kreuger forging a few bonds for a million."

[11] See **EP37** note 2.

[12] Pound's "The Jefferson-Adams Correspondence" appeared in the *North American Review* (Winter 1937/38), pp. 314–24.

[13] **Edmondo Rossoni**

[14] This book was *Inside India* (1937).

JD18

TSL GS (YCAL)

March 10, 1938

Dear Mr. Pound:

This note is definitely extra-curricular. I am enclosing two pamphlets from my growing collection of your books, plus your Abdication and Eliot's book.[1] With these is an envelope with sufficient return postage. Would you do me the great honor of personally signing these? Did you receive the February-March issue? Your most recent letter has been received. Whether or not there is time to get it into our next issue I can't at the moment say.

But more at a later date. George Antheil has sent in a manuscript by his wife[2] —it seems pretty good. I've only had a hasty glance at it, for it only arrived yesterday.

Thank you for anything you may write in the enclosed booklets.

Sincerely yours,

[Signature]

James Taylor Dunn

[1] It is not clear which pamphlets Dunn sent to Pound to sign. "Abdication" was Pound's first article to run in *Globe* (see Contribution #1). The "Eliot's book" is probably a copy of *Ezra Pound: His Poetry and Metric* (1917).

[2] **George Antheil**'s wife, Böske, wrote "Arabs: Noisy, Nosey, and Nice" for the July 1938 issue of *Globe*.

JD19

TSL GS (YCAL)

March 12, 1938

Mr. Ezra Pound
Via Marsala 12/5
Rapallo, Italy

Dear Mr. Pound:

Have as yet heard nothing about Gingrich and his offers. Ken is not on the stands; but it's appearance is scheduled for the 31st of March; though that's not saying it will appear on that date.[1]

I am sending you under separate cover past copies of the main digest-size magazines. Notice the tone of all these; what an important part sex and the sensational play – also the purely factual and informative. Mr. isn't, of course a competitor, but just a sample of what Americans will read. Digest and Review and World Digest are the best of their kind, after the first to be published and the first in the public's eye, The Reader's Digest. For Men Only (that's the title now) is partially invading our field, though only partially. Coronet and Photo Facts are more like GLOBE; and they are both pretty good mags, in their way. Esquire is so bulky, I couldn't send a copy this time. Scribners and Story, plus The Atlantic and Harpers are definite competitors. And then in some ways so are Life, Pic, Focus, Click, Look, etc. Do you want me to send you examples of some of these? Scribner's is running an article on "Magazines That Sell" (the first called "Sex, Esq." – about Esquire, of course), written more from the history angle than anything else.

No clipping from England has as yet been received here.[2] Many thanks, however, for the puff. Do you happen to have an extra copy? If not, I can write to the weekly that published it, requesting a tear sheet.

Much luck on the success of your new book.[3] We will await its publication with interest. Did you receive my other package?[4]

I wish now I could have squeezed more into that one envelope.

Read with interest the ads for your festival. Purcell, Vivaldi, etc. are at last coming into their own.[5] Excellent record releases here (Victor, Gamut, Timely, Columbia, Musicraft) show decided trends in that direction.

The article on micro-photograph in Broletto; Periodico della Citta di Como was received. Also noticed that Katue Kitasono[6] had an article in the same issue. We have recently heard from him. Several months ago he translated "The Sun Helmet" by Harold Armitage (from our July, 1937, issue) and published it in Vou.[7] I only by chance ran across it.

A new manuscript by Christopher Hollis is on hand.[8] After reading it one is inclined to say, "So what," but the whole thing is so amusing and very well written that we can't help wanting to publish it. We've recently been able to use John Groth[9] as an illustrator; he used to be Art Editor of Esquire – also several other capable and well known men.

A letter came in from Henry Miller a few days ago.[10] In part he says, "So much emphasis is placed on the sensational aspect of 'place' that writing is almost ignored." This concerning GLOBE, of course. But he does have the following to say; "Everybody here admires the efficiency with which you master technical difficulties."

Others, besides Hollis, in the next issue? (It's on the press now). There's a Louis Adamic sketch about America;[11] and Stephen Leacock has written a very good article on French Canada.[12] Jerre Mangione (author of "Sicilian Policeman") is with us again;[13] and there are others, of course – lesser known, but none the less, on the average, pretty good.

Sincerely yours,
GLOBE MAGAZINES, Inc.

[Signature]

James Taylor Dunn

Assistant Editor

P.S. Thought it would help you if I were to write, for The Colophon – a book collector's quarterly, an article on the events leading up to and concerning the publication of your first book. Aren't there some facts about it not generally known? Some points in the book itself, perhaps?[14] And such an article would prove of great interest to many bookmen, and furthermore be of great value. This is especially timely, I believe, because of the publication of your recent books. There's the anniversary angle, too.

JTD

[1] For *Ken* see **EP40**.
[2] In **EP40**, Pound asked the question: "did you get my puff of Globe in New English Weakly?" No copy of the article could be found in *Globe* files.
[3] Pound's *Guide to Kulchur* was published in July 1938 by Faber & Faber. See also **EP40**.
[4] These are the books that Dunn sent to Pound for his signature. See **JD18** note1 and **EP41**.
[5] See **EP40** note 8.
[6] Pound forwarded a copy of the Italian journal *Broletto; Periodico della Citta di Como* which reproduced a Vivaldi manuscript score. The article was apparently by **Olga Rudge** and based upon her work on Vivaldi manuscripts at Dresden (see Conover, *Olga/Ezra,* p. 131). Pound's description of the article is found in his *Globe* essay "Milestones" (Contribution #14). **Katue Kitasono**'s article, which was placed in *Broletto* by Pound, was a version of Kitasono's introductory essay to the VOU Club poetry which appeared in the first issue of **Ronald Duncan**'s *Townsman.* Pound wrote to Kitasono on January 18, 1938: "Yesterday I saw proofs of *Broletto* with 'The Hand of Summer Writes' printed large and in the original four ideograms, with the Italian version of your manifesto from *Townsman...*"
[7] This was not the first time **Kitasono** simply translated and printed a piece that he fancied without asking for permission from or informing the copyright owner. He apparently did this with Pound's material also (see **EP10**).

[8] This manuscript was "Cannibals for Art's Sake." It was published in *Globe* (April–May 1938, pp. 48–51) and concerned **Christopher Hollis**' trip to Fiji.
[9] **John August Groth**
[10] **Henry Miller**
[11] **Louis Adamic**
[12] **Stephen Leacock**'s "French Canada: Revenge of the Cradle" appeared in the April/May 1938 issue of *Globe* (pp. 22–9).
[13] **Jerre Mangione**'s "A Man's Best Audience Is His Horse" appeared in the May 1938 issue of *Globe* (pp. 30–3).
[14] *The Colophon: A Book Collectors' Quarterly* was established in 1930 and ran through 1940. Dunn never wrote this article. For Pound's comments on his first book, *A Lume Spento*, see the response to this letter **(EP41)**.

EP41

TSL GBS (BL)

30 March

Dear JTD

Thanks for yours ofI2 th inst. / will await the packets of muggyzeens/[1]
How MUCH sex crap do you need or want to keep the flag or prong UP ??
I hadn't started on THAT line/ I had been lookin for milk bars/ and rude health/
I might stir up Ludovici/[2] Rodker/ etc:etc/ plenty of'em[3]
can't write on anything else.
After all I don't have READ all the Globe/
Sorry have no copy of N.E.Weekly[4] with the note on Globe/ the blighters OUGHT to exchange it with you BUT it has <(N.E.W.)>
"action" much more alive.[5]
I wonder WHAT packet you referred to/ last Globe came single copy/ and then a pack/ of 6 two weeks later. <vide infra>

about my FIRST book/ A Lume Spento, printed in Venice I908.[6]

I landed in Gibraltar with 80 bucks/ the Yusuf, &
and two suit cases/ one full of mss//
Mohameed Ben Abt el Hjameed, etc/ Liceo Calpe, in Canto XXII[7]
<in fact a Globe Canto>
refer to that period.

No poems accepted perviously in America/ save about 6 lines in Munsey's.[8]
Introductions to a missionary named Elson/ damn good guy in Tangier/[9]
And to the
REVEREND Cavaliere Dottore AleXXXandeRRR RRRRRobertson[10] of the Scotch KiRRRk in Venice/ author of a worrrrk in Paolo Sarpi/[11] and really convince<d> that the chuRRRRch ov RRRRome was the ScarrrrleTT Wummun ov the Apocalypse.
everything in the bbook written before leaving the U.S. earliest about 1906 I think/ and the best and body of the book/ done in Crawfordsville mud flats/, <Indiana> [12]
Most of what has been kept in later edtns/ from that time 1907/ or about that.
I think 1906 about the earliest.

<Haaavud Treasure Room>

Believe last known copy sold for 75 dollars/ naturally I didn't get it. I did however sell my last duplicate for I think 150% of printing bill.
orig/ price One dollar/
This what you a want?
I think "E.P. his Metric and Poetry" notes gathered by Eliot and printed buy Quinn[13] / has something about FIRST London real publication/ the better parts of A Lume Spento and what had been done during interval .

<"Personae"
1909">[14]

Oh yes/ you MEAN packet of Your books/ yes, I signed 'em and sent them along.[15] or were they your bro's ??
Attempt to stir American Insteroot of Aht and Letters[16]
into doing something USEFUL, already leads to private suggestion from fellow member that) shd/ resign.

mebbe the Colophon[17] cd/ use THAT.

Colophon MIGHT be sufficiently solemn to take up the PROBLEM of the Institute and its functions, actual, imaginary and possible. Telling its readers a little of what, say, the French Institut DOES.[18]

and what the American Instertoot hasn't tried.

<& lemme know about
the ST. Crap

Yr

EZ P>

[1] See Pound's request in **EP40**.

[2] **Anthony M. Ludovici**

[3] **John Rodker**

[4] For *The New English Weekly* see **EP16** note 29.
[5] For *Action* see **EP16** note 28.
[6] *A Lume Spento* was published in Venice in 1908 by A. Antonini in an edition of 150 copies. Pound arrived at Gibraltar on March 23, 1908. He proceeded to Spain and, after returning to Gibraltar for a short time, sailed to Genoa and made his way to Venice. There he settled in at 861 Ponte San Vio. At the suggestion of the Reverend Alexander Robertson (see note 10 to this letter) Pound went to Antonini to have his manuscript printed at his own expense. Pound had questions as to the book's worth. Much later in Pisa, Pound remembers in Canto 76:

> ...by the soap smooth stone posts where San Vio
> meets with il Canal Grande
> between Salviati and the house that was of Don Carlos
> shd/I chuck the lot into the tide water?
> le bozze [the proof sheets] "A Lume Spento"/..."

However, doubts were put aside and the book was printed. At the end of the summer of 1908, Pound set out from Venice for London and took the books with him—*A Lume Spento* came only to about 72 printed pages. There Pound put them to good use as a kind of calling card, giving copies to literary figures and reviewers he met in London, as well as sending copies back to American to friends like W. C. Williams and to his family for them to place for review in the United States.

[7] Canto XXII first appeared in *The Dial* (84.2 [February 1928]). In part it narrated events from Pound's trip to Gibraltar in 1908. The opening lines of this section of the Canto has Pound being recognized as "Meestair Freer" by an unnamed native of Gibraltar (probably Yusuf Benemore) who had become acquainted with Pound when he visited Gibraltar with his Aunt Frank in 1902. Aunt Frank's name was Francis Amelia Weston, but she apparently traveled under her maiden name Freer—hence, Pound was remembered as "Mr. Freer." It was through this old acquaintance that he met,

> ...Mohamand Ben Abt el Hameed,
> And I that evening he spent his whole time
> Queering the shirt seller's business
> And taking hot whiskey. The sailors
> Come in there for two nights and fill up the café
> And the rock scorpions cling to the edge
> Until they jes' nacherly can't stand it
> And then they go to the Calpe (Lyceo)

The scene was that of a "social club" named the Lyceo Calpe—Lyceo Calpe being equivalent to "Café Gibraltar" (Mt. Calpe is the Spanish name for Mt. Gibraltar). Gibraltar, in turn, is derived from the Arabic *Jebel Taraq*, a designation Pound also used in the following lines of the Canto in the form of the slightly inaccurate "Gibel Tara." As the action unfolded, tension developed due to Mohamad's accusation that a certain merchant's goods were shoddy. The merchant's business dried up and a few days later the merchant came back to the club and a fight took place, as a result of which Mohamad took the merchant to court. Later in the Canto, Yusuf Benemore, now mentioned by name, took Pound to one of Gibraltar's synagogues. Pound's experience of the service made a positive impression on him. This was reflected in the enthusiasm with which Pound rendered the scene in this passage of the Canto. In Canto 76, Pound remembered the synagogue while being held at Pisa thirty-seven years later:

> So that in the synagogue in Gibraltar
>   the sense of humor seemed to prevail
>   during the preliminary parts of the whatever
> but they respected at least the scrolls of the law...

Concerning Benemore, Noel Stock wrote of him: "When he [Pound] landed in Gibraltar he was lucky to fall into the hands of a Jewish guide, of whom he later wrote, 'Life saved by Yusuf Benemore.' It is not clear how Yusuf saved him, whether figuratively or actually" (Stock, *Life*, p. 74). For this and other details, see Carpenter, *Serious Character*, pp. 88–9.

[8] Pound was referring here to the somewhat longer "A Dawn Song," *Munsey's Magazine*, New York 36.3 (December 1906), p. 380 :

> God hath put me here
> In earth's goodly sphere
>   To sing the joy of the day,
> A strong glad song,
> If the road be long,
>   To my fellows in the way.
>
> So I make my song of the good glad light
>   That falls from the gate of the sun,
> And the clear cool wind that bloweth good
>   To my brother Everyone.

See Michael John King (ed.), *Collected Early Poems of Ezra Pound* (New Directions) 1976, p. 204.

[9] It is not clear to whom Pound was referring here. Accounts of Pound's 1908 trip to Gibraltar do not mention a trip to Tangier. However, the context of Pound's comments to Dunn, that he mentioned an introduction to Alexander Robertson in Venice, would seem to imply that he at least intended and possibly did go to Tangier on the 1908 trip. Pound did go to Tangier in 1902 with his Aunt Frank and on his 1908 trip he did retrace some of his steps from that previous journey.

[10] The Reverend Dr. Alexander Robertson (1846–1933), pastor for the Church of Scotland in Venice, was another of Pound's contacts from his trip to Venice in 1908. Pound was fascinated by this eccentric clergyman's burr and theology. Robertson was very anti-Roman Catholic and wrote pamphlets such as *The Harlot of the Seven Hills* warning of the evils of the Roman Church. Pound portrays him in Canto 76. He is overheard admonishing the young Pound:

> "Dawnt let them git you" burred the bearded Dottore
> when was the Scottch Kirrk in Venice
> to warn one against the Babylonian intrigue
>   and there have been since then
> very high episcopal vagaries...

Pound also mentioned Robertson in his *Guide to Kulchur* (p. 259).

[11] **Paolo Sarpi**

[12] Pound was referring to the time he spent teaching at Wabash College, located in Crawfordsville, Indiana. Pound left Philadelphia in the fall of 1907 and began to teach his classes in Romance languages and literatures. The appointment was not a good fit. A scandal arose around Pound over having an "actress" allegedly spend the evening in his lodgings. However, there were probably more reasons than simply this that led the trustees of the college to terminate Pound's employment in the spring of 1908. Pound responded to his dismissal by setting out for Gibraltar in March 1908.

[13] T. S. Eliot's *Ezra Pound His Poetry and Metric* (1917), published as a separate volume by Pound's publisher A. Knopf, was originally intended as an introduction to the American edition of Pound's *Lustra* (1916). **John Quinn** paid for the publication of the essay (for details, see Carpenter, *Serious Character*, pp. 302–6).

[14] The *Personae of Ezra Pound* was published by Elkin Matthews in London in April 1909. This book is not to be confused with the *Personae* of 1926 issued by Boni and Liveright which was to become the standard collected "shorter" poetry.

[15] For Dunn's request for Pound's signature on his first editions, see **JD18**.

[16] In 1938, Pound was elected to the National Institute of Arts and Letters. The National Institute was formed in New York City in 1898. In 1904, the

American Academy of Arts and Letters was founded as its subsidiary. In 1976, the two bodies were consolidated as the Academy of Arts and Letters. The membership of the Academy-Institute is limited to 250 American citizens (native born or naturalized) and honorary membership to 75 foreign artists and writers.

[17]For *The Colophon* see **JD19** note 12.

[18] Pound is referring to the Académie française founded in 1635 by Cardinal Richelieu during the reign of Louis XIII. It is restricted to 40 members. The American National Institute of Arts and Letters was founded in 1898 to provide the United States with an analogous learned body.

JD20

TSL GS (YCAL)

March 31, 1938

Mr. Ezra Pound
Via Marsala 12/5
Rapallo, Italy

Dear Mr. Pound:

As I said to you in my letter of March 12, I did not think we would be able to get your complete letter into the current issue because of the very short time left. This turned out to be quite correct. The whole magazine was defiantly set and unfortunately there was room left over for only a half page short.

Accordingly, we are enclosing our check for $5.00 and hope that our putting the Notes on Micro-Photography[1] into that half page was not too presumptuous of us.

Many months ago you made a very cryptic statement about business managers, which we have found out is all too true.[2] Our business manager has read over the rest of your manuscript, as he does everything that goes into the magazine, and does not believe we should publish it.[3] Our financial condition is such that we find it impossible to publish invective material concerning a country that is advertising in GLOBE. It is a definite case of money speaking louder than words.

Sincerely yours,
GLOBE MAGAZINES, Inc.
[Signed]
James Taylor Dunn
Assistant Editor

[1] Dunn was referring to the unpublished manuscript "Milestones" (see Contribution #14) and "Notes on Micro-Photography" (see Contribution #9).
[2] See Pound's comments in **EP2**.
[3] Dunn apparently was referring to a manuscript contribution that was subsequently marked indicating obscure and offensive passages and sent to Pound for review (see **JD22**). This manuscript seems to have been lost. The business manager was James Keith (**JK1**). By the spring of 1938, *Globe*'s financial situation had become dire, and J. W. G. Dunn Jr. was facing increasing pressure from his father, the principal backer of the magazine. Circulation had never reached the initial goal of at least 20,000 per issue. Advertising, never consistent or plentiful in the magazine, began to dry up. To save money, the magazine went to bi-monthly. Pound's response to this letter was explosive and reverberated through several letters sent to Dunn (see **EP42**, **EP43**, and **EP44**).

JD21

TSL GS (YCAL)

April 7, 1938

Mr. Ezra Pound
Via Marsala 12/5
Rapallo, Italy

Dear Mr. Pound:

Many thanks for the pamphlets. I really appreciate the trouble you took on my behalf.[1]

Well, GLOBE keeps on; how I don't exactly know, but it struggles along. Advertising is slowly coming in, and every little bit helps. But it takes a long time to build up a magazine, far longer than we at first anticipated. And with advertisers using GLOBE, you are more or less in their hands. For fear of losing even one, we have to watch closely everything we publish. Take our last issue as an example. The dude ranch article was put in there to get the Northern Pacific to advertise.[2] We had a devil of a time finding even a mediocre story on Mexico ("Prayer in Earnest") to go with the Mexican Railway ad, etc.[3]

In spite of all this, though, we feel that the April-May issue is our best one to date. Our two lows have been the September '37 and the December-January issues, with the latter on top. And Hipple definitely was a mistake – the sort of thing we will try to avoid in the future![4]

After twenty years with the "Christian Science Monitor," Sisley Huddleston[5] has resigned ("because it hampered me in the expressions of my views"). He is now finishing a book IN OUR TIME, O LORD, to be published by Dutton, and plans to send us something very soon. He goes on to say, "Anyone who can't see that the world is going headlong to war and that the chief war mongers are not Hitler and Mussolini (though they will furnish plenty of opportunities) but the agitators in the so-called "Democratic" countries, passes my comprehension." He is sending us another article, after quite a long silence.

Montgomery Butchart[6] has sent in a number of manuscripts by himself and others. They're out being read now. We have also received from him a copy of "The Townsman" containing the Japanese poems.[7] I'm glad he published them, but as interesting as we found the two introductions and a few of the poems, we still feel that they were definitely not for GLOBE.

Charles Duff is silent.[8]

And you have most likely already noticed that Mangione[9] is back with us again, in our latest issue.

Alfred Perlès [10] has written a light and amusing bit of ephemera which should help balance our next issue. And George Antheil has sent us a manuscript by his wife entitled (by her) "A Summer in North Africa."[11] It's definitely not as deadly as the title. At present we plan on using it, too, in our coming number.

Vardis Fisher's reportage on Boise[12] raised quite a stink in his part of the country. A follow-up article says "What the world needs is bigger and lustier scandals....I wrote the GLOBE a little essay on the lovely and charming city where I now live; and when the magazine hit the newsstands the roof was blown off the town. Boise hasn't had so much to talk about since the treasurer embezzled a hundred thousand to give to her worthless son who did a high society fling in distant places and came down on his face and landed in an asylum."

Charlie Flandrau,[13] Saint Paul's most famous literary figure, died on the 28th of March. He was planning a return to writing with a series of travel articles for which he was so famous. These were to be for us – a great loss!

Harriet Munroe's A POET'S LIFE is a masterpiece.[14]

We all hope you understand the reasons for out last letter. It's just another case of being "shit on by business managers."[15]

Sincerely yours,

GLOBE MAGAZINES, Inc.

[Signature]

James Taylor Dunn, Assistant Editor

JTD/dl

[1] Dunn was referring to pamphlets and books he sent to Pound for his signature (see **JD18** and **EP41**).

[2] The April/May 1938 issue of *Globe* ran the article "Whoopee I'm a Dude" by Dorothy Laidlaw (pp. 116–27). Northern Pacific ran a full-page color ad on page three of the issue. The CM Ranch in Dubois, Wyoming, did take out a full-page ad on page 129.
[3] "Prayer in Earnest" by Thayer Waldo appeared in *Globe* (May 1938, pp. 99–103). The National Railways of Mexico took out a half-page advertisement on page 127.
[4] William H. Hipple, Jr., a Minnesota-born reporter, wrote one article for *Globe*, "The Empty-handed Emperor" in the March/February 1938 issue. The article was about the Ethiopian emperor **Haile Selassie**, then exiled in London.
[5] **Sisley Huddleston**'s book actually was entitled *In My Time: An Observer's Record of War and Peace* (1938), his views of European politics and political leaders during the interwar period.
[6] **Montgomery Butchart**
[7] Poems by **Katue Kitasono** and the members of the Japanese VOU Club. The *Townsman* was a journal edited by **Ronald Duncan.**
[8] **Charles Duff**
[9] **Jerre Mangione**'s "A Man's Best Audience is His Horse (A Story)," *Globe* (May 1938, pp. 30–3).
[10] **Alfred Perlès**' "The Necktie Strikes Back" in *Globe* (April/May 1938, pp. 38–43). The novelist Henry Miller had recommended Perlès to *Globe*. Miller himself published a photo essay "Eye On Paris" in *Globe* (November, 1937). The photographs included in this essay were taken by Brassaï, who was a friend of both Perlès and Miller. Brassaï contributed photographs to an earlier feature entitled "Paris not in the Guidebooks" which appeared in the September 1937 issue of *Globe* (pp. 45–53).
[11] **George and Böske Antheil**
[12] **Vardis Fisher**'s article "Overalls or Tails?" which poked fun at Boise, Idaho, appeared in *Globe* (February/March 1938, pp. 82–5).
[13] **Charles M. Flandrau**
[14] **Harriet Monroe**'s memoir, apparently published posthumously, appeared in 1938. It was entitled *A Poet's Life: Seventy Years in a Changing World.* In it Monroe wrote:

> It is not entirely his fault [Pound's] if he has become somewhat embittered and has spent upon trivial quarrels and temperamental exaggerations the energy which should have gone into important progressive work. The power which would have been stimulating has become explosive, and like many another man of genius, Pound has been thwarted and diverted into passionate reactions against human dullness. *Poetry's* first few years came in the period of his greatest power—a controversial statement, perhaps, for those who prefer the *Cantos* to the poems in *Lustra* and earlier volumes. At

> any rate, *Poetry* was the first of the numerous "little magazines" which he has fostered or founded and then tired of. Its editor has always acknowledged gratefully what she owed to his help during those first diverting and experimental years. (p. 268)

[15] Dunn was referring to **JD20** and to Pound's use of the scatogicial phrase in **EP2**.

EP42

TSL GBS (BL)
<12 April>

[Stamped] April 23 1938

Dear J.T.D

What you and ALL other ever heard of Americans DON'T GET is that it is utterly impossible FROM HERE to know what is considered detremntal by bizniz managers .
Fer garzake send me a BACK a few ms/ WITH the passages MARKED.
INVECTIVE. You can't send a straight BOOST of Daladier[1] for his honest intentions and occasional ACTS without pointing out that he is surrounded by SHIT (or the polite verbal terms conveying the same idea.)
What bloody countries except Italy and the U.S. Advertise. <?>
Esquire putt me out for saying three years ago what Chamberlain NOW says.[2]
The great wild of kike choinulism thinks D<ot>/Thom<p>son a choinulist fer saying Hitler wd/ never make a career in Germany.[3]
WHICH is invective against WHAT?
I am no more anxious to kill the paper than you are.
The packet of small mags you sent does NOT arouse terror (nor pity for that matter)[4]
The Tirol stuff by M. R. wasn't invective. In fact the <manuscript of> whole little book, of which I sent you chap. I. is being translated in Tokio. so I suppose <J>apan will beat you to it.[5]

ALSO once again/ when I am NOT writing CANTOS
I do not care a hoot how much I am EDITED.
I am not touchy about the elimination of a phrase.
WHEN I EDIT <other people> I CUT OUT what I don't want. when I am edited I give the editor similar leeway. That is what EDITING is. The writer provides the ammunition and the editor shoots it TOWARD the target.

I agree to 240 bucks a year/ if the paper can't pay it thazzatt/ If it is only issued 6 times a year that halves the remuneration till further notice. But I shd/ like to work out a system for I20 bucks annual. Then I wd/ not have to think about THAT part of the rent.
NOT charity/ the wyper has got to earn it. You passed over a proposition I made re/ INTERESTING writers by offering 'em STOCK in small dabs/ to bear interest WHEN the paper begins to pay.
I still think the plan wd AUGMENT yr/ intake of manuscripts that WOULD make the paper SELL. It wd/ temp<t> me to send enough stuff so you WOULD be able to use 20 bucks worth per <issue>~~month~~ ETC..
I still have NO idea WHAT yr Biz Mgr found INVECTIVE.
jHeeZuss NO ONE know<s> what CLARITY of expression means.
everyone THINK<s> the other guy is GOING to understand him.
[typewritten in the left margin:] I dont NOW know whether you have anything of mine IN RESERVE or whether you want something NOW invective for JEWlie

<Yr E.P>.

[1] **Édouard Daladier**
[2] **Neville Chamberlain**
[3] **Dorothy Thompson**
[4] See Pound's request in **EP40**.
[5] Pound was referring to an article, "Grais or the Beauties of the Tyrol," written by Mary Rudge (later **Mary de Rachewiltz**), daughter of Pound and **Olga Rudge**. The article was rejected by *Globe*, but was eventually translated and published in Japan in the magazine *Reijokai*, vol. 18, no. 1 (January 1939), pp. 98–11.

EP43

TSL GBS (BL)

24 April

[stamped received:] May [ ] 1938

Dear J/T/D
YES I understand all that (yrs/ 7th inst)
and the NEED to be practical/
What you and yr/ sr/ BRO can do and haven't DONE is to ORGANIZE and NURSE yr/ writers/
TELL 'em what you CAN print/ ask them CLEARLY to do this and that/ return 'em ms/ with

UNPRINTABLE passages MARKED so they can UNDERSTAND what you are up against/ and
WHAT yr/ biznczts managur thinks will stop sales.
Do realize that most authors have not the foggiest idea WHAT an editor CAN use/ especially when editor is in far country among inexplicable obstacles.
<a> kid named B/Comstock might be trained/[1]
last of his I saw was a few pages too long for Globe, I think.
ask the Bizniz mg/ whether he think's Gingrich's[2] authors will write What HE (the biz Mg/ wants
for Globe rates ?? (this is to keep him in order === not in unsympathy wiff his trails

<Ez>

[1] **Boyd L. Comstock**
[2] **Arnold Gingrich**

JD22

TSL GS (YCAL)

April 27, 1938

Mr. Ezra Pound
Via Marsala 12/5
Rapallo, Italy

Dear Mr. Pound:

We definitely did not want to intimate that your letters were no longer desired.[1] On the contrary; we still feel that contributions from you are an integral part of GLOBE.

But our magazine has up till now been for the few (and very few at that). The time will come, we hope, when ours will be the privilege of dictating, but, unlike "Poetry,"[2] we have no guarantors and so have to tody [sic] to the so-called man-of-the-street who is most of the time looking for temporary entertainment and not for solid worth.

Your first article, "Abdication,"[3] definitely met the approval of many of our readers. Later letters, however, have been called "obscure." You cannot underestimate the public's intelligence, and many would say re. your last letter: "Who are Baxter, Andrews, etc." "What is meant by the phrase 'after Baxter sold out his church!'"[4] And so forth. In your "Deflation Benefit" (August, '37) you said, "I trust I am not being too technical."[5] Another reader stated at the time that that was exactly it, you are too technical. Of course, I don't mean by this that you should prostitute your art and write about no account subjects just to appeal to people. But we would prefer articles that can be followed a little more easily, that won't require of our readers a thorough background in, and complete understanding of foreign affairs. There are very few such Americans.

As for the sex angle,[6] we don't necessarily want articles such as appeared in the magazines sent you. Those were merely to show where the public's mind is today. Of course, a certain amount of such stuff, in a milder, pleasanter way, is bound to help. We feel that in GLOBE have appeared far too many of the morbid sex stories (Francis Frost, Jesse Stuart, Ed Bell, etc.),[7] which type we want to avoid.

[Page two]

These stories with the same angle, but a more pleasing outlook, have met with far more favor, like Bob Brown's "Dr. Francisco,"[8] or Andre Roosevelt's "Monumental Patient."[9]

I am enclosing your latest letter and have red pencilled it quite thoroughly. For instance, on page two, passages like, "And a bit later Rothschild horned in on the racket" need historical elaboration. The transition from the war in Spain to brothels in England is rather brusque (is the theme economic motivation? Not too evident to the reader). Also there should be additional stuff preceding the paragraph on page five beginning, "And as to the government." These church and state paragraphs aren't linked up too well. In short, the theme of this article is Economics.

Italy and Germany face the question. Rotted, rotten, and rottener: France, The Church of England, England, Spain, Canterbury, York, all Britons, English and French press, etc. We hope that this is "clarity of expression."[10]

As for the money part. We will make the same arrangement as before – twenty dollars an issue, which will be raised as soon as possible, for we all realize the value you have been to GLOBE and want to try and pay you back in some measure, though of course anything we can do will hardly be what is due.

Very sorry I unintentionally overlooked the suggestion about payment of authors [11] (those that won't take the limit of fifty dollars, which price we have paid a few from time to time; not more than one a month). Before any such arrangements are made, however, we will have to be pretty damn sure about the article. And it's not a question which can be decided in a moment. But it won't be forgotten and you'll hear from me later about it. I'm not the one to decide and will have to talk it over with others.

We have nothing in reserve, and the June-July issue is locked up on the 18th of May. Anyway, we hope you will send us something for the next number. And in the meantime, may this letter help clear things up.

Sincerely,

GLOBE MAGAZINES, Inc.

[Signature]

James Taylor Dunn
Assistant Editor

JTD/dl

encl.

[1] See **EP42.**
[2] Dunn was referring to Harriet Monroe's Chicago-based journal *Poetry* (established 1912), with which Pound was closely associated early in his career.
[3] "Abdication" appeared in the first issue of *Globe* (March 1937) (see Contribution #1).
[4] This reference appears to be to a passage of a lost essay sent by Pound to Dunn or a passage edited out of a published or unpublished essay, since this reference to Robert Baxter is not found in existing published or unpublished material Pound sent to *Globe*. For Robert Baxter and further details, see Pound's response to this letter **EP44** notes 1 and 2.
[5] "Deflation Benefit" (Contribution #5) appeared in *Globe* (August 1937, pp. 66–71).
[6] See **EP41.**
[7] **Frances Frost**'s contributions were "Lady in The Taxi" (March 1937, pp. 12–15); "Rainy Sunday" (May 1937, pp. 56–61); "Down a Dark Street" (October 1937, pp. 30–4). **Jesse Stuart**'s contributions were "Kentucky Constables" (March 1937, pp. 49–52); "Against the Sunset" (June 1937, pp. 17–22); "The Faded Flag" (July 1937, pp. 84–6). **Ed Bell**'s contributions were "Country Grunt's Boy Friend" (May 1937, pp. 71–7 and "Nashville 'Nanners' " (August 1937, pp. 44–9).
[8] **Robert Carlton Brown**'s "Dr. Francisco" appeared in *Globe* (February–March 1938).
[9] **André Roosevelt**
[10] Again Dunn seems to have been referring to a passage of a lost essay sent by Pound to Dunn or a passage edited out of a published or unpublished essay, since the references in these two paragraphs do not appear in existing published or unpublished material Pound sent to *Globe*. For further details and the reference to the Rothschilds, see Pound's response to this letter (**EP44**).
[11] Dunn may be referring to Pound's comments in **EP43.**

EP44

TSL GBS (BL)

I0 May

Waaal naow young DUFF !

Yrs of 27 th ult; is helpful but it is still OBSCURE to me just like ME am obskewer to the antipodes./

Now WOULD the article you have sent back[1] have been printable IF I has added footnotes (or explained in the text) that Baxter[2] was the son of a bitch who brough<t> tolerance of usury into the Bloody Church of England/ and that Morgan the Elder was[3] <a> crook dragged into court <& condemned> for a dirty deal (as recorded in Corey's <u>House of Morgan</u> ?[4]
And that Necker brought in a set of Swiss bankers/[5] and Rothschild didn't break into the centre office of the Bank of <France.>

<Till along in the 1840's.>[6]

papa KUNG[7] : is the degenerate bastard who is finance minister of China/ tool of international finance/ or at least playing their game.
gombeen man, irish term for extortionate mortgage holders.
Not the least clear from your letter whether you want me to rewrite the article/ or whether you want to exclude the whole <u>subject matter</u> of it.
Do get it that I have never objected to tempering by expressions. I am interested in establishing a sane news service to the U.S. even if it is limited to 24 pages a year.
I look at my earnings BY THE <YE>AR, it was worth tying at 240 bucks/ that mean<t> that much income/ new arrangement means that is cut in half. essentially the SAME amount of work/ as the difference in number of words makes NO diminution in the amount of sanity <or news> that shd/ be conveyed.
There IS NO european news without perspective. <W>ithout historic perspective its its just GUNTHER[8], i;e; bloody BUNK..
asses talking about the Negus coming back to Abyssinia[9] (and the more drivvling <ly> idiotic, about Mussolini trying to intrigue to get him back.)

Look at my old Esquire stuff/ years ago[10] I had to TELL 'em that Italy and Jugoslavia wd/ NOT go to war.
Of course one Esquire article pays more that Globe now offers for a years service. That is the MINIMUM Ginrich/ <rate> and if one chose to KEN, and do waht they want it goes UP and UP.
$500 and $I000, and Colliers $I500 a fahrticle.
Tjis dont mean anything except that if I am to go on, we have got to understand each other.
Seveal people read "Resposibility, shucks".[11]

Hitler, by the way, has said two things during the season. One was about money. Both are important.[12]
England and france ARE rotten. Nobody but Mosley[13] has the COURAGE <To think> that England is anything but INCURABLE.
If you want anything from Rapallo/ we have I take it till July I3 to concoct it.

Yrs. < EP>

with the Globe coming out only every two months/ you and yr/ bro/ might even send me a list of questions about Europe to be answered/ if you that that wd/ guide me.
ONLY get it straight that the Rome-Berlin axis EXISTS[14] and any attempt to blink that fact is just CRAP/

<That is the Europe you have got to get news FROM.>

[1] This submission to *Globe* was sent back to Pound by Dunn with editorial queries (see **JD22** note 4). Pound apparently never revised or resubmitted the piece and it does not seem to have survived.
[2] **Richard Baxter**
[3] **John Pierpont Morgan, Sr.**
[4] *The House of Morgan: A Social Biography of the Masters of Money* (1930), by Louis C. Fraina (1884–1953), who wrote under the name Lewis C. Corey.
[5] Probably **Jacques Necker**
[6] Pound may have been referring to a loan in 1841 which James de Rothschild negotiated with the French government of Marshal Soult. This loan to the French Treasury was for the purposes of rearmament and the improvement of the defenses of the city of Paris. (For details, see Ferguson, *The House of Rothschild*, pp. 379–405.)
[7] **H. H. Kung**
[8] **John Gunther**
[9] "Negus" is the Amharic word for the title "king" or "ruler." The reference is to the Ethiopian Emperor **Haile Selassie** (1892–1975). Selassie had assumed the throne in 1930 and after failing to turn back Mussolini's invasion, he was forced to flee Ethiopia in 1936. He spent the next five years in exile in Britain. Backed by the British government, Selassie regained control of Ethiopia in 1942.
[10] See **EP1**.
[11] See Contribution #7.
[12] See "...And Excursions" (Contribution #4).
[13] **Sir Oswald Mosley**
[14] Mussolini and Hitler signed the Berlin–Rome Axis agreement on October 25, 1936.

EP45

TSL GBS (BL)

21 May

Dear Dunn

I haven't yet seen a way to save anything save the news/ straight and IN PROPORTION, the main things first. will wait yr/ answer to my last letter.

If I have got to twist and squirm to get something thru I might as well Esquire or Ken[1] and get it to more people. (at immensely different stipendium).

In the interim/ I suggest you young highbrows note that a REVOLUTION has been occuring under your noses where you least look for it.

The Delphian Society[2] prospectus which I have just seen (though I have been writing for 'em for some years) CONTAINS at least one proposition that is NEW in american Anschauung./ Why don't you get Mis Burd[3] <herself> or one of 'em to write it up. Quite as interesting as Boise and them Towns/ and of course wd/ carry Globe to many homes as yet unGlobed.

I leave it to you to find out WHICH plank in their platform raises hell with the constituted and supinely accepted fugg which has shit the country for the past 40 or more years.

Minor point, a young bloke named Spranklin[4] has been ON THE spot in Czzkoslovakia/ Viena/ Roma/ may be able to send you something if it dont slip his active mind.

at any rate I told him to send in.

The Delphian bizniz concerns the business mgr/ as well as the etds//

<yr E P>

[1] For *Ken* see **EP40**

[2] For the Delphian Society see **EP2**

[3] **Mary Burd**

[4] **Spranklin**: unknown

EP46

TSC (BL)

3/Aug

[stamped] AUG 13 1938

dear Dunn
I have just happened on something
non=economic and non political/
will send it along today or tomorrow.

<E>

EP47

TSL GBS (BL)

23 Nov.

[stamped received] OCT 4 [1938]

Dear Dunn

There hasn't been much CONTACT lately / from the home office to European outpost; but I hear from Tweddell[1] that the rumor of suspension of publication/ is false, and that No. issue is out.

I never have approved of CHILD stuff, but I am sending on a translation of letter from a 12 year old in the Tirol.[2] The opening is very clear/ it is quite as good as a lot of the accounts in Frazer.[3]

I am trying out this sample. I have another letter, not about local feasts, which I can also translate if wanted.

The stuff is perfectly straight and very much SO.

yrs E.P. <EP>

At any rate is personal and simple letter/ Quite different from anything yet, and country unexploited, although quite near.

I have nothing TO it. It is in Italian
<Title and all.>
I think exactly as I have given it. I can't recall having ever made a closer translation of anything.
<The "etc." is the original "ecc."
I haven't altered anything>

[1] **Dr. Francis Tweddell**
[2] Mary Rudge (later **Mary de Rachewiltz)**
[3] **Sir James Frazier**

EP48

TSL P (BL)

[December 15, 1938]

Pleased to see Globe after so long interval/ /evidently feeling the s train/
damd hard to send correspondence / NEWS service from Europe when the whole of Munich agreements etc/[1] can intervene between time of writing But will take another shot soon.
and try to be up to date (i; e; up to date of probably publication.)
On the practical side/ a kid named R. J. Lowry [2]
is printing "Little Man"
3747 Hutton St., Conncinnati [sic].
I see no reason why you shdnt ABSORB / as he must be wasting production costs/ has no aims distinct from globes/
wants to buck Coronet etc.
Believe he is still in college/ but SOMEONE must be paying his printer.
There is NOT enough lively stuff for two such mags/ and you need cheap copy as well as etc./
Anyhow he has writ/ to me, and I pass this on to YOU.
I of course dont KNOW what he wd/ do/ but i shd/ do a lit work for nothing with "prospects"

EP

[1] The Munich Conference, which decided the fate of Czechoslovakia, took place September 29-30, 1938. The international agreements signed at this conference allowed Germany to annex the Sudetenland on October 1, 1938. Within a year this led to the incorporation of the whole country into the German Reich.
[2] **Robert J. Lowry**

EP49

TSL GBS (BL)

I8 Dec.

Dear Dunn the younger

Does present issue mean that GLOBE is down to bed rock and means to carry on/?

IF yr/ bro/ now sees his way to doing the REAL thing instead of thinking he can compete with SLOP by a compromise I might make a few suggestions.

I mean to say I can't think a magazine can print a certain amount of TRUTH, that is a mag cant have ANY real value at all and still buck the punk mags/

I dont want to be too sure of this statement/ but a little virtue is dangerous.

A commercial practical mag/ MAY be able to be honest in aim/

I don't know.

stang/ keeping down the over head and determined to carry on somehow/

what about trying I00% or as much as can be got of A. Is stuff with a periphery of honest student stuff that is easy to get for 2 dollars an article ?

In present format you cd/ use travel stuff and a line up of W.C. Williams (as in Passaic River)

Huddleston / e/e/cummings/ Bunting (if he will write)[1]

If you are hard up and want to try THIS kind of mag/ and can give me as much liberty as I now have in "ACTION" and the British Union Quarterly,[2] and dare use a monthly letter from me, I will cut my rate from 20 bucks to 5 bucks per article for a series of I2 articles.

of mu own kind, I e; getting the paper SEEN by various people, not always the same people for each issue.

Can you send MARKED copies of current issue to

Ubaldo degli Uberti,[3] Corso Degali 3/4 Geneva.

(he writes he has stopped his
subscription)

A. Raven Thomson[4], "Action" Sanctuary Building's
Gt Smith St. London S.W. I;)

Odon Por,[5] 5 B. Via Angelo Masina, Rome, Italy.

shd/ also like three more copies (or even 5) here IF you can at all PLAN a GLOBE for 1939, different from earlier Globe ; one might announce a series of I2 issues with I2 special features BY known authors

among whom Williams (W.C.) Cummings/ Claude Bowers, if being Ambassador dont prevent him and if it does, the an article ABOUT his various books of U.S. history) W. E. Woodward

say Maranini .[6]

I know you wrote you wanted PRESENT news. But ONE historic article of the right kind in each issue, taking past history ONLY IN SO FAR as it is topical NOW, i;e; bears on some present crisis / some present conflict that is IN THE NEWS of the month/

it wd/ raise the value of the mag.

and not be at all like academic troy artices in the canned conserved magazines. what the hell is the use of news from Corsica to people who don['t] know what Corsica IS. Let alone whether Napoleon was Italian.

and if so, how far, and if not; WHY not and by h[o]w narrow a technical margin.

R.C. Large/ another; recently noticed by old UptonSinclair[7] send him current issue of GLOBE

address 8 Thornton Rd. Wimbledon

London S.W.I9

England

what about that Tyrol stuff by M.R. [8] / I thought thta t worth printing, and cost wd/ be next to newt.

Of course Lin Yutang is MADE for what Globe started out to be. likewise the unreachable Halide Edib.[9]

try sample copy to J.P. Angold,[10] with request for impressions of Scandanavia .

address

Oaklyn, The Mildens

Westcot, Surrey, England.

of course I cd/ even ASK people to write for nothing during a lean IF yr/ bro intends or agr res even partly to my proposal for a better and smaller Globe with a bit of intention (not about theory) but of carrying vital INFORMATION

and so o forth <EP>

[1] **William Carlos Williams, Sisley Huddleston, Edward Estlin Cummings, Basil Bunting**

[2] For *Action* and *The British Union Quarterly* see **EP16.**

[3] **Ubaldo Degli Uberti**

[4] A. Raven Thomson (1899–1955) Director of Policy for the BUF.

[5] **Odon Por**

[6] **Giuseppe Maranini**

[7] **R. C. Large**: unidentified

[8] **Mary de Rachewiltz** Also see **EP46.**

[9] **Lin Yutang, Halide Edip Avidar**

[10] **John Penrose Angold**

EP50

TSL GBS (BL)

Dear M/Dunn

Xmas present vurry nearly hit the day.
The end of yr/ letter also on the UP.
Now damn it, as you have (GLOBE has) been drug thru a knot hole, why go out for making it a REAL paper that will get free advertising be reason of BEING ahand of the snot.

If you are going to UNIFY the foreign, news, why not git Wyndham Lewis[1], who saw Hitler coming back in I93I
// address Studio A;
Kensington Gardens Studies
29 Notting Hill Gate, London W. II.
England.
Author of Mysterious Mr. Bull etc//[2]
a letter from him monthly would be the BEST news of england/
or Generral Fuller[3] who was in Abyssinia and SAW what was done in the way of provisioning troops and busting the army text book dry rot.
also Tanks/ also onto economics.
As for Home news/ Ham and Eggs polled a million and a quarter votes[4]/ NEWS of the local colour in Calif/ would have been welcome to them one millyum and more kallyfornicators and as the press wuz boycottin 'em you wd/ have built up a grateful public.
try Luther Whiteman[5]
I shd/ pussnly be grateful if you cd/ git one of them bustards to say coherently WHY the bleedin hell they want a consumptive WEEKLY weakly sticker / which iz NUTZ
instead of a sane MONTHLY stamp.
Anyhow ham and eggs wuz for Globe omlet/
and SCENES during the election wd/ have been as non political as even yr/ venerable bro/ cd/ have wished.
One millyum and 25 the/ peeples in'rested in it/ dont tell me it waz just a subjek fer a few flatchested highbrows.
why didnt a Globe staff go WEST to broaden his blinknik mind during that elexshum ??

cordially and Happy gnu yr/
<EP>

[1] For **Wyndham Lewis**'s *Hitler* see **EP39.**

[2] *The Mysterious Mr. Bull* (1938) was a critical analysis of British society and

politics which included, as was most common in **Wyndham Lewis**' work, a jaundiced discussion of the class system in Britain.

[3] **John Frederick Charles Fuller** (1878–?), British major-general, journalist, and author. Fuller first served in the British army in the Boer War. He was one of the first military strategic thinkers to formulate what would later come to be known in World War II as the German "Blitzkrieg." In 1934, Fuller became a member of Sir Oswald Mosley's British Union of Fascists (BUF) and was a frequent contributor to the BUF's periodicals *Action* and *Fascist Quarterly*. Fuller covered the Spanish Civil War as a journalist and traveled with the Italian army in its 1935 invasion of Ethiopia. The result of his efforts was *The First of the League Wars: Its Lessons and Omens* (1936).

[4] The so-called "Ham and Eggs" pension scheme was developed by economist Roy G. Owens and promoted in California by two brothers, Willis and Lawrence Allen. The plan dictated that any unemployed person fifty years of age or over would receive from the state thirty pieces of scrip a week with the value of a dollar each. This scrip could be spent like money. But if any individual held on to the scrip beyond a week, he or she had to affix a two-cent revenue stamp, which was sold by the state, to the piece of scrip each week it was held in order to maintain its value of one dollar. Any piece of scrip held throughout the year would be redeemed by the state for its face value of a dollar in cash only if $1.04 in revenue stamps had been affixed to the piece of scrip through the year. The stamps then financed the state's payout and administrative costs of the pension program.

If it had adopted this pension plan, the State of California would have in effect created an alternative, local currency—and this did not sit well with the federal government. The plan was actually brought forth as an initiative during the 1936 elections. It was defeated, but it received 1,430,000 votes.

The appeal of this type of scheme to Pound is clear when one considers his interest in the stamp scrip experiment made by Michael Unterguggenberger, burgermeister of the village of Wörgl in Austria (see "Interview with Mrs. Unterguggenberger," Contribution #6 and **EP29**).

[5] **Luther Whiteman**

CODA

When *Globe* collapsed, the Dunn brothers headed off to separate parts of the world to cool off after the familial sparring caused by the magazine's demise. Jack went on to write travel articles and promotional material for resorts around the world, particularly Mexico. Montfort, a Yale graduate who had studied art in Paris, became an art collector and also traveled to Mexico in the winters.

James Taylor Dunn did what he initially had planned to do when he graduated from Hamilton College—get a library science masters from Syracuse University. In 1942, Dunn was drafted. Shortly before joining the army, he left his *Globe*/Pound correspondence to Hamilton College.

Dunn served in Europe during World War II, utilizing the French that he had learned in college. In Luxembourg, he met his future wife, Maria Bach. After the war, the couple settled in Cooperstown, New York, where Dunn worked as librarian of the Farmer's Museum, which is affiliated with the New York State Historical Association. He was associated with the folklore movement of New York historians, and wrote about upstate New York folktales.

During that time, the Dunns occasionally headed up to Hamilton to chaperone dances. In the late 1940s and early 1950s, they met a young Omar Pound, Ezra's son, then attending the school.

More than two decades after they had last corresponded, Pound wrote Dunn from Rapallo, a year after he was released from St. Elizabeths.

EP51

TSL on Albergo Grande Italia
& Lido stationery (RUT)

[June 23, 1959]

Dear Dunn

I don't know whether the farmer's museum buys anything but old models of farm machinery.

You might annoy the swine by going in for Van Buren, a legitimate N.Y. interest though Ives [1] and co/ and the rustees of Ham/ col. wouldn't LIKE curiousity re/ so disturbing a character.

As outlets are being one carefully CLOSED for all contempory thought . No where to treat any subject more than ONCE. etc.

No curiousity permitted in Clinton[2] re/ problem of issue (of $) no interest in what a tax system SHOULD be.

No suggestion of applying ang/sax heritage INSIDE labour organizations

which might derive from Mafia via Al Capone,

etc. am thinking of
turning antiquary, and selling off items.

such as G.Santayana's
pencil notes in margine of presentation copy of Guzzo's Dialoghi di Bruno.[3]

etc.

Have you ever done yr duty by the Sq $, series.[4] Or has Barnes ?[5]

Librarian at ham. col. has rather toned down since i suggested to the Prex(who, I take it, did NOT deliver my note to trustees to them,)[6] to put some american HISTORY(as distinct from brainwash)

into the criKIm.

Get any news from La. up in yr/ county ?

I spose I ought to keep old Loomis Court docket in the family.[7] tho no one likely to read it in Brunnenburg.[8]

Find file of Globe in Rap/ on return here.[9] Is that in the Farmers' Mus ? or in cellarage. "A noble effort."

cordialky yrs/ E Pound

It was clear from this letter that Pound was reaching out to Dunn just as he had twenty-one years earlier—as someone who could disseminate his ideas to his *patria*.

Dunn, however, never received the note. He had left New York in the early 1950s to become librarian of the Minnesota Historical Society in his hometown of St. Paul.

Louis Jones, then director of the Farmer's Museum and also a Hamilton alumnus, wrote back to Pound in an attempt to acquire material from the poet, but he never forwarded the letter on to Dunn. Pound did not write back to Jones.

Pound never attempted to correspond with the Dunns again. He remained in Italy slowly fading from sight—visiting America once, in 1969, to attend the opening of the exhibition of the "rediscovered" manuscript of T. S. Eliot's *The Waste Land*. He then went on to attend the conferral of an honorary degree upon James Laughlin by Hamilton College and was also honored at the ceremony as an illustrious—even lionized—alumnus. The successful and impressive event was in marked contrast to his last visit to Hamilton in 1939, when, with much controversy and fuss, he had received his own honorary doctorate. Pound's last years were spent in silence and reclusiveness in Italy. He died in 1972.

The Dunn brothers continued their separate lives, but all retained summer homes in the Minnesota village of Marine-on-St. Croix, north of St. Paul along the river that divides part of Minnesota and Wisconsin.

James Taylor Dunn went on to a distinguished career as the librarian of the Minnesota Historical Society. His numerous publications on Minnesota history included *The St. Croix: Midwest Border River*, part of the Rivers of America series published in 1965. In 1998, he edited *The Far Islands and Other Cold Places: Travel Essays of a Victorian Lady* by Elizabeth Taylor, a distant relative. James Taylor Dunn died on September 8, 2002.

Endnotes

[1] Irving M. Ives (1896–1962), trustee of Hamilton College, 1942–60, also served as New York State Assemblyman, 1930–46 (served as Speaker in 1936) and as US Senator (Republican) for New York, 1947–59. He graduated from Hamilton College Class of 1920. It is not clear why Ives would be interested in Martin Van Buren, outside of the fact that Van Buren was also a US Senator from New York before becoming the eighth President of the United States.
[2] Clinton, New York, where Hamilton College is located.
[3] Pound is referring to Augusto Guzzo's *I dialoghi del Bruno* (Torino: Edizioni de "L'Erma," 1932). It is not clear how Pound acquired a copy of this book annotated by the expatriate American philosopher George Santayana (1863–1952). Pound and Santayana had a kind of association in Italy beginning in 1937. It was largely carried on by correspondence, but was punctuated by occasional meetings. It is possible that Santayana lent Pound his copy of the book—both were very much interested in Neo-Platonism and the Renaissance. As in many cases, the book may have been forgotten and left with Pound. Exactly where this book finally found its home is unknown.
[4] Pound was referring to the "Square $ Series" which he brought out in the early 1950s while he was resident in St. Elizabeths. The series was published by John Kasper and T. D. Horton. Six books/pamphlets were issued for $1.00 each. These included reprints of Pound's *Unwobbling Pivot*, *The Great Digest*, and Ernest Fenollosa's *The Chinese Written Character* in one volume, and *Analects of Confucius*. The rest of the volumes were short texts by authors such as Del Mar, Senator Thomas Hart Benton, and the nineteenth-century anti-Darwinist Harvard biologist Louis Agassiz, each representing one of Pound's hobby-horses. Pound was apparently asking whether Hamilton College had acquired these texts for their library.
[5] Harry Elmer Barnes (1889–1968), American educator and sociologist who lived near Cooperstown.
[6] Robert Ward McEwen, president of Hamilton College from 1949 to 1966. Pound sent McEwen several letters from St. Elizabeths and from Italy urging the college to incorporate more economics and constitutional history into its curriculum.
[7] The location of this document is unknown. Pound claimed descent from a gang of horse thieves who terrorized upstate New York in the nineteenth century. Carl Carmer wrote about the gang's exploits in *Listen to a Lonesome Drum* (1940), see pp. 229–37.

[8] Upon his arrival in Italy after his release form St. Elizabeths in 1958, Pound took up residence with his daughter Maria de Rachewiltz and her family, Olga Rudge and his wife Dorothy at Brunnenburg castle in the Italian Tyrol.

[9] After Pound settled down in Italy, he began to go through his extensive personal archive sorting and often annotating with dates and comments incoming correspondence, as well as carbons of his own outgoing letters. It is likely that Pound was prompted to get back in touch with Dunn in 1959 when he came across his correspondence with *Globe*. Pound could easily have gotten Dunn's address through his connections with Hamilton College. Pound had always stayed in touch with the college and he could have read of Dunn's position at the Historical Society in the *Hamilton Alumni Review*, which he regularly received in Rapallo and St. Elizabeths. He could also have gotten Dunn's address from his son Omar. Pound's *Globe* file, as well as the major portion of his personal archive, went to Yale University. Today it is among the Ezra Pound Papers in the Yale Collection of American Literature (YCAL 43) housed in Yale's Beinecke Library. The letters from Pound to Dunn, along with his Pound-related collection of books and other associated materials, are in the Burke Library at Hamilton College.

PART TWO

Pound's Published and Unpublished Contributions to *Globe* Magazine

PUBLISHED ARTICLES

Contribution #1: "Abdication"
Globe March 1937 issue, pp. 82–7

For "Abdication," see **EP11, EP12, EP19, EP22, JD11, JD13, JD14, JD22, JWGD1**

Before any man sick with the love of power writes any more in judgment, let him put against the ten brief paragraphs of The Farewell, a sentence of Remy de Gourmont's: "To write frankly what one thinks is a writer's sole pleasure." [1]

Consider that even a banned and loathed writer like myself can always speak in one way or another, can see his passion in print after a fortnight if important,[2] *after a year or two if it really lands a right to the jaw of some pet stupidity of the gang or the multitude and needs a whole book or long essay to hold it. Never believe a word in the daily press. That is axiomatic for any reader who wants to get any sort of understanding of my monthly letters.*
Ezra Pound

ABDICATION

Rapallo, Italy

On the evening of December 11th, at a moment or not more than two moments after eleven o'clock (Italian Time), the radio in the Albergo Rapallo[3] began with perfect clarity and no static to render a voice as of a man just coming out from under an anaesthetic. And because of the honesty and sincerity in that voice England forbids the sale of the disc and forbade gramophone companies to record it.[4]

You must remember that England has been rotted and made putrid for two hundred years by the sixty per cent racket on money. That is absolutely basic for any comprehension of what goes on there; of the millions of starved and half-starved; of the absolute evil concentrated in Baldwin and Chamberlain[5] and their popinjays, Eden,[6] son-in-law of the banking Becketts,[7] Duff-Cooper, son-in-law of the Duke of Rutland,[8] Sasson the parsee,[9] also of a usurious family—Baldwin concentrating in his person the great refusal, which in the IDEAL of that England which assumes that man ought to be something less than human, an unthinking clod, having the astuteness of the sow hunting truffles.

The reader, in order to find a parallel to the "mind" of Chamberlain, must imagine that a codfish died of constipation some time in the Ice Age and was petrified, the fossil's intestine dug up—and you have Chamberlain's mind.

The one thing that unites Baldwin's cabinet is the absolute determination that millions of Englishmen are to be kept at or below starvation level; that the true history of money either in the past or in the present is NOT to be printed in the daily papers, and that no change in the present nauseating conditions shall occur.

It is an error to suppose that Empires necessarily renew themselves by revolution. Empires often decay and their parts fall leprously off. Thirty years ago the English might have studied the slow descent of Venetian power. Today you must look into the state of Austria, eighty years ago, and Bourbon Naples of 1859, if you want to examine pathologies analogous to that of England in 1936-37.

Baldwin's spiritual home is Cicero (Illinois), [10] but neither the pig and pipe fancier nor any or all of his accomplices could have put out Edward, had Edward decided to stay. On that point you can, I believe, take Edward's remarks on "decision" as wholly authentic.

Some forty years ago Edward Windsor was sat down firmly on Victoria's lap. And he DECIDED AGAINST IT.

They used him twenty years
To quiet people's fears . . . .
He was put to make excuses
For the most gawdamed abuses
And they pinned a dukedumb to his britches
When he left'em. [11]

Concerning all this, the Italian papers printed articles more thoughtful than appeared anywhere else. *The Gazzetta del Popolo,*[12] looking at the affair from short time range, spoke of the contest between Baldwin, the old statesman utterly cold, and the king in an abnormal or over-excited mental state.

My solid and thoughtful English colleague writes me "the King's preconditioned mind." Therein is the root.

Of the statements printed in England, two are significant: One from an old actor who "had seen it coming" when he heard Edward at a war memorial speaking well and conscientiously but with a hurried ending, as a performer who wants to throw up his part; the other, from an ex-cabinet minister, to the effect that Edward had no friend of outstanding intelligence.

The Archbishop of Canterbury,[13] taking a cad's chance to kick his ex-sovereign, also had a go at Edward's circle. Let us consider a moment the people whom Edward did NOT make friends with. Viccy used to have old Alf. Tennyson in to tea.[14] His verse was no worse than that admired in those decades by all except a few highbrows. Henry James' impressions of Browning and Tennyson weren't printed till years after Vic's death.[15]

Edward VII was supposed to read the "Pink 'Un"[16] and Marie Corelli.[17] George V was always held up to the people as a model of imbecility. If he ever read a book the fact was most carefully concealed from the public. Nothing but stamp collecting was considered safe enough for Royal attention. Nevertheless, the keepah of the Imperial Stamp collection found George quite intelligent.[18] Here at any rate was a common topic of conversation. George was not a moron. But the "faithful custodian," so far as I know, never betrayed this secret to anyone save his cousin Miss C.

On the death of his elder brother, George V was pitchforked out of his normal life.[19] He was told what was his duty. Under the drizzle and the half-light of armistice day, George's face was the face of a man who had willed no evil.

After having begun his reign as "this damned unINteresting King,"[20] he ended with the solid affection of his people. Mr. Baldwin thought Edward VIII was too intelligent for the job.

There is no sense in excited critics condemning Edward for having made the "grand refusal;" that is precisely what he had not made. Edward refused to be a stuffed rabbit.

And in those very words my Tory friend G. hammers the table and says: "The King OUGHT to be a stuffed rabbit, that is his job, that is what he is paid for."

The fury and backbiting in England is due in large measure to fear. Some of 'em are afraid, *even now,* and quite wrongly, I think, that Edward might want to come back.

It is the old story of the Emperor's clothes. The absent-minded Emperor had forgotten to put on any clothes. Embarrassed courtiers were doubly anxious to compliment the Emperor on his apparel. A small boy said: "He hasn't got any on."

In this case Edward took both roles, i.e., of the small boy *and* the Emperor. Result: public fury and consternation.

A handful of fascists, a handful of social creditors, a handful of communists refused his abdication. In Parliament three communists, one socialist and one liberal voted to refuse abdication.

But the official press ignores the utter ABDICATION of PARLIAMENT. The quickness of the hand deceives the eye. Edward was kept off the radio until after his abdication. The report that he would reply to the prelate over the air has not had confirmation. Who is the Prelate and what is the Church of England? For the latter see Anthony Trollope's "The Warden."[21]

The last Church Assembly[22] made quite a shot at economic investigation, the first intellectual act since the reign of Elizabeth. The Church of England actually defined one difference between "work" and "employment," stating that the latter was "the sale of work, often under economic pressure." Whereupon the Archbishop went on a cruise. Not on a little uncomfortable thirty-foot yacht.

In contrast to the British bishop's, the Pope's broadcast on December 24th was enlightening. It may be contended that his statements were generalities. One does not expect scintillating novelty from a man who is over eighty or sudden newness from millenniar institutions, but here was in any case a prayer for peace, pity and the general decencies. The Holy Father had the grit to keep at it for half an hour against failing breath.[23] Belonging to neither congregation I can say fairly that here was a message to make any Catholic proud of his fellowship. What Mr. Morgan[24] thought of his friend Canterbury's discourse I know not, supposing that he took the trouble to hear or read it. The Pope spoke for one part of truth (and a great part); Edward Windsor, for his small parcel of reality against overwhelming dead sham, against a crushing mass of false values.

But the emphasis amid Farewells falls on the two abdications. Edward consciously and avowedly giving the power into the hands of a brother who values his friendship, and who is, to Edward's mind, in better position to wield the power than he, Edward, would have been. But beyond that is the abdication of Parliament, surrendering its power to no avowable successor, to no acknowledgeable body, leaving the people of England without representative government.

Supposing George VI [25]to be the tenth part of a man (and he has certainly the advantage of a more vigorous physique than his brother), supposing him to have any respect whatsoever for the last promise his brother made in Wales,[26] it would be the greatest joke on the powers of hell and reaction in England since Columbus discovered America, or since we pitched their tea into Boston harbor.

Edward Windsor is today in a position more powerful than when on the throne. He has but to whisper to some cub reporter: "Let the TEN MILLION EAT," and the massed corruption of Britain has dithers. Dave Windsor on his own feet can do more than he ever could have done on a throne surrounded with flummydiddles and gold braid and flunkies. I mean if the man has it in him to want his ex-subjects nourished, to want the fruits of the Empire delivered and eaten, and the spun cloth of his ex-realm worn, and the fuel used to heat poor men's houses, he can now say so.

All of this is within his oath of allegiance. All of this is 100% constitutional. The ruling clique wouldn't like it. English gentlemen don't know, and don't *want* to know that London Acceptance Houses help Stalin;[27] that the city has a hand in the rearming of Germany. They don't even want to admit that Napoleon (dead as he is) got money in London to arm his troops against England.[28]

If George, on the other hand, does nothing, the weight of Royalty's function in England will be seen to be that of an ant on a ten ton fly-wheel.

Among the Trivialities of Gossip:

Eden's role is obscure. His wife didn't like Wally.[29] Eden's father-in-law is the banker Beckett. The pretty, once-young secretary married and then got into Parliament, and as they say "since then his rise has been rapid." The anti-Edward stuff ran in the *Yorkshire Post,* which is under Beckett influence.[30] Most British newspapers represent Industrial Chemicals, or the Birmingham Small Arms,[31] or our dear expensive Astor's[32] or some other "influence" that prefers personal profit to the welfare of the British people. I can't think Eden is pronoboskos[33] or the big noise in any of this god awful mess. The heavy hippopotomi in England don't take the limelight.

I suspect that Wallie's secret is that she was the first woman to treat Edward as a human being and not a brass image with feathers.

As far as the cabinet goes, I suspect only one of 'em (Sam Hoare)[34] of common honesty. Since his remarks on rearmament, I can now only consider him as a man who would have preferred a better world had nature provided one for him to inhabit. His god is respectability.
It was interesting to note that Hoare heard the identical phrase in Durham that I heard here in Rapallo: "now IF he had married the poorest single girl out of the mills. . . ."

Ezra Pound [Signature]

[1] The "Farewell" Pound referred to was Edward VIII's abdication radio speech. According to a comment Pound made in a Rome radio broadcast on May 10,

1942, the quotation came from a personal letter Remy de Gourmont sent to the poet. This letter seems not to have survived.

[2] Pound intended the sentence to read: "...after a fortnight if *un*important..." See **EP22** where he complained that *Globe* had made the mistake.

[3] Ezra and Dorothy Pound lived above the Albergo Grande Italia & Lido Hotel in Rapallo.

[4] On December 11, 1936, Edward VIII, after less than a year on the throne, delivered a radio address entitled "A Farewell" in which he made the now famous statement: "I have found it impossible to carry the heavy burden of responsibility and to discharge my duties as King as I would wish to do without the help and support of the woman I love."

[5] For **Stanley Baldwin,** see EP11 note 13. For **Neville Chamberlain,** see EP42 note 2.

[6] For **Anthony Eden** and his marriage to the daughter of **Sir William Gervase Beckett,** see EP12 notes 4 and 7.

[7] For the Beckett family and their connections, see **EP12.**

[8] **Alfred Duff Cooper**

[9] Pound probably was referring to **Baron Philip Albert Gustave David Sassoon** as a "parsee" because his family could trace its family to Iraq, where, according to local tradition, it had settled after the *Reconquista* of the Iberian peninsula in 1492. Sassoon's grandfather Sir Albert Abdulah David had been born in Baghdad.

[10] Pound's reference to Cicero, Illinois, was meant to compare Stanley Baldwin with the gangster Al "Scarface" Capone. Capone had his residence in this Chicago suburb.

[11] An excerpt from Pound's longer doggerel sent to Dunn four days after Edward VIII abdicated, see see **EP11.**

[12] *The Gazzetta del Popolo* was a Turin-based popular political newspaper founded in 1848.

[13] **Cosmo Gordon Lang**

[14] **Alfred Tennyson.** Pound refers to Queen Victoria here as "Viccy."

[15] The novelist Henry James (1843–1916) published *William Wetmore Story and His Friends*, a remembrance of the sculptor Story and his circle, including Browning, in 1903. James also published accounts of his friendships with various writers and artists, including Browning and Tennyson, in his posthumously published *The Middle Years* (1917).

[16] *The London Sporting Times* was printed on pink sheets and was known popularly as the "Pink'un."

[17] **Marie Corelli**

[18] **Sir Edward D. Bacon**

[19] Edward VII died in 1910 and George V assumed the throne at the age of 45.

[20] Pound is probably paraphrasing **H. G. Wells'** famous and widely publicized

remark that George V ruled over an "alien and uninspiring court." Wells made the comment in 1914, reflecting not only his distaste for the dull and uninspiring person of George V, but also emphasizing the German origins of the royal house as well as the fact that Kaiser Wilhelm II and the Russian Czar Nicholas II were his first cousins. It was due to such anti-German sentiments, which the British people shared, that at the outbreak of World War I, George V abandoned the family name Saxe-Coburg and Gotha, inherited from his grandfather Prince Albert, Victoria's consort, and changed it to "Windsor."

[21] Anthony Trollope's *The Warden* (1855) focused on a local pastor's battles with the hierarchy of the Victorian Church of England.

[22] Pound was referring to an Archbishop's Commission convened by Cosmo Lang, Archbishop of Canterbury. However, any number of commissions were ongoing at the time, including the Commission on the Relations Between Church and State which was instituted in 1930 and ran for most of the following decade, occasionally generating reports on various subjects. It is not clear precisely to which of these various commissions or church assemblies Pound was referring.

[23] On December 24, 1937, Pope Pius XI made his Christmas broadcast to the world. In the speech he declared "atheistic communism" to be "a new menace" threatening Christian civilization. He also obliquely criticized fascist dictatorships: "We see with sorrow not a few allowing themselves to be dominated and guided by false and fatal ideas, both in their choice of remedies and in the appraisal of their adversaries."

[24] **J. P. Morgan, Sr.**'s father, J. S. Morgan, after having taken over the business from his former partner George Peabody, established the operations of the London and Paris branches of the Morgan family securities and banking business. J. P. Morgan, Sr. consolidated the company's activities in New York. In 1910, the London branch of J. P. Morgan & Co. became Morgan, Grenfell & Co. which replaced it and became the London center of **J. P. Morgan, Jr.**'s investment banking activities.

[25] Edward VIII's slightly younger brother, who became George VI, succeeded him on the throne after Edward's abdication.

[26] In November 1936, Edward VIII made a visit to Wales and, observing the plight of the urban workers, was reported to have commented: "Something must be done." This simple comment did cause some consternation among his ministers as it was perceived by some as an "unconstitutional" intrusion into domestic politics (see Ziegler, *King Edward VIII*, p. 262).

[27] Acceptance houses are investment banks and financial houses in London that make high-risk loans to foreign governments, importers, and other entities. Several British acceptance houses made loans to the Soviet Union in the 1930s.

[28] Pound was referring to the legend that London banker Nathan Rothschild learned of Napoleon's defeat at Waterloo in 1815 before other bankers in

London and purchased British government bonds at a low price on the basis of this "insider"information, reaping a huge profit. The House of Rothschild did indeed profit greatly from the Napoleonic Wars, but it was through financing Britain and its allies *before* Napoleon's return in 1815. In fact, the Rothschilds were more likely caught holding rapidly depreciating assets after Napoleon's Waterloo defeat. Anticipating another extended round of war on the Continent after Napoleon's return from Elba, the Rothschilds had begun to accumulate assets to once again finance Britain and its allies for the duration. Napoleon's abrupt and complete defeat at Waterloo was unexpected and sent the Rothschilds scrambling to control the financial damage. They made moves to rid themselves of gold and other assets they and Napoleon's former adversaries now no longer needed. Nathan Rothschild's speculation in British consols after Waterloo seems to have been an attempt to partially cover their losses and reaped only modest profits to this end. (For details concerning the Rothschilds' financing of Britain and its allies during the Napoleonic Wars, see Ferguson, *The House of Rothschild*, pp. 83–110.)

[29] **Wallis Warfield Simpson**

[30] See **EP12.**

[31] Created in 1861, Birmingham Small Arms was one of the largest armament concerns in Great Britain during the 1930s.

[32] Pound was referring to the wealthy British–American family descended from the German-born American businessman John Jacob Astor II (1763–1848). William Waldorf Astor I (1848–1919), the son of John Jacob II, established the British branch of the family when he became a naturalized British subject. He eventually became a member of Parliament (1910), and was created 1st Viscount Astor (1917). William Waldorf's business was in newspaper and magazine publication and he was not without literary ambitions himself, writing two rather unsuccessful novels. His son, William Waldorf Astor II (1879–1952) followed him into conservative British politics and inherited his title as Viscount. William Waldorf II's son, John Jacob Astor V (1886–1971) bought a major share of the Times Publishing Company and became the chairman of its board. He was also created 1st Baron Astor of Hever.

[33] An error by the typesetter. Pound meant the Greek term "pornoboskos." See **EP16** note 3.

[34] **Sir Samuel John Gurney Hoare**

Contribution #2: "Europe MCMXXXVI"
Globe May 1937 issue, pp. 106–10
Reflections written on the eve of a new era

For "Europe 1936," see **EP3, EP9, EP16, JD10, JD5, JD6, JD13, JD14, JWGD1**

Rapallo, Italy

There is no use in writing about Europe as if it had been founded by the Pilgrim Fathers in 1620, nor in seeing it second-handed through the eyes of English weekly reviewers. And there is certainly no use in my writing about it if I am merely to tell GLOBE readers what they already know or believe.

If I am to write for GLOBE we may as well understand each other. I have been right several times in the past. Plenty of people have thought me crazy. But they always think me crazy for what I am actually saying at the moment, not for what I SAID fifteen or twenty years ago.

Ezra Pound

You can only see a country straight by looking at it through its own history. Essential parts of history get mislaid. The Leopoldine Reforms[1] are as little known to the present Anglo-Saxon world as is the real work and meaning of Jackson and Van Buren to Europe. And yet all the Manchester school of thought[2] was thought out and tried out in Tuscany in 1785 and, what is much more interesting, Leopold's successor[3] had already started correcting the errors and excesses of the free trade cranks before Napoleon upset all Europe.

Cobden,[*(4)] a crank, came down to Siena to lay a wreath on the tomb of Sallustio Bandini;[†(5)] but a less advertised investigation was set on foot by Palmerston,[6] and has been conveniently or inconveniently forgotten. The New Economists may look into this.[7]

Your present correspondent is looking ahead, not prophesying that anything will happen, but trying to open the general eye to a few possibilities of the European situation.

Balzac and his followers have given a good deal of publicity to the dream of a United States of Europe.[8] But there is an older dream based on perceptions and instincts far more vigorous than rough analogy with the U.S. Constitution and the Articles of Confederation.[9]

The watchful reader should not fall into the error of supposing this dream to be purely, or merely, Italian. The Roman Empire civilized the occident as

[*] **Richard Cobden** (1804–65), English Liberal and economist.
[†] **Sallustio Bandini** (1677–1760), Italian economist.

we know it. The IDEAL was so solid that it persisted in Constantinople for centuries. It persisted in German Europe, in the very terminology of the Rulers. It was an ideal of ORDER, not of bunk, not of humanitarian illogicallity but of a POSSIBLE ORDER functioning amid very perfect human beings without any calculations being made on their sudden and/or total amelioration before next Saturday fortnight.

Obviously no man will be able to THINK the revival of the Roman Empire clearly unless he have fairly clear and articulate idea of what the old Roman Empire was and how it came into being.

Dr. Walton McDaniel writes to me[10], "Few people realize what a disease usury was in the (Roman) Republican period."

My own hypothesis is that the Roman Empire became possible when the Greek (maritime) usury system gave way to the more moderate agrarian usury of the Romans. I am not going to try to condense the economic history of 900 or 1200 years into one paragraph.

As news of the month I am telling you that nonsense is being talked about the Roman Empire A.D. 1937.

An European Empire will not come into existence by anyone's conquering anyone else. A new Europe worth living in will not be welded by brute force or the efforts of French gun merchants to enlarge the market for their contrivances.

An ideal order and justice rose with the Roman Empire. That doesn't mean that Caesar made it. The Empire started before Caesar and went on through the processes of Antoninus, Constantine and Justinian.[11]

A new Empire can only come into being with the rise of a new concept of ECONOMIC JUSTICE, a higher and finer and saner justice than mankind has yet thought could be workable.

If you are watching Europe from Saint Paul, Minnesota, you should first know what NOT to believe. Be Missourians. Make them show you. Believe nothing in ANY paper until it is proved. Believe nothing until you find out how much of that paper's news is *selected* by the Birmingham Small Arms or Imperial Chemicals.[12] I should never believe a line in the London "Daily Herald." Europe is full of left wing papers that are worked by finance.

The Raffalovitch documents,[13] official papers of the Russian who was hiring the French press before 1914, have been printed (L'ABOMINABLE VENALITE DE LA PRESSE).[‡] I made a check up, once, and found that there were four French

---

[‡]Published by Librairie du Travail, Paris.

papers not run by the gun makers union (*Comité des Forges*) and even those four got a bit of advertising now and then.

Raffalovitch, toward the end of his very busy-busy career, thought the French press was too rotten to buy. Not enough suckers still believed it.

The real function of most French newspapers is purely emotional. Somebody who dislikes Mr. So-and-So is a blue-eared son of a sea cook's mate, etc. and pays a few centimes for the pleasure.

The English press is much subtler. The low papers print plenty of lies of all sizes, but the honorable organs OMIT. They have developed to an arch-angelic grade of perfection the art of omitting every vital idea.

The "Times" and "Telegraph" are cited in the Raffalovitch papers. The best-doctored news is due to the Shipping Interests. They run a legitimate business and have hardly any need to print lies, though do not advise any trusting widow to believe their financial experts and so-called economists.

The possibility of a Roman Empire is measurable by ATTRACTION. The worst elements in English high life keep trying to stir up friction between Italy and Jugoslavia.[14] There is no more reason for hostility between Jugoslavia and Italy than between Canada and the U.S.A.

All the civilization that there has ever been in the Dalmatian and Balkan countries went in from the Roman Empire and from Venice. Jugoslavia is a natural agricultural reserve and Italy its natural partner in exchange for art, culture and manufacturies.[§]

The movement for the so-called Universality of Rome[15] was started either in Poland or up in those parts. Hungary and Austria are already feeling the pleasant effects of Mussolini's solid intelligence.

Nobody but the vendors of powder and shot wants ructions in the Dalmatian segment. There is no part of the world where peace would be more likely to occur of itself if the populations were left free from fussers and meddlers. Or at any rate the shootings would have no more effect on international calm than have family feuds in Kentucky on American foreign relations.

AS FOR RUSSIA. It is pointed out that the late executions[16] bear close resemblance to the time-honored Slavic pogrom. Russia is very Russian; very, very Russian!

If the executions were faked and the celebrated collection of victims is now held in reserve to be distributed under a new set of aliases to gladden the world

[§]Events have caught up with this article, written before the Italo-Jugoslav agreement.

heart of world reds, that comedy is scarcely one that will impress the old world with the seriousness of Russians as Russians.

What counts in any country is the degree, the close, hard grain of its civilization. That lasts. There was—past tense—a pogrom in Siena in 1799[17] after they had had a particularly nasty piece of work called Aaron or something of that sort as commissar for the French revolution. There is today no anti-semitism in Italy. When trying to understand a foreign country, try to know what it has already LIVED THROUGH.

The last heretic was burnt at the stake in Portugal when the Inquisition was revived in 1824 or '26. The Russians will in time live through certain phases of violence, so will the Spaniards. But nations that have already passed through their chicken pox and measles probably will not go back and do it again.

Nobody or almost nobody who hasn't lived for a long time in Italy, in different parts of Italy, realizes the amount and density of Italian knowledge. We have constant impressions of exuberance. An exuberant Venetian carried my suitcases three quarters of a mile only last evening because he wasn't prudent enough to wait and watch me buy him a ticket on the little steamboat that carries people along the Grand Canal. He got to my door five minutes after I did and the steamboat company has four lire less this morning. That is due in part to their courtesy in refunding the price of the tickets when I pointed out that man and baggage had disappeared.

Some of the men and books worth notice for any traveler who wants to understand what is going on in the Europe he visits are: Christopher Hollis' TWO NATIONS, Professor H.C.F. Bell's LORD PALMERSTON and Montgomery Butchart's MONEY.[18]

Ezra Pound (Signature)

[1] See note for **EP1.**
[2] "Manchester School" was a term that British Prime Minister Benjamin Disraeli popularized in referring to the United Kingdom's Liberal free trade movement in the nineteenth century. The movement's followers advocated that government take a laissez-faire approach to the economy.
[3] **Holy Roman Emperor and Grand Duke of Tuscany, Leopold II**
[4] **Richard Cobden**
[5] See **EP3**
[6] **Henry John Temple**
[7] Group of economic theorists led in large part by British economist **John Maynard Keynes,** who argued that governments needed to intervene to guide and restrain capitalist forces. Keynes' evolving ideas on these matters were first disseminated widely in 1926, when he published his essay "The End of Laissez

Faire." During the world Depression of the 1930s, "New Economics" gained prominence in Europe and the United States.

[8] Pound's reference to "Balzac" in this context is obscure.

[9] The Articles of Confederation were agreed to by the Continental Congress on November 15, 1777. They were ratified and went into effect on March 1, 1781. The Articles were comprised of a preamble and thirteen articles. The Articles provided for a very weak central government, according the maximum amount of power to the states to control their own internal affairs. This was reflected in the provisions dictating that any measure of Congress had to be passed by consent of nine of the thirteen states and that all thirteen states had to agree to any modification of the federal government's power. This loose coalition of the former colonies proved to be almost unworkable as far as mutual defense, federal legislation, taxation, and international and interstate commerce was concerned. Inevitably, a convention of the thirteen states was convened to amend the Articles in Philadelphia in 1787. However, rather than simply amend them, the convention decided to scrap the Articles and created the present Constitution of the United States. It was ratified in 1789.

[10] **Walton Brooks McDaniel**

[11] **Antoninus Pius, Constantine I, Justinian**

[12] See "Abdication" (Contribution #1) note 31.

[13] **Arthur Germanovich Raffalovich**

[14] Pound wrote this article as Italy and Yugoslavia were making diplomatic overtures toward one another. On March 25, 1937, Italy and Yugoslavia signed a treaty guaranteeing the existing borders and maintaining the status quo in the Adriatic. However, relations between the two nations were tense throughout the interwar period. Italy participated in the invasion of Yugoslavia by Germany in 1941 and seized Yugoslav territory along the Adriatic.

[15] In 1933, Mussolini's fascists launched the Comitati d'Azione per l'Universalità di Roma, a kind of fascist "international" to help organize fascist movements outside of Italy. By the mid-1930s, the committee had contact with about forty such groups across the world, including a fledgling fascist movement in Poland. Despite Pound's assertion, the committee was financed, organized and directed primarily by Italian fascists.

[16] Beginning with the murder of his rival Sergei Kirov on December 1, 1934, Stalin launched what came to be known as "The Great Terror." In his study of the period, Robert Conquest gives this assessment of Kirov's murder: "This killing has every right to be called the crime of the century. Over the next four years, hundreds of Soviet citizens, including the most prominent political leaders of the Revolution, were shot for direct responsibility for the assassination, and literally millions of other went to their deaths for complicity in one or another part of the vast conspiracy which allegedly lay behind it" (Conquest, *Terror*, 1990). The Terror cut through all of Russian society. The

victims of the purge included many high-ranking Communist Party officials, military personnel, writers, intellectuals, scientists, and academicians, as well as common people. Others were sent into exile or to labor camps. Beginning in 1936, Stalin held several notorious "show trials" in which high-ranking members of the party were charged with and condemned for conspiring with Leon Trotsky to assassinate Stalin as well as other conspiracies to overthrow the government of the Soviet Union.

[17] The Jewish community in Siena is an old one, dating back before 1229. There was opposition to the Jewish community in Siena, especially from the Franciscans, because of their financial and commercial importance to the city. But the Jews held their own and had fairly free range of the city. It was Duke Cosmo I, who, under Church pressure and looking for a grander title, introduced the ghetto into Tuscany. Siena was one of the cities in which a Jewish ghetto was established. When in the spring of 1799 Napoleon's troops entered the city, the Jews were granted full citizenship and the ghetto was dissolved. However, in the summer of that year, angry rioters from an adjacent region entered Siena and attacked the Jews, killing thirteen. After the riots, many Jews left the city.

[18] **Christopher Hollis'** *Two Nations* (1935); Herbert C. F. Bell's *Lord Palmerston* (1936); and **Montgomery Butchart's** *Money: Selected Passages Presenting the Concepts of Money in the English Tradition 1640-1935* (1935). At the time, Hollis was doing economic research at Notre Dame University; Bell was a professor of European History at Wesleyan University; and Butchart, who had taught at several American universities, was living in London.

Contribution #3: "Revolution by Radio"[1]

Globe June 1937 issue, pp. 95–7

If the GLOBE reader would turn his mind to the serious and constructing parts of Europe, he must pardon me for writing in a less snappy and sparky manner. It is impossible to send on real news without at least a few technicalities.

EZRA POUND

Revolution by Radio

Rapallo, Italy.

In our time the real revolutions have gone on unhindered. I have never read one single line of propaganda against the REAL REVOLUTIONS.

Marconi won the 1918 revolution in Russia. You can find that in John Reed's "Ten Days."[2] Nothing was further from Marconi's[3] mind when he carried on the development of wireless from where the American Loomis[4] had left it in the 1860's.

Without radio Lenin could not have won. In Italy, Mussolini threw out an exotic parliamentary form[5]. In the 1850's Cavour* had introduced this northern violet and spent a decade teaching the Piedmontese how to be parliamentarian.[6] In England in 1936 parliament resigned, gave over what shreds of power it had to a secret committee of usurer's pot boys.

The real revolution HAD OCCURRED. In our time the jaw house system, the system wherein delegates of the people govern by argument in a "chamber," gave way to government by newspapers.

Parliamentary government ceded to newspaper government. In 1936 Roosevelt beat the press[7]—that is, he beat the most corrupt forces in the U.S.A. then in control of the printed page. The real fight was by radio.

Newspaper government gives way to radio government. The bank pimps in England kept Edward OFF the radio until he ceased to be Edward VIII. Morgan's pal, the arch-noise of the English Church, was at once on the air.[8]

So far as I know, Italy has preceded all the pretendedly democratic countries in putting a session of her chamber on the air in the autumn of 1936.

Herein is the REAL REVOLUTION now evolving in Europe. The ideological war is by comparison isolated. More really isolated than the mass barbarism in Spain. The gun-makers' game is to keep trouble in process as long as possible for the natural sake of a larger munitions market.

If the reader is trying to understand Europe 1937, let him see the thing in three planes:

1. BASIC: the revolution from parliamentary to newspaper, and thence to radio government.

2. OBSCURANTIST: the pseudo-ideological tosh in all newspapers and in all printed matter having a large circulation; the false issues that the British press feeds its readers; the perpetual betrayals of the "left" of the popular parties by Macdonalds, Atlees†, and Blums,[9] either from natural and slimy corruption or from blockheadedness.

3. THE REAL struggle in the domain of intellect, which is and has for a decade been in the monetary domain. Mistrust every editor, every writer however celebrated who won't answer straight questions about the nature of money and its mode of issue. He is either a knave or a fool. In most cases he may be the dirtiest kind of knave, one who damps down his and other men's curiosity. H. G. Wells stalls,[10] the Archbishops of England put their tails

---

*Count Cavour (1810–61), great constructive statesman of modern Italy.

†C. R. Attlee, a temporary leader of the English Labour Party.

between their fat and thin legs and ran to cover after the Church Assembly had opened the question.[11] There is not a newspaper in England on EITHER side whose letter columns are open to free discussion of money. There is no real news in the French papers.[‡]

The victory of the Opposition in the London elections[12] doesn't or wouldn't necessarily mean anything in itself, save that the contrivers of British misery find it more convenient to use one set of straw-men than another. But the chance that there after all may be "something in it" was first indicated by a statement in "Reynolds"[§] for February 14th, when their Political Correspondent assured their readers that the Opposition does not object to interest on genuine loans—that is, loans in which the lender parts with his own money. It will certainly ask the House of Commons: "Why must the Government pay interest to a bank for creating and lending money which the Government can create for itself?"

The enlightened American reader will see that England in 1937 has drooled along to where our forebears were in the 1830's or in the time of Tom Jefferson: Jeff, Andy Jackson, and Van Buren all having observed that a government needn't pay interest.[13]

EZRA POUND (Signature)

[1] "Revolution by Radio" was a truncated and slightly modified essay taken from two sections of a longer, unpublished essay that Pound entitled "...And Excursions" (Contribution #12).
[2] In Chapter 9 of *Ten Days that Shook the World* (1920), American journalist John Reed related how Lenin and the Bolsheviks issued radios to all regiments, divisions, and soldier committees to efficiently convey propaganda and directives.
[3] **Guglielmo Marchese Marconi**
[4] **Mahlon Loomis**
[5] In 1922, Mussolini and his Black Shirts staged the so-called March on Rome that initiated the dissolution of the Italian Parliament with the sanction of Italy's King Victor Emmanuel II, and the foundation of Mussolini's government.
[6] **Count Camillo Benso di Cavour**
[7] A survey of the US newspapers showed that in the 1936 election 57 percent endorsed Alfred Landon, the Republican candidate for president, while only 36 percent endorsed Franklin Roosevelt. Roosevelt did not have the majority of newspaper endorsements in the 1932, 1940, or 1944 elections.
[8] **Cosmo Gordon Lang**

[‡]Editor's note: An excellent book on English newspapers is *The English Press* by Jane Soames (London, 1936).
[§]*Reynolds's Illustrated News*, English weekly newspaper.

[9] **Ramsay MacDonald** and **Clement Richard Attlee**
[10] **H. G. Wells**
[11] See "Abdication" (Contribution #1), note 22.
[12] The Labour Party took control of the London County Council in 1934, and strengthened its position in subsequent elections in the 1930s. Meanwhile, the national government was led by the Conservative Party. This section came from the beginning of "...And Excursions" (Contribution #12).
[13] Pound was referring to the notion that governments should not have to depend upon private banking institutions, which charge interest, for loans to undertake projects or provide services that further the common good of the nation. Pound saw this as an unnecessary encumbrance and was, as were the presidents he mentioned, against a national banking system which might give private financiers too much power over the federal government and the national economy. Perhaps still one of the most important books on these issues in early American history is Arthur Schlesinger, Jr.'s *The Age of Jackson* (1945).

Contribution #4: "Net Result"

Globe July 1937 issue, pp. 101–5

Rapallo, Italy

Whoever is right or wrong, 50/50 or 45/45 wrong, right, mixed or fictitious in Spain,[1] the net result in England is that all the active hot heads are neatly drained out of the country and the chances of disturbing the fugg reduced to the level most likely to please the present owners of privilege.
Instead of peppering his obese uncle in the bosom of the pants with a little bird shot, on the off chance it would make him think, Winston Churchill's nephew takes his best gal to Spain to shoot Spaniards.[2]

A young society lady (Spanish) deeply shocked at Spanish reds, tells me they weren't shooting HER friends and the rich but merely the small town baker and drugstore proprietor. She wouldn't have blamed 'em for shooting the rich.

The neat balance between number of "national" and "governmental" troops allowed to infiltrate[3] might seem to the sarcastic eye very nicely contrived to maintain munitions sales as long as possible under the circumstances; whatever ideology be used to cover the maneuver, and whichever side was out for tin mines, oil markets, etc.

The dirt I got two years ago on Catalonia was "straight." One gang in Barcelona dislike Madrid's collecting taxes and "governing" and the other side dislike the idea of having to pass manufactured goods across a customs barrier [sic]. Hence the continuing local "warmth" re separation and union [sic].

Several events have occurred that might be said to have cheered men of my persuasion. 1. Blum,[4] whom I consider a thoroughly bad lot, ran true to form in advocating a tax on books. I consider Blum an undercover man for the money monopoly. And the usurers' party has ALWAYS and unfailingly been against verbal expression. It has always done its utmost to hamper true writing of history, free speech and an effective communications service.

2. The attempt to sell out India to "Imperial Chemicals"[5] produced a certain amount of friction. This definition of the "New Constitution for India" is not my own. I had it from one of the few high Indian officials whom I have been able to meet.

3. "The King" (George VI) annoyed the sons of hell and corruption by proposing to visit the Fenland flooded districts.[6] The British Government decided that such sign of humanity on George's part would be untimely. It would in fact bring his departed brother to mind. I trust these little similarities will be multiplied.

4. The continental press openly speculates on the direct profit to Baldwin's firm,[7] and connections in the steel trade, likely to result from the rearmament racket.

In the face of continuous lying, voluntary and involuntary, the reader might do well to sift for himself the undeniable and established, from any rumors and explanations.

1. Spain provides a gun market. Any gun market is profitable to gun makers. There is no record of gun makers trying to diminish their own market. Pacifists (I mean the professionals) have done, I think, NOTHING to make peace desirable.

2. I suggest that the lower the state of a nation's culture the easier it is for more highly organized nations (or groups in such nations) to cause trouble inside the less civilized states. Nations having a very small group of civilized or hyper-refined inhabitants are peculiarly unstable. I mean not only in respect to nations where there is a high literacy level (meaning very few analphabetics) but in relation to say Bulgaria, where there is supposed to be a "peasant level" . . . and considerable immunity to naval persuasion. (Nothing for the blighters to bombard, as in case of Greece or nations with seaboard culture.)

3. I notice, for what it may imply, that the French or frog franc dropped three or four points against sterling and lire the day BEFORE the papers carried the news of red reverses at Madrid. "People" do not maintain an expensive information service for nothing.

On the other hand "Socialists" whose habit it is to maintain a bourgeois level of life do not take an interest in elimination of interest on money save the theoretical total abolition of interest (which is unjust and impractical). I would gladly receive data re any writing socialist who isn't looking for a state or university job maintained now by money interest on endowments or by taxes levied by the state or on private investments, like Millionaire Blum, the French stool pigeon.

Taking Fuller's report,[8] with impressions conveyed from the other side, one must suppose that there are decent men on both sides of the Spanish fighting line. Those of them that ARE decent want very much the same things. The war profits ONLY the foreign, chiefly frog, gun-sellers. Every day that it continues is a loss to Spain as Spain, and to Spaniards. The longer it can be kept going, the more even the opposed forces can be kept, the greater the gun-sellers. The reader of these letters must decide whether he wants me to send the real news or mere "colorful items." The real news is of necessity technical. Nothing is easier than to say Europe is going to hell. Every country has its chiselers.

The deadly and undying war is between life and the money-monopolists. The latter fear EVERY sort of order and organization. Politics, head lines, etc., do NOT matter in the sense that the monopolist don't care WHAT the people "call it." He must have disorder.

The American reader who won't read Martin Van Buren's autobiography[9] and a few hundred pages of American history as was in the 1830 simply can NOT understand the subsequent events in American and European history.

These letters are not written to teach the reader kindergarten economics, but he must know that such subjects exist or his view of Europe will be no more intelligent than that printed by the luxury trades or the "Why don't they eat cake?" of Madame de Lamballe or whatever other lady friend of Marie Antoinette said it.[10]

From now on we must have the new news sense. Every railway bookstall on the continent is covered with WAR FOR OIL, WAR FOR COTTON by Messrs. DGHKZ and Mr. Ktlzp etc. atrocities and unprincipled romance, translated into six languages. These things are no longer left to highbrows and heavy professors. But the real wars, the wars for money monopoly haven't yet got onto the stalls.

The tribute to one of my ABC's which I prize above all others came from the brilliant hard-boiled Paris correspondent of a string of American newspapers: "HELL! This can't be economics! I can understand this."[11]

There is nothing highbrow about it. It is as simple as 3 card monte, and a million suckers bite every week. The news is hard to get in some cases. Ever since Albert Londres wrote LA CHINE EN FOLIE,[12] French publishers have had out their drag nets trying to equal that story of "China gone crazy" which perhaps even Londres could never again have matched had he lived. "Paris Soir," despairing of staff reporters, mobilized Jean Cocteau with results: MON PREMIER VOYAGE, tour of the world in 80 days.[13] (GLOBE stuff, all of it, that anyone can read.)

Ezra Pound [Signature]

[1] In July 1937, the Spanish Civil War had been under way for slightly more than a year.
[2] Eighteen-year-old Esmond Romilly, the nephew of Winston Churchill's wife Clementine, eloped to fight for the Republican cause in Spain with his second cousin Jessica "Decca" Mitford, 19, daughter of Lord and Lady Redesdale. Romilly and Mitford were both members of the Communist Party, and the British newspapers trumpeted Churchill's "red nephew." The couple later sailed to America. In 1939, Romilly joined the Canadian Air Force. In 1941 he was killed on a World War II combat mission. Mitford eventually remarried and settled in the United States. Later she became the author of *The American Way of Death,* an exposé of the funeral industry. She died in 1996.
[3] Pound may have been referring to the Non-Intervention Committee (NIC). In 1936, the French and British governments formed NIC to try and enforce an arms embargo of the Iberian Peninsula. Later NIC worked out proposals for the withdrawal of foreign combatants from the conflict. Though Italy and Germany eventually signed agreements to this effect, in the end, Italy, Germany, and Russia did not comply with the terms.
[4] For **Léon Blum**, see **EP29** note 12.
[5] The Government of India Act 1935 was a British plan to create semi-autonomous states and provinces in India. Only part of the whole plan went into effect in April 1, 1937, granting limited autonomy to several of India's provinces. The act favored investment in India by British corporations like Imperial Chemical Industries (today ICI), which worked out deals with separate provincial governments.
[6] The Fens is a region of England bordering upon the Wash. It includes Cambridgeshire, Lincolnshire, and West Norfolk. Though this swampy, inhospitable region is under control today, before World War II it was prone to frequent and disastrous flooding. Pound was apparently referring to a proposed royal visit to one such flood site in the Fens. The consternation Pound reported among government officials may have reflected the fear of an incident similar to that created by Edward VIII's sympathetic, but supposedly unconstitutional, comments on the plight of Welsh miners when the king visited impoverished regions in Wales in November 1936 (see "Abdication" [Contribution #1] note 26).
[7] After retiring from politics in 1937, **Stanley Baldwin** became chairman of Imperial Relations Trust. Also see **EP11**.

[8] **Major-General John Frederick Charles Fuller**
[9] *The Autobiography of Martin Van Buren* (1833).
[10] **Marie-Thérèse-Louise, Princesse de Lamballe**
[11] Pound could be referring to **Guy Hickok** of the *Brooklyn Daily Eagle*.
[12] **Albert Londres**
[13] **Jean Cocteau** published *Mon Premier Voyage, Tour du Monde en 80 Jours* in 1936. The book was an account of his efforts to repeat the journey of Jules Verne's character Phineas Fogg in the 1873 classic *Around the World in 80 Days*. Cocteau's trip and book arose from a challenge from an editor at *Paris Soir.*

Contribution #5: "Deflation Benefit"[1]
Globe August 1937 issue, pp. 66–71

For "Deflation Benefit," see **EP21, JD15, JD16, JD17, JD22**

I can not repeat too often my conviction that the only way to understand Europe (or any other continent) is by a collection of details, though most of them will appear irrelevant and unconnected. Under any news there is money. Anything whatever that gets a headline is probably red-herring. Coronations, Abdications, Supreme Courts, Riots in Clichy, Trouble in Morocco, all take the public mind off the one basic issue, which is the monopolization of claims against wealth, mandates against the harvest. There are probably not two hundred men in all Europe who keep their eye on the root problem. Men who ought to know better are led off into by-paths; they are duped either by the great cinema flim-flam or caught in sectarian theories.

Rapallo, Italy

At the cost of enormous human suffering, deflation has conferred one, and so far as I know only one, benefit on cultured Europe—it has formed the New Hungarian Quartet.[2] It has taken the deflation at least a decade to do this, and the most block-headed reader will see quite quickly that such a benefit is preferential: i.e. it can affect only the minute part of European public that could afford 20 lire for a biennial concert ticket in Venice or ten lire in less exclusive (economically speaking) congregations.

About 15 years ago the Inflation was beneficial to a somewhat larger segment of the privileged class. During the inflation, at the price of enormous human suffering, it was possible to print *de luxe* books. Money was going down in value per unit, and people had to BUY something, or as result lose for a few years the stifling censorship exercised by the cheap publishers; and the big distributing agencies (sometimes unconsciously) could be broken by printing magnificently what could not be made to pay in wood pulp editions. With the end of the watered money came the end of this campaign for books which AS BOOKS tried to equal those of Soncino and Bodoni as issued in 1500's and 1700's.[3]

"Concert life is dead." This is the other side of the story. Ten or more years ago Germany had 80 state operas. As a measure of *economy* (that is, of folly) the number was cut down to 40. This didn't, or at least didn't immediately mean an improvement in quality. Germany lost Maestro Piccadri (Cologne director). I have not heard that the quality of Cologne performances improved.

It was only last September that I drew my first cultural dividend on the deflation. Four soloists: Sandor Vegh, Laszlo Halmos, Denes Koromzay, and Vilmos Palotai in 1935 gave up solo careers and got together.[4] And let your aged friend tell you they make a QUARTET spelling the whole word in capitals. And those who only heard them in Venice don't know the 'arf of it, dearie.

In a period of inflation they in all probability would have been out starring, each on his own. There is no way of proving that even men of their musical integrity with an interest in music exceeding an interest in personal limelight would have coalesced, had they been young in 1925 instead of the present decade. There is no use my reporting in GLOBE the facts already divulged in the N.Y. "Herald-Tribune" Telegraph Service unless such events have been "interpreted" out of all relation to fact (which is unlikely) or out of all relation to significance, which is almost unavoidable.

The most significant events are not usually in the much printed news. I don't mean hidden events in the world of art which "are to mean to our children," but statal events, which will certainly mean MORE almost immediately.

Among cultural events is the drive toward microphotographic editions of vast music treasures now hidden in the libraries of Europe from Turin to Upsala, a drive due in large part to the researches of the American Violinist Rudge,[5] though the fact has hardly percolated her native Ohio. In fact even the New York reader may know her only as a name credited with translations of Vivaldi's correspondence lavishly quoted by Lawrence Gilman in the N.Y. "Herald-Tribune" for January 3.[6]

All of which dates back to the propaganding of the very amiable and "crazy" Bob (Robert Carlton) Brown[7] who years ago bored all his friends with the theory unkindly summarized as "the conviction that if we only read FAST enough, we needn't bother to understand ANYthing." Brown's propaganda for a "reading machine" has had one result, or ran concurrently with a result known to every wide-awake American librarian. Newspapers are now filed in microphotographic records. Newspapers, since wood pulp came into use, do not keep their natural state.

Europe is slowly awakening to the fact that vast quantities of musical composition quite as good as the "best culturally known" are lying unusable in the archives, or get published in silly editions which merely irritate better performers.

In another ten years ALL serious publications of Vivaldi, Bocherini,[8] Porpora,[9] and the hundred other masters of European Music from 1200 to 1750 will be accompanied by a little strip of micro-photoreproductions, even midget film size. American participation in this reform or renaissance will be counted as further proof of the GLOBAL form of the planet.

I don't see how my news is to be intelligible unless the reader has at least a vest pocket guide to the Continent that I *think* I am writing from.

Starting with Russia, I am a Leninite. I like Lenin's writing. I do NOT like Trotsky's essays on literature.[10] When I say I admire Lenin, I mean it. Italians admire Lenin. Lots of Italians speak well of him. When Mussolini lately told a bunch of Americans that "all Italians respect Jefferson and Franklin," I regard that as politeness or as what is called "rising to the occasion." I don't believe that more than a handful of Italian highbrows have ever heard of Thomas Jefferson. Back in 1850 a lot of Europeans had heard of him, but they mostly thought of George Washington. Anyhow, that lot has died off.

I trust I am not being too technical. Secondly, I believe what an old English general told me. I'd have believed it even if he hadn't told me. He said the mainstay of peace in Europe is this Italo-German friendship. The Italians call it the "Rome-Berlin axis." Old "Bib" Ibbotson blew through Rapallo on his way *hin und zuruk* from Germany.[11] His nephews are in all sorts of businesses in Germany, his wife having been German. He gasps and says: "The LIES that you read about Germany!" He was full of enthusiasm for what he had seen there in the way of their being well fed and eating, in the way of being well housed.

So far as I know there are only two countries that will provide one with any FACTS. If I want to know something in particular I write to somebody at the Forschungsinstitut, Frankfurt-am-Main (where is the Afrikaarchiv) and I get back in 48 hours, or say three or four days at the outside, a monograph on African drums or monetary usage in the South Seas; along with a letter and a few references to bulkier volumes.[12] This contrasts favorably with news from a young man in Cambridge (England), sic: "He (the student's advisor) admitted that it had nothing to do with real life, but said the course couldn't be changed." Or the Professor from Cambridge, Massachusetts, who said you couldn't hurry the changes because you had to wait for seniority (i.e. for the old blokes to die off).

Or else (I mean when I want facts) I write or go down to Rome, where there are a half dozen monthly magazines run by Cabinet ministers or edited by some man whom they advise. I heard a foreign office chap teasing Por about writing for "clandestine reviews."[13] Por is the brightest economist in this country. These reviews are (my suffering Tom Cats! ! !) dull. They are written NOT for the casual reader, but for blokes who have got to do something about it.

Distinguish between TWO very distinct sets of phenomena. The Italian writing about literature is in the main small town piffle, for example in Valitutti's "Civilta Fascista"[14] we have Julien Benda's "Trahison des Clercs" dated as 1933.[15] Fifteen years ago this work was being noted in the "Dial" and "Criterion."[16] Italian literary organs are full of stale fugg about French books that died in the early 1920's. But on the other hand, almost any Italian magazine which touches sociology or questions of government structure makes any English paper on the same subject read like infantile twaddle or the maunderings of adolescent ignorami. The same issue of the "Civilta Fascista" contains phrases on the state which are definitely outside the grasp of the normal English and American reader. They dig down to a strata of seriousness which no English or American writer can count on finding in his audience. And they are written for a kind of reader with whom it is almost impossible to communicate in our periodicals.

Two or three decades ago the name of Mme. Montessori rang through the world of children's schools.[17] When the Fascist Regime took over, the idea that infants of six might be amused rather than developed in gloom made another step forward. The idea that reading was funny entered the primary text books in Italy. A bit later a wail ascended from the "advanced" (Italian and other) that Religious Instruction had been put back into the schools, and that another era of darkness and superstition was being imposed on the Italians.

It is unlikely that the "advanced" will look into one of the actual text books. Having done so, I think they won't do very much harm. *That* (for children of eleven) might even indicate why Christianity has not, as a rule, in Italy degenerated into that pest, eccentricity, incentive to oppressions and witch-burnings, as it has so often become in countries not built on a "classic" basis. Mediterranean moderation appears in a prayer for rain:

O God, in whom we live and move and are, concede a restoring rain so that we, aided sufficiently in our earthly needs, may reach up with greater trust to eternal things. So be it.

A prayer for serenity (that is, fair weather) :

We implore, omnipotent God, thy clemency so that thou, having made to cease the flooding rain, shalt show to us through the calm sky the hilarity of thy face. In the name of Jesus Christ our Savior. So be it.

These seem to me to belong rather to the universal religion of all men than to any sect or fad of religion. This universality was, and perhaps still is, one of the ideals of the "Church."

After these and a few more prayers I find "Il Cantico del Sole" of St. Francis;[18] here and there a verse quotation; Fogazzaro on the bells;[19] a bit of Manzoni;[20] "I Templi" of Silvio Pellico;[21] a bit of psalm, and a rather beautiful passage from the Mass translated into Italian so that the reader shouldn't think that the Mass is mere mumbo jumbo in Latin. St. Francis' poem is, or should be, in any early Italian anthology. The anecdotes of the few Saints are such as could be in any school reader: they tell of commendable human actions, not of eccentricities or excesses. It is impossible to get everything in to one school book: if Mazzini [22] is not attacked for fanaticism, his constructive acts are recorded; and Cavour [23] is praised with masterly succinctness, sic: "Through deep study and long travels he came to understand the needs of the Italian people . . . As head of the government he improved with wise provisions the condition of agriculture, industry, and commerce. . . "

Space does not permit me to give an exhaustive study of the Italian school system, but I do not think the present regime has anything to fear for equanimous examination of it . . . until one gets up to the somnolent universities, and there, if you compare them with those in our own "blessed" etc. country . . . I dare say we should not be found better off. I have no idea where "the text book racket" has now got to in America. I do know that I have on my desk a child's schooling for a grade. One book, eleven lire, 648 pages plus a geographical supplement; illustrated by not very brilliant halftones of a nature to interest anyone. Cathedrals, paintings, savages, farm machinery, animals, magnets, fossils, an appalling amount of arithmetic aimed at practical life. Cover: the Victory (antique statue) of Brescia,[24] and an airplane. Also, by chance, the GLOBE (or a Globe) as background.

King Edward was a card,
But ladies were debarred
From the precincts of the Castle,
so he left 'em.[25]

The triumphant passage of the Windsors across Europe has been very pleasant, the people just like 'em. There has been nothing fixed. The press has known the news value, but the popular good will has been utterly spontaneous.[26]

EZRA POUND [Signature]

[1] In this title Pound used the term "deflation" to refer to the Depression of the 1930s. Deflation is defined as a simultaneous drop in the money supply and in prices for goods and services. The overall value of the economy thus "deflates."
[2] The New Hungarian Quartet, founded in 1935. Its original members were

Sándor Végh (1912–97), László Halmos (1909–97), Denes Koromzay (1913–2001), and Vilmos Palotai (?–?). The group quickly developed a reputation throughout Europe. The quartet was formed in part due to the fact that it was increasingly difficult for individual musicians in Europe to find sufficient employment. In 1950, the group moved to the United States, where it remained until disbanding in 1970. Pound wrote of the Hungarian Quartet, its performance at the 1936 Venice Biennial, and its upcoming concert (February 18, 1937) in Rapallo in an Italian article in the local paper *Il Mare* (see Schafer, *Pound and Music,* pp. 420–1; also see pp. 399–401).

[3] The Soncino family of Northern Italy were Renaissance Jewish printers who began produced books in the 1400s. Giambattista Bodoni (1740–1813) of Parma, Italy was renowned for the quality of his editions.

[4] See note 2 above.

[5] **Olga Rudge**

[6] **Lawrence Gilman**

[7] For **Robert Carlton Brown,** see **JD15** note 16.

[8] **Luigi Boccherini**

[9] **Niccolo Antonio Porpora** (1686–1766), Italian composer and teacher of singing. Franz Joseph Haydn was one of Porpora's pupils.

[10] Pound was probably referring to **Leon Trotsky**'s *Literature and Revolution* (1924).

[11] For **Joseph Darling "Bibb" Ibbotson,** see **EP16** note 9.

[12] The Afrikaarchiv is still housed at the Frobenius-Institut in Frankfurt am Main. The Frobenius-Institut is the successor institution to the Forschungsinstitut für Kulturmorphologie, founded by **Leo Frobenius.**

[13] **Odon Por**

[14] Probably a reference to an article by Salvatore Valitutti (1907–92) in the journal *Civilita fascista: Rivista mensile organo dell'Istituto Nazionale fascista di cultura* in which the author made an error as to the publication date of Julien Benda's novel.

[15] **Julien Benda** (1867–1956), French author. His *Trahison des clercs* was published in 1927.

[16] For *The Dial*, see **EP2** and **EP4** and **Marianne Craig Moore.** For *The Criterion*, see **EP4** and **John Cournos.**

[17] **Maria Montessori**

[18] "Il Cantico del Sole" of St. Francis of Assisi (1182?–1226). Pound provides a translation of this poem in his *Spirit of Romance* (1910).

[19] **Antonio Fogazzaro**

[20] **Silvio Pellico**

[21] **Alessandro Manzoni**

[22] **Giuseppe Mazzini**

[23] **Count Camillo Benso di Cavour**

[24] Pound was referring to a first-century bronze Nike in the collection of the Brescia Museum. It was excavated from the Temple of Vespasian in Brescia, Italy.
[25] For Pound's doggerel on the abdication of Edward VIII, see **EP11**.
[26] **Edward**, now the Duke of Windsor, and his soon-to-be wife **Wallis Simpson** traveled to several European cities after his abdication, and according to press accounts were greeted by friendly crowds everywhere.

Contribution #6: "Interview with Mrs. Unterguggenberger"
Globe October 1937 issue, pp. 70–4

For "Interview with Mrs. Unterguggenberger,"see **EP3, EP29, EP32**

Ezra Pound

I am, in these letters, trying to let the globe reader know a few things that happened before GLOBE started, and in ignorance of which nobody can get the real hang of Europe

Five years ago a little Austrian town in the mountains[1] (whose key note is solid simplicity), up there more or less near Salzburg and Innsbruck, put the wind up all the worst skunks in Europe. A bloke with a six barrel name started to print local money marked (in German) EASES NEED, GIVES WORK AND BREAD. Also *Als Notabgabe ist monatlick 1% in Marken zu entrichten*, meaning "you got to put on 1% of the face value in stamps per month to keep this valid." Little town of four to five thousand inhabitants.

And Mrs. Unterguggenberger[2] (I told you it was a six barrel'd name) said to me in her little shop where she sells mountaineer shirts and those funny little short-laced panties that the Tyrolese wear to display their nobbly big knees: "My husband knew it was money, but he pretended it wasn't." The gent with the name[3] was having a walk up the mountain, so I got the side lights from his missus.
This you understand was *the* stamp scrip demonstration. *The* proof that the dang'd stuff will *work*. The town got on its feet and out of bankruptcy. They gave work to more people, though the main point of course was that the new school teachers etc. could *eat* before or after their labors. And people began to come into Wörgl from the surrounding countryside. At first they used the scrip in the shops in Wörgl, then the shops in the surrounding villages began to accept it, and then it got up to Innsbruck, and the thunder started. The bank blighters in Innsbruck got the wind up;[4] they complained to Vienna, and Vienna said to Wörgl, "Get rid of that buggymeister." And the Wörglese said: "Wotter hell! We *like* the burgomeister we got. . . ."

So the bank blighters had a pseudo sham government in Vienna suppress the local government in the town of Wörgl, but the *news* had leaked out.

And as Mrs. Unter-etc. said to me: "He (Mr. U. etc.) said 'Nobody *knows* about Gesell.[5] If I do it, they'll at least have to talk.' "

Write they couldn't. I asked why didn't they write about it in the papers. Said Mrs. U.: "Do you realize that there is nobody in this village that is *able* to write a newspaper article?"

So Senator Bankhead talked in the U.S. Senate and even brought in a bill,[6] which his home state has apparently never heard of, and which the bright snappy boys in Paris "representing" (and how!) the alert go-getting American newspapers, hadn't heard of the year after Bankhead had proposed it.

And Mons. Daladier,[7] now French minister of War, went over to Wörgl, and Milford the Whoosis of Medici[8] went up to Wörgl. Mons. Daladier got up in the French Radical caucus and gave the old bustard Caillaux[9] the scare of his doddered senility by talking of stamp scrip. All out of a little town in the mountains. And ever since then Mr. Daladier has been kept *employed* on some job, like the frog war office, to keep him *out* of the treasury and to keep the frog farmers from gittin' frogskins.

And you can *not* tell E.P. that plain folks can't understand economics. They can get the real thing quick as blazes. I said to Mrs. Unterguggenetc.: "Now in Rapallo we've got *buoni di lavoro* and *buoni viveri*."[10]

Says she bright as a dollar: "Do they *circulate*?"

"Well," said I, "you can't exactly say that they *cir*culate. A bloke gets a work-ticket and that means he can be taken on for a day's work on the roads, and at the end he gets a food-ticket which he can spend in a Rapallo shop, and the shop, at the end of a fixed time can use it in paying its taxes. It circulates through a one, two, three circuit."

This was no use to an orthodox Gesellite, whose husband ran a milk route and was mayor of a small town in the mountains, while she kept a shop that sold cheap shirts and such like to the villagers. But don't tell me that she didn't understand scrip-money.

And Doc Fisher[*] wrote a book on the subject (like he does about everything).[11] And there is a nice big half tone of the Wörgl money in "La Stirpe" for Xmas 1935 by Mr. Por[†] who knows eggs from onions.[12] And so forth. . . . And

---

[*]**Irving Fisher**, Profesor of Political Economy, Yale; author *Stamp Scrip*, 1933 (ed.).

[†]Por is the brightest economist in this country (E.P.).

this year the mayor went and died on us. But for a small town mayor he had cut the danged largest notch of any small town mayor in Europe. And it ain't the *end*, not by no means. Johnnie Brown[13] wasn't all killed when they killed him.

I CAN'T with six pages per month get the news of Europe to the GLOBE readers unless they help, at least to the extent of knowing where else to look for the news. The plain people, often the active reformers among them, are prejudiced against highbrows. I've seen enough highbrows to know why. But I say: "Overlook it." The literary guy, when he is a good one, gets the *news* first.

Don't think I am crabbing the English. Here is what the liveliest living Englander has to say of his country:

> *. . . present system of government in England is a fake antique. It is a machine-made grandfather's clock. It is cleverly "faked" to look old; with eighteenth-century works; with a big wheezy tick; with a weatherbeaten face of bogus respectability and age. A full parliamentary cast performs for our benefit, . . . and all the rest of it, possessing as little political power as screen-stars in a House of Rothschild film. A disarming facade of 'democracy' conceals what is in fact a Money Trust, which runs us like a national waxworks, but for whom we are a side-line, not their main concern. We are not by any means the biggest pebble on the beach. As a 'nation' we have ceased to exist.*

That is Mr. Wyndham Lewis in *Count Your Dead—They are Alive*. His motto or slogan is, "Let us be free men again. Why not?"[14] He is as quick as I am to spot and debunk the fake Europe that John Gunther[15] pretended to be "Inside" of.

AS our old Swedish cook used to say, "dhry tdo bleaze,"[16] and if our editor wants what I know about the Near East, etc., I can get through it in a very few words. I once amused an ex-colonial governor. I don't think I knew he was an ex-governor. He was, to me, a pleasant sort of bloke I'd met at a lunch party in London. He said before I got through that he had long been that lowest of creatures, a bureaucrat. I quoted him Gertrude Bell.[17] "I believe," wrote Gertie to her mama or to someone, "that when not contrary to the interests of the Empire, our promises to the Arabs should be kept."

That is the voice of the Empire. Sir X. said, "Did Gertrude say that?"

And two months later I picked up "Vu"[‡] [18] and saw a piece about Sir X., "England's Authority on Mediterranean and Near Eastern affairs." But I had

‡ Snappy Parisian news weekly.

time to quote Gertrude, and to speak fairly plainly about Abyssinia,[19] he having put up some of the usual official Genevan cobwebs (that being in 1935).

I said, "A nation with low civilization, a nation of six hundred or two thousand or even less years behind contemporary civilization, cannot exist indefinitely along side of a higher civilization."
So he came down to brass tacks and admitted, "Yes, I suppose it will have to go." He is a sane man, and has read a few books fit to read more than once.

When it comes to stuff one can read in the papers, I notice that the last English scheme, according to the Continent, implies the shift of 250,000 Arabs from the coast, or comparatively habitable parts of Palestine,[20] to the uninhabitable or back-mountain districts. I don't see why they should like this.

"Waaal," says the editor, "what about Malta?"[21]

"Not so good," says your correspondent.

They were talking a mixture of Arabic and early Italian down in that island before the British language was heard of. Walter Scott's pet king (Richard Lionheart) went sailing out to the Holy Land and a pasha held up his best gal; but made his excuses in Turkish. Richard then made his only known effort to speak anything but his native Provençal. He said, "Ee spik lak a fole Britain."[22] However, the British seem to object to the Maltese speaking Italian; but the gun-range has now got so long that what the foreign office calls "the bloody ice-creamers" can sit right on the toe of the boot and chuck shells into Malta harbor, so maybe the *base* ain't so first.

Travelers should know that at least a decent mode of transport exists between Paris and London. The nastiest and most putrid characteristics of all nations show in their frontier parasites. Nothing can exceed the niggardly and blub-nosed degradation of frontier formalities. Ever since America was diddled by Colonel House[23] into electing our most deleterious and fish-faced President, Woodie Wilson,these inconveniences have festered. The turnstile at a French channel frontier would alone have justified the annihilation of that unhappy country as a political unit. And the British channel-boat flunkies have for years furnished a good basis for Anglophobia.

At last a channel train ferry carries or can carry a few privileged to and fro. And the customs-noses function only at Victoria Station No GLOBE reader should ever go soft and pardon legislators who cause the idiocies at frontiers. Before the late war, there were almost no passport formalities. We who remember that comparatively clean state of things should not allow the young to think the present festers have always existed.

Our own government has been chief among the spreaders of the passport and visa disease. No nation has worse frontier manners, though ours are, for obvious reasons, no filthier than the French and English. The bureaucrats put in by Wilson have done infinite harm to international minor relations. And his successors have got to be either eager or clever in curing the damage.

[1] In 1932, the Tyrolean town of Wörgl launched a brief stamp scrip experiment led by the town's Burgermeister, Michael Unterguggenberger (1884–1936). Pound visited the town twice, in 1935 and 1936. Pound's daughter Mary was living near the town in Gais at the time. Pound mentioned the Wörgl experiment in Canto LXXIV.

[2] Pound met Unterguggenberger's second wife, Rosa Schnaiter Unterguggenberger. Unterguggenberger's first wife, Maria Ender, died in 1917.

[3] Unterguggenberger died of heart failure on December 19, 1936. It is not known whether Pound ever met him.

[4] Unterguggenberger and the Wörgl government decided to issue stamp scrip as the Depression hit Austria in 1932, but press coverage of the decision caught the attention of Austrian National Bank officials. They pressured the state government, which forced the provincial government to prohibit Wörgl's "value coupons." After about a year of court wrangling over the prohibition, the coupons were withdrawn and the experiment stopped.

[5] Silvio Gesell (1852–1930), German economic thinker and author of *The Natural Economic Order*. Gesell argued the establishment of "Free Money," a form of stamp scrip which would be required to be used in a certain period of time, therefore limiting accumulation. Gesell's goal, advocated by many supporters throughout Europe and North America in the 1930s, was to eliminate accumulation of interest and force the rapid circulation of money.

[6] **Senator John Hollis Bankhead II** submitted legislation in 1933 supporting the idea of stamp scrip. The bill died in committee. Further efforts by Bankhead to attach stamp scrip amendments to legislation failed.

[7] In 1937, **Daladier** was working as vice-president of Council for the French Ministry of National Defense. Prior to that post, he held several positions, including in the Public Works Ministry.

[8] Not clear to which banking institution or official Pound is referring.

[9] **Joseph Caillaux**

[10] Pound seems to have been referring to a system of tickets issued as work permits (*buoni di lavoro*) which, after the work was completed, could be exchanged for a ticket/voucher for food (*buoni viveri*) at local Rapallo shops. The shop-keepers could then use them for tax payments. See next paragraph in article.

[11] **Irving Fisher**

[12] **Odon Por**

[13] **John Brown**

[14] *Count Your Dead—They Are Alive! Or, A New War in the Making* (1937).
[15] **John Gunther**
[16] This last part of the essay was lifted from sections of Pound's unpublished essay "On Pleasing." For notes on this portion, see "On Pleasing" (Contribution #11).
[17] **Gertrude Margaret Lowthian Bell**
[18] *Vu* was a Paris-based illustrated journal sympathetic to the French right. In 1935 Pound wrote a review article entitled "'Vu,' No. 380, and Subsequent Issues" for *The New Age* (October 31, 1935). This article focused upon articles for *Vu* by Francis Delaisi.
[19] Relations between the independent African nation of Ethiopia, headed by Emperor Haile Selassie, and Italy, which had colonies adjacent to Ethiopia in Eritrea and Somalia, were increasingly tense throughout the early 1930s. After a border clash in 1934, the League of Nations intervened and tried to negotiate a settlement. Mussolini, however, had no intention of peace and on October 3, 1935, Italian troops invaded Ethiopia. On October 7, the League of Nations declared Italy the aggressor in the conflict and on October 11, the League imposed wide-ranging sanctions, which were largely ineffective. Meanwhile, the modern, mechanized Italian army (using tanks, airplanes, and poison gas) swept through Ethiopia, defeating the poorly equipped Ethiopians. On May 5, 1936, the Italians occupied the Ethiopian capital Addis Ababa and on May 9, Italy formally annexed the country into the Italian empire. The invasion was seen as a prime example of the inability of the League of Nations to mediate international disputes.
[20] In July 1937, the Palestine Royal Commission, chaired by the Rt. Hon. Earl Peel, issued its report calling for the partition of Palestine (then administered by Great Britain) into Arab and Jewish sections. Palestinian leaders rejected the report.
[21] Malta was an important British naval port in the Mediterranean at the time. British military experts questioned the loyalty of the Maltese population, and also worried about the port's proximity to Sicily. In the mid-1930s, the British navy based much of its Mediterranean fleet in the port of Alexandria, Egypt, as a result. An edited version of this section of the text, from "Waaal,...." to "... the BASE ain't so first," formed a latter portion of the published *Globe* essay "An Interview with Mrs. Unterguggenberger" (Contribution #6).
[22] Though born in Oxford, Richard the Lionheart spent much of his youth at his mother's court in Poitiers, France, where he spoke Provençal. He never became proficient in English.
[23] **Colonel Edward Mandell House**

Contribution #7: "Responsibility? Shucks!"
Globe February–March 1938 issue, pp. 108–11

For "Responsibility? Shucks!" see **JWGD3** and **EP44**

Ezra Pound

THE WHY AND WHEREFORE OF "PUTTING IT OVER" AND "WIPING IT OFF"

There is one (at least one) absolute and utter barrier between an European wanting to understand an American and *vice versa.* Any or almost any European has traces of a sense of responsibility: somebody once told him he had a duty, and he still thinks that things have consequences and possibly causes.

This may not apply to a few Spanish anarchists. "Europe ends," said a wise guy, "with the Pyrenees." The Iberian peninsula was invaded by some border Europeans and Granada fell when Chris. Columbus discovered San Domingo.[1] When I first got to Tangier (1902)[2] there were still Moors carrying big keys, and these were said to be the keys of their houses in Granada, — take it as joke, Moorish irony, patent of nobility, boast of ancient lineage, or whatever.

The normal American is convinced that nothing matters, and more than convinced that there is no use doing anything in particular. All my generation was brought up to be humorous. There is no American of my generation or of Woollcott's[3] whose fond parents didn't tell him about the usefulness of a sense of humor.

"No, boss, there is *no one* in this country who is interested in taking life as seriously as you do," writes to me a brilliant compatriot with the advantage of 30 years or so of juniority.

Take a particular illustration from our literary (God help us for the word) "life." It is a narsty way to speak about anything but what can you call it? There once was Bohemia. Right in old New York.[4]

What does the young generation know of it? I can *still* get sentimental over Carmen and Hovey; back in 1905 what was there native except "Songs from Vagabondia?"[5] I wonder what young have read them. I wonder who now reads or reprints Bruno's Chap Book.[6] Note that Sadakichi Hartmann once raised about 25 dollars for Walt Whitman.[7] I forget whether they fed him on oysters or if it was strawberries, but they did a good turn to old Walt.

Who could now dig up, or how, a collection of the poems Sadakichi put in the *Chap Book*? Would anyone print them? Could I myself still read them if they were available?

There was, a dozen years ago in Paris, a chap named Dunning [8] who wrote a few good poems in a then out of date manner. Mr. Hemingway, realist, assured me that I would never "put 'em over," which was perfectly true. A later amateur publisher wanted to print the "whole of D's poetry" and then found so much of it bad. I don't deny it. My point being that the kind of badness was instructive, and belonged with the quality. Also there is a very great difference between badness and merely being out of fashion.

I am not here concerned either with poetry or any other specific topic, but with the American ideas of "putting it over" and "wiping it off." Against which I set the attitude of the European local *commissario*, to whom I doubted if it were any use printing a note on local concerts in a local paper. "No matter," he said, "if *nobody* reads it. It will be there in the records."

That remark comes from a very different way of taking things, it comes from a very different way of looking at life.

"Not interested," said the Semitic prosecuting attorney of one of our great eastern American cities, "in anything but bunk! I mean in seeing what you *can* put over." That may be either racial or geographic, I leave the reader to think it over. I don't myself think that remark was one inch more Jewish than American. The fun of putting it over?

Take it a notch higher up. For twenty years I was told that certain ideas were eccentric or exotic. They weren't. They were just horse sense. By and by one had a list of authorities, one had a stack of proofs that a whole series of intelligent and practical men had seen and held these ideas.
Comes now 1938 and I point out to one of our most brilliant American publishers that you can get Marx, Lenin, Trotsky, and Stalin, all of them exotics, for 10 cents or a quarter a volume, and that no American can buy the best of J. Adams, Jefferson, and Van Buren at any price; or maybe he can dig up an uncirculated publication of the Historical Association for three dollars. All of these guys were 100% U.S.A.-ers.
"But," says the publisher, "Nobody would be interested in what they said. Now if you were to write out exactly the same words as your own, I think we could sell it."

In Europe you couldn't. Some bloke like Francis Picabia,[9] or some librarian like Manlio Dazzi[10] would call it. The former would say something bright and snappy about: Who discovered the moon. And the latter would with chapter and verse observe that Marco Polo, or Bacon, or as the case were, Mr. Adams, had on the 3rd of January, 1803, written to Mr. Whoosis a letter containing on page three, lines 9 to 14, the remarks used by . . . .

And if you in Europe wanted to verify something before you released it you might get from Professor V. a note to the effect: "Not knowing, I asked Prof.

Z.G.T. Neither I nor my wife can read his abominable handwriting, but here is his answer; it seems that in 151 B.C. the Roman Senate *etc. etc.*"

Mr. Yeats,[11] hearing the helluva shindy down the street, asked his hotel keeper what the row was about.

"Shoore," said his Irish host, "and they're fightin' about the Earl."

Further enquiry showed that the subject of the dispute had occurred about 1480 A.D. There are countries where houses are without running water. There are still in Europe public spigots out in the street used by a number of families. A view of modern Italy is incomplete unless the viewer compare the number of houses now having running water with the number that had it in 1920.

The dirtiest places in Italy and in all Europe are little hill hamlets where the water runs down hill as fast as it falls. Then there are flies. There was recently a good piece about Indian hygiene (minus) in the "Magazine Digest" of Canada.

In 1912 I walked all about the South of France with no documents except an unstamped membership card of the Touring Club.[12] I never used it. I used the club button once when they took me for a hobo, not on the "authorities" but on a landlady in the little burg where they had killed off King Richard back in 12 hundred and whatever.[13] The only man who took any interest in my *état civil* was a peasant, puzzled as hell as to what I had in my sack. My spare clothes? Yes but what had I got to sell? Not selling anything! Was I a baker? He'd never seen white pants on any man but a baker.

After the great filth of 1914 I had to ask a couple of gendarmes if they thought the German Fleet would get up the Dordoigne from Bordeaux, but my only arrest was for counterfeiting.[14] I am not supposed to know that. It was mistaken identity, and the local beak called down his subordinates at first sight of me. *"c'est pas celui-lá"*

The flics excused themselves, got out the photos of a sort of gorilla and said I could see that their mistake was quite understandable. But what a comfort to be had up for mere crime. Suppose one's papers had been out of order?

A man, Tommy E.,[15] once lost his carte. *"On ne perd pas sa carte d'identité,"* said the Parisian authority. "No one loses a card of identity."

For years the only comfortable way to get them in Paris was via the porter who was sweet on the secretary (or *vice versa*) of the fellow who issued them. When Triebitch Lincoln[16] was finally pinched he had seven passports of seven different countries, all in perfect order, all with his photograph on them, an each made out in a different name.

When it comes to "putting it over" we are not so far ahead of the decrepit old civilizations.

Ezra Pound [Signature]

[1] Granada, the last stronghold of Moorish culture and military power on the Iberian peninsula, fell to Ferdinand II of Castile in 1492. Columbus discovered the island of San Domingo that same year.

[2] Pound's visit as a teenager to Europe and North Africa with his Aunt Frank in 1902 included Tangiers. Incidents from this trip are described in Canto LXXIV. In this Canto Pound describes a bizarre scene involving a fakir's magic:

> but in Tangier I saw from dead straw ignition
>   From a snake bite
> Fire came from the straw
> from the fakir blowing
> foul straw and an arm-long snake
> that bit the tongue of the fakir making small holes
>   and from the blood of the holes
>   came fire when he stuffed the straw into his mouth...
>
> (Canto LXXIV 242-49)

[3] **Alexander Woollcott**

[4] Pound was rather nostalgically "remembering" a period in the American avant-garde that he only knew through his connections with the "little magazines" of the period, such as *The Little Review* and *Poetry*. Based primarily in New York and concentrated in the Greenwich Village area of the city, it included the salons of Mabel Dodge, the Stettheimer sisters, Walter Arensberg, Max Eastman's *The Masses* circle, and Alfred Stieglitz's Gallery 291. It is usually said that the climax of this "first American avant-garde" came with the 1913 New York Armory show of contemporary art. Pound had settled in London in 1908 and preferred avant-garde circles there and on the Continent. The only exception to Pound's long-distance participation in this ferment was his short visit to America from June 1910 to February 1911. He would only return for another brief stay in 1939. His impressions of America during his earlier trip are recorded in *Patria Mia,* which appeared as a series in *The New Age* in 1912.

[5] Canadian poet Bliss Carman (1861–1929) and American poet/musician Richard Hovey (1864–1900). After meeting at Harvard, the two collaborated on the popular book *Songs from Vagabondia*.

[6] **Sadakichi Hartmann**'s poetry appeared in the *Bruno's Chap Books* edited by **Guido Bruno**. The series ran from January 1915 to May 1916.

[7] Pound had been receiving begging letters from **Sadakichi Hartmann** and

his family. His mention of Hartmann and *Bruno's Chap Books* was certainly spurred by these pathetic letters.
[8] **Ralph Cheever Dunning**
[9] **Francis Picabia**
[10] **Torquato Manlio Dazzi**
[11] **William Butler Yeats**
[12] In the summer of 1912, Ezra Pound hiked the troubadour region of southern France. His notebooks from that trip were published in 1992 as *A Walking Tour in Southern France: Ezra Pound among the Troubadours,* edited by Richard Sieburth (New York: New Directions).
[13] English King Richard the Lionheart, born in 1157, was fatally wounded by an archer while besieging Chalus.
[14] Pound seems to have been talking of an arrest made due to mistaken identity in France sometime soon after World War I. The current Pound biographies do not make mention of this incident.
[15] Pound might be referring to an incident involving T. S. Eliot.
[16] **Ignatius Timothy Trebitsch-Lincoln**

Contribution #8: "United States of Europe?"
Globe November–December 1938 issue, pp. 42–4

For "United States of Europe?" see (tangentially) **EP49**

An American traveler said to me last week: "Facts favorable to the corporate states are propaganda; facts unfavorable to them are news."

This was certainly a sincere statement on his part but does not assist me in sending letters to GLOBE and at the same time conciliating the current superstitions (or whatever they are) of American news service.

There is the FACT of Europe, bounded naturally on the West by the Atlantic, on the South by the Mediterranean and on the East not so very well bounded by nature, on the North there is ice, the North Pole, and the Scandinavians who have never, or seldom ever, constituted a menace.

Some years ago Rudolf Hess[1] said it should not be beyond European intelligence to work out a system of living together, meaning between European peoples.

The most intelligent men in Europe are now thinking EUROPE. I mean even men who hold political office, not merely a few dreamers and intelligentia.

Europe WAS civilized from the Mediterranean. This is not an idle THEORY. It is history. A lot of sapheads have for years tried to limit literature to fiction and picking daisies. If there are any adult readers perhaps they will consider the possibility of including authors like Constantine and Justinian in literary history.[2] I have for some time said that J. Adams, T. Jefferson, Van Buren and Co. wrote parts of American literature as well as history. In any case Europe exists, some men, even if they are politicians, are thinking about a possible PEACE instead of ineluctable war. That annoys pacifists to no end. Or put it another way, the old style pacifist is completely discredited. The men who have worked and are working for peace are a different breed. The old style subsidized pacifist never asked, "Who gets it." Only recently has a newer kind of pacifist society gone in *even* for being curious as to how much it costs.

There are a whole squad of niggers in several woodsheds. The reds for example won't show up concession hunters even when the concession hunters are following Franco.

Franco's "Charter of Labor" damns usury.[3] I haven't seen that fact advertised in the hostile papers. And so on. Ribbenthrop has had a bad press in England.[4] They always say the man used to be a salesman for Champagne (French beverage). Nobody prints what Rib. said at the Leipzig Fair last year. Even though Hitler has recently let it out of the bag, no longer a kitten, but a full sized tom cat with whiskers.

As to bro Hijalmar Horace Greely Schacht[5] a lot of people think him a rascal, but no one thinks him a saphead. He recently said, "If money were merely dead metal." But don't let's go into that. He recently said, "Money that doesn't represent commerceable goods, meaning goods you can buy and sell, is mere paper *valuta*."

Don't let's go into that, unless of course "we" have business interests and want to know what is going on in old Europe.

But politically speaking, now that it is twenty years since Picabia[6] wrote: "Europe, exhausted by the conquest of Alsace Lorraine," people, even Chamberlain,[7] are beginning to worry as to whether it is really worth while to bleed Europe white again by conquisting yet again a bit of its (Europe's) lights and liver. There are plenty of MAPS, such as Delaisi printed in *Vu*[8] showing who owns what. For example there is SKODA[9]—what price Skoda and soda?

Well at any rate, the fact that the price of the League of Nations is now ZERO points out what I quoted to GLOBE readers two years ago, when nobody liked me. And I assure you once again that Europe NEVER for ten minutes intended Russia to have Barcelona. Take that as FLAT. Some things just don't make sense. Wars are largely made to keep up a market for war material. War scares are largely made to sell material.

A lot of people are also wondering whether representation by trades isn't more EFFECTIVE than representation by geographic areas, at least AFTER the interests of people living in big towns like New York and Chicago are all mixed up *inside*, let us say, congressional districts. Sure, there has been a lot of fireworks and manoeuvres, and moral evolutions that astonished old style naval techniques. And there have also been lots of books, Wyndham Lewis in 1932 printed one about Hitler,[10] he has now spilled some beans, a novel: REVENGE FOR LOVE,[11] about Spain that aren't to be found in Mr. Hemingway's bull stories.[12] The undersigned keeps on writing books that will some day bust the present ninety-three per cent dead university curricula wide open like a soft melon.
Europe doesn't yet read Mr. Cummings.[13] Some bright lads just don't know what is ON. Bill Williams has written about "Life on the Passaic River,"[14] that is news TO Europe. Mr. T.S. Eliot has gone to Portugal for the Camoens celebration,[15] thereby causing an outcrop of limericks, etc. Prof. Maranini is writing books about Robespierre.[16] Fenollosa's tomb is still visited by Japanese neighbors,[17] which shows that American expatriates aren't always detested. If GLOBE has any Italo-American readers, or reaches students who read Italian, I can recommend 'em *Broletto* and *Rivista del Lavoro*, to start on, and supply a longer list of Italian reading matter if wanted. I sometimes wonder why GLOBE readers don't write in and TELL one what they want to hear about Europe. The old place is still here. There is still water in the Gulf of Tiguillio,[18] and I suppose in other parts of the Mediterranean.

Ezra Pound [Signature]

Globe readers are invited to address personal letters to Ezra Pound care of Globe Magazine, 1033 Lincoln Ave., St. Paul, Minn., U.S.A.

[1] **Rudolf Heß**
[2] **Constantine and Justinian**
[3] On March 9, 1938, the Spanish dictator Francisco Franco (1892–1975) issued the so-called Labor Charter. This document outlined the social and labor policies of his regime. It defined the mutual responsibilities that existed between the state and its citizens. All citizens were obligated to work, but the state was obligated to provide them with the right to work. The charter also provided for fair wages, limited working hours, and paid vacations, but it also declared strikes to be treasonous offenses against the regime.
[4] **Joachim von Ribbentrop**
[5] **Hjalmar Horace Greeley Schacht**
[6] The source for **Picabia**'s quote is not known, but Pound made the same reference in his essay "For a New Paideuma" (*The Criterion*, January 1938).
[7] **Neville Chamberlain**
[8] See "Interview with Mrs. Unterguggenberger" (Contribution #6).

[9] The Skoda Works was a Czechoslovakian armaments firm.
[10] **Wyndham Lewis**' *Hitler* actually appeared in 1931.
[11] **Wyndham Lewis**' novel, *The Revenge for Love*, was published in 1937.
[12] **Ernest Hemingway**'s book, *Death in the Afternoon* (1932), is a somewhat eccentric work. In it Hemingway provides a kind of impressionistic guidebook to Spain, but it is also an expression of his own musings on life and writing. Central to this book is his love of bullfighting, all aspects of which are treated in detail. Hemingway began writing his Spanish Civil War novel, *For Whom the Bell Tolls*, in the spring of 1939. It was published in 1940.
[13] **Edward Estlin Cummings**
[14] **William Carlos Williams**' *Life On The Passaic River* (1938).
[15] In 1938 **Eliot** traveled to Lisbon for a festival honoring Luis De Camões (1524–80), Portugal's most famous poet and author of the epic *Os Lusiadas*.
[16] **Giuseppe Maranini** (1902–69), Italian professor of politics, wrote several books on the French Revolution.
[17] **Ernest Fenollosa**
[18] Rapallo overlooks the Gulf of Tigullio.

Contribution #9: "Notes on Micro-Photography"

Globe April-May 1938 issue, p. 29

For "Notes on Micro-Photography," see **JD19**. This contribution seems to be an edited version of "Milestones" (Contribution #14).

Ezra Pound

As to what the "intellectuals" are doing God-blessum: BROLETTO, monthly magazine of the City of Como, Italy, in January published a complete concerto (of Vivaldi) in small half-tones taken from "microfoto" Leica films—an enormous saving over the old system where half-tones were made from full size photos.[1] Dr. Sayce of Kings College, Newcastle,[2] calculates he can register 500 pages of music on a grid of grainless film the size of a post card. This means an absolute revolution in all study of unpublished music, and the whole problem of the musical library enters a completely new phase. For the technical side of this, refer to the American Documentation Institute, Science Service, 2101 Constitution Ave., Washington, D. C. The Science News Letter last year (March 20, 1937) mentioned the process, but the musicians didn't get a look in. The two fields where the process means most are music and oriental studies, neither being cheaply reproducible by anterior printing systems. Music is getting ready to have its ears washed and its teeth scrubbed.

[1] See **JD19** note 6.
[2] Professor Leonard A. Sayce, pioneer in the development of microphotography.

UNPUBLISHED ARTICLES

Contributions in typescript signed by Pound but rejected by *Globe*.

Contribution #10: "That League in Calvin's Home City"[1]
October 18, 1936. Signed by Pound.

For "That League in Calvin's Home City," see **EP16, EP17, EP18, EP19, JD9, JWGD1**

All this will have to be got over sometime/ regardless of date of issue, if readers of Globe to get clear perception of Europe. Ezra Pound

---

Mr Anthony Eden a nasty and over-dressed "young" man had by Sept. 25 got round to discovering a phase of the "Covenant" long since known to the outer world. He discovered that it stood for the status quo.[2]

During the first 48 hours after the first publication of that document,[3] Congressman George Holden Tinkham read it. He read it before Knox and Lodge had done so.[4] Some day this fourty eight hours will be recorded in American History. Tinkham saw that the document meant called for an offensive and defensive alliance; that no nation signing it could honourably keep out of any future war, however silly its cause, however corrupt its motivations, or however disasterous its consequences were likely to be.

Eden is on the surface produced by the English edu- or snobi-cation. He is in substance the synthetic creation of his father-in-law's bank, the Westminster.[5] He stood unsuccessfully for parliament before forming that tie. After it his "rise was rapid."

A supple ape in the limited arena of British fixed politics he is less loathesome than Baldwin,[6] who is <u>de facto</u> and professedly an enemey of all thought. Eden is less nuisance than Neville Chamberlain,[7] who personifies a harder + as you might say petrified malignity.

Chamberlain is, I think, firmly convinced that millions of Englishmen ought to be underfed for the preservation of a small clique of officials, semiconsciously, or even in a state of complete unconsciousness, kept "employed" by very obscure interests.

(Some of these men + interests have been listed in a book called "The Old Lady Unveiled,"[8] but that "aint the 'arf of it, dearie.")

Intellectual progress on the English front can be registered by the fact the Brit. Foreign minister, by Sept. 25 of the year 1936 had reached the peak of perception attained by Tinkham, Lodge, and Philander Knox, sixteen or seventeen years or whenever it was, sooner. Let us say sixteen years sooner. In Europe this triad and Borah[9] are still remembered as having saved the U.S.A. from the con game of Versailles.[10]

At the end of Sept. the most acute English observation of detail was shown in a paragraph on the British Railway equipment boom, which suggested that Railway Equipment cos. could make, and had often made, shells. New Zealand's declaration of independence from the Bank of International Settlements (i.e the root of, and force behind, the Geneva League)[11] was followed by demand from long oppressed Austria for freedom to run her own monetary and credit business.

The devaluation of the French franc was long overdue.[12] Any such Devaluation is always sub specie aeternitis unnecessary but as long as the powers of any country uphold a certain group of black lies, such devaluations will occur. They are part of the rules. The hat trick consists in saying any boat must sink. The unalterable rule is that boats do sink if you smash big enough holes in their bottoms when at sea.

Krassin's daughter married into an ancient "noble" family, as Krassin's gold was removed from Russia, before Czarist bonds and currency were sunk.[13] This event given munitions to anti-semites. They were given a lot during the autumn of 1936. Nevertheless men like Neimeyer [14] are enemies of ALL mankind, jew and gentile alike.

The racial question is not basic to the economic dispute. The most significant paragraph printed during Sept was apropos of New Zealand's recognition of the plot of the Bank of International Settlements to dominate N. Zealand without assuming one ha'penny's worth of responsibility.

The Bank of International Settlements can be most briefly defined as a clique of financiers, including Neimeyer who wished to govern the whole world without responsibility to any nation, government or people whatsoever.

This bank aimed at being the supreme self-elected world authority. The forces behind it had, years ago, alarmed the Pope, who denounced them a bit vaguely as to their identity, but accurately as to their nature, in the encyclical "Quadrigessimo Anno."[15]

===

Item British "acceptance houses" in low water, held up by Stalin who borrowed at high rate of interest in order to obtain political influence.[16]

===

Schacht's[17] method for fooling nearly all the people, is asserted on the best possible authority, to be that of telling the truth in a nation so given to persistent mendacity that "no one believes him."

SCHACHT'S proposals for international exchange made during his visit to Paris are eminently sound. Using present date line, we can report no such sincerity and clarity in internal monetary issue or credit program inside the Reich.

ITALY keeps pumping purchasing power into the Italian masses. The corporate system, that is the system of huge guilds, with representation based on the kind of work a man does, as distinct from geographicly divided representation, is so organized that the delegated authority, the state, can discipline prices. Hence the raise in the wages of millions of Italians, by 8%, 9%, 10% does not, and can not cause INFLATION, using the word "Inflation" in the old pejorative sense. There is more money about but its value per monetary unit does not go DOWN.

The value of any nation's monetary unit is determined by WHAT IT WILL BUY INSIDE the country.

For foreign exchange it depends on what the foreign market can force a country to hand over in respect to the given measured claim.

Put it another way, under inflation, in the old sense, the dollar or lire buys less.

There is no use in my sending news items, unless I put the reader in condition to understand them.

Under the mediaeval "just price" system, with Charlemagne's commodity denar,[18] or under the projected C.H. Douglas system (now working in respect to N.Zealand butter)[19] or in contemporary Italy, an increase in the total money (and/or credit) available for the WHOLE PEOPLE can increase (enormously) without the evil effects of inflation.

Again we define inflation as: increase in total mass of currency and/or credit, accompanied by rise in prices of commodities especially of necessary staple commodities: food, clothing, heating and transport.

The wisdom of the framers of the AMERICAN CONSTITUTION becomes more apparent with every HOUR of European history in our time.

The clearest thought in Europe is leading all Europe, some of it via blood and calamity, to the perception of certain sanities known to Jefferson and to John Adams, sanities followed by a few of their successors up to about 1840, AND unknown to most of America in our time, those preserved in the minds of a few hard headed Americans who are in control neither of press nor of government.

The man who wants to see European events TODAY can have no better watch tower and telescope than our own CONSTITUTION. Men under forty never read it. Half our congress, at least half and probably 80%, don't know what it signifies.

Ezra Pound

<Venezia.
18th Oct.
1936>

<will use decent typing when get back to my own typewriter>

[1] **John Calvin**

[2] Covenant of the League of Nations. **Anthony Eden**

[3] On September 25, 1936, the governments of the United States, Great Britain, and France issued simultaneous statements from their respective capitals announcing that France was preparing to devalue the franc in an effort to stabilize international trade. The tripartite agreement, made without participation of the League of Nations, did not stabilize the economy.

Pound rewrote this sentence and dropped the following passage: "This discovery was made during the first 48 hours period subsequent to the first publication of that egregious and mess document. Nothing in history perhaps will so summar [sic] summarize the mental sloopingess [sic] of the Lord Lloyd George Woodrow Wilson ** activities during Versailles."

[4] **George Holden Tinkham** was one of the senators who led the fight to keep the United States from signing the Covenant of the League of Nations. Republican Sen. Philander Chase Knox (1853–1921) of Pennsylvania and Republican Sen. Henry Cabot Lodge (1850–1924) of Massachusetts were leaders in the fight against President Woodrow Wilson's efforts to make the United States a signatory of the Covenant of the League of Nations.

[5] John Strange Spencer Churchill's daughter Anne Clarissa married **Anthony Eden.**

[6] **Stanley Baldwin**

[7] **Neville Chamberlain**

[8] *The Old Lady Unveiled: A Criticism and an Explanation of the Bank of England*, by J. R. Jarvie (1933).

[9] **William Edgar Borah**

[10] The Paris Peace Conference to end World War I was held from January 12, 1919 to January 20, 1920 in and around Paris. The Versailles Treaty that arose from the discussions led by the victorious Allied powers placed numerous requirements on the defeated Central Powers (Germany, Austria, Turkey, and Bulgaria) including the surrender of all German colonies; the return of German-occupied region of Alsace-Lorraine to France and the surrender of

other German and Austrian lands to Lithuania, Belgium, Poland, and the newly created Czechoslovakia; demilitarization of the German Rhineland; and German reparations to the Allies of £6,600 million.

[11] The Reserve Bank of New Zealand was created in 1934 as a private bank, but the Labour government took it over in 1936. The New Zealand government refused to go along with efforts by the Swiss-based Bank of International Settlements (BIS) to coordinate monetary policies of the world's major central banks. Created initially to coordinate reparation payments by Germany to the various Allies, the BIS quickly became an organization to coordinate central banks during the global Depression.

[12] In September 1936, the French government devalued its franc by 25 percent to attempt to stabilize the nation's, and Europe's, faltering economy.

Pound rewrote this sentence and dropped the following passage: "The devaluation of the French franc long over due will [?] be followed by unending wrangles and wriggles to tie the dollar to sterling. That is to subject the average American citizen to a clique of international *infamie* [?] (same old Basel contingent). New York agents of British Banks etc."

[13] **Ludmila Mathias**

[14] **Ernst Otto Niemeyer**

[15] Pound was referring to Pope Pius XI's "Quadragesimo Anno," an encyclical issued on May 15, 1931: "On Reconstruction of the Social Order." The document reaffirmed the Catholic Church's opposition to socialism and supported the right to private property, but supported "the sacred rights of workers" and condemned excesses of capitalism. Part of the encyclical dealt vaguely with how capital serves only itself, not humankind.

[16] For "acceptance houses," see "Abdication" (Contribution #1) note 14.

[17] **Hjalmar Horace Greeley Schacht**

[18] **Charlemagne**

[19] Pound was referring to the economic system of Social Credit advocated by Clifford Hugh Douglas (1879–1952). In 1935, the Labour Party was elected in New Zealand. In 1936, the government took control of the New Zealand Reserve Bank and began a series of economic reforms. The government also set up price controls on dairy products, including butter. Douglas' ideas had wide circulation in New Zealand. In 1954, the country's newly founded Social Credit Political League won 10 percent of the popular vote in parliamentary elections. The party continued to be one of the larger minority parties in New Zealand until the 1980s, when it changed its name and dropped in popularity. In 1993, it merged with several other small parties and disappeared.

Contribution #11: "On Pleasing"

Postmarked July 24, 1937. Signed by Pound.

For "On Pleasing," see **EP35**.

Said S...n the dhirty jew to B.... the dhirty yidd:
"Our English politcians will do as the
bankers bid."
Said B;;;;t the dhirty yidd to S...n
the dhirty kike
"All vfrencch goffervments
are ahlike."[1]

"I," as our old swedish cook used to say "dhry tdo bleaze,"[2] and if our editor wants what I know about the Near East etc. i can get thru it in a very few words. I once amused an ex-colonial governor. I dont think I knew he was an ex-governor He was, to me, a pleasant sort of bloke I'd met at a lunch party in London. He said before I got thru that he had long been "that lowest of creatures, a bureacrat." I quoted him Gertrude Bell,[3] "I believe" wrote Gertie to hez mama or to someone, "that when not contrary to the interests of the Empire, our promises to the Arabs shd/ be kept."

That thaaar iz the voice of Empire. Sir X. said: "Did Gertrude say that?" Getrude had bored him. She was "marvelous," knew everything that the sheik Ibn Jbn had said to the Sheik Muley Wbn in 1897 and what agreements existed between the Buj and Juj tribes etc/, but WOULD talk about these things at dinners to people who didn't.

Waaal, it was a happy half hour, waitin fer the antient figures to lift their hammers and smack the bell on the clock tower next to S.Marco, which they didn't, cause they was bust.[4] And two months later I picked up "VU"[5] [There is a mark here in the text and an illegible margin note in Pound's hand at this point in the ms.]and saw a piece about Sir "England's Authority on Mediterranean and Near Eastern affairs. " But I had had time to quote Gertrude, and to speak fairly plainly about Abyssinia,[6] he having put up some of the usual offical Genevan cobwebs (that being in 1935).

I said ; "A nation with low civilization, a nation six hundred or two thousand or even less years behind contemporary civilization, can not exist indefinitely along side of a higher civilization."

So he came down to brass tacks and admitted: "Yes, I suppose it will have to go." He is a sane man and has read a few books fir to read more than once.

When it comes to stuff one can read in the papers I notice that the last

English scheme, according to the continent, implies the shift of 250,000 arabs from the coast of comparitively habitable parts of Palestine, to the uninhabitable or back mountain districts.[7] I don't see why they shd/ like this.

Apart from that I heard a bit about the country from Col. Tom Lawrence's brother,[8] way back before the Globe readers were born. And I didn't learn much one evening when Lawrence "of Arabia" dined with me after a narsty afternoon with the very greasy character Llard George and the frog-bassador,[9] because the Col. was so damnd fed up with their shifting and sheistering that he wd/ talk of almost nothing but second rate art. He wanted to get down to the country and do de luxe editions of greek authors, presumably to get Arabia out of his mind. But he did have, years later in Oxford, a swell set of photos of temples cut in the face of those rocks.

"Waaal," sez the eddytor: "Wot erbout Malter?" "Not so good," says yr/ correspondent.[10] They were talking a mixture of arabic and early eyetalian down in that island before the British language was heard of. Walter Scott's pet King (Richard Lionheart) went sailing out to the holyland and a pasha held up his best gal, but made his excuses in turkish. Richard then made his only known effort to speak anything but his native Provençal. He said: "EE spik lak a fole britain."[11] However the British seem to object to the Maltese speaking Italian, but the gun range has now got so long that what the foreign office calls "bloody ice-creamers" can sit right on the toe of the boot and chuck shells into Malta harbour, so medde the BASE ain't so first. Then there is the subject of air-lines.

An' I hear from the middle of Afrika that colonial "society," in the high sense, is still spittin' mad that there was an unconquored country that someone else went and took.[12] This pen picture comes from a British subject who had found the official view somewhat wearing.

With which kind words mebbe bro. Dunn will allow me to postpone my epitaphs upon Rhoosia, and to say that a sense of EUROPE arises. Take me too long to go into that now, and I want in any case to deal with brother HUDDLESTON not for what he said in July but for what he didn't say back before that,

A QUARREL WITH HUDDLESTON[13]

It need remain no longer a secret. I have been wanting to wring Huddy's neck for three months, all for his ommission of one two-syllable word. I shd/ have said, "journalists are punk because they are not EVEN superficial."

The pseudo-high-brows among em are a nuisance because they pass on clichés; that is, dead prejudice, points of view which are based NEITHER on direct perceptions of details NOR on any acquaintance with historic process or any attempt to understand why anything happens or WHICH men are making decisions, I mean decisions which really DECIDE.

About five years, or was it longer ago, the Paris boys got orders from home to HOLD DOWN. That means: "No European news WANTED. Write funny stuff about the birth of a six-legged calf or the bees that nested in grandma's pyanny, but don't send any real news about Europe."

A practical journalist is a bloke that knows enough to bribe the telegraph operator to send his stuff FIRST. A normal journalist, according to his city, is one who leans over a bar waiting for someone to TELL him, or, in centres for mimeograph slips to come in from the agencies...

There are London editors who don't yet know enough to see the joke in the word "Innsbruck" as a date line. I was sitting in a Whatever Café with Fodor (who is a better journalist than some others, because he was a steel engineer first, and thereby got used to reality).[14] There were a couple of other boys with us, including Mr Beee ——— or let that stand for his name ——— from down Alabama or thereabouts. And he had suspicioned one of the Viennese agencies. So when he went out of his office he had left a slip on his desk as follows:

Phone the XYZ Agency to ask if there is any confirmation of the attentat contre Zogu. Only——he pronounced it "att-en-TATT conter Zogu."[15]

The reader will understand that there had been one or two attempts to shoot up King Zog a year and a couple of years before this, but that on the date mentioned the attentat existed only in Mr Beee's fertile imagination. At 1.15 A.M. on the morning of whenever was it, as I was seated, as per above, with the very able Fodor, Mr Beee, and some others, a slip was delivered and Mr Beee burst into expletives, which the blushful reader is spared.

The XYZ agency had reported (from Innsbruck, naturally) an attentat contre Zogu.

And that my deerly lebuvved brevvrem is how things get to be news, unless your daily paper is represented by inquisitive fellows like Beee and Fodor.

As to WHY writers turn journalist, my answer is, they are so fed up with the stuff in the newspapers, which stuff is supposed to be due largely to journalists, that they have been DRIVEN to take a hand in the shindy. The late mons. Gustave Flaubert[16] said that a novelist's job was to write "the history of contemporary custom," or of contempary habits and ways of living. I have emended that or gone on with it by saying, "literature is news that stays news."[17]

Journalists have given us stuff that isn't even news on the day it is written. X, Y, and Z have come to Europe in deepest and smeariest ignorance of everything under heaven. They have NOT reported the surface of things. They have NOT had the faintest taint of what Huddy seems to fear as profundity. They are neither fish, fowl, nor animal.

Their attitude is that nothing matters and that nothing can be done about anything. And yet there is a very great European "journalist" who has said "The indifferent have never made history."[18]

Idiots like Mrs L. and Mr G.X naturally make the most utterly piffling forecasts because they fail UTTERLY and absolutely to understand the nature of WILL when applied to historic process. They count on the resolute man being just as flabby and slobby as they are.

They know, as it were, all about what makes an automobile stop and nothing about what makes it go. And they blame their own lack of guts on their owner or editor.

As to France in this bad year for Frenchmen, a french bloke and patriot who knows the whole lot, I mean the ministers, big politicians etc. said to me: "France is governed by two ex-typists, Mrs Bloom was a typist, Mrs Mosch [19] "and damn well named was a typist" and these two hags drive on those unfortunate slobs to avenge every insult they (the ex-typists) have received from the bourgeoisie when they were typists.

Note the frenchmen's use of the word "bourgeoisie" meaning people with larger incomes than stenographers, and families where the wives don't go out to do office work.

"Mosch!" says the frenchmen, "Blum's chef de cabinet, well named!" (Mosch means a slob, in french slang.)

These remarks were a bit of SURFACE. It may be more than surface. At any rate the fact that a french author said it is a fact about France. There were similar facts about Rousseau in the 18th. century.[20]

A couple of years ago M.Delaisi printed a sort of dial in VU (things seen)[21] of the Bank of France showing how the 12 regents of the Bank had the whole of French heavy industry, steel works, gun works, banks chemicals etc. by the short hairs. That article finally trickled into England and possibly into the U.S.A. several times without M.Delaisi being given the credit for his persistence and spade work.

Nobody outside the inner ring in Paris has today the faintest notion of whether the "reform" of the bank of france was real or all camouflage. The man from Cairo who had been seeing the high British officials was sure that

Jouhaux wd/[22] end up by sending 'em all (that is Blum and co.) to the guillotine. This estimate you can take as being coloured by the very strong sunshine of Egypt. The more cautious view was in June that Blum wd have to clear out by October.

This view was "sustained" by complete ignorance of monetary necessity. But if a form of dense ignorance is shared by a sufficient number of people, that blithering ignorance will "make history."

A general commanding 10,000 men who thinks there are a hundred thousand enemy troops in an empty valley, will probably not try to pass through that valley, if he thinks there is some other road less encumbered.

I repeat that the big french press is all OWNED, and that when a revolutionary paper is run by M.Hennessy[23] or some other reactionary, you can't trust it for news. And the small press is run by cranks, that is fellows who know some particular gadget in economics or "sociology" and usually have no sense, and a very sketchy conception of history.

I object to race prejudice, because it is blighting red-herring, it serves only to get people's minds off real issues.

But nobody can be in Europe today without thinking of race prejudice as a problem. And the rarest bird in the occident is a jew who will think about the NATURE of money. Marx didn't.

There is no use in merely "connecting the idea" jew " and the "idea " money" and then getting into a lather. Meyer Anselm was a genius or very high power.[24] he used craft against sheer brutal force. It was his ONLY possible chance. And intelligence is, in itself, highly respectable. his refusal to analyze money. And this is all the more curious because back in Deuteronomy or Exedous or wherever the author of those books clearly distinguishes the fruit from the corrosive. marbis from neschek. [25] And the orthodox jew or his rabbi, will often be quite sound on the problem of interest.

On the other hand anybody who had ever read Trotsky's literary criticism[26] would know, from the generally messy quality of the thought, that Leon wd. never get the strangle hold on Joe Stalin. He has survived by escape. He may stick it out till Joe [Joseph Stalin] dies.

In the mean time the frog government is at least shortening the hours of labour.[27] This is NOT the answer to an economic problem. It don't increase the total pruchasing power of the french people one blasted centime, though it may spread out the insufficient power to buy. And it is humanly decent to split up the needed work among as many people as possible.

People eat when they have MONEY. Nobody yet ever ate a slice of work stuck between two slices of labour.

All of which is becoming slowly (oh molassessly up-hill-in-winterly) apparent to an increasing part of the population. Some blokes in the International Labour Office (Gen-bloody-eva) have heard about Milhaud. (ref. my long translation of Por's bdy. dull article on the Milhaud plan, in the British Union Quarterly for this summer.[28] (Aug. Oct. if they print it. At any rate they've got it set up, and the proofs have been corrected.)

If there are any econ/ sharks, professors, stewd-dents of history etc. among the Globe's multitudinous readers, who really want to know about Europe, they'll have to start reading Italian. Rassegna Monetaria, Rivista di Politica Economica, La Stripe, Relazioni Internazionali, Rivista del Lavoro and a half dozen others.) Just like if they want to be hep to literature 1937 they'll have to start learning japanese becasue Tokio is the livest spot just at present.[29] This paper is labelled GLOBE, it is not just a New York extention or a Dorcas Soc. journal[30] for a few Americans in London and Paris (where most of 'em have never learned to speak either language). Frank MA is a winner.[31] Langston Hughes is wherever he happens to be at the moement.[32] I wish Kumrad cummings wd. go down to Washington, and tell us about that SURFACE.[33]

I am all for writers telling us ALL about surfaces. Tell a man about the surface and he'll think about CURVATURES, and then he'll have to think how it gets thatta way. Of course I don't see how the Hell N Blazes any American is going to understand Europe until he or she makes at least a stab at understanding U.S. History (past if not present). Any american can get the writings of Lenin, Marx, Stalin, for ten cents or a quarter. Nobody can get the writings of John Adams, Thos. Jefferson, J.Q. Adams or Van Buren without special effort and special knowledge of where. A lot of 'em are utterly out of print and unobtainable. This is democracy?

Anyhow you won't understand Europe till you know what LED to 1776, and what 1776 led TO in Europe. There is plenty of Europe that goes BACK to the American Colonies. There was a little, a very little, Europe, back in 1760 to 1780 and 1790 that was mentally contemporary with our american ancestors of that time.

Fifty years later Savage Landor wrote a rhetorical and unintelligible ode to Andy Jackson.[34] Does any bright school boy know WHY?

If a few more journalists knew WHY, it might help 'em to be "superficial" in an intelligent manner.

FRENCH POSTSCRIP on arrival of Chautemps[35]

After searching a pile of french nooz-wypers for indications and a possible leakage of news as to whether the difference is between flea and louse I found in the lot ONE line.

"Chautemps accompanied by the Senator Israel."[36]

This was confirmed by the appointment of Bonnet (photos showing probiscis).[37] Suspiscion that the french people had again been sold down the river, thereby consolidated, but the frogs have added a picturesque touch (acc/London account) they are going to make Alfons and Gaston pay for the fluid. "Among the proposals for revenue, a raise of one penny (2 cents American) per cubic meter of water.."

Ezra Pound

Travel note (to be added to whichever letter of mine you use next.)

Travellers shd/ know[38] that at least a decent mode of transport exists between Paris and London. The nastiest and most putrid charasteristics of all nations show in their frontier parasites. Nothing can excede the niggardly and blub-nosed degradation of frontier formalities. Ever since America was diddled by Col. House [39] into electing our most deleterious and fish-faced president Woodie Wilson these inconveniences have festered. The turnstile at French channel frontier wd/ I alone have justified the annihilation of that unhappy country as a political unit. And the British channel boat flunkies have for years furnished a good basis for anglophobia.

At last a channel train ferry carries or can carry a few priviliged to and fro. And the customs noses function only at Victoria station. No GLOBE reader shd/ lose opportunities of rubbing it in. No GLOBE reader shd/ ever go soft and pardon the legislators who cause the idiocies at frontiers. Before the late war, there were almost no passport formalities. We who remember that comparatively clean state of things shd/ NOT allow the young to think that the present festers have always existed.

Our own government has been chief among the spreaders of the passport and visa disease. No nation has worse frontier manners, though ours are, for obvious reasons filthier than the french and english. The bureaucrats put in by Wilson have done infinite harm to international minor relations. And his successors have not been either eager or clever in curing the damage.

[1] This anti-Semitic doggerel, most probably Pound's composition, might be referring to **Sir Philip Sassoon** and the **Beckett** banking and publishing family. However, the Becketts were not Jewish.

[2] A slightly edited first section of this essay was published in the latter portion

of the published *Globe* essay "Interview with Mrs. Unterguggenberger" (Contribution #6).

[3] See "Interview with Mrs. Unterguggenberger" (Contribution #6) note 17.

[4] Since 1497, two bronze Moors, when they are operating properly, mechanically hammer a large bell on the hour in a tower overlooking St. Mark's Square in Venice.

[5] See "Interview with Mrs. Unterguggenberger" (Contribution #6) note 18.

[6] See "Interview with Mrs. Unterguggenberger" (Contribution #6) note 19.

[7] See "Interview with Mrs. Unterguggenberger" (Contribution #6) note 20.

[8] **William George Lawrence**

[9] Pound had Chirstams dinner with and others in December 1918, while Lawrence was in London accompanying King Faisal as he met with British and French officials.

[10] See "Interview with Mrs. Unterguggenberger" (Contribution #6) note 21.

[11] See "Interview with Mrs. Unterguggenberger" (Contribution #6) note 22.

[12] Pound was referring to the Italian conquest of Ethiopia. During the colonial period, Ethiopia and Liberia were the only two independent African nations on the continent, and Liberia had been founded by American ex-slaves.

[13] In the July 1937 issue of *Globe*, **Sisley Huddleston** published an article entitled "Hoi Polloi in the Palace," about working-class French vacationing in previously exclusive sections of the Riviera. But Pound was angry about Huddleston's article in the June 1937 of *Globe*, entitled "Why I am the World's Worst Journalist." In that article, Huddleston complained about how American journalists, gathered in wine cellars and cafes in Paris, all were taking sides on political issues in the 1930s. He also felt too many journalists were writing books while too many writers were trying to become "newspapermen." Pound was particularly agitated by the following section in the article about an argument that Huddleston had with Ernest Hemingway about newspaper reporters: "It appeared to me the appropriate moment to explain, at great length, that newspapermen should quit their jobs when they began to lose their greatest asset—their superficiality. I fancy Arthur Brisbane said that before me. He said most things about journalism. And paradoxical as it sounds, it is absolutely necessary that the daily writer should prevent himself from becoming profound. If he really penetrates below the surface he is lost. By which I mean—to make a long story short—that newspapermen have no business to be Red or White, to express opinions on whether it is better to have a Jewish Prime Minister or an anti-Semite Dictator, on whether the fate of democracy is somehow involved in the Spanish fighting, on whether Russia is in the advance-guard of civilization, on whether Fascism is the latest sort of Devil without which men don't seem able to live, on whether better or brighter atrocities are committed in the name of liberty or in the name of order, and all

the rest of the tripe that is nowadays put forward in the place of old-fashioned straightforward reporting of good downright concrete facts recorded without any particular slant or propagandist purpose" (pp. 93–4). Also see **EP33**.

[14] **John Gunther** wrote an introduction to **Fodor**'s *Counterplot in Central Europe: Conditions South of Hitler* (1937).

[15] **Ahmed Bey Zogu**

[16] **Gustave Flaubert** (1821–80), French writer.

[17]*ABC of Reading* (New York: New Directions, 1960), p. 29.

[18] It is possible that this was a remark made by Mussolini, who worked as a journalist from 1904 to 1914. After being wounded in World War I, he returned to civilian life to edit the right-wing journal *Il Popolo d'Italia.*

[19] Possibly **Jules Moch.** Pound possibly was punning upon "Blum" and "Bloom," implying that Léon Blum is as henpecked by his wife as Joyce's Leopold Bloom is by Molly in *Ulysses.*

[20]**Jean Jacques Rousseau**

[21] See "United States of Europe?" (Contribution #8)

[22] **Léon Jouhaux**

[23] Possibly **James Richard Charles Hennessy**

[24] **Mayer Amschel Rothschild**

[25] Pound was referring to Leviticus 25. "Marbis" and "neschek" are Pound's transliterations of the Hebrew words for "increase" or "profit" and "interest". These Hebrew terms appear in Leviticus 25, where Moses issues regulations to the Israelites prohibiting usury. Pound uses "marbis from neschek" to mean the unlawful gains made from usury. For more information, see *Pound/Zukofsky: Selected Letters of Ezra Pound and Louis Zukofsky,* edited by Barry Ahearn (New York: New Directions, 1987), letters 74 and 75.

[26] Leon Trotsky

[27] In June 1936, **Léon Blum**'s government introduced a government-regulated 40-hour work week for all workers plus two weeks vacation.

[28] **Odon Por**

[29] The VOU Poetry Club

[30] The Dorcas Society was the name of a group of charitable church organizations founded by Protestants in Great Britain and North America during the Victorian period.

[31] In the June 1937 issue of *Globe*, **Frank Ma** wrote from Shanghai reporting on a failed coup against Chinese General Chiang Kai-shek in an short letter simply entitled "China."

[32] At this time **Langston Hughes** was in transit to Spain to report on the fighting from Republican Madrid.

[33] **E. E. Cummings** made a trip to the Soviet Union in the 1930s which resulted in his book *EIMI* (1933).

[34] **Walter Savage Landor**

[35] In June 1937, **Camille Chautemps**, who had been **Léon Blum**'s minister of state, replaced him as premier of France in 1937. Blum became vice-premier. Chautemps' coalition government collapsed in March 1938.
[36] **Alexandre Israël**
[37] **Georges Bonnet**
[38] A slightly edited version of this traveler's note was published as the last portion of published *Globe* essay "Interview with Mrs. Unterguggenberger" (Contribution #6).
[39] See "Interview with Mrs. Unterguggenberger" (Contribution #6) note 23.

Contribution #12: "...And Excursions"
Postmarked August 3, 1937. Signed by Pound.[1]

For "...And Excursions," see **JD15**

The "victory" of the oppostion in the London elections doesn't,[2] or wouldn't necessarily, mean "anything in itself" save that the contrivers of British misery find it more convenient to use one set of straw-men than another. But the chance that there after all may be "something in it" was indicated first by a statement in "Reynolds" [3] for Feb. 14 when their "Political Correspondent" assured their readers that "the Opposition does not object to interest on geniune loans—that is, loans in which the lender parts with his own money—it will certainly ask the House of Commons:

"Why must the government pay interest to a bank for creating and lending money which the Government can create for itself?"

The enlightened American reader will see that England in 1937 has drooled along to where our forebears were in the 1830's or in the time of Tom Jefferson; Andy Jax and Van Buren all having observed that a government needn't. Yet one reads the happey choirboy in Reynolds with scepticism. Will the opposition do anything of the sort?

Hitherto the "Opposition" i.e. Peter Pan Dalton[4] has for the most part contented himself with sticking out his PeterPanish nose just far enough for barbor's Toney[5] to tweak it with greater convenience. But on the land a quick one on the tip of Eden a-Beckett WOULD[6] the thoroughly rascally newswypers of Hengland "give equal prominence to the Debate?"

Chance is they wdn't. They wd. stuff in another two cols. of crLpe aout the horrible future of Aberhart[7] which topic already gives 'em bed-time stories and takes the London reader's attention away from the black misery in Wales and the starving districts.[8]

But on the other foot, the GLOBE'S favourite "Red Ellen"[9] (Wilkinson) says she don't see why a nation shd/ pay rent for its own credit. She has even printed this sprightly sentiment. Ef this keeps on, breverem and my sisterem, the 'Owse of very Commons may yet again become the seat of serious debate and vivid repartee.

Other sections of God's gloomiest Island are speculating on the next Frame Up. At what point is an Englishman loco? In any other country if a bloke crawled round on his kness barking one wd. say he was bug-house. But that don't necessarily work in olde England. The robust William Morris [10] was found on the floor of his dining room biting the table leg. He had got the worst of an argument with Bill Mike Rossetti[11] on the subject of Nordic Sagas, and was heroicly relieving his feelings. Nobody ever suggested that Morris was goofy. otherwise excellent printing. He believed that books during the Victorian decadence shd/ not be inferior as typework to books printed three centuries earlier. He even invented an adjustable armchair.

However, the northern press in England is speculating on how to get rid of Georgie V as there is no chance to frame him on scandal bis.

Scotland Yard's city chief is up for investigation, elaborate preparations are being made to have two policemen present for every coronation spectator. That pantomime said to interest Hollywood rather more than it does the starved areas (vide sopra) of England.

My only bet is that if "George Fifth the Second" (as they call him in Paris) shows the faintest inclination to live up to Edward's promise to the miners,[12] Baldwin's gang will subject him to unpleasant strain.

If the Globe reader wd. turn his mind to the serious and constructing parts of Europe he must pardon me for writing in a less snappy and sparky manner. It is impossible to send on real news without at least a few technicalities.

SEEDLINGS

On Nov. 30 a writer in "Rivista del Lavoro" declared that Hitler's preceding Nuremberg speech contained the central idea of the New Economics, namely that of the National Dividend. Hitler, as a matter of fact, said that production and not the rate of wage, determined the amount of product that wd. go to each "contracting party in the economic process."

And the argument hasn't stopped yet . Did Hitler mean EVERYMAN? His original words were "*und damit jener Anteil der auf den einzelnen Kontrahenten am Wirtschaftsprozess trifft.*"

Does the Führer consider Jedermann, everyman, a contracting party in his state?

The Italian economist is perfectly clear in his statement of what "totalitarian regimes" do (or ought to do). By program or profession they "will the prosperity of the whole people." Question is whether their picture of prosperity is adequate.

German agriculture 1932/3 got 6.4 billion; 1935/6 it got 8.8 billion.

The National Dividend idea means that EVERY CITIZEN (or every citizen of certain age, etc.) gets an even share in the national TOTAL material profit for the year. If Hitler really means this, it is an highly commendable meaning. The "Revista del Lavoro" critic states without any ambiguity that this idea is "slowly but surely gaining ground more or less all over the place."

NOTHING but a ticket system can make this idea effective. Let the reader hold it quite in mind that the word billet in french and biglietto in Italian is used for a railway TICKET and for what we call a treasury note.

The sanest definition of MONEY is P.Larranaga's "a measured claim."[13] It must be transferrable and it bears no intereast when hoarded.

The present tax system is an infamy and based on barbaric ignorance of the nature of money AND of the state.

When the STATE provides a valid state money, that is a measure of value stamped on paper or metal or anything else and which functions as medium of exchange, the STATE does a job of work.

And if the state is paid for that work, such payment differs FUNDAMENTALLY from taxes, as now understood. All present taxes are a dirty grab. The states takes 'em in a number of ways, mostly vicious, and in most countries they are levied by irresponsible swine, unknown to the public, anonymous, hidden, half-witted.

In England the various Banking racketeers are well represented at the controls. Baldwin's camarilla contains representatives of most of the worst English Banks. The most sinsister figure in the late dirty deal is Lord Wigram,[14] permanent Lord in Waiting, now put back where he can whisper sweet nothings into young George's VI credulous ear. British edtr asks whether Lord Wigwam is still a director of the Midland.

It doesn't matter. There is no representative of the British people or nation in Baldwin's cabinet.

Nevertheless the REAL REVOLUTION goes on. Revolutionaries know nothing about it. Revolution need not be conscious. Professed revolution may in some cases have coincided with a real revolution.

In our time/ the real revolutions have gone on unhindered. I have never read a single line of propaganda against the REAL REVOLUTIONS.

Marconi won the 1918 revolution in Russia. You can find that in John Reed's Ten DAYS.[15] Nothing was further from Marconi's[16] mind when he carried on the development of wireless from where the American Loomis had left in the 1860s.[17]

Without radio Lenin cd. not have won. In Italy, Mussolini threw out an exotic parliamentary form. In the 1850s Cavour[18] had introduced this northern violet, and spent a decade teaching the Peidmontese how to be parliamentarian. In England in 1936 parliament resigned; gave over what shreds of power it had, to a secret committee of usurer's pot boys.

The real revolution HAD OCCURRED. In our time the jaw house system/ the system wherein delegates of the people govern by argument in a "chamber" gave way to government by newspapers.

Parliamenterian government ceded to newspaper government. In 1936 Roosevelt[19] beat the press, that is he beat the most corrupt forces in the U.S.A. then in control of the printed page. The real fight was by radio.

Newspaper government gives way to radio government. The bank pimps in England kept Edward OFF the radio until he ceased to be Edward VIII. Morgan's pal and the arch-noise of the English Church was at once put on the air.[20]

So far as I know Italy has preceded all the pretendedly democratic countries in putting a session of her chamber on the air, in the autumn of 1936.

Herein is the REAL REVOLUTION now evolving in Europe. The idealogical war is by comparison isolated. More really isolated than the mass barbarism in Spain. Europe is not going to tolerate Russian power in Barcelona. The gun-makers' game is to keep trouble in process as long as possible for the natural sake of a larger munitions market.

If the reader is trying to understand Europe 1937 let him see the thing in three planes:

1. BASIC, the revolution from parliamentary to newspaper, + thence to radio government.

2. OBSCURANTIST: the pseudo-ideological tosh in all newspapers and in all printed matter having a large circulation; the false issues that the British press feeds its readers, the
perpetual betrayals of the "left" of the popular parties by Mcdonalds, Atlees, and Blums, either from natural and slimy corruption or from blockheadedness.[21]

3. THE REAL struggle in the domain of intellect which is, and has for a decade been, in the monetary domain. Mistrust every editor, every writer however celebrated who wont answer straight questions about the nature of money and its mode of issue. He is either a knave or a fool. In most cases he may be the dirtiest kind of knave, one who damps down his and other men's curiosity. H.G. Wells stalls,[20] the Archbishops of England put their tails between their fat and thin legs and ran to cover after the Church Assembly [23] had opened the question. There is not a newspaper in England on EITHER side whose letter columns are open to free discussion of money. There is no real news in the French papers.

Take it from papa that Leon Blum is no good, a sort of kike version of Ramsey Mcdonald, no more glory to Judea than Ramsey to Scotland.[24] In poetic phantasy one might imagine a France run by a Laval-Daladier[25] combination, i.e. with at least some knowledge and guts. One frog tells me this isn't impossible. One can learn NOTHING from their papers. They are still in the state they were when Raffalovitch[26] used to hire them to sell Russian bonds to French suckers back in 1905, 1909, 1913, right up to the time the Turks borrowed French money for guns they hadn't time to buy from Schneider Creusot [27] and had got to from the other side of the border.

The other news item is A. de' Stefani's[28] appointment to China. The appointment of this honest, and to my mind slightly conservative statesman and economist as Chief Financial Advisor to the Nanking government is another crack on the snout for Ernst Otto Neimeyer[29] and swine of Basel (that is of the League of Nation's control center). At least a few Chinamen have at last got wise to Geneva.

[typed note on lower left margin]
This shd/ be long enough to cut if necessary.

[1] Pound wrote this essay and mailed it on April 3, 1937. *Globe* accepted the manuscript but then ran a truncated and slightly altered version of it later under the title "Revolution by Radio" (Contribution #3).
[2] The Labour Party took control of the London County Council in 1934. The national government of the time was led by the Conservatives.
[3] *Reynolds's Illustrated News* (London).
[4] **Hugh Dalton**
[5] **Anthony Eden**
[6] "Eden a-Beckett" is a punning reference to the relationship between the **Beckett** family, **Anthony Eden** and "Thomas a Becket."
[7] **William Aberhart**
[8] See "Abdication" (Contribution #1) note 26.
[9] **(Cecily) Ellen Wilkinson**

[10] **William Morris**
[11] The story Pound related here was also mentioned in his essay for *Poetry* (March 1918) "Swinburne Verses His Biographers" (see *Literary Essays*, p. 290). In the earlier version it was Dante Gabriel Rossetti and not **William Michael Rossetti**, his brother, who was involved in this incident.
[12] See note 8 above.
[13] **P. J. M. Larrañaga**
[14] **Clive Wigram**
[15] See "Revolution by Radio" (Contribution #3) note 2.
[16] See "Revolution by Radio" (Contribution #3) note 3.
[17] See "Revolution by Radio" (Contribution #3) note 4.
[17] See "Revolution by Radio" (Contribution #3) note 5.
[18] See "Revolution by Radio" (Contribution #3) note 6.
[19] See "Revolution by Radio" (Contribution #3) note 7.
[20] See "Revolution by Radio" (Contribution #3) note 8.
[21] See "Revolution by Radio" (Contribution #3) note 7.
[22] See "Revolution by Radio" (Contribution #3) note 8.
[23] See "Abdication" (Contribution #1) note 22.
[24] Though this section was reprinted in "Revolution by Radio," this remark was dropped by the *Globe* editors concerning **Léon Blum** and **Ramsay MacDonald.**
[25] **Pierre Laval**
[26] **Arthur Germanovich Raffalovich**
[27] The firm of Schneider-Creusot was one of the largest producers of iron ore in Alsace-Lorraine.
[28] **Alberto de Stefani**
[29] **Ernst Otto Niemeyer**

Contribution #13: "Opry out of Doors"
Postmarked August 4, 1938. Signed by Pound.

For "Opry out of Doors," see **EP40**

And we are all so familiar with the usual 200 kilograms of female meat emitting a few liquid high notes but unable to contract any of her musicles sufficiently to express any of that understanding of the composer's meaning (which she probably never had)...that...in short the idea didn't tempt me. They did it here last year in my abscence and I expected the same sort of thing that had drvien me out of more than one building in Florence or Venice. BUT (with capital letters) I saw they were doing the "Barbiere di Siviglia"[1] and thought I'd better look in on the home town effort. Setting: one football field where Boyd Comstock,[2] late of Harvard or Yale and/or California, trains his Olympic athletes, the valley of the "BOGO" spelled Boato, moon as per picture post cards, and an occasional lighted train on the railway embankment passing between one's seat and the sea. One's feet in the grass among the violin cases. The orchestra looking as if the family had got there, grandma, and the children sharing the music stands.

I had however done right (by myself). Paolo lo Monaco is a very neat and tidy conductor. And, to relapse into musical criticism, it is quite probable than no one whosoever has ever so well understood that art of suing orchestra WITH voices as did "old twinkle" Rossini,[3] who stopped writing operas in 1829, and lived on for 39 years more refusing to participate in the steadily worsening mess of XIXth century operaticism.

A fact which might make people think. I am not talking about melodic line, at which Mozart can beat him as he wd/ have been the first to maintain. And I will admit that various composers developed this that, and the other, while losing the very precious art of using Instruments WITH the voice, instead of against it, or of merely repeating insignificant noise in the hope that the stage or the Yowling of the singers wd. keep people from noticing how much trash they had given the instruments.

The tourist may as well know that out door opera is having a boom all over Italy, some of it is probably bad but if anything as good as Anita de Alba (as Rosina) Angelo de Dristina as Figaro,[4] with Guido Guidi, late of the Civic Opera Co. of Chicago as an inimitable Don Basilio and Pietro Medici holding up his end as Almaviva,[5] then it is worth taking your chance on any well composed opera that is billed out of doors when you are in summer in Italy, the maximum cost here in Rapallo is 15 lire (about 80 cents) and gets down to 3 lire (approx. fifteen cents). And for the economical there is the river parapet past the fence where the voices are still quite audible though the orchestra sounds a bit faint.

La Traviata[6] is a very undistiguished piece of work, proving that Verdi at his worst is as "bad as Wagner" and on just those counts on which Verdi revial sets him against Wagner. And I dont care what happens of Boheme and Butterfly.[7] I admit they are at some times better done than at others. If it is news than the flop of Boheme in this Rapallo season caused the compartive smallness of the attendance at the Barbiere, and that the enthusiasm for the Barbiere got a full field for Traviata, make the most of it. It suits my belief all right. I think the people will take good stuff when they get it.

And the older I get the more convinced I am that musicians "fall down because they haven't learned the FIRST page of the excercise book." They think is it is so easy that it don't matter.

House artist please copy

and that don't mean maybe! It dont mean almost. It means that and are the SAME length not more or less.

And I have known musicians who have studied 30 years and given concerts for 20 who haven't yet found it out. Just as there are prominent and/or protuberant orchestra conductors who have always counted one, two, three, four, ie

(printer don't omit dot.) because three is a longer WORD than one or two, and therby caused a great lot of vague and indefinite boredom. The French and Germans don't do it, because they count in their own languages where trois and drei, are NOT longer than deux and zwei.

There were singers in the season with higher priced names, but I am not boosting the season, I am talking of a particular chance. Some reader may know of Guido Guidi (born in Tolentino, studied in Rossini's home town (Pesaro) and learned to sing by NOT permitting teachers to ruin him more than temporarily. P. Medici who speaks well Piccoli, and the Spanish (Cadiz) Amita de Alba who sings like a bird. I am using the term technically and don't know that the lady will appreciate the application. A bird has a narrow beak and opens it wide. The de Alba appears to open her mouth to an enormous extent, say six inches up and down and about one inch wide, out of this quite rectangular ablong the notes precede with most saticfactory clarity and precision. Personal tastes of the singer: Rossini, Verdi, Donizetti[8] and Pergolesi,[9] has sung in Milano, Roma, the rest of Italy and the orient, Tokio Shanghai, Singapore and Hong Kong. if she disarmed her Technique from Pizzi. Viva Pizzi.

Take a chance, brother, if you see these or Angelo de Cristina on a program, or Lo Monaco billed as conductor.

I sat for four hours train trip to some home for Rossini' s Barbiere, but didn't expect to be satisfied. The sense of duty has often failed to keep me in my seat more than ten minutes at an opera.

The Podesta is quite right in saying that these are popular spectacles. I couldn't expect him to run nothing but what I personally want to hear, and I don't expect Strawinsky just yet,[10] but I do think there will be in Rapallo at least one good (in my sense) show every summer opera week, plus something respectable and possibly a period piece by Mercadante.[11] I see nothing nothing to stop Cav. Tadini from doing the Seraglio or the Nozze di Figaro [12] next August. At any rate there is more than a point of contact between these "popular" shows and the extremely high brow concerts that we put on here during the winter. I am not guaranteeing the big musical fetes all over Italy. There was good stuff in Venice when I last tried their annual, but there was also etc....

Are they doing it all over America? Would they like it all over America?

At any rate we hope to have a week's Mozart this winter and a week of Vivaldi the next.. I don't know why American towns of our size shouldn't do likewise. May be there do.

Continuing my vest pocket course for intending musicians and composers. Lesson A. first page of the excercise book (as above) with implications of Carl Fleschier and his methods, note also that Rossini told Lavignac that he, Rossini, had learned his job by copying out the parts of Hadyn's quartettes.[13]

I don't say that if the distracted reader does it he will write a Bianca e Faliero [14] or a William Tell [15] or a Barbiere, but it might suggest to him (or her) unless he or she has a conservatory spoliation, that the knowledge of PARTICULAR details of a masterpiece is worth years of theory. Microphotographic editions of inedited masterwork would provide a basis for an immense reawakening in efficient composition and discrimination in music. The student copying the parts or filling the bass, ciphered and unciphered, could learn a great deal that he commonly does not learn about the thought of the masters. It is all very well to read a score, some people have, but nobody but God Almighty could read a score with the same attention a man has to give it in copying it out note by note. Hence the inundation of musical soupiness which occurred when musicians stopped a doing this.

Other items of local excitement. Ed Windw Windsor looks less peevish than formerly or than might be expected. His missus has pretty eyes (perhaps that shd/ have been told in an earlier article) correspondent apologizes for delay in transmission. Gen Badoglio[16] plays an old fashioned game called "bocchi" (or bowls without nine pins).

AND make no mistake about it, Anita can act, which might be news to some manager wanting a Rosina or a Serva Padrona.[17] Comin' down along the river last night the children were talking about Don Basilio as if he were a real person. I bet they didn't do that about the characters in any of the other operas of this series, and I take it as at least a strong hint concerning that vitality of Rossini's work (and his libretist's, who was a bloke named Sterbini[18]) I also take it as a tribute to the way Guido Guidi puts it over. EVVIVA.

Ezra Pound

[1] **Gioachino Rossini**'s comic opera, *Il barbiere di Siviglia*, was first staged in 1816.

[2] **Boyd Comstock**

[3] **Gioacchino Rossini** (1792–1868), Italian composer. Rossini began writing operas at the age of 18 and quickly achieved fame. Many of his operas are still

standard repertoire. After working with theater opera companies across Italy and France, he stopped writing operas at age 37.

[4] In the plot of the opera *Il barbiere di Siviglia*, the character of Figaro is taken into the service of Count Almaviva to help Almaviva court Rosina, daughter of the forbidding Dr. Bartolo.

[5] In the plot of the opera *Il barbiere di Siviglia*, the character Don Basilio is a music teacher in the household of Dr. Bartolo.

[6] **Giuseppe Verdi**'s opera *La Traviata* premiered in 1853 at the Teatro La Fenice.

[7] **Giacomo Puccini**'s opera *La Bohème* premiered in 1897 in Venice and his *La Madama Butterfly* premiered at La Scala in 1904.

[8] **Giuseppe Verdi, Domenico Gaetano Maria Donizetti**

[9] **Giovanni Battista Pergolesi**

[10] **Igor Stravinsky**

[11] **Giuseppe Saverio Raffaele Mercadante**

[12] **Mozart**'s opera *Die Entführung aus dem Serail* premiered in 1782 and his *Le Nozze di Figaro* in 1786.

[13] **Albert Lavignac**

[14] **Rossini**'s *Bianca e Falliero o sia Il consiglio dei Tre* was first staged at La Scala in 1819.

[15] **Rossini**'s *William Tell*, which premiered in 1831 in Paris, was based upon Schiller's drama of the same title.

[16] **Pietro Badoglio**

[17] Rosina is one of the main characters of *Il barbiere di Siviglia*. Pound is probably referring to the central character Serpina (the Serva Padrona, the "maid-mistress") in the opera *La serva padrona*.

[18] **Cesare Sterbini**

Contribution #14: "Milestones"
Date unknown. Signed by Pound.

This short manuscript is a draft or version of "Notes on Micro-Photography" (Contribution #9)

As to what the "intellectuals" are doing, God-blessum! BROLETTO, monthly magazine of the City of COMO,[1] in January published so far as we know, for the first time in history, a complete concerto (of Vivaldi) in small half tones taken from "microfoto" Leica films——in enormous saving over the old system where half tones were made from full size photos. Dr. Sayce[1] of King's College, Newcastle, calculates he can register 500 pages of music on a rigid grainless film the size of a poscard. This means absolute revolution in all study of unpublished music, and the whole prolmem of the musical library enters a completely new phases.

BRANCUSI has been to Indore to see about building a temple and his "Endless Column" has been set up in Jargu jiu Gory, Roumania.[2] Where they cleared out a slum, made a new park as set up a sixty foot high metal section of this form, which the imagination can prolong as far as it likes.

Painting about where it was in 1917, music getting ready to have its ears washed, and its teath scrubbed. Licherchoor? oh well LICHERCHOOR is the domain of mr e.e.cummings for the moment.[3]

Ezra Pound

FOLLOWING QUOTE

verbatim as follows:
"As regards general economic questions, these are not within the scope of the Society of the Friends of National Spain,[4] which exists to enlighten English public opinion regarding the Nationalist movment in that country. We are not out to deal with economic questions, about which no doubt our members have different views."
signed E.E. Beare, secretary.
53 a St Stephen's House, London S.W.I.

another page

AND you have the Van Zeeland "report,"[5] Oldsmobile model 1896, and de'Stefani

and every continental writer worht a damn laughing at it, and you have the British press solemnly slobbering along as if Hitler and/or Mussolini was going to BUY it for a Rolls-Royce 1940.
Such, my children, IZ forces.

[1] See **JD19** note 6.
[2] See "Notes on Micro-Photography" (Contribution #9) note 2.
[3] **Constantin Brancusi**
[4] **Edward Estlin Cummings** published his *Collected Poems and New Poems* in 1938.
[5] Society of the Friends of National Spain was a pro-Franco organization that raised money for the Nationalist cause in Great Britain.
[5] In 1938, ex-premier of Belgium, Paul Van Zeeland (1893–1973) issued a report calling on a conference of world powers to restore a system of economic cooperation.

Contribution #15: "A Continent or"

Date unknown. Signed by Pound.

For "A Continent or," see oblique references in **EP9**

If you are trying to make your own map of Europe, you might start by recognizing Jugoslavia[1](Serbia etc as was); a solid agricultural country, such as Horace Greely[2] might have told young men to go to. Loads of wood, planks cut to specific length, specified quality, deliverable by motor boat to Ancona, within 24 hours of being ordered. Simple and natural commercial relations between producers of certain raw materials and handy Italian market.

And by contrast Czeko-Slovakia. Private bailywick of London and of Imperial Chemicals.[3] The last country where people will swallow a London Times editorial.

I mean that by the time every boob in Poland and every peasant in Clabria is onto Printing House Square there will <u>still</u> be Czeko-Slovaks thinking of Gladstone[4] and believing that England is today Queen Victoria's England.

And if I may quote more or less from a poem "Djekko-Slovaks! Tdere ArHre gno Djekkoslovaaaks! It iss ligke dtalkink apout deh Kento-Welsch."

Masaryk[5] was a good guy, but simple minded. Any kind of honesty looks simple minded to some. In 1937 Czeko-Slovakia looks to everybody except a few friends of "the professor" like a flimsy jerry-built country invented by England and ideologues.

Note that their best and biggest gun-works[6] were bought up in the spring for London via the Vienese Rothschilds[7] or something of that sort. The people who want war and/or who still have a nice retrospective letch toward Metternich and/or the Congress of Vienna[8] (whatever that was) wd/ call it "the powder magazine." Some of it was once was Bohemia (without a sea coast). Now it's Poland that has no sea coast except up by Danzig. And so forth. My advice to people in powder magazines wd/ be don't explode. Anyway, if England needs a goat, that goat will be tethered in Praaaag [Prague] . But let's hope it won't happen. I personally am against it, for whatever that matters. A few clean men can prevent a war. I mentioned one of 'em to an Ambassador[9] (a compatriot). I said how often HAS he prevented a war. "Dunno," said his respectable Excellence, "Two or three times in the last couple of years."

Thank god America has had at least ONE good ambassador since Farley became postmaster general.[10] I take off my hat to ONE U.S. Ambassador. But I have no idea whether that remark was intended for publication. And I cd do without a lot of his friends.

I am not talking about PAN-Europa, or Dr Kuddleguggle Kurrumbi, but a sense of Europe arises.

T.S. Eliot wrote long ago that Henry James had become a good European,[11] with an aside that no Englishman ever had. For a year there has been talk of the Rome-Berlin axis.[12] Even that isn't quite what I mean.

I mean that people in Jugoslavia, Hungary, the hither or selected Balkans, Italy, Germany have definitely a level of civlization, and certain common grounds, not merely of interest but of disposition. They have no more reason for poisoning each other with gas or dropping bombs out of air planes on each others women and chillins than people in Ohio have about fighting Toronto.

The bloke who gimme the dope on Blum said, "The french peasant is very CLOSE. ("Il est tres avare") Sense of personal property very high, ingrained. Down in Toulouse when we were eating A.I. (I will say, AYE ONE) veal chops during the armistice after meat cards in London, I used to say I cd/ feel the whole city go out and GROAN whenever a train of good food went to Paris.

Communism is a state of tribal feeling belonging to nomads, it become again real in certain industrial conditions when a lot of men collaborate in an end product, none of 'em making it all, but each of them functioning in a general process. Under these two conditions it has a basis in REALITY, and forms a coherent ethic.

It don't work on the small holder. It is emphatically NOT an agricultural emanation. "You can NOT conquer a map." The amount of gol-basted hooey written about Mussolini's opposition to farm machinery cd. be possible only to liars and ignorant apes. You try running a tractor over a ligurian hill side, where the stuff is grown on terraces 20 to 6 feet wide, held up by a lot of hand built walls! Try it!

As for French dislike of the Germans, you might temper the news-lords' views with old Marie's opinion. She had been prisoner behind the German lines, they had put her to do hard work, she had no use for sloppy Bavarians but a Prussian had knocked out her front teeth with a gun butt because she didn't step to it, and her idea of the Prussian was HIGH. "Mais le Prussien!! C'est un chic homme!"

A man running open air political meetings in London (July 1937) writes me "But you wd. be amazed at the pro-German feelng among the working men here."[13]

France can't be the centre of Europe. France WAS European culture from 1830 to 1914, mebbe a bit before than and mebbe for a few months longer. But Paris is NOT all France.

"What, you have been to Paris, and you have come here to Rochechoart? Ils n'ont pas vous corrumpu le bas?"

I have seen 'em down in the Pyrenees thinking that: "all the harm comes from Richelieu.[14] WHY shd/ we be under Paris."

There is a perfectly EUROPEAN part of France, it stretches from the Pyrenees up to Tours, and as far East as the Rhone. I don't know enough about the parts east of the Rhone, so I will say nothing about 'em.

Then there is the France of the biologically fixed. "Bigod you've hit it," said the exRussian exgeneral[15] "biologically FIXED!" Waal that type of frog is a black-out. He has got a set of dead ideas, smooth as the curate's egg before breaking.

Vienna has always been European. They've got NO good art, they are way back of beyond. And coming out of Arthur Schnitzler's one day, sez young Antheil: "But how a MAN, can go on like that, livin' in a one horse town like Vienna!":[16]

Wich iz my sentiments. But Vienna is European, I wont [illegible word] its Europeanity, it was about 1897 when I was there ten years ago. Rome is European. I have evidence by letter that there ARE Europeans living "all over the place." Frankfurt am Main has for long been, but often in a sinister sense, "European." You can use the word nastily or you can use it with a smile: "European." But there is nevertheless an European common sense. Not quite "le bon sens français." But certain kinds of ideological bunk just don't hook the real European. He has a certain moderation, and a certain immunity from the excessive abstractions.

This works in agricultural France as well as in middle Europe and Italy.

Now with all gentleness toward the dead, You can't say that pore ole Geo. V was much more of man than our own peanut-faced Coolidge. He was poor bloke who got stuffed into a job by calamity of his birth, he was very English, typical and beloved by "his" people. But when a EUROPEAN idea, the channel tunnel was proposed, he thanked God for "Glorious Insularity,"[17] opposed it and thereby set back his country, with full connivance of its pastors, and masters.

Half the English head is chock full of suet. If you find an Englishman thinking, suspicion him, in 90% of all known exemplars there is somehing WRONG with the bloke. And the racial British intelligence KNOWS this and suspects, therefore, ALL mental activity. It saves time, trouble and attains 90% of effenciency in the general weighing of mundane affairs. (But the Wimmen... say Hank! (as Mr Hemmingway[18] sez)

"I," sez I "can't be bothered about a lot of bhloddy middle-aged wimmen?!"

"There," sez Aunt Nellie [19] when I was a whole lot younger, "is where you yr/ MIStake my deah Ezra. The world is ENtirely bedevild and managed by middle-aged wimmen."

"The hell!" said yr/ correspondent without phazing her. And she continued "From cradle to the grave! They wheedle it out of their fathers. they pester their husbands, and they bring up their sons. They stuff'em with whatever they want. They pester their husbands. A man doesn't CARE. He don't care about anything. All he was wants is to be left there in peace and quiet. If a wommun pesters him long enough he will say YES to ANYthing."

Well, there are in the feminine island, three million "superfluous" rendered lively by competition. They believe in polygamy. They are expert conversationalists. That is to say they ask questions. Such soothing questions! They wd. ask Baalam's ass about politics. They wd. ask YOU about writing or music, or politics, and look interested in yr. platitudes.

"But wd/ you," said Balfour of Burleigh[20] by no means to be confused with the late downy bird and slick guy Arthur James Balfour[21]) to Lady B;;n.nk, "abandon the enormous benefits of monOGamy?"

Sez she: "I might. If I had ever encountered it." (meanin' monogamy) "Fingers," she said to me, his were " fat and white like big stalks of asparagus." And by contrast Europe is masculine. Demographic average und so weiter. French 'arf n' arf, got a price mark on EVERYTHING.

I shd/ say the present Europe has a lot of <u>unconscious</u> agreements. Non-English, non-Parisian. Over and above these there are a few formulae. Note for example the charter of labour: That means roughly a minimum wage, by law established. It means a limited number of hours of work. It means that the owners are supposed to have responsibilities, more important than sheer competition with some other firm trust or company. That is part of new Europe.

When the left side frogs got in, all they had was a few proposals already working in Italy. When the reform sharks of all kinds in Californy got together, Townsendites, Doug/ites etcs.[22] they had some points of agreement (all of 'em <u>old stuff</u> in Italy, + now starting in Hun-land I% on rural housing loans north of the Alps, that is European at present.

There is also a sense of NOT being Russians. An' if yr/ present correspondent knows anything he is telling you that the gorrrdam slavs have NOT had the sense to think out a money system. They have NOT had the sense to set up a money system or even to HEAR OF what we in America knew 1780 to 1840 and FORGOT with the Civil War.

This, more than anything else, is why Russia is having jitters, and why Uncle Joe is, if we may trust press accounts, pluggin' so much lead into "old kumrads."[23] They just wouldn't think about money. What, sonny, IS money?

As to frogs, there is no need wastin' sympathy on the frog governink classes. Either they lie, or they are criminally ignorant. Just as a dentist or stable boy would be CRIMINALLY ignorant instead of plain and honestly ignorant, if he attempted to perform a complicated operation. The NEWS, if real, is bound be technical, I mean the BIG news, as distinct from the merely loud. Rossoni's speech[24] on the amassi, that is on passing the grain to centrals, and guaranteeing a price to the farmer; Rossoni telling 'em that he sees a chance for a completely different concept and system of taxation is NEWS# It wasn't there the year before last. Gun sales are always with us. They are habit. There are two sides, salesmanship on one side, and cannon-fodder the other.

It might also be noted that the present era England has reached an exotic, not in form of Island imitation of continental externals, trappings, coloured shirts etc, but as a local growth belonging to the times, in the little advertised National Socialist League.[25] This is a party believing in correlated guild organization. It is not a "merely monetary" group but at the same time it keeps the money question in front line. Whether it is too sane and moderate to please the wild and woady Britons must be left to the year after the year after next to show, but at any rate they have an intelligent program, without fads, without rosettes and trimmings.

As to WHERE we have got to, summer and autumn 1937. No one writing for England or America can be considered other than a blithering ass, a four-flusher or pertaining to the Gunther[26] class of those who merely parrot and pass on fixed ideas and superstitions unless he, or she, desist from general terms, such as fascism, communism# etc/ and talk of specific measures. As rough and approximate statement, the real men who think at all are divided as to the PROPORTION IN WHICH there has got to be organization and monetary reform. Some want more emphasis on honest money and no private monolopy, or anti-social wangling of same, others expect to leave finance till the last and advance via guild organization more or less coordinated to centre.

Obviously "specialists" who avoid defining the terms, especially the basic, initial and most necessary terms of their subjects are mere lice. There are more elaborate and "parliamentary" ways of making this last statement, but they do not affect its main meaning.

A great deal of "organization propoganda" is fake, that is, it proposes impractical organization merely as a means to stave off honest money. Sometimes one gazes back westward and seems to perceive that this modus operandi is not limited to "the old world."

[1] See "Europe MCMXXXVI" (Contribution #2) note 14 and **EP9** notes 3–4.
[2] **Horace Greeley**
[3] See "Abdication" (Contribution #1) note 31.
[4] **William Ewart Gladstone**
[5] **Tomáš Garrigue Masaryk**
[6] See "United States of Europe?" (Contribution #8) note #9.
[7] The Viennese branch of the House of Rothschild was founded by Salomon Rothschild (1774–1855), who had a personal and business relationship with **Prince von Metternich.**
[8] **Prince von Metternich**
[9] Possibly **Claude Gernade Bowers**
[10] **James Aloysius F. Farley**
[11] In 1918, **T. S. Eliot** wrote of Henry James in his essay "Henry James: In Memory": "It is the final perfection, the consummation of an American to become not an Englishman, but a European, something no European, no person of any European nationality can become" (*Little Review*, August 1918, as quoted in Gordon, *T. S. Eliot*, p. 102).
[12] Mussolini and Hitler signed the so-called "Rome–Berlin Axis" pact. They also agreed on common policies in Spain in Central Europe. The Axis was expanded in 1937 with the Anti-Comintern Pact between Germany and Japan which Mussolini joined in 1937.
[13] Pound was possibly referring to a letter from **Oswald Mosley**, Leader of the British Union of Fascists. If so, this letter seems not to have survived.
[14] **Armand Jean du Plessis**
[15] **Honore Golijewsky**
[16] **Arthur Schnitzler** was Böske Antheil's uncle.
[17] By "Glorious Insularity", Pound was referring to the 19th century British attitude and foreign policy of "Splendid Isolation." This policy emphasized the avoidance of all treaty ties and entanglements.
[18] **Ernest Hemingway**
[19] **Edith Ellen Hyde-Lees** of Dorothy, Pound's wife.
[20] Possibly **Alexander Hugh Bruce**
[21] **Arthur James Balfour**
[22] Pound appears to have been reading **Luther Whiteman** and **Samuel L. Lewis**'s *Glory Roads: the Psychological State of California* (1936), which deals with economic reform movements in the state in the 1930s. By Townsendites, Pound was referring to supporters of Dr. Francis E. Townsend of Long Beach, California. In 1934, Townsend founded the organization "Old Age Revolving Pension, Limited," and advocated a pre-social security plan to set

up government pensions for retirees. By Doug/ites, Pound was referring to supporters of the Social Credit theories of Clifford Hugh Douglas. See note for "That League in Calvin's Own City."

[23] Pound was referring to Joseph Stalin's purges.

[24] **Edmondo Rossoni**

[25] National Socialist League headed by **Sir Oswald Mosley.**

[26] **John Gunther**

Contribution #16: "SIENA"

Date unknown. Handwritten. Signed by Pound.

For "SIENA,"see **EP36**

Very optional p.s. (date to suit) no typewriter with me.

A monthly letter can not compete with cable news in the domain of cable news. One of the simplest means of not being surprised by cable news is to pick the key phrases in Mussolini's radio speeches.

On this line i have not yet made any very wild errors.

The speech at Palermo (Aug. 20) underlined several points already made in these letters.

1. Europe will not have Russia "or anything like it" in the mediteranean.

2. The Rome-Berlin[1] axis will not be chucked. Italy intends it as an implement of peace.

The phrase "a fatto" means "not a bit of it." and referred to the League of nations. Italy just don't give a bosh whether the League does or doesn't.

"We do not go to Geneva to register births." "We might perhaps register a demise."

[edtr. omit this p.s. if daily papers have already worked the subject to death.]

Note that there was no ideology, no theorectic discussion in the Palermo speech. The "problem of Sicily" is water-supply. I take it the "25% done, 25% in process," refers to this subject specificly as well as to things in general. + The remaining 50% "will be accomplished."

As to the juxtaposition of the words via (highway) and vita (life) anyone who saw the effects of the bombardment of Ancona[2] (done before declaration of war.) or anyone whose front veranda is so near the mediterranean that he can (as I can) shoot orange pips into it.

can see why Italy is interested is the Mediterranean problem.

As to rumours. The head of the government is not going to be diddled by a British dude in a tail coat. I shd. discount cable news to that effect.

Ezra Pound

(gets too long if I try to explain why this that + the other.)

[1] See "A Continent or" (Contribution #15) note 12.
[2] On May 4, 1915, Austro-Hungarian ships shelled the Italian port city of Ancona, killing civilians and damaging buildings. Italy formally declared war on the Austro-Hungarian Empire on May 23, 1915.

Contribution #17: "Railway Station SIENA"
Date unknown, with three photos of station. Signed by Pound.

SIENA now has a new building as well proportioned as her mediaeval cathedral.[1] The 20th century oust the horrible architectural mess of the 19th Italy. Interest not only in the form but in comprehensive use of new materials. Other railway stations such as that of Viareggio and Firenze will give chance of testing the new Tiros, bricks, metals against the old tufa and travertine, now competing with boom in italian marble.

this third photo not much use for Globe. But I include it. for edt. instruction rather than for reprod.

[1] Il Duomo di Siena was built from 1284 to 1377.

BIOGRAPHICAL APPENDIX

William Aberhart (1878–1943), Canadian politician. Aberhart was a Canadian high school principal and radio preacher who founded the Social Credit League of Alberta in 1932. Aberhart was elected premier of the province of Alberta in 1935 and established the first Social Credit government in the world. Social Credit theorist C. H. Douglas served for a while as economic adviser to Aberhart and in 1937 he wrote the book *The Alberta Experiment: An Interim Survey.*

Louis Adamic (1898–1951), Slovenian-born American author. His best-known work is *The Native's Return* (1934) which was highly critical of the regime of the Serbian king Alexander I of Yugoslavia (1888–1934).

B. M. G. Adams, pen name of **Mrs. Evelyn St. Bride Scratton** (1882–1964), English writer. Pound met Scratton about 1910 in London. The two formed a long friendship—her letters to Pound continued well into the late 1950s. Pound promoted Scratton's writing and through his influence she appeared in *The Dial*, *The Criterion*, and the *transatlantic review*. Though the character of their relationship is unclear, Pound was named as a co-respondent in Scratton's divorce proceedings in 1923. Pound included a collection of Scratton's prose sketches entitled *England* (1923) in a series of books edited by himself and published by William Bird's Paris-based Three Mountains Press.

Brooks Adams (1848–1927), American historian. Brooks Adams was the grandson of President John Quincy Adams and brother of Henry Adams.

Adams was a strong critic of the capitalist economic system and expressed these views in his book *The Law of Civilization and Decay* (1895). Pound read this book with enthusiasm in the mid-1930s.

Samuel Hopkins Adams (1871–1958), American journalist and author; graduate (1891) and trustee of Hamilton College. Adams began his career as a journalist at the New York *Sun*, but soon joined the staff of *McClure's Magazine*. He made his reputation as a muckraking investigative reporter at *McClure's*, writing on the conditions of public health in America. It was his series of articles for *Collier's Weekly*, entitled "The Great American Fraud" (beginning October 1905), that had the most influence. In these articles Adams exposed the ineffectiveness and even the danger of patent medicines. These pieces led directly to the passing of the 1906 Pure Food and Drugs Act.

Halide Edip Adivar (1885–1964), Turkish novelist, autobiographer, politician, educator, and feminist leader. In 1901, she was the first Turkish Muslim woman to graduate from the American College for Girls at Üsküdar. She became involved in the Turkish nationalist struggle and wrote for the left-wing journal *Tanine*. In 1910, political conditions forced her to flee Turkey, but she returned in 1912. During World War I she worked in Syria and Lebanon. When the Turkish War of Independence broke out, she was allied with Mustapha Kemal Pasha (later known as Atatürk), who, in 1923, became President of the Turkish Republic. However, she eventually broke with Atatürk and withdrew from political life. She lived in France, and did not return to Turkey until Atatürk's death in 1938. Her primary books were *Memoirs of Halide Edib* (1926) and *The Turkish Ordeal* (1928).

John Penrose Angold (1909–43), English poet and writer. During the 1930s, Angold wrote on economic topics for *The New English Weekly*. He also had a deep interest in classical Greek poetry and published a volume of his own verse in 1933, entitled *NYX Apocalyptike*. Angold initiated a correspondence with Pound in 1932 and kept in constant touch with him until 1939, when he joined the British military. Angold was killed in action as an RAF pilot in 1943. His death is lamented in Canto 84. Angold published Canto 45, which first appeared in his journal *Prosperity* (4:3 [February 1936]) as "WITH USURA."

George Antheil (1900–59), American composer and author. Antheil left America in 1922 on a concert tour under the patronage of a wealthy patron, Mary Louise Bok. On June 13, 1923 he arrived in Paris and settled into a small second-floor apartment above **Sylvia Beach**'s Shakespeare and Company. Soon afterwards, through **Margaret Anderson**, editor of *The Little Review*, Antheil met Pound. A collaborative relationship developed between the two. Antheil helped with the notation and orchestration of Pound's opera *Le Testament* and later, in 1926, assisted in the first performance of the work. In October 1924, Pound published *Antheil and the Treatise on Harmony*, which combined his appreciation and assessment of Antheil's music with his own thoughts on music theory.

Falik Rifki Atay (1894–1971), Turkish journalist. Atay contributed an article entitled "As We Are, Not Were" to the June 1937 issue of *Globe*. Atay was a member of Atatürk's inner circle and was a political theorist for his regime.

Clement Richard Attlee (1883–1967), British statesman, 1st Earl Attlee of Walthamstow, Viscount Prestwood and prime minister. He served as under-secretary of war in **Ramsay MacDonald**'s first government (1924), and as chancellor of the duchy of Lancaster and postmaster general in the second. When MacDonald formed his coalition government in 1931, Attlee resigned. He then became the deputy leader of the Labour Party and, in 1935, its leader. In the Churchill government he held a number of posts including deputy prime minister (1942–5). Attlee succeeded Churchill as prime minister in 1945 and served until 1951.

Pierre Audiat (1891–?), a French author and journalist whose works include *Trois amours de Louis XIV: Madame de Montespan* (1938) and *Paris pendant la guerre: juin 1940-août 1944* (1946). Audiat held various editorial positions during his career. These included *Paris-Soír* (literary director), *Le Figaro* and *Le Figaro Littéraire*, *Le Monde,* and editor-in-chief of *Paris-Midi*.

Edward D. Bacon (1860–1938), British philatelist. Bacon became curator of the Royal Stamp Collection (then known as the King's Collection) in 1913 and held the post until 1938.

Pietro Badoglio (1871–1956), Italian general and statesman. Under Mussolini, Badoglio directed the Italian invasion of Ethiopia. Though he was considered a military hero by the fascists, Badoglio opposed Italy's entry into World War II. During the war, Badoglio was blamed for Italy's disastrous attempt in 1939–40 to invade Greece. As a result, he was relieved of his command. When Mussolini was overthrown in 1943, King Victor Emmanuel II named Badoglio prime minister and tasked him with trying to negotiate a peace with the Allies.

Stanley Baldwin (1867–1947), British Conservative politician, 1st Earl Baldwin of Bewdley, Viscount Corvedale. Stanley Baldwin was prime minister three times between 1923 and 1937. Baldwin came from an industrial family invested in mining, steel, and railroads. While prime minister for a third term (1935–37), Baldwin faced Hitler's remilitarization of the Rhineland, the outbreak of the Spanish Civil War, the Ethiopian Crisis, and the abdication crisis.

Arthur James Balfour (1848–1930), British philosopher and statesman, 1st Earl of Balfour. Balfour was prime minister from 1902–5.

Sallustio Bandini (1677–1760), Italian economist. Bandini began his career as a soldier but soon took holy orders and turned to the career of economist concerned with agriculture, markets, taxes, and other problems. His best-known work is an essay on the potential economic benefits of the swamp region of Tuscany known as the Maremma (*Discorso economico* 1737, published 1775). He presented this work to Francesco III, Grand Duke of Tuscany, and father of Grand Duke Leopold I, whom Pound celebrated in *The Fifth Decad of Cantos* for the so-called Leopoldine Reforms. Bandini would be largely neglected by Francesco III, but would be a primary inspiration for his son Leopold I's economic policies in Tuscany. Given Bandini's interest in land reclamation in the Maremma region, in Pound's historical imagination he stands in line with Mussolini's over-touted draining of many swamps in the Maremma, as well as with the Chinese land reclamation projects mentioned in the "Chinese Cantos" LII–LXXI.

John Hollis Bankhead II (1872–1946), American politician. John Hollis Bankhead II was a three-term Democratic senator from Alabama. He came from a powerful political Alabama family. His father was John Hollis Bankhead ([1842–1920], Democratic senator 1907–20) and his brother was William Brockman Bankhead ([1874–1940], Democratic representative 1917–40 and speaker of the house 1936–40). His niece was the well-known actress Tallulah Bankhead. Pound corresponded with Bankhead between 1933 and 1940.

Joseph Bard (1892–1975), Hungarian-born journalist and author. Bard was a correspondent for Associated Press and Reuters. He was the first husband of the journalist **Dorothy Thompson**, whom he met in 1921. The marriage ended in divorce in 1927—the year Bard met Pound in Rapallo. Soon after meeting Bard, Pound wrote to **Marianne Moore** at *The Dial* recommending that she take Bard's poem "Aurea Mediocritas" for the journal. Bard shared Pound's interest in **Leo Frobenius** and proposed to translate some of Frobenius' work in Bard's new journal *The Island*, which he started in 1931. Bard solicited contributions from Pound for the journal, which in 1932 was renamed *Axis*. Pound was skeptical of Bard's endeavors and there is no evidence that he contributed anything to Bard's journal.

Jean Barral (1912–?), French right-wing writer and editor. Barral was editor of *L'Economie Franchiste* based in Nice. Barral published on the Jewish question, economics, and European politics. In 1935, he became secretary of an organization known as the Université International de Nice. Pound produced two pieces concerning Barral's work during this period: a "Press Notes" letter which appeared in the June 15, 1934 issue of *New Democracy*, and a short piece entitled "Jean Barral with Us" which appeared in the December 5, 1935 issue of *The New English Weekly*. This latter piece was a review article of Barral's book *La Révolution Economique* (n.d.) which appeared in a series entitled Nouvelles Editions Latines. At that time this series included eight other right-wing volumes on European history and economics.

Herbert Ernest Bates (1905–74), British novelist and short story writer. Beginning with his *The Two Sisters* (1926), Bates gained a reputation for his depiction of English country life. His short story "No Country," about a German Jewish immigrant in Great Britain afraid of being deported back to Germany under the Nazi regime, was published in *Globe* (May 1937, pp. 8–10).

Richard Baxter (1615–91), English priest, bishop, preacher, author, and chaplain to the Army of Parliament. Baxter was ordained to the priesthood in 1638, but by 1640 he had allied himself with the Puritan cause. However, after the Restoration in 1660, Baxter served as chaplain to Charles II and was elevated to Bishop of Hereford. Later, Baxter lost both of his positions and was charged with "libeling" the Church in his writings. After a dubious trial, Baxter was convicted and spent eighteen years in prison. Pound seems to have associated Baxter with the rise of British mercantilism in the wake of Cromwell's revolution and Calvinist capitalism.

Sylvia (neé Nancy Woodbridge) Beach (1887–1962), American publisher, author, and bookseller. In 1919, Beach settled in Paris and established her famous bookstore and lending library Shakespeare and Company. Beach became a hub in the lives of many expatriate writers in the 1920s and '30s in Paris, including Ezra Pound. Beach is best known as the publisher of James Joyce's *Ulysses* in 1922. She maintained Shakespeare and Company until she was forced to close it in 1941 after the Germans occupied Paris. As in the case of so many others, Beach lent and sold Pound's work in her bookshop and provided a space where he could meet with many of the other writers and artists resident in Paris at the time.

Charles Austin Beard (1874–1948) and **Mary Ritter Beard** (1876–1958), American historians and social activists. C. A. Beard's approach to history emphasized the role economic interests played in the formation of political movements and institutions. He wrote a body of large-scale, synthetic works such as *The Development of Modern Europe* (1907 with James Harvey Robinson), *An Economic Interpretation of the Constitution* (1913), *Economic Origins of Jeffersonian Democracy* (1915), *American City Government* (1912), and *A Charter for the Social Sciences in the Schools* (1932). Though considered a political radical earlier in his career, Charles Beard was a strong critic of Franklin Roosevelt and the New Deal. Mary Ritter Beard was an historian in her own right. She met Charles Beard while attending DePauw University. They married in 1900 and Mary became involved in the British suffrage and labor movements. Her commitment to the labor movement and women's movements is reflected in her books: *Woman's Work in Municipalities* (1915), *A Short History of the American Labor Movement* (1920), *Understanding Women* (1931), *America Through a Woman's Eyes* (1933). Pound possibly was made aware of the Beards' work by Odon Por (cf. Surette, p. 213 referring to a letter from Por to EP dated April 25, 1935).

Rupert Evelyn Beckett (1870–1955), deputy chairman of the Westminster Bank, director of the Yorkshire Penny Bank, and chairman of the Yorkshire Conservative Newspaper Company for thirty years. The *Yorkshire Post* was one of the company's papers. The *Post* was founded 1754 as the *Leeds Intelligencer*. It adopted its current name in 1866. In November 1939 it merged with the *Leeds Mercury*, which was founded in 1718.

Sir Henry Maximilian Beerbohm (1872–1956), English critic, author, satirist, and caricaturist. Max Beerbohm began building his reputation for intellectual and sartorial sophistication as an undergraduate at Oxford. He soon became a younger member of literary and artistic circles associated with the Decadent movement's journal *The Yellow Book*. Aubrey Beardsley, Oscar Wilde, William Rothstein, Reginald Turner, and **W. B. Yeats** became his friends. Beerbohm's social set also included the aristocracy as well as those belonging to the world of the arts and politics. He became a leading British caricaturist, satirizing most of his friends and acquaintances of whatever level of society or reputation in his smart, witty drawings. Pound certainly knew of Beerbohm in the pre-World War I period in London, and he is said to be one of the inspirations for the poem "Brennbaum" in Pound's *Hugh Selwyn Mauberley*. Max Beerbohm went to live in Rapallo in 1911 after he married the actress Florence Kahn. In 1921 and 1923, exhibitions of his caricatures caused controversy in London and Beerbohm went into semi-retirement at his Italian retreat. After Pound moved to Rapallo in the 1920s, Beerbohm became a cordial, but distant, acquaintance.

Ed Bell (1910–56), American novelist. His books include *Fish on the Steeple* (1935) and *Tommy Lee Feathers* (1938).

Gertrude Margaret Lowthian Bell (1868–1926), British archaeologist, traveler, diplomat, and advocate of the Arab cause. She played a key role in Iraqi politics in the first part of the twentieth century.

Julien Benda (1867–1956), French author. His *Trahison des clercs* was published in 1927.

William Rose Benét (1886–1950), poet, novelist, anthologist, editor, and brother of the poet Stephen Vincent Benét. William Rose Benét was an editor at *Century Magazine*, the *Literary Review* of the *New York Evening Post*, and the *Saturday Review of Literature* (which he helped found in 1924). He won the 1942 Pulitzer Prize in poetry.

Louis Berman (1893–1946), American physician, medical journalist, and endocrinologist. In 1935 and 1936, Berman was endocrinology editor of the *Journal of Medical Practices.* In 1922, Pound read and favorably reviewed Berman's book *The Glands Regulating Personality: A Study of the Glands of Internal Secretion in Relation to the Types of Human Nature* (1921) in *The New Age.* He was impressed enough with the work that Pound arranged to have Berman examine James Joyce in Paris in July 1922. Berman recommended endocrine treatment and the extraction of Joyce's teeth to ease Joyce's glaucoma.

Heinrich Besseler (1900–69), German musicologist. Besseler, a professor at the University of Heidelberg, specialized in Medieval, Renaissance, and Baroque music with an emphasis on Bach studies. Pound contacted Besseler through **Douglas Clayton Fox** and the staff of **Frobenius**' Forschungsinstitut für Kulturmorphologie and conducted a brief correspondence concerning Antonio Vivaldi manuscripts and Vivaldi scholarship in Germany.

Léon Blum (1872–1950), French statesman. Blum formed the "Popular Front" governments of the late 1930s. The Popular Front was formed by a coalition of the Communist, Socialist, and Radical parties. In 1936, Blum became the first Jew to become prime minister of France. During his first ministry, he succeeded in passing significant labor reform legislation. However, under pressure from Britain and the French right, he decided not to intervene in the Spanish Civil War. The Communist Party then withdrew from the coalition and the Blum government fell in 1937.

Luigi Boccherini (1743–1805), Italian composer. Boccherini's best-known work today is perhaps his String Quintet No. 5 in E major. He adopted Franz Joseph Haydn's style to such an extent that Neopolitan violinist Giuseppe Puppo nicknamed him "Haydn's wife."

Georges Bonnet (1889–1972), French politician and diplomat. Bonnet was French ambassador to the US from 1937 to 1938, when he became French minister of foreign affairs.

Emilio De Bono (1866–1944), Italian field marshal, colonial governor, and member of the Italian Fascist Grand Council. De Bono was the commander-in-chief of Italy's armed forces during the initial phases of the invasion of Ethiopia in 1935. De Bono had fought in North Africa during World War I and was one of the organizers of the so-called "March on Rome" that inaugurated Mussolini's regime in 1922. In the 1920s, De Bono served as governor of Libya and minister of colonial affairs. He was successful as commander-in-chief of the Italian forces in Ethiopia, but due to his age was relieved of his duties. As a sop, Mussolini promoted him to the rank of Marshal. In reality, De Bono played no significant role in the regime after 1935. However, as an honorary member of the Fascist Grand Council, he participated in the coup that overthrew Mussolini on July 25, 1943. German occupying forces later took De Bono prisoner. Along with Mussolini's son-in-law, Galeazzo Ciano, he was executed in Verona on January 11, 1944.

William Edgar Borah (1865–1940), American politician. Borah was Republican senator for Idaho 1907–40. He opposed the US joining the League of Nations, but worked to write legislation and create international treaties to outlaw war and to establish a world court to settle conflicts. Pound conducted a correspondence with Borah in the 1930s.

Jozef Borowik (?–?), director of the Baltic Institute of Gdynia, Poland. Borowik wrote and traveled to promote improved international relations, especially American relations with the Baltic region. He published two pieces in *Globe* (May 1937): "Poland" and "Poland on a Powder Keg."

Giuseppi Bottai (1895–1995), Italian Fascist politician. Bottai was an advocate of corporatism and professor of comparative politics at the University of Pisa.

Claude Gernade Bowers (1878–1958), American historian, journalist, and diplomat. Bowers was an influential spokesman for the Democratic Party and especially for Franklin D. Roosevelt's New Deal. He also served as ambassador to Spain (1933–9). Bowers remained in Madrid throughout the Spanish Civil War and supported the Spanish Republican cause. He then served as ambassador to Chile (1939–53). Bowers' historical writing, which appealed to a popular audience, was decidedly partisan, emphasizing the accomplishments of past Democratic leaders. His works include *Jefferson and Hamilton: The*

Struggle for Democracy in America (1925), and *The Tragic Era: The Revolution after Lincoln* (1929). Stock relates in his biography of Pound (pp. 455–6) that the poet especially admired Bowers' *Jefferson and Hamilton*. Pound quoted a snatch of a letter from Bowers (CB to EP, May 10, 1938, YCAL) on the Spanish Civil War in Cantos LXXXI and LXXXV.

Constantin Brancusi (1876–1957), Romanian sculptor. Brancusi visited India in 1937 and proposed building a "Temple of Meditation" for the Maharajah of Indore, but the project never happened. In 1935, he built a war memorial for a park in Turgu Jiu, Romania. The installation included an "Endless Column."

James Henry Breasted (1865–1935), American orientalist, Egyptologist, archaeologist, and author. James H. Breasted was the first American to receive a doctorate in Egyptology. With the aid of John D. Rockefeller, Jr., Breasted was able to found the Oriental Institute of the University of Chicago in 1919. Breasted promoted a wide range of studies at the Institute, including numerous archaeological expeditions to Egypt, Central America, and Mesopotamia. He also founded the Chicago Assyrian Dictionary Project. As an author, Breasted is perhaps best known for his *A History of Egypt*, first published in 1905.

Pound wrote to Breasted on December 27, 1931, suggesting that he might wish to collaborate to establish an interdisciplinary journal unifying all fields of learning and providing the reader with news summaries in these various fields. Breasted responded cordially with mild encouragement in a letter dated January 13, 1932, emphasizing his many responsibilities. Pound's second letter was answered by a secretary. This note was polite, but firm, brush-off, stating that Breasted was in the Yucatan on an expedition and overwhelmed with responsibilities.

D. G. Bridson (1910–80), British journalist, broadcaster, and producer. Bridson was a young poet from Manchester, England, when he began a correspondence with Pound in 1931 or 1932. Pound thought enough of his work to include him in his *Active Anthology* (1933). That same year Bridson did a review of the *Cantos* for the October 12, 1933 issue of *The New English Weekly*. In 1935, he joined the BBC and was put on E. A. F. Harding's Research Unit staff. Harding had been involved in the development and broadcast of Pound's opera *Le Testament de Villon* in 1931. Bridson kept up a long correspondence with Pound. However, he met Pound only after Pound had been confined at St. Elizabeths.

Arthur Brisbane (1864–1936), American newspaper editor. Brisbane was influential as a columnist for Hearst papers.

John Brown (1800–59), American radical abolitionist. Brown was convicted and hanged after his failed raid on a federal armory at Harper's Ferry.

Robert Carlton Brown (1886–1959), American writer and inventor. About 1928, Brown developed a machine that anticipated the modern microfilm reader. Brown thought that a kind of mechanized speed scrolling through loops of texts with "unnecessary" words and particles eliminated would increase readers' speed as well as improve comprehension of texts. Brown commissioned a number of avant-garde writers to provide him with "readies" (so named in hopeful response to the "talkies" which had just replaced silent film). These authors included Pound, Mina Loy, Laurence Vail, James Farrell, Samuel Putnam, and Nancy Cunard. The anthology was entitled *Readies for Bob Brown's Machine*. It was published in 1931 by Brown's own Roving Eye Press. For a detailed treatment of Brown and his work, see Dworkin, "'Seeing Words Machinewise': Technology and Visual Prosody," *Sagetrieb* 18:1 (2001), pp. 59–86.

Alexander Hugh Bruce (1849–1921), British statesman. Bruce was the 6th Baron Balfour of Burleigh and Secretary for Scotland 1895–1903.

Guido Bruno (1884–1942), American editor and publicist. Bruno has been described as the "P. T. Barnum of Greenwich Village." A flamboyant figure, Bruno was an entrepreneur and exploited the "Bohemian" scene in pre-World War I Greenwich Village. He established Bruno's Garret which staged avant-garde evenings for visitors to the Village, who paid him a ten cent admission fee. Bruno's magazine, which published the first work of writers such as Hart Crane and Djuna Barnes, frequently changed names. At various times it was known as *Bruno's*, *Bruno's Review of Life, Love and Literature*, *Bruno's Review of Two Worlds*, *Bruno's Bohemia*, *Bruno's Weekly*, and *Bruno's Scrapbook,* as well as *Bruno's Chap Books* (see Watson, *Bedfellows*, p. 375n).

William Christian Bullitt (1891–1967), American diplomat. Early in his career, Bullitt served as a member of the American delegation to the Paris Peace Conference after World War I. Bullitt was dispatched by President Woodrow Wilson on a secret mission to Russia to assess whether the United States should recognize the Communist government. Bullitt recommended recognition, but his advice was rejected. He resigned and became vocal critic of the Treaty of Versailles. In 1932, Bullitt became special assistant to Cordell Hull and then served from 1933 to 1936 as America's first US ambassador to the Soviet Union. After his tenure as ambassador to Moscow, he took up the position of ambassador to France from 1936 until 1940, when France fell to Nazi Germany.

Basil Bunting (1900–85), British poet, journalist, intelligence officer and diplomat, Persian scholar and translator. After leaving the London School of Economics without graduating, Bunting wandered to France working as a "road digger, artist's model, and barman" (Forde, *Poetry of Basil Bunting*, p. 24). Bunting met Pound in Paris in 1923. In February of 1924, he made his first trip to Rapallo to visit Pound. He stayed in Italy until 1925 when, upon his father's death, he left for England. Over the next decade, Bunting and his American wife Maria lived intermittently in Rapallo. During this time Pound placed Bunting's verse in *Poetry* and included his work in the *Active Anthology* (1933). In 1933 Bunting and his family left Rapallo for the Canary Islands. During the late 1930s, Bunting published poetry, reviews, and articles in *The Spectator*, *The New English Weekly*, and *The Criterion*.

Mary Burd (?–?), American editor. Burd was the editor of *The Delphian Quarterly*, the journal of the Delphian Society. She was also a former social worker and a general supervisor of educational activities of the Society.

Montgomery Butchart (1902–69), British author. Butchart was an associate editor of **Ronald Duncan**'s *The Townsman* and an economic historian. Extant correspondence suggests that Butchart and Pound became acquainted sometime around 1934, possibly through a mutual association with or interest in **A. R. Orage**'s *The New English Weekly,* to which Pound was a regular contributor. Butchart assembled an anthology of some Orage's pieces from *The New English Weekly (Political and Economic Writings from* The New English Weekly *1932–1934, with a Preliminary Section from* The New Age *1912,* [1935]). Pound valued another of Butchart's anthologies, *Money: Selected Passages Presenting the Concepts of Money in the English Tradition, 1640–1935* (1935).

Lina Caico (1883–1951), Italian journalist and translator. Pound promoted Caico and had her published in the local Rapallo paper *Il Mare* in the 1930s. Caico lived in Palermo, Sicily. Contacted by Pound directly to write for *Globe*, Caico eventually published several articles for the magazine.

Joseph Caillaux (1863–1944), French Popular Front politician. Caillaux served in several French governments as finance minister. He supported a policy of appeasement in dealing with Hitler. He opposed stamp scrip.

Erskine Caldwell (1903–87), American author. In the early 1930s, Caldwell's short stories began to appear in prominent modernist and left-wing literary journals such as *This Quarter*, *Blues*, *Front*, *transition*, *Hound & Horn*, *Pagany*, *American Caravan*, and *Scribner's Magazine*. In 1932, he achieved his first major success with publication of the novel *Tobacco Road.* He followed up with the equally successful and controversial *God's Little Acre* (1933). At the time *Globe* editors contacted Caldwell, he was involved with photographer Margaret Bourke-White. In 1937, the couple produced *You Have Seen Their Faces,* a book of photo-reportage documenting living conditions for the South's poor.

Morley Callaghan (1903–90), Canadian novelist and journalist. Callaghan was brought to Pound's attention by their mutual friend Ernest Hemingway. Hemingway, who was foreign correspondent for the *Toronto Star*, met Callaghan, a reporter for the newspaper, in Toronto when Hemingway and his wife Hadley went to Canada so she could deliver their son there instead of Paris. Hemingway found out that Callaghan wrote fiction and asked to see some of his stories. He was impressed.

When Hemingway returned to Paris he remained in contact with Callaghan and circulated his work. Pound, about to launch his journal *The Exile,* accepted two of his short stories, "A Predicament" and "Ancient Lineage." In the end, "Ancient Lineage" appeared in *The Exile* but "A Predicament" was picked up by Maxwell Perkins for Scribner and Sons' prestigious literary magazine *American Caravan* in 1927. Callaghan's career was launched.

Callaghan, a prolific writer, published nine books between 1928 and 1937. After 1937, his career entered a slump. Beginning in 1948, he resumed writing, producing fifteen more books until his death in 1990.

John Calvin (1509–64), French Protestant theologian. Calvin, born in Picardy, France, resided from 1536 in the Swiss city of Geneva.

Francis Carco, pseudonym of Tusoli Carcoppino (1886–1958), French novelist and poet.

Carl Carmer (1893–1976), American folklorist. A graduate of Hamilton College 1914, he was known for his nonfiction, especially *Stars Fell on Alabama* (1934), a popular work about Southern life and society seen through the eyes of a Northerner, and *Listen for a Lonesome Drum* (1936), a book recounting anecdotal history and folklore of upstate New York. Carmer, along with Harold Thompson, Louis Jones, and others formed a group of folklorists known as "the Hamilton School," which led an upstate New York folklore renaissance from the 1930s through the 1950s. Carmer published numerous books on folklore, particularly ghost stories. In 1939, he became general editor of "The Rivers of America" series for Farrar & Rinehart. James Taylor Dunn, who met Carmer while working as librarian of the Farmer's Museum in Cooperstown, New York, in the 1950s, was chosen by Carmer to write about the St. Croix river for this series. *The St. Croix* was published in 1965.

Count Camillo Benso di Cavour (1810–61), Italian statesman. Cavour was largely responsible for the creation of the unified Kingdom of Italy. Cavour used his newspaper *Il Risorgimento* as a prime means of communicating the ideology of Italian unification and independence to his public.

Blaise Cendrars, pseudonym for Frédéric-Louis Sauser (1887–1961), French-speaking Swiss novelist, poet, and traveler.

Neville Chamberlain (1869–1940), British statesman and prime minister. Chamberlain became mayor of Birmingham in 1915 and became a member of Parliament in 1918. He held ministry positions in two of the governments formed under Prime Minister Stanley Baldwin (1924–9, 1935–7). He became prime minister in 1937, following Baldwin's resignation. Chamberlain advocated a policy of appeasement in dealing with Hitler and Mussolini and was the primary negotiator with Hitler in creating the Munich Pact, signed in September 1938. The pact gave Germany the Sudeten area of what was then Czechoslovakia. This concession set into motion the German territorial expansion that led to the Polish crisis of 1939. Chamberlain's govenment ended in 1940 and he was succeeded by Winston Churchill as prime minister.

Charlemagne (750–814), first emperor of the Holy Roman Empire. Around 812 CE, Charlemagne issued a law which has become known as the *Capitulare de Villis*, that defined and regulated the economic life of his empire. This decree laid down standards for accounting in government matters, standardized the monetary system, and regulated weights and measures. These standards and regulations were strictly enforced. The standardization of money was guaranteed by the royal mint, which had a monopoly on the production of coins.

Camille Chautemps (1885–1963), French Radical Socialist politician.

Richard Cobden (1804–65), British businessman and politician from Manchester. One of the founders of the "Manchester School" of economics, Cobden was an ardent opponent of British imperialism.

Jean Cocteau (1889–1963), French poet, critic, prose writer, artist, and film maker. By the time Pound met him, Cocteau had already forged connections with Pablo Picasso, Erik Satie, Marcel Proust, Igor Stravinsky, and Serge Diaghilev, the impresario of the Ballets Russes, among others. Cocteau published his first book of poems, *La Lampe d'Aladin*, in 1908 and in 1920 brought out a volume of collected poems, *Poésies (1917–1920).*

George D. H. Cole (1889–1959), British economist, journalist, academic, and novelist. During the 1930s, Cole was a member of the Economic Advisory Council and the Committee on Economic Information. He wrote for a time as labor correspondent for the *Manchester Guardian*. Cole was as a Fabian socialist who had an interest in the guild and syndicalist movements. He was also reader in economics and then professor of social and political theory at Oxford.

Boyd L. Comstock (?–1950), track coach and athlete. Comstock came from the United States to Italy in the 1930s to train track athletes. He trained several Italians for the 1936 Olympics.

Constantine I (272–337 CE, ruled 306–37 CE), Roman emperor. Constantine was declared "Augustus" in Britain in 306, but he had to consolidate his power through war with imperial rivals; he became sole emperor in 324 CE. In this position he moved the capital of the empire from Rome to what was to become Constantinople on the Bosphorus Strait. He also undertook a massive overhaul of the imperial administration, military organization, and legal system. Constantine is best known, however, for making Christianity the empire's state religion and suppressing the old Roman religion.

Alfred Duff Cooper (1890–1954), British politician, 1st Viscount Norwich. He and his wife Lady Diana, daughter of the Duke of Rutland, were close friends with **Edward VIII** and **Wallis Warfield Simpson**. Cooper was secretary of state for war in the cabinet of prime minister **Stanley Baldwin**. During the abdication crisis, he was one of the few cabinet ministers whom Baldwin allowed Edward VIII to consult. Realizing that Edward would not give up marriage to Wallis Simpson, Cooper strongly advised that he put off the wedding until after his coronation. Edward rejected this advice. In 1938 Cooper was First Lord of the Admiralty in prime minister **Neville Chamberlain**'s government. He resigned in protest in after Chamberlain signed the Munich Pact with Hitler.

Marie Corelli, the pseudonym of Mary Mackay (1855–1924), British author. Corelli was a popular and prolific author of melodramatic novels.

Charles E. Coughlin (1891–1979), Canadian priest and political propagandist. Coughlin was pastor of the Roman Catholic National Shrine of the Little Flower in Royal Oak, Michigan. In 1926, Coughlin began his broadcast career with a religious program entitled *The Golden Hour of the Little Flower*. Later, his agenda became more political. He founded the National Union for Social Justice, which published *The Social Justice Weekly*. Couglin also supported the

Christian Front, an anti-Semitic, pro-fascist organization. In 1933, he began to attack Franklin Roosevelt and his New Deal policies. His broadcasts also became increasingly anti-Semitic. In 1938, Coughlin publicly stated that the Nazi movement was a necessary curb on the alleged Jewish influence in international finance. Beginning in 1939, church authorities in the United States and the Vatican, the Roosevelt Administration, and the Code Committee of the National Association of Broadcasters all brought pressure to curtail Coughlin's broadcasts. In May 1942, Coughlin ceased broadcasting by order of his bishop.

John Cournos (born Johann Gregorievitch Korshoon, 1881–1966), Russian-born American journalist, novelist, poet, playwright, and translator. Cournos immigrated to the United States from Russia in 1891. In 1912, he traveled on assignment for the *New York Times Book Review* to England. He met Pound in London and interviewed him for the *Philadelphia Record.* Pound published one of Cournos' poems in his anthology *Des Imagistes* (1914). Cournos remained in England and became involved in Pound's London circle and activities. He also helped to bring Pound into contact with the sculptor Gaudier-Brzeska.

Pound and Cournos were close during 1912–14. However, in 1915, after the death of Gaudier-Brzeska, the two quarreled over the disposition of the artist's estate. Pound wrote to Alice Corbin Henderson at *Poetry* that "I am very much displeased with Richard [Aldington], more displeased with [F. S.] Flint, and within the last week I have found it necessary to eliminate Cournos also from my list of acquaintance (re/Brzeska's death, not on a point of style or literary activity)" (Nadel, EP to ACH, August 6, 1915). Pound's displeasure was further aggravated by Cournos' later defection to Amy Lowell's camp of Imagists.

René Crevel (1900–35), French surrealist writer. The 22-year old Crevel entered André Breton's Dada/surrealist circle soon after World War I. He became known for his narcoleptic ramblings, but went on to produce more substantial works such as *Babylone*, *La Mort difficile*, and *Les Pieds dans le plat* as well as critical appreciations of Paul Klee and Salvador Dalí. During the 1920s and '30s, Crevel formed close relationships not only with the surrealists, but also with Gertrude Stein, André Gide, and others in the Paris literary scene. Crevel became caught up in the intrigues that riddled the surrealist movement. In a bizarre gesture just before a major literary convention in Paris, Crevel committed suicide. See Pound's "René Crevel" *Criterion*, 18:71 (January 1939), 225–35.

Benedetto Croce (1866–1952), Italian philosopher, critic, historian of ideas, and politician. Croce's work primarily concerned the philosophy of aesthetics.

His best-known work today is perhaps his *L'Estetica come come scienza dell'espressione e linguistica generale: teoria e storia* (1902). He was openly anti-fascist and was forced from public life by Mussolini's regime. After the war, Croce became a member of Italy's Constituent Assembly. In 1947, Croce was elected president of the Italian Liberal Party.

Edward Estlin Cummings (1894–1962), American poet, painter, and playwright. Cummings met Pound in Paris in July 1923, but they saw each other infrequently. After 1924, when Cummings took up residence in New York City, Pound only occasionally corresponded with him. The correspondence picked up after 1933 when Cummings published his book *EIMI*—a "novel"/memoir based upon diaries Cummings kept of his visit to the Soviet Union in 1930. This novel fired Pound's imagination. It represented for Pound all that travel writing and journalism should embody. Pound wrote to Cummings in the 1930s in part to get him to write a similar book about contemporary American culture.

Édouard Daladier (1884–1970), French Radical Socialist politician and French prime minister. In 1927 Daladier became leader of the Radical Socialists and served as minister of war under several Radical and Popular Front governments in the 1930s. He served as French prime minister in 1933, 1934, and 1938–9. Daladier helped to negotiate and then signed the Munich Pact. He generally supported a policy of appeasement toward Hitler, and in 1939, when Russia invaded Finland, Daladier took a non-interventionist position, as a result of which he was forced to resign as prime minister. He remained in the French government until its collapse in 1940. He was arrested and imprisoned by the Vichy government, liberated in 1945, and remained in French politics until 1958.

Hugh Dalton (1887–1962), chairman of the National Executive of the Labour Party (1936–7).

Joseph Edward Davies (1876–1958), American diplomat and author. In 1937, Davies replaced **William Bullitt** as the US ambassador to the Soviet Union. Davies served in this position until 1938, when he became ambassador to Belgium (1938–40). He then served as special assistant to secretary of state Cordell Hull. In 1945 he participated in the Potsdam Conference. He was also the author of a widely read book, *Mission to Moscow* (1941). Pound was reported to have been reading this book on November 17, 1945 when he was summoned for transport from the Detention Training Camp in Pisa to Washington, DC, to stand charges for treason.

Torquato Manlio Dazzi (1891–1968), Italian librarian and translator. Dazzi was a close friend of Pound. They corresponded from 1925 to 1960.

Paul Henry De Kruif (1890–1971), American bacteriologist and author. De Kruif was a Rockefeller research fellow and then professor of bacteriology at the University of Michigan 1912–17. He then became an associate in pathology at the Rockefeller Institute in New York City 1920–2. De Kruif left the academic world in the 1920s to become a highly successful author, writing popular accounts of major biological and medical discoveries. Among his best-known works were *The Microbe Hunters* (1926), *Hunger Fighters* (1928), and *Men against Death* (1932). In August 1933, after reading *Men against Death*, Pound began a correspondence with De Kruif. De Kruif was influenced by Pound's economic interests, and by November 1933, he was enthusiastically reading C. H. Douglas on Social Credit. In a letter to Pound dated January 27, 1934 (YCAL), he wrote: "Mr. Pound I want to make trouble for you. You have opened a new world for me, with your confounded little ABC, and thank you." The "trouble" De Kruif wrote of was his efforts to get his publisher, Harcourt, Brace, & Co., to publish Pound's *ABC of Economics* and *Jefferson and/or Mussolini*. De Kruif only succeeded in getting Pound an offer for an expanded edition of *How to Read*.

Adele de Leeuw (1899–1988), prolific travel writer and children's author. De Leeuw wrote numerous books throughout her life, as did her sister Cateau. They both lived most of their lives in Plainfield, New Jersey. The two traveled the world extensively, spending a great deal of time in what was then the Dutch East Indies. Adele de Leeuw's "Cremation in Bali" was published in the inaugural issue of *Globe* (March 1937, 71–3).

Mary de Rachewiltz (b. 1925), daughter of Ezra Pound and Olga Rudge.

Carlo Delcroix (1896–1977), Italian author and Fascist official. Blinded in the Fascist uprising in 1922, Delcroix was president of the Italian Association of War Wounded and Invalids.

Domenico Gaetano Maria Donizetti (1797–1848), Italian composer. Donizetti is best known for his operatic compositions, especially *L'elisir d'amore* (1832), *Don Pasquale* (1843) and *Lucia di Lammermoor* (1835).

John Drummond (1914–?) began to correspond with Pound as an undergraduate at Queens College, Cambridge in 1932. In his initial letter he asked Pound's permission to print excerpts from a *Draft of XXX Cantos* for a review he was doing of the book for a student-run journal, *Contemporaries and Makers*. Pound put Drummond in touch with Ronald Duncan and articles by Drummond appeared in Duncan's *The Townsman*. Duncan and Pound corresponded frequently during the 1930s and beyond. Drummond helped

Pound to choose representative Cantos for Pound's *Active Anthology* (1932). Later, Drummond translated some of Pound's Italian articles. He also helped with the proofs and indexing of *Guide to Kulchur* (1938). Duncan served in the British army during World War II in North Africa and southern Italy. He provided aid and information to Pound, Dorothy Pound, and Olga Rudge after Pound was taken into custody by the American army in 1945. (See Pound and Spoo, *Letters,* "Introduction," pp. 1–33; and especially note to "Document 7", 72, 74.)

Charles Duff (1894–1966), British author and translator. Under the pseudonym Carlos Prieto, Duff, who had served in the British Foreign Office in the Iberian Peninsula, wrote a fairly well-known book on the Spanish Civil War entitled *Spanish Front* (1936). He also wrote for various publications, including *The New English Weekly*, where Pound probably read him.

Ronald Frederick Henry Duncan (1914–82), British pacifist, poet, librettist, essayist, playwright, autobiographer, and editor. Duncan came into contact with Pound at the same time he came into contact with Gandhi. In 1936, having recently joined the Peace Pledge Union, Duncan sent a copy of a recently composed pacifist pamphlet (*The Complete Pacifist*) to both Pound and Gandhi. According to Duncan's autobiography, *Every Man Is An Island*, the pamphlet provoked a scathing reply from Pound and an invitation to visit from Gandhi. Duncan decided to take Gandhi up on the invitation and set out for India in January of 1937 via Paris and Marseille. After visiting Gandhi, Duncan visited Pound on the return journey in Rapallo and began to discuss the possibility of starting a new literary magazine. This discussion resulted in the journal *The Townsman*, which Duncan published from 1938 to 1944. Pound was a regular contributor to the journal. Duncan contributed two articles to *Globe*, "Visit to Gandhi" (August 1937) and "Funk in a Fog" (October 1937).

Ralph Cheever Dunning (1878–1930), American poet. Dunning, a friend of **Sisley Huddleston** and **Ernest Hemingway**, contributed to Pound's *The Exile*. Pound was an enthusiastic supporter of Dunning and helped him get established as a writer. Dunning won *Poetry* magazine's Levinson award in 1925.

Armand Jean du Plessis, Cardinal Richelieu (1585–1642), French statesman, cardinal, and Duc de Richelieu. Cardinal Richelieu was chief minister of French king Louis XIII and a key figure in centralizing the French royal government. He was also founder of the French Academy.

Sir Anthony Eden (1897–1977), British statesman, 1st Earl of Avon, foreign secretary, and prime minister. He was appointed foreign secretary in 1935 by prime minister Stanley Baldwin. Baldwin resigned as prime minister in 1937 after the abdication crisis. Eden resigned as foreign secretary in 1938 after differences arose with Neville Chamberlain, Baldwin's successor as prime minister. Though one would suspect that Eden was sympathetic to Baldwin's position that a marriage was impossible between Edward VIII and Mrs. Simpson, Eden seems to have taken little part in the political machinations behind the crisis.

T. S. Eliot (1888–1965), American-born British poet, critic, and editor. Pound maintained a close friendship and an extensive correspondence with Eliot from their first meeting in London in September 1914 until Eliot's death in 1965.

Max Ernst (1891–1976), German surrealist artist and author. Pound became familiar with the surrealists while in Paris in the early 1920s and was enthusiastic about several of the visual artists in the movement, including Ernst, Picabia, and Man Ray. Pound remained tepid about the work of most of the writers in surrealist circles. As Pound wrote to the editors of the magazine *Demain* in 1934: "Nothing much against the Surrealists, save that a lot of 'em are French, and therefore bone ignorant, like the English. I believe they write, but none of 'em has ever been known to read, and it is highly doubtful the alphabet is personally known to most of them."

Hugo Robert Fack (1885–1954), economic reformer and practitioner of homeopathic medicine. Based in San Antonio, Texas, Fack pursued a colorful career. Along with his wife, Manuela D. Fack, he ran Dr. Fack's Health Institute and Sanitarium in San Antonio. He also ran the Free-Economic Publishing Company which issued his economic reform journal *The Way Out*. He is perhaps best described in his own words in a flyer from this period:

> Hugo R. Fack, ND, DNSC, Orthop. Ph.D.—Vice President of Texas Naturopathic Association. Author, Lecturer, Pioneer advocate of numerous specific natural treatment methods, now adopted by the profession at large. Pioneer advocate of the Natural Economic Order by means of Freed Money and the Freed Land, the economic system of Freedom and Justice, Plenty and Peace. Editor of "The Way Out," the free-economic monthly, read by progressive thinkers in all parts of the world.

Fack began writing to Pound in 1934. Their shared interests included the economic theories of Silvio Gesell (1862–1930), which formed the basis for Fack's own theories. Fack translated Gesell's work and it is through his translations that Pound became familiar with Gesell's economic theories.

Peter Fanning (?–?), British writer. Fanning was an old associate of **Alfred Richard Orage.** He seems to have worked on the staff of Orage's *New Age* before World War I.

Roberto Farinacci (1893–1954), Italian journalist, lawyer, and deputy of Parliament.

James Aloysius Farley (1888–1976), American politician. A staunch political ally of Franklin Roosevelt, Farley served as postmaster general (then a cabinet post) during the first two Roosevelt administrations (1933–40). Farley was also chairman of the Democratic National Committee from 1932–40 and managed Roosevelt's first two presidential campaigns in 1932 and 1936. Farley is mentioned at the end of Canto 46.

James T. Farrell (1904–79), American novelist, short story writer, and critic. Farrell was one of the new post-World War I generation of socially conscious, politically committed writers whose fiction dealt with the struggle of the inner city working class. A frequent contributor to avant-garde periodicals like *Blues* and *This Quarter* in the 1920s, Farrell later turned to leftist venues like the *Partisan Review* in the 1930s. Though as a thinker and writer Farrell was sympathetic to Marxism, he was an independent intellectual. At the time Pound suggested him to Dunn as a possible contributor to *Globe*, Farrell was one of the organizers of the American Committee for the Defense of Leon Trotsky. In 1937, Farrell traveled to Mexico with the Dewey Commission to gather evidence from Trotsky himself to counter the charges that Stalin had lodged against him in the Moscow Trials. Among the best known of Farrell's many works is the trilogy made up of *Young Lonigan* (1932), *The Young Manhood of Studs Lonigan* (1934), and *Judgment Day* (1935).

Ernest Fenollosa (1853–1908), American-born scholar of Japanese art, language, and literature. Fenollosa studied Japanese language and culture at Harvard University and the Imperial University in Tokyo. Eventually, he rose to the position of imperial commissioner of art in Tokyo.

Irving Fisher (1867–1947), American economist, mathematician, and author. Though Fisher earned his doctorate in mathematics at Yale in 1891, he went on to write on a wide variety of social and political topics, including public health, mathematics, international relations, diet, political economy, and monetary reform. Fisher spent his academic career at Yale, becoming professor of political economy in 1898 and remaining in that position until his retirement in 1935. Fisher's book *Stamp Scrip* (1933) was an important text for Pound. (For a detailed discussion of Fisher's impact upon Pound's thinking in the

1930s, see "Silvio Gesell and Irving Fisher," in Surette, *Pound in Purgatory*, pp. 178–97.)

Vardis Fisher (1895–1968), American educator and novelist. He was author of the novel *Children of God* (1939).

Charles M. Flandrau (1871–1938), American author. Flandrau was a Harvard-educated travel writer who lived in St. Paul, Minnesota. He was author of the travel essay collection *Viva! Mexico* (1908).

Gustave Flaubert (1821–80), French writer. Flaubert's novels, along with the works of Voltaire and Henry James, were Pound's favorite prose works.

Marcel William Fodor (1890–?), American journalist. A leading journalist on international affairs, Fodor wrote *Plot and Counterplot in Central Europe; Conditions South of Hitler* (1937) with an introduction by **John Gunther**.

Antonio Fogazzaro (1842–1911), Italian poet, novelist and psychologist.

Ford Madox Ford (1873–1939), English novelist, poet, editor, essayist, and memoirist. Ford was the author of almost eighty books. Pound was introduced to Ford in 1909 by a mutual friend, May Sinclair, while Ford was the editor of *The English Review*. Ford, whose grandfather was the Pre-Raphaelite painter Ford Madox Brown, provided Pound with a living link to the Rossetti circle as well as to contemporary literary circles which included Henry James and Joseph Conrad.

André de Fouquières (1876–1959) French travel and fashion writer. Among his many works are *Au paradis des rajahs* (1912), *Les amours de Lauzun* (1931), *Cinquante ans de panache* (1951), and *Mon Paris et ses parisiens* (1954).

Douglas Claughton Fox (1906–?), American journalist, author, and museum curator. Fox was an assistant to the German anthropologist, archaeologist, and folklorist **Leo Frobenius**. In 1933, Douglas Fox became Pound's primary contact with Frobenius' Forschungsinstitut für Kulturmorphologie (see Introduction pp. 24–5). According to a letter to Pound dated December 17, 1933 (YCAL), before Fox joined the Forschungsinstitut he worked for seven years in New York as a journalist reporting for several newspapers and magazines. It seems that Fox spent his childhood on Long Island, New York.

During 1934 and 1935 Fox went on several expeditions with Frobenius, traveling to the Transjordan, the Libyan desert, eastern Spain, and south-western France—all with the purpose of gathering data on prehistoric rock art.

Fox wrote to Pound from Kharga, Egypt, on April 4, 1935 (YCAL), that Iris Barry, an old friend of Pound's now working at the Museum of Modern Art (MOMA) in New York, had written to him about the possibility of an exhibition of African rock art at MOMA. Frobenius assigned Fox to help him organize the exhibition. Fox traveled to the United States to supervise the installation of the exhibition in the spring of 1937 and to finalize the arrangements for the publication of *African Genesis,* a popular book of African folklore compiled by Fox and Frobenius. The MOMA exhibition opened on April 28, 1937.

Frobenius died in Italy in 1938, and, given the political conditions in Germany and the outbreak of war in 1939, Fox left Germany. On October 15, 1939 (YCAL), Fox wrote to Pound that he was the curator of Walter P. Chrysler's art collection in New York. It is possible that this is the result of contacts Fox made while in the city supervising the MOMA exhibition. In the 1940s, Fox went on to become a curator at the Baltimore Museum of Art.

Bruno Frank (1887–1945), German writer and poet.

Harold Franklin (?–?), American journalist. A writer for the Chicago-based *Delphian Quarterly*, Franklin was living in Milan in the spring of 1933. That March he attended Pound's lectures on economics at the Bocconi University in Milan. A little over a month later, Franklin wrote to Pound and reminded him of their encounter. He requested an interview with Pound for the *Delphian Quarterly*, for what was to be the first in a series of interviews of "outstanding American and non-American literary figures in Europe" (HF to EP, May 4, 1933 [YCAL]). Pound consented and the interview took place on June 15, 1933. From 1936 until 1940, Pound contributed pieces to the *Delphian Quarterly.* The Delphian Society was a women's club which described itself as dedicated to the promotion of "higher education, personal improvement and social progress."

James Frazier (1854–1941), Scottish classicist and anthropologist. Author of *The Golden Bough* (1890).

Leo Frobenius (1873–1938), German anthropologist, archaeologist, and folklorist. Frobenius originally established the "Afrika-Archiv" in Berlin as a center for his African studies. In 1920, Frobenius moved the Archiv to Munich and renamed it the Forschungsinstitut für Kulturmorphologie. Ultimately, in 1925, the Forschungsinstitut found a home at the Johann Wolfgang Goethe Universität in Frankfurt am Main. It still exists there today as the Frobenius-Institut. An often-quoted letter from **W. B. Yeats** to Sturge Moore (WBY to SM, April 1929; see for example Stock, *Life*, pp. 371–2) suggests that Pound came across Frobenius and his work through Spengler's *The Decline of the West*. However, Pound must have known of Frobenius somewhat before the date of this letter. Pound's correspondence with Frobenius and his Institute begins in early 1928. Pound made Frobenius' personal acquaintance when Pound traveled to Frankfurt to attend the premiere of George Antheil's work *Transatlantic* in 1929.

In the 1930s, Pound was interested in getting funds for the English translation and publication of Frobenius' major work *Erlebte Erdteile*. Pound sent out letters to the presidents of Fisk, Tuskegee, and Howard to enlist their support for such a translation. Pound's search for support for this project also led him to contact **Langston Hughes**, which initiated a cordial correspondence between the two poets. (See Introduction, pp. 23–4; for the full correspondence between Pound and Hughes, see David Roessel, "'A Racial Act': The Letters of Langston Hughes and Ezra Pound," in *Ezra Pound and African American Modernism*, edited by Michael Coyle [2001], pp. 207–42.)

Frances Mary Frost (1905–59), American novelist, poet, and children's writer. Frost wrote extensively for *Globe*. At the time of her contributions to *Globe*, she was just beginning to rise in prominence. In 1934 she had won the Shelley Memorial Prize for Poetry and in 1936 she published her novel *Innocent Summer*. She was also mother of the well-known "Lower East Side" New York poet Paul Blackburn (1919–72), who would correspond with Pound during the 1950s.

Varian Fry (1907–67), American writer and editor. Fry had helped **Lincoln Kirstein** edit *Hound & Horn* at Harvard. Pound came to know Fry through this work on the journal. After the Nazi defeat of France, Fry would play in important role in aiding European intellectuals in their escape from Nazi-controlled France. In 1940, Fry arrived in Marseille as an agent for the Emergency Rescue Committee. Between 1940 and 1941, with the support of Hiram Bingham IV, an American vice-consul stationed in Marseille, Fry managed to help between 2,000 and 4,000 refuges obtain visas allowing them to escape Nazi-controlled France.

John Frederick Charles Fuller (1878–1966), British major-general, journalist, and author. Fuller first served in the British army in the Boer War. During World War I he rose to the position of chief of staff of the British Tank Corps. Fuller was one of the first military strategic thinkers to formulate what would later come to be known in World War II as the German "Blitzkrieg." In 1934, Fuller became a member of **Oswald Mosley**'s British Union of Fascists (BUF) and was a frequent contributor to the BUF's periodicals *Action* and *Fascist Quarterly*. Fuller covered the Spanish Civil War as a journalist and traveled with the Italian army in its 1935 invasion of Ethiopia. His writings include *The First of the League Wars: Its Lessons and Omens* (1936), *Tanks in the Great War* (1920), and *Memoirs of an Unconventional Soldier* (1936).

David Lloyd George (1863–1945), British statesman, 1st Earl of Dwyfor, and prime minister. During the first phases of World War I, Lloyd George served as minister of munitions and secretary for war in H. H. Asquith's coalition government. Asquith was ousted in 1916 and Lloyd George became prime minister. After the war, Lloyd George was a principal participant in the negotiations at the Paris Peace Conference (1919–20). He played a key role in the political reorganization of the Near East after the collapse of the Ottoman Empire. He served as prime minister until 1922.

Lawrence Gilman (1878–1939), American music critic and author. Gilman was music critic for *Harper's Weekly* (1901–13) and the *North American Review* (1913–23), before becoming music critic at the *New York Herald Tribune* in 1923, a position he held until his death. He was succeeded as music critic at the *Herald Tribune* by the composer Virgil Thomson.

Arnold Gingrich (1903–76), American editor and author. Gingrich was editor at *Esquire* magazine from 1935 to 1945. In early 1934, perhaps at the instigation of Ernest Hemingway, Gingrich contacted Pound and suggested that he contribute to *Esquire*. An exchange of letters followed developing ideas for contributions. They finally agreed on a series of articles about the artists Pound had known in Paris. *Esquire* would pay $150 for each. Pound submitted his first article to *Esquire* in June 1934 entitled "Gaudier: A Postscript." It appeared in August 1934, but Gingrich was not entirely comfortable with the piece.

When the next installment on Brancusi arrived, Pound was paid for it but the piece was rejected. The next article that Pound wrote was published by the magazine, but Pound then sent a piece critical of Britain. Gingrich wrote to Pound that *Esquire* was about to run articles on Canada and the British Empire, so a piece critical of the English was ill-timed (AG to EP, November 13, 1935 [YCAL]). Pound took this as an indication that Gingrich was toadying to British interests. (Also see Donald Gallup, "Ezra Pound's Experiment for *Esquire*," *Paideuma* 22:1/2 [Spring/Fall 1993], 181–90.)

William Ewart Gladstone (1809–98), British statesman. Gladstone served as prime minister four times (1868–74, 1880–5, 1886, and 1892–4). Gladstone was an advocate of Irish Home Rule (which caused the collapse of his third government in 1886). He entered parliament in 1833 as a Tory but was later drawn to a Liberal agenda—especially on the issue of free trade, which he supported as chancellor of the exchequer (1852–5, 1859–66).

Michael Gold, pseudonym of Isaac "Irwin" Itzok Granich (1893–1967), journalist, editor, and novelist. See Introduction, pp. 1–35.

Honor Goleyevsky (?–?), an ex-general exiled from Czarist Russia during the Russian Revolution and in residence in Paris in the 1920s, where Pound made his acquaintance.

Joseph Ferdinand Gould (1889–1957), Greenwich Village personality. After attending Harvard, Gould drifted about until he took up a job in New York in 1917 as a cub reporter for the *Evening Mail*. During this job, he was inspired to write what he called *An Oral History of Our Times*. It was to be an immense collection of all the stories that he was told and all the conversations he overheard as he made his way about New York City. With this plan in mind, he quit his job and, though he came from a well-off New England family, became indigent. Gould lived off the charity of those who took an interest in him and his project. E. E. Cummings, who moved to 4 Patchen Place in the Village in 1924, was one of his supporters. Alleged excerpts from the *Oral History* appeared in the *Dial*, *Broom*, *Pagany*, and Pound's own short-lived journal *The Exile*. Pound and Cummings tried to place Gould's work elsewhere with no success. After Gould's death in 1957, the manuscript of the *Oral History*—by Gould's report, over 9,000,000 words in length—was nowhere to be found.

In 1964, the journalist Joseph Mitchell, who had written a profile of Gould for the *New Yorker* in 1942, wrote a two-part follow-up article entitled "Joe Gould's Secret" (September 14 and 26, 1964). In this piece, Mitchell gave strong evidence that the *Oral History* never existed—or at least remained, unwritten, in the mind of Joe Gould.

Remy de Gourmont (1858–1915), French novelist, literary critic, and columnist. De Gourmont arrived in Paris from his native Normandy in 1883, and took up a position as assistant librarian at the Bibliothèque Nationale. In his twenties, he became afflicted with a disfiguring skin disease often described as lupus. Though something of a recluse, he was active in most of the modern literary movements that swept through Paris during the 1890s and the early part of the twentieth century. He helped found the *Mercure de France* for which he wrote a column. Early in his career he was immersed in the Symbolist movement, but his erudition and interests were very wide. Pound became intensely interested in de Gourmont's work very early on in his London career, translating and serializing a portion of de Gourmont's 1897 novel *Les Chevaux de Diomède* for *The New Age*. Pound's admiration for de Gourmont was shared by such diverse critics/artists as **T. S. Eliot**, Kenneth Burke, Richard Aldington, and Amy Lowell. Pound's best-known homage to de Gourmont was his translation of the writer's 1903 essay *Physique de l'amour, essai sur l'instinct sexual.*

Horace Greeley (1811–72), American journalist, reformer, author, and politician. Greeley was the editor of the *New York Tribune*. The famous words attributed to him, "Go West young man," were penned by an editor of an Indiana paper John Soule. However, they reflected perfectly his support for westward expansion and settlement of the American frontier.

Marcel Griaule (1898–1956), French anthropologist. Griaule specialized in the cultures of south Saharan and sub-Saharan Africa. His many works include *Calebasses dahoméennes: Documents de la Mission Dakar-Djibouti* (1935) and *Dieu d'Eau, entretiens avec Ogotemmêli* (1948).

John Groth (1902–88), illustrator. Groth was known for his illustrations of sports and war. During World War II he worked with **Ernest Hemingway**.

John Gunther (1901–70), American author and journalist. Foreign correspondent for the *Chicago Daily News* and NBC. Author of best-selling books, especially *Inside Europe* (1936).

John Hargrave (1894–1982), British leader in the international Boy Scout movement, political activist, author, illustrator, and cartoonist. Though later his in his career he concentrated on political activism and monetary reform, in 1908 Hargrave became involved in the Boy Scout movement in Britain. He quickly became a leading figure in the movement. As "White Fox," he wrote a regular column for the Scout magazine, *The Trail*. His career with the Boy Scouts was interrupted by his service in World War I. Hargrave, a Quaker, served as an officer in the Royal Army Medical Corps. He saw action in the Dardenelles and Sulva Bay. After the war, he returned to the Boy Scouts, but found himself in conflict with the mainstream movement. In 1920 he founded his own version of the Scouts which he named "Kibbo Kift."

In 1923, he met C. H. Douglas, the founder of the Social Credit movement. This meeting would eventually transform Hargrave's thinking. In 1927, Hargrave integrated Social Credit into his Kibbo Kift philosophy, and as Clement E. Vose wrote in *Gorham Munson: Papers on the American Social Credit Movement and* New Democracy (1977):

> He [Hargrave] quickly became the most prominent social credit man in England, apart from Douglas, leading a movement with a succession of different titles: Economic Party, 1929–1930; the Crusader Legion in Coventry, 1930–1933; an inner elite known as the Iron Guard and then as the Green Shirts; the Green Shirts Movement for Social Credit, 1933–1935; and finally, the Social Credit Party of Great Britain ... Hargrave feuded with Douglas, and the Green Shirts, in uniform, broke up a Social Credit reception for one of Douglas's associates. Hargrave

> had become an hysterical mystic, and the militant Green Shirts was largely ended by the Public Order Act outlawing the use of uniforms for political purposes. For some years, Hargrave edited *This Week's Message from Hargrave*. He rejected both Fascism and Communism and believed that only a monarch could stand up to the conspiracy of the money trust and, on this ground, took the side of Edward VIII in the abdication crisis. (Vose, *Gorham Munson*, p. 8)

Pound carried on an extensive correspondence on Social Credit matters with Hargrave from 1935 to 1939.

Sadakichi Hartmann (1867–1944), Japanese-born American author, critic, photographer, painter, playwright, and journalist. Hartmann was born on Dejima Island in Nagasaki Harbor, Japan. He was sent to Europe by his German-born father and was educated in Germany. After a quarrel with his father, he left for America. At 14, Hartmann settled in Philadelphia and made the acquaintance of the elderly Walt Whitman, who lived in nearby Camden, New Jersey. He wrote a memoir entitled *Conversations with Walt Whitman* (1895). After 1896, Hartmann wrote frequently for the New York photographer Alfred Stieglitz's *Camera Notes* (later, *Camera Works*). Beginning in 1900, Hartman wrote a number of books on art and art history, including *Shakespeare on Art* (1900), *Japanese Art* (1903), *The Whistler Book* (1910), and his influential *History of American Art* (1901, revised edition 1938). In the 1920s, he relocated to the West Coast for health reasons and tried unsuccessfully to break into scriptwriting for Hollywood.

Hartmann wrote to Pound on November 27, 1929, as editor of a periodical called *The Motion Picture Blue Book*. Pound knew of Hartmann and his poetry from *Bruno's Chap Books*. Soon after this initial exchange Hartmann became an invalid. Most of the remaining "correspondence" with Pound is made up of letters begging for money.

Heinrich Hauser (1901–55), German novelist.

Harold W. Hawk (?–?) was a former student of Pound's at Wabash College in Crawfordsville, Indiana. According to extant correspondence, Hawk attended Pound's French class during the short time Pound taught at Wabash College in 1907–8. On February 15, 1936, Hawk wrote to Pound that he was about to publish a review of *Jefferson and/or Mussolini* for a "Texas newspaper." This led to a sporadic exchange of letters until 1939. Dunn dutifully followed up on Pound's suggestion and Hawk wrote back to Pound: "It was kind of you to tell the nascent St Paul Globe about me. I appreciate it. Perhaps I can pick up a few dollars there" (HWH to EP October 16, 1936 [YCAL]).

Ernest Hemingway (1899–1961), American novelist and journalist. Hemingway was introduced to Pound by **Sylvia Beach** in 1922 in her Paris bookstore, Shakespeare and Company. The two men became close friends and even occasional boxing partners. Pound joined Gertrude Stein and Sherwood Anderson as major and lasting influences upon Hemingway's writing. In 1923, at Pound's urging, Hemingway was put on the board of **Ford Madox Ford**'s *transatlantic review*. Ford published three of Hemingway's stories in the pages of the *transatlantic review*, including "Up In Michigan." Pound also included Hemingway's booklet *Three Stories and Ten Poems* (1923) in the Contact Press series he was editing for **Robert McAlmon**. Hemingway's friendship with Pound was to last throughout Hemingway's life. Yet, Hemingway's close association with *Esquire* and its editor **Arnold Gingrich**, as well as his celebrity status, soured the relationship a bit for Pound in the 1930s.

James Richard Charles Hennessy (1867–1945), French statesman and editor. Hennessy entered the Chamber of Deputies in 1919 and became senator in 1921. He remained in this position until 1938. He was also political director for the journal *Liberal*.

Abel Hermant (1862–1950), French novelist, essayist, journalist, and Academician. A prolific writer, he is considered one of the finest novelists satirizing and chronicling French society of the Belle Époque. At the end of the nineteenth century, Hermant served as drama critic for both *Gil Blas* and *Le Figaro*. It was at this time that he befriended Marcel Proust. Hermant was made a member of the French Academy in 1927. He was removed from the Academy in 1945 after his conviction as a Nazi collaborator. Hermant defended his conduct during the occupation in one of his last works, *Le Treizième Cahier* (1949).

Édouard Herriot (1872–1957), French Radical Party politician and writer. Premier of France three times, 1924–5, 1926, and 1932.

Rudolf Heß (1894–1987), German Nazi official. Heß was private secretary to Adolf Hitler and Deputy Führer of the National Socialist Party. On May 10, 1941, on his own initiative, Heß flew alone to Scotland to present an ultimatum to the British government to make peace. Hitler immediately dismissed the incident and rejected any connection with Heß's "mission." He was taken prisoner by the British and tried after the war at Nuremberg. He was sentenced to life imprisonment in 1947. In 1987 he committed suicide in Spandau Prison, the last of the inmates convicted of war crimes at Nuremberg.

Hermann Hesse (1877–1962), German writer and winner of Nobel Prize in 1946.

Guy Carlton Hickok (1888–1951), American journalist. After graduating from Oberlin College in 1914, Hickok joined the staff of the *Brooklyn Daily Eagle*, becoming the head of its Paris Bureau in 1918. The connection between Pound and Hickok probably developed through **Ernest Hemingway,** who became friends with Hickok in Paris. Hemingway, who arrived in Paris in late 1921 as a foreign correspondent for the *Toronto Star,* made Hickok's acquaintance through weekly meetings of the Anglo-American Press Club in Paris. Hickok shared Pound's disdain for the American culture of the 1920s and wrote an article, "On Those Synthetic States," in the first issue of Pound's short-lived journal, *The Exile*. Hickok returned to the United States in 1933 and joined the McClure Syndicate. Hickok later worked for *The Literary Digest, Newsweek*, and as coordinator of inter-American affairs for NBC broadcasting. Pound kept up a correspondence with Hickok until the outbreak of World War II.

Hilaire Hiler (1896–1966), artist, and his father **Meyer Hiler** (?–?), American painter and an authority on costuming. In 1939, in collaboration with his father, Hiler wrote a well-received reference work, *Bibliography of Costume: A Dictionary Catalogue of About Eight Thousand Books and Periodicals Compiled by Hilaire Hiler and Meyer Hiler* (1939). Hiler was associated with the Precisionist movement in the visual arts. Hiler, who was active in Paris during the 1920s, along with an ex-jockey by the name of Miller, took over the defunct Café Caméléon at the corner of Boulevard du Montparnasse and rue Champagne Première, transforming it into the Jockey Club in 1923. It was an overnight success, and was frequented by avant-garde writers and artists. Pound became part of this lively Parisian crowd. Hiler forwarded a photograph to Dunn. It was taken in the fall of 1923 outside what would soon open as the Jockey. Besides Pound, the group includes Hiler, Jean Cocteau, Margaret Anderson, Jane Heap, Man Ray, Kiki of Montparnasse, Tristan Tzara, and Mina Loy.

Hiler returned to America in the mid-1930s, living briefly in New York and then in California. He worked on WPA projects and then entered academia, working at several colleges and universities throughout the southwestern United States. He later moved back to Paris where he died in 1966.

Charlotte Teller Hirsch (1876–?), American novelist, playwright, suffragette, and freelance writer. Hirsch met Pound in London prior to World War I. She was also a friend of the poet Khalil Gibran and had corresponded with Mark Twain. In 1935, she published the travel book *Everybody's Paris* under the pseudonym John Brangwyn.

Sir Samuel John Gurney Hoare (1880–1959), British statesman, 1st Viscount Templewood. Hoare was foreign secretary from 1931–5. He was notorious for developing the so-called Hoare–Laval Plan, which championed Italy's claims in Ethiopia after its 1935 invasion. The plan met with such general disapproval that Hoare had to resign his post. He later played a central role in developing the equally ill-considered Munich Pact under Prime Minister Neville Chamberlain.

Maurice Christopher Hollis (1902–77), British economist, politician, and author. The Oxford-educated Hollis taught at Stonyhurst College, England from 1925–35 and became an exchange professor in economics at the University of Notre Dame from 1935–9. He served as Conservative member of Parliament from 1945–55.

John Holroyd-Reece (1897–1969), British publisher. Holroyd-Reece established several European publishing ventures, including the Paris-based Pegasus Press. In 1928, the Pegasus Press became embroiled in publication and trial of Radclyffe Hall's lesbian-themed novel *The Well of Loneliness* (see most recently, S. Cline, *Radclyffe Hall*, pp. 245–67). After the Pegasus Press folded, Holroyd-Reece went on to more successful enterprises such as the Albatross Press in England and the later acquisition of Tauchnitz, Leipzig.

Miriam Hopkins (1903–72), well-known actress of stage and screen. Hopkins was probably at the peak of her career in the 1930s, performing in Noël Coward's *Design for Living* (1933), and the movies *Becky Sharp* (1935) and *Barbary Coast* (1935). Pound was fond of the movies and especially enjoyed the films of Fred Astaire and Ginger Rogers. **George Antheil**, now in Hollywood, was writing detective novels and music for the movies; he had just become head of the music department for Selznick International when he wrote to Pound on June 26, 1937 that Miriam Hopkins collected editions his works. Pound wrote back: "Gawd bless Miriam and give me her address and I'll send her a li'l one she ain't got. At least I bet she aint got it. Only I'll she mussn't be disappointed on account of it being my smallest" (EP to GA, July 1937 [YCAL]). Unfortunately no correspondence from Hopkins to Pound seems to exist.

William Horgan (1914–?), American journalist. Horgan was a regional writer living in Oakland, California. His article, "California's Greenwich Village," appeared in the October 1937 issue of *Globe*.

Colonel Edward Mandell House (1858–1938), American diplomat and presidential advisor. House represented the Wilson administration at many conferences during and after World War I. House had been instrumental in Wilson's successful campaign for the presidency in 1912, and thereafter became a close and trusted adviser to the new president.

Mary Howell (?–?), American journalist. Howell wrote for the Paris edition of the *Chicago Tribune* in the 1930s. She interviewed Pound in 1930. Her article appeared in the *Tribune* under the headline: "Pound Paints Peccadilloes of Pedant in Murdered Marts of Learning" (April 19, 1930). Howell became familiar with Pound's circle and his parents in Rapallo. In her letters to Pound she also tried to interest him in various plans for an English language literary journal aimed at an Italian audience. Howell seems to have lived at least part of the time near Genoa and was well connected with highly placed Italian officials. She was in occasional contact with Mussolini himself—at least enough to be able to report in a letter of February 3, 1934 (MH to EP [YCAL]) that several Italians including Mussolini were enthusiastic about *Jefferson and/or Mussolini*.

Bronislaw Huberman (1882–1947), Polish violinist. Acclaimed throughout Europe, Huberman openly criticized Nazi Germany's persecution of its minorities—refusing to perform with the Berlin Philharmonic at the invitation of Wilhelm Furtwängler. In 1935, after a visit to Palestine, Huberman founded the Palestine Symphony Orchestra (the predecessor of the present Israel Symphony Orchestra), which was exclusively made up of Jewish refugees. Arturo Toscanini (1867–1957), the renowned Italian conductor, who had broken with Mussolini's Fascist regime in the late 1920s, conducted the first performance of the Palestine Symphony Orchestra held in Tel Aviv in December 1936. It was that inaugural concert that Pound offered to review in a note to Dunn.

Sisley Huddleston (1883–1952), American journalist, political commentator, and essayist. Huddleston was stationed in Paris from World War I through the 1930s. He served as Paris correspondent for *The London Times* and later was chief European editor of the *Christian Science Monitor*. Huddleston was associated with Ernest Hemingway and his circle when Hemingway was correspondent for the *Toronto Star* in Paris. It was probably through Hemingway that Pound was introduced to Huddleston. Huddleston wrote for various other American and British publications including *Atlantic Monthly*, the *New York Times*, and the *New Statesman*. He wrote memoirs about Bohemian and literary circles in Paris during the 1920s such as *In My Time: An Observer's Record of War and Peace* and *Bohemian Literary and Social Life in Paris; Salons, Cafés, Studios*.

(James Mercer) Langston Hughes (1902–67), African American poet. Pound began a correspondence with Hughes in 1931, soliciting his support in getting an African American college or university to financially support a translation of the African archaeologist and ethnologist Leo Frobenius' work *Erlebte Erdteile*. See Introduction pp. 23–4 for details.

Lt. Colonel Graham Seton Hutchison (pseud. Graham Seton, 1890–1940), English novelist, military historian, memoirist, and biographer. As a leader of the National Workers' Party in Britain, Hutchison carried on a significant correspondence with Pound from 1934–6. In 1936, Pound granted permission to Hutchison to quote extensively from his *ABC of Economics* (1933) in his novel *Blood Money* (London: Hutchinson & Co., 1934).

Edith Ellen Hyde-Lees (1868?–1941), Dorothy Pound's aunt. After the death of her first husband, Hyde-Lees married Henry Tudor Tucker, Olivia Shakespear's brother. Hyde-Lees was also the mother of Georgie Hyde-Lees who married **W. B. Yeats.**

Joseph Darling Ibbotson (1869–1952), Hamilton College professor of English Literature, Anglo-Saxon, and Hebrew. Later he became librarian of the college. For Pound's correspondence to Ibbotson, see Vittoria I. Mondolfo and Margaret Hurley (eds), *Ezra Pound: Letters to Ibbotson, 1935–1952* (Orono, Maine: National Poetry Foundation, University of Maine Press, 1979). Ibbotson and his family traveled to Europe in 1937, visiting relatives in Germany and Pound in Italy.

Alexandre Israël (1868–1937), French politician. Israël was elevated to the position of senator in 1927 and held the position until his death in August 1937. He was a close associate of **Camille Chautemps,** who had appointed him as minister of health in 1933.

Carlo Izzo (1901–79), Italian writer, professor, and translator of Anglo-American literature. Izzo was associated with the Venetian newspaper *Il Gazzettino*. In the mid-1930s, Izzo began translating selections of Pound's poetry into Italian, the earliest published examples appearing in the journal *Anteneo Veneto* in 1935 (excerpts from Cantos II and III, "Ballad for Gloom," "Night Litany," and "The Return"). He continued to translate Pound's poetry, later often in association with Pound's daughter Mary de Rachewiltz. Izzo also translated Charles Dickens' *Autobiography,* an anthology of African American poetry, and some of Thomas Hardy's poetry into Italian.

Eugene Jolas (1894–1952), European editor, poet, and critic. Born of immigrant parents in New Jersey, the family resettled in Europe. Eventually, Jolas and his wife Maria made their home in Paris. From 1927 to 1938, Jolas and his wife edited the influential Paris-based journal *transition*. Jolas knew most of the

Paris avant-garde, but was especially close to James Joyce. He was a staunch defender of Joyce's *Finnegans Wake*, which appeared in serial form in the pages of *transition*.

Léon Jouhaux (1879–1954), powerful French trade union leader and key backer of Léon Blum's government.

Justinian (born 482 CE, ruled 527–65 CE), Byzantine emperor. Justinian is best known for commissioning a compilation of all the imperial constitutions from the emperor Hadrian. This commission resulted in the publication of what is now known as the Justinian Code (530 CE). The *Digest* (533 CE) was later compiled under Justinian to excerpt and codify the works of the classical jurists. Justinian also introduced many fiscal and administrative reforms into the government of the empire. Pound mentioned Justinian and his code repeatedly in the *Rock-Drill* section of *The Cantos*, which he wrote while he was held at St Elizabeths. In the section, Pound associated the emperor and his code with crystal and light.

Dr. Ludwig Kast (?–?), president of the Josiah Macy Foundation. Pound wrote to Kast on July 23, 1937, inquiring: "Would the Foundation entrust me with the spending of a sum of money for the printing expenses of a series of 32 page brochures on the following conditions. I shd\receive no money whatsoever, I shd. act solely as selector of the material, and the authors of the particular brochures wd\receive normal 10% royalty for their work" (YCAL). Pound then went on to indicate that the brochures would be economic in subject, though they would relate to health issues including one about Francis Tweddell and his calcium cure for tuberculosis.

Joseph Elie Kessel (1898–1979), Argentina-born journalist and foreign correspondent. Traveled widely. Author of *La Rose du Java* (1937).

John Maynard Keynes (1883–1946), British economist, patron of the arts, and diplomat. Keynes is one of the most important economic theorists of the twentieth century, specializing in monetary theory, the behavior of financial markets, and employment. He participated in the treaty negotiations after World War I and became disillusioned with the economic policies and reparation payments imposed upon Germany. He expressed his views in *The Economic Consequences of the Peace* (1919). He also published the influential *A Tract on Monetary Reform* in 1923. His best-known work is *The General Theory of Employment, Interest, and Money* (1936).

Pound's biographer Humphrey Carpenter quotes a letter from Pound to his father, Homer, where he remarks that Pound "managed a meeting between

[Major] Douglas and Keynes on Thursday last. Douglas the real mind. Keynes fairly courageous in his book [*The Economic Consequence of the Peace*], but has invented whole Roman Apostolic Church of economics, just as bad as the old Whore of Babylon" (quoted from EP to HP, February 22, 1920 in Carpenter, *Serious Character*, p. 357). For a summary and discussion of Keynes, social credit, and Pound, see Surette, "The Keynesian Revolution and Social Credit," in *Purgatory*, pp. 108–35.

Lincoln Kirstein (1907–96), American author, editor, critic, librettist, and founder of the New York City Ballet. Kirstein came into contact with Pound shortly after he founded, along with **Varian Fry**, his influential magazine of the contemporary arts *Hound & Horn* (1927–34), while still an undergraduate at Harvard. The title of the journal was inspired by lines from Pound's poem "The White Stag": "'Tis the white stag, Fame, we're a-hunting,/Bid the world's hounds come to horn!" Often Pound referred to the magazine as "Bitch and Bugle," and was a regular contributor. Pound also kept up a steady correspondence with Kirstein into the early 1930s.

Egon Erwin Kisch (1885–1948), Czech journalist and author. Kisch started his reporting career in 1903 as a local reporter in Prague, where he developed a critical, "hard-hitting," realistic style of reporting. After 1933, Kisch, who was Jewish, went into exile in Paris and agitated against Nazism. When World War II broke out, he fled Europe and settled in Mexico. From 1927 on, Kisch wrote from a Marxist perspective, as in his *Zaren, Popen, Bolschewiken* (1927) and *Paradies Amerika* (1930).

Annette Kolb (1870–1967), German novelist and biographer. Kolb was born in Munich. Her mother was a French pianist and her father a German landscape architect. In 1933, she emigrated from Germany to live in Paris. Her autobiographical novel *Die Schaukel* appeared in 1934 and was followed by biographies of the composers Mozart (1937), Schubert (1941), and Wagner (1940). Kolb was also a close friend of Rainer Maria Rilke.

Leonid Borisovich Krasin (1870–1926), Bolshevik and Soviet commissar. Krasin was a member of Lenin's circle, who rose from electrical engineer in St Petersburg to commissar for foreign trade in talks with Britain that led to the Anglo-Russian Trade Agreement of 1921. He became Soviet ambassador to London and served in the Soviet government as commissar for trade and industry. His daughter was Ludmila Mathias.

Ivar Kreuger (1880–1932), Swedish-born American industrialist and financier. At the of age 20, Kreuger immigrated to the United States. In 1908, he founded a construction firm. Later, he branched out into manufacturing matches. Kreuger began acquiring factories throughout Europe and his wealth grew to such an extent that he was able to make significant personal loans to various small countries during World War I at favorable rates in exchange for match monopolies. After 1922, he diversified his enterprises, creating a bewildering empire of over 400 interlocked subsidiaries. He stretched his resources by making huge loans to larger countries such as France and Germany. The aftershocks of the 1929 stock market crash severely damaged Kreuger's financial empire. When its books were examined as part of the negotiations, Kreuger's empire was found to be millions of dollars in debt and it fell apart. In 1932, Kreuger shot himself in Paris.

H. H. Kung (or K'ung Hsiang-Hsi, 1881–1967), Chinese politician and government minister. Kung served as finance minister for the Chinese Nationalist government 1933–8. He was the brother-in-law of General Chiang Kai-shek.

Marie-Thérèse-Louise, Princesse de Lamballe (1749–92), French noblewoman and intimate friend of Marie Antoinette.

Alfred ("Alf") Mossman Landon (1887–1987), American politician. In 1912, Alf Landon, often described as a "liberal" Republican, entered politics as a supporter of Theodore Roosevelt's bid for the presidency as a candidate for the Progressive Party. In 1922, he was appointed as private secretary to the Governor of Kansas. In 1928, he became chairman of the Kansas State Republican Party. Landon also served as Republican Governor of Kansas 1933–7. During the 1930s, he was an important unifying figure in the splintered Republican Party. Though he experienced a crushing defeat by Franklin Roosevelt in the 1936 presidential elections, Landon remained an influential figure in American politics.

Walter Savage Landor (1775–1864), English poet and prose writer. Landor wrote a tribute to President Jackson in his *Imaginary Conversations of Literary Men and Statesmen,* which was published in sections from 1824 to 1829.

Cosmo Gordon Lang (1864–1945), British ecclesiastic, Archbishop of Canterbury (1928–42). As Archbishop of Canterbury during the abdication crisis, Lang insisted that **Edward VIII** could not marry twice-divorced **Wallis Simpson** and remain on the throne as head of the Church of England. He clearly sympathized with prime minister **Stanley Baldwin**'s effort to secure Edward VIII's abdication and to install his brother as George VI if the king could not be persuaded to give up his intent to marry Simpson.

P. J. M. Larrañaga (1883–1956), Basque mining engineer and amateur economist. Larrañaga was the author of *Gold, Glut and Government* (Allen & Unwin, 1932) which Pound found much to his liking. Larrañaga, who was allied to the social credit movement, was sufficiently talented to catch J. M. Keynes' attention. Robert Skidelsky, Keynes' biographer, writes that Larrañaga "struck Keynes as a brilliant amateur, but not a crank" (*John Maynard Keynes: The Economist as Savior: 1920–1937*, Vol. 2 [1991], 141).

James Laughlin IV (1914–97), American publisher and poet. The 1930s marked the beginning of Pound's relationship with Laughlin. After visiting Pound in Italy in 1933, Laughlin returned to Harvard as an undergraduate and, as a member of the editorial board of the *Harvard Advocate,* published Canto 38 in the February 1934 issue of the journal. Laughlin returned to Italy to stay with Pound during the summer of 1934. He returned to America in the fall and, beginning in September 1935, was briefly with **Gorham Munson**'s social credit journal *New Democracy* based in New York City. Finally, Laughlin put together funding and began New Directions. On November 16, 1936, his first publication came out: *New Directions in Prose and Poetry*. This was an anthology volume which was to become an annual "journal." The first issue included Pound's Canto 46, along with the work of such writers as **E. E. Cummings**, Elizabeth Bishop, Gertrude Stein, and **Marianne Moore**. *Guide to Kulchur* (1938) was the first New Directions edition of one of Pound's books. Laughlin became a lifelong friend as well as Pound's American publisher.

Pierre Laval (1883–1945), French statesman. Laval was French prime minister from 1931–2 and 1935–6. He started his career in 1914 as a Socialist member of the Chamber of Deputies. As his career progressed he became more and more disenchanted with the liberal democratic form of government. After the invasion of France by Germany, Laval was the key player in the formation of the Vichy regime and collaborated closely with the Nazis. He fled with the Germans when they retreated from France in 1944. Laval escaped to Spain just before the German surrender, but was arrested by the Franco regime and turned over to the Allied forces. He was tried and executed in France.

Albert Lavignac (1846–1916), French author of *Théorie complète des principes fondamentaux de la musique moderne* (1909).

T. E. Lawrence (1888–1935), British writer, scholar, and soldier, known as "Lawrence of Arabia." Lawrence was the author of *The Seven Pillars of Wisdom* (1926), a famous account of his participation in the Arab Revolt against the Turks during World War I. An archaeologist and classicist, Lawrence wrote a monograph on the architecture of Crusader castles in the Near East, excavated with Leonard Woolley at the Hittite ruins of Carchemish in Turkey, and published a literary translation of the *Odyssey*. Lawrence planned for years to set up a small publishing company when he retired from the Royal Air Force. He retired in 1935 and was killed in a motorcycle accident that same year. Pound had an acquaintance with Lawrence and the they corresponded on occasion. See B. K. Martin, "Ezra Pound and T. E. Lawrence," *Paideuma* 6 (1977), 167–73.

William George Lawrence (1889–1915), brother of the British writer and soldier Thomas Edward (T. E.) Lawrence. As vice president of St John's College Essay Society, Cambridge University, William Lawrence had invited Pound to speak to their group in 1912. He was killed in action on the Western Front during World War I. He is mentioned in Canto 74.

Stephen Leacock (1869–1944), Canadian humorist and professor of political economy at McGill University.

Fernand Léger (1881–1955), French painter and writer. Léger and Pound became friends during the 1920s in Paris. They collaborated on film projects (see **EP29** note 6). Léger directed a film of George Antheil's *Ballet Mécanique* (1923–4).

William Lemke (1878–1950), American lawyer and politician. Lemke was attorney general of North Dakota (1921–2), and then Republican representative for North Dakota (1933–41, 1943–50). He was the Union Party candidate for president in 1936, which probably brought him to Pound's attention. Pound carried on a brief correspondence with Lemke from 1936–7.

Dominic Bevan Wyndham Lewis (1894–1969), British biographer, satirist, screenwriter, and anthologist. After World War I, Lewis emerged as a writer associated with the Catholic Literary Revival movement in England. He was closely connected to the writer and Catholic apologist Hilaire Belloc and his circle. Lewis is probably best known today for his anthology of extremely bad poetry, selected from the work of both well-known and obscure authors, entitled *The Stuffed Owl*. He also produced biographies of such diverse figures as Molière, Cervantes, Louis XI of France, Villon, and the Emperor Charles V of Austria/Hungary. Much to **Percy Wyndham Lewis**' chagrin during his lifetime, the two writers were often confused.

Percy Wyndham Lewis (1882–1957), Anglo-American writer and painter. Lewis pursued both his painting and writing, developing uneasy associations with Bloomsbury through the Omega Workshops and the critic and artist Roger Fry, as well as Augustus John and Lady Ottoline Morrell. In 1908, Pound was introduced to Lewis in London in the Vienna Café by Lawrence Binyon. The introduction later led to the creation of the so-called Vorticist movement in the literary and visual arts. The movement included Pound, Lewis, Jacob Epstein, Dorothy Pound, David Bomberg, Henri Gaudier-Brzeska, the photographer Alvin Langdon Coburn, Edward Wadsworth, and others. Vorticism's best-known publication was the journal *Blast* which appeared in April 1914 and lasted for only one more issue. Pound played a central role in producing *Blast* and promoting the artists in the movement—especially Lewis and Gaudier-Brzeska. In 1916, Lewis registered for service in World War I and entered the Royal Garrison Artillery as an officer and served as an artist for the Canadian War Records Project. Lewis published his first novel, *Tarr*, in 1917. As his career developed he showed himself as prolific a writer as a painter. During the 1930s he turned to political themes in his writing, including a Spanish War novel, *The Revenge for Love* (1937), an admiring book on the Nazi movement, *Hitler* (1931), *Count Your Dead: They Are Alive* (1937), and a repudiation of his earlier admiration of Hitler, *The Hitler Cult* (1939). Pound and Lewis remained close friends and corresponded frequently until Lewis' death in 1957.

Carlo Linati (1878–1949), Italian author, translator, and poet. Linati was an editor of a Milanese journal, *Il Convegno*, and translator of Irish literature into Italian, including works by Yeats, Synge, and Lady Gregory. He was a friend of James Joyce and translated *Exiles* (1920) and sections of *Ulysses* (1926) into Italian. In 1921, he was the recipient of the famous "Schema" outlining the thematic structure of *Ulysses*. In June 1920, while Pound was in Italy that year, it appears that he may have had his first personal contact with Linati in Sirmione at the same time he first met Joyce personally after seven years of correspondence with the Irish writer. (See Read, *Pound/Joyce*, pp 164–79; Pound seems to have been in contact with Linati by letter as early as 1915.) Pound then quickly recommended Linati as a contributor to *The Dial* in a letter to Scofield Thayer dated June 16, 1920 (see Sutton, *The Dial*, p. 36).

Eduard Christian Lindeman (1885–1953). In response to a letter from Pound, **Dr. Ludwig Kast** suggested that Pound refer to Lindeman's book *Wealth & Culture: A Study of One Hundred Foundations and Community Trusts and Their Operations During the Decade 1921–1930* (1936) so that Pound could better focus his requests to foundations for grant monies.

Walter Lippmann (1889–1974), American journalist, columnist, author, and political pundit. Lippmann was member of an elite, well-connected group of media-affiliated political insiders who both reported upon and shaped politics at home and abroad. As a young man Lippmann had connections with the Greenwich Village avant-garde and was a regular at Mabel Dodge's Fifth Avenue salon. In 1913 Lippmann published his first important book, *A Preface to Politics*, and in 1914 he and Herbert Croly founded the political weekly *The New Republic* which supported and, though a "current affairs" journal, occasionally published the literary left. A strong advocate for Woodrow Wilson and his policies, Lippmann was appointed in 1917 as an assistant to Newton Baker, Wilson's secretary of war. Lippmann worked closely with Wilson and Edward House in drafting the "Fourteen Points" peace program. He was also a member of the American delegation to the Paris Peace Conference of 1919 and helped to draft the covenant of the League of Nations. In 1920, he left *The New Republic* to work for *The New York World*.

Harold Loeb (1891–1974), American author and editor. Loeb first became acquainted with Pound while he was editor of the little magazine *Broom* (1921–4). He associated with Ernest Hemingway's circle in the early 1920s in Paris. In the 1930s, Loeb became deeply involved in an economic reform movement known as Technocracy, founded by Howard Scott and the economist Thorstein Veblen in 1919. Technocracy held that the advent of mechanized labor would lead immediately to the elimination of the economic condition of scarcity. Loeb organized and headed the movement's Continental Committee for Technocracy. Loeb also wrote *Life in a Technocracy, What It Might Be Like* (1933) and *The Non-Production of Wealth* (1933).

Albert Londres (1884–1932), French journalist and author. Londres published *La Chine en Folie* in 1925.

Leo Longanesi (1905–57), Italian journalist, painter, and editor. Though he had trained for the law, from 1926 on Longanesi was involved in editing and directing a number of magazines including *L'epermesso*, *Il Toro* and *L'Italiano*.

Mahlon Loomis (1826–86), American dentist and inventor. In 1860, Loomis pioneered experiments in wireless telegraphy. He incorporated the Loomis Aerial Telegraph Company in 1873 but could not secure enough capital to pursue his experiments.

George Lewis Lorimer (1868–1937), American editor. Lorimer was editor of the *Saturday Evening Post* from 1899 until his death. Though conservative in his taste in politics and literature, under Lorimer's editorship the *Post*

Robert J. Lowry (1919–94), American short-story writer, editor, and novelist. Lowry operated a small Cincinnati, Ohio-based press called "Little Man" in the late 1930s. He also was the author of the novel *The Big Cage* (1949).

Kurt Lubinski (1900–55), German-born travel writer. Lubinski wrote about various countries, including Ethiopia and the Soviet Union. He settled in the United States in 1939. He did not publish in *Globe*.

Anthony M. Ludovici (1882–1971), British author and translator. Pound came to know Ludovici while he was at A. R. Orage's *The New Age*. Ludovici was a frequent contributor to and book reviewer for *The New Age*. He also acted as *The New Age*'s art critic. Ludovici also served for a year as secretary to the sculptor Auguste Rodin and wrote a memoir of this time, *Personal Reminiscences of Auguste Rodin* (1926). He spent much of his career translating the works of Friedrich Nietzsche. As well as working on a team which translated the *Complete Works of Nietzsche* (1914) for Macmillan and Company, Ludovici produced other translations of Nietzsche's works in the 1920s and edited a selection of Nietzsche's letters.

Frank Ma (?–?), Shanghai-based Chinese writer. Contributor to *The China Critic* and feature writer for *The China Press*.

Robert McAlmon (1896–1956), American writer and publisher. McAlmon, born in Clifton, Kansas, arrived in Paris in the fall of 1921. Prior to his appearance in Paris, he had published a small book of poems, *Explorations*, with Harriet Weaver's London-based Egoist Press. McAlmon helped James Joyce with the typing of *Ulysses*, frequented Sylvia Beach's Shakespeare and Company (which he used as his mailing address in Paris), drank with Hemingway and his circle, and came to the amorous attention of Kay Boyle. While in England McAlmon had married the heiress and writer Winifred Ellerman, known as "Bryher." Bryher's father settled a trust of £14,000 on McAlmon which allowed him to combine forces with another American expatriate, William Byrd and his Paris-based Three Mountains Press to publish a number of books by avant-garde writers under the imprint of the "Contact Editions" between 1922 and 1931. His authors included Gertrude Stein, Mina Loy, W. C. Williams, Marsden Hartley, Ford Madox Ford, and Nathaniel West.

Although McAlmon was energetic and enthusiastic about publishing and editing other writers' work, his own writing languished. His binge drinking necessitated escapes from Paris to Switzerland or the Rivera. He is best known today for his memoir of his Paris years, *Being Gensiuses Together* (1938). In 1939, he returned to the United States, ill with tuberculosis, and joined the family business in El Paso, Texas, where he remained until his death.

Walton Brooks McDaniel (1871–1978), American academic. McDaniel was professor of Latin at the University of Pennsylvania. He tutored Pound in Latin poetry when Pound was doing postgraduate work at Penn.

Ramsay MacDonald (1866–1937), British statesman, Labour Party leader, and prime minister. One of the most prominent figures in the Labour Party after World War I, MacDonald was prime minister in 1924, 1929–31, and 1931–5. He was Labour prime minister in his first two ministries but in 1931 he became prime minister in a coalition government with the Conservatives. In 1935, the arrangement broke down and he resigned, and **Stanley Baldwin** took over as Conservative prime minister. MacDonald died suddenly in November 1937.

John Angus McNab (1906–77), British editor, official of the British Union of Fascists. McNab served as associate editor of the *The Fascist Quarterly* from 1935–6 which, in January 1937, became *The British Union Quarterly* (1937–40). This was a publication of the British Union of Fascists headed by Oswald Mosley. McNab's first contact with Pound was a letter he wrote the poet to solicit a contribution for *The Fascist Quarterly* (JM to EP, July 30, 1936 [YCAL]). McNab resigned as editor of the journal in 1937 when Mosley purged the paper and reorganized its staff.

Jerre Mangione (1909–98), American author and educator. Mangione worked as a book editor at Robert M. McBride & Co. in New York from 1934–7. From 1937–9, he was a coordinating editor for the Federal Writers Project. He taught at the University of Pennsylvania from 1961–78. A son of an immigrant family, Mangione is best remembered today for his novel of Sicilian immigrant life, *Monte Allegro* (1943).

Heinrich Mann (1871–1950), German novelist, staunch anti-Nazi and brother of Thomas Mann. H. Mann lived in exile in France from 1937 to 1940.

Klaus Mann (1906–49), German author and son of Thomas Mann. Klaus Mann left Germany in 1937 and eventually settled in the United States. Author of the novel *Mephisto*.

Alessandro Manzoni (1785–1873), Italian novelist and poet.

Giuseppe Maranini (1902–69), Italian professor of politics. Maranini wrote several books on the French Revolution.

Riccardo Marchi (1897–1992), Italian writer and journalist.

Guglielmo Marchese Marconi (1874–1937), Italian scientist and inventor. Marconi was a major figure in the development of the wireless telegraph, precursor to the radio. Marconi was a strong supporter of the Fascist regime. He was nominated to the Italian Senate in 1929 and became head of the Royal Italian Academy in 1930. Marconi also served as an Italian delegate to the Paris Peace Conference in 1919. He received the Nobel Prize in physics in 1909.

Isaac Frederick Marcosson (1876-1961), American journalist, editor, and author. Born and raised in Louisville, Kentucky, Marcosson began his career there, working for various publications, before moving east. From 1913 through the 1930s, he was special European correspondent for the *Saturday Evening Post*. Marcosson's stock-in-trade was securing interviews with key political and business leaders across Europe. He was the author of numerous books, including *Adventures in Interviewing* (1919) and *Turbulent Years* (1938).

Filippo Tommaso Marinetti (christened Emilio Angelo Carlo Marinetti, 1876–1944), Italian poet, editor, aesthetic theorist, and founder of the Futurist movement. Marinetti founded the Italian journal *Poesia* in 1905—through this, he hoped to promote the avant-garde in Italian poetry. But he is best known for issuing the "Foundation and Manifesto of Futurism" in *Le Figaro* on February 20, 1909, which brought him international recognition. Marinetti lectured in London for the first time in 1910, but he caught the attention of the British media in 1912 at the opening of an exhibition of Futurist paintings at the Sackville Gallery. From that time on, Futurism became a fixture in the international avant-garde. Initially Pound, as well as **Wyndham Lewis**, were cool to him and the Futurist movement. Over the years, however, Pound followed Marinetti's activities and approved of his support of the Italian regime. Marinetti achieved considerable prominence as a writer under the Italian Fascist government and had met Mussolini in the early days of the Fascist movement—as early as 1919. In 1944, Pound "honored" him by making him a central figure in the "Italian" Canto 72, where he is found wishing to be brought back from death to fight the Allied forces in Italy.

Tomas Garrigue Masaryk (1850–1937), Czechoslovakian academic and statesman. Masaryk was a member of the Vienna Parliament of the Austro-Hungarian empire in 1891–3 and again in 1907–14. After expressing his support for the creation of individual, ethnically define nations from the multi-ethnic central European empire, Masaryk had to flee to Germany in 1914. After World War I, Masaryk convinced President Woodrow Wilson to support the creation of Czechoslovakia, of which he was the first president from 1918–35.

Hajime Matsumiya (?–?), Japanese diplomat. At the request of Katue Kitasono, Ken Yanagisawa, an official in the Japanese Ministry of Foreign Affairs, contacted the Japanese Embassy in Rome on behalf of Pound. The contact resulted in a meeting with Matsumiya, who is described in the Kitasono/Pound correspondence as either a "councillor" or "secretary" and served in the Japanese Embassy in Rome from 1936–9. Pound wrote to Kitasono on January 1, 1937: "In Rome I had a three hour conversation with Mr. Hajime Matsumiya, Councillor of the Embassy. He has done a book in English on Japanese poetry, which I shall try to have published in England." Whether Pound was successful in placing the book is unknown. (See Kodama, *Ezra Pound & Japan,* especially pp. 32–7.)

Jacqueline Maury (?–?), French author. Maury seems to have been an acquaintance of Pound's during the 1920s in Paris. Pound may have met Maury while attending Natalie Barney's salon in the rue Jacob. In the spring of 1932 Pound suggested that she send a story entitled "Those Dear Gentlemen" to Lincoln Kirstein for publication in his *Hound & Horn*. Kirstein rejected the story and in a letter of April 12, 1932, wrote to Maury suggesting that she submit it to W. C. Williams' journal *Pagany* (LK to JM, YCAL). This same Jacqueline Maury may also have been responsible for a translation of the Upanishads published in France in 1943.

Giuseppe Mazzini (1805–72), Italian patriot and leader of the Risorgimento.

H. L. Mencken (1880–1950), American journalist, essayist, political commentator, humorist, and amateur philologist.

Giuseppe Saverio Raffaele Mercadante (1795–1870), Italian composer. Mercadante is primarily known for his operatic compositions. His most noted opera is perhaps *Il giuramento* (1837).

Prince Klemens von Metternich (born Clemens Wenzel Nepomuk Lothar, 1773–1859), chancellor of the Austro-Hungarian Empire. Metternich was one of the driving forces behind the European peace brokered at the Congress of Vienna (1814–15) after Napoleon's fall from power.

Henry Miller (1891–1980), American novelist. Miller published the photo-essay "Eye on Paris" in the November 1937 issue of *Globe*, pp. 45–52. The photos were credited to "Brassaï from Black Star." Miller had already become well known in the United States for the publication of his controversial *Tropic of Cancer* (1934). *Globe* editors used a photograph from the article on the cover of the November issue.

Jules Moch (1893–1985), French statesman. Moch was a member of Blum's first government in 1936. Blum was widely criticized for including other Jews in his cabinet, though only Moch and one other member were Jewish. Moch later jointed the French Resistance during World War II and became French minister for public works (1945–7), minister of the interior (1947–50), and minister of defense (1950–1).

Walter Molino (1915–97), Italian illustrator for several major Italian publications, including *L'Intrepido* and *Il Popolo d'Italia*. Molino went on to become a comic strip artist and later a chief illustrator for *Domenica del Corriere*.

Sir Leo George Chiozza Money (1870–1944), British economic journalist, Parliamentary private secretary, member of Parliament, and economist. Money's most prolific period was just before World War I, when he published his best-known work *Riches and Poverty* (1910). Money also served as Parliamentary private secretary to Lloyd George when he was minister of munitions (1915–16). He served as Labour MP for Paddington North and then for East Northants from 1906–10 and 1910–18 respectively. Money sat on numerous boards and committees for the British government dealing with trade, taxes, industrialization, and munitions. He was knighted for his services in 1915. His first book of poetry was titled *The Immortal Purpose and Other Poems* (1924). In 1932, he published a book of poetry titled *Sonnets of Life*. Pound suggested to Money that he send a sonnet to Dunn for *Globe*.

Henri de Monfried (1879–1974), French author and adventurer.

Francesco Monotti (?–?), Italian journalist. Monotti wrote for the Genoese magazine *L'Indice*, edited by Gino Saviotti. Pound also contributed to this journal in the early 1930s. Monotti may have first met Pound around 1931 when he interviewed him for the magazine *Belvedere*.

Harriet Monroe (1860–1936), American poet, founder and editor of *Poetry*. Pound maintained a strained, but productive, relationship with Monroe as *Poetry*'s "foreign correspondent" in London before World War I.

Maria Montessori (1870–1952), Italian physician and educator. Famous for developing a system of education for children based upon spontaneity and loosened constraints.

Marianne Craig Moore (1887–1972), American poet and editor. In 1918, Moore wrote to Pound when he was editor for *The Little Review*. This led to a lifelong personal and professional relationship, conducted almost exclusively through letters. In the 1930s Pound promoted Moore's work whenever he could, including two of her poems in his collection *Active Anthology* in 1933. Moore, in turn, published a major review of *A Draft of XXX Cantos* in the October, 1933 issue of *Poetry*.

Paul Morand (1888–1976), Russian-born French novelist, poet, and diplomat. Pound became acquainted with Morand and his work in Paris during the early 1920s, perhaps through their mutual friend **Jean Cocteau.** Pound promoted Morand's work through *The Dial*. Pound also translated several of Morand's shorter works. Morand became the Paris contact for *The Dial* after Scofield Thayer fired Pound from the position in 1923.

Marino Moretti (1885–1979), Italian poet and novelist. In 1901, Moretti moved to Florence. He abandoned his initial theatrical ambitions and turned to literature, publishing his first short stories and poetry between 1902 and 1903. Soon he was contributing to journals like *La Riviera Ligure* and, in the early 1920s, *Corriere della Sera*. His first novel was *Il sole del sabato* (1916). His early book of poetry, *Poesie scritte col lapis* (1910), marked the appearance of a particular poetic tone in his work which became known as "crepuscolare."

John Pierpont Morgan, Sr. (1837–1913), American financier and founder of the Morgan financial empire.

John Pierpont Morgan, Jr. (1867–1943), American financier and son of J. P. Morgan, Sr. He became senior partner in J. P. Morgan & Co. upon his father's death.

Henry Morganthau, Jr. (1891–1967), US Secretary of the Treasury during most of the Roosevelt administrations from 1934 to 1945.

Frank Vigor Morley (1899–1980), American author and editor. Frank Vigor was the youngest of three sons of the noted mathematician Frank Morley (1860–1937). In 1924, after receiving his degree from Haverford College, he went to study at Oxford as a Rhodes scholar. He subsequently settled in England, becoming associated with Faber & Gwyer, the publishing house later to become known as Faber & Faber. Morley became a director of the publishing company along with his close friend **T. S. Eliot**, who joined the firm in 1925. He returned to America in 1939 at the outbreak of World War II. Morley became a vice president of the publishing firm Harcourt Brace & Co. in New York. He also collaborated on T. S. Eliot's literary journal *The Criterion: A Quarterly Review*, which ran from 1922 until 1939. During the 1930s, Morley seems to have been Pound's primary business contact/editor at Faber. Much of Pound's correspondence with Morley in this period concerns publishing projects for the firm.

William Morris (1834–96), British artist, author, designer, and craftsman. William Morris was an influential member of the Pre-Raphaelite movement. His vision was one in which industry was restricted to craftsmanship for the production of goods. Industrialized mass manufacturing was a degradation of the value of labor and the products it produced. Morris believed that all objects, if individually crafted, could reflect a deep sense of the spiritual and the beautiful. Furniture, dinnerware, wallpaper, and fabrics all could share the aesthetic value associated with the "fine" arts. Morris saw this extension of the beautiful and spiritual into the everyday world as having its precedent in the Middle Ages. He set up several studios during his career to produce craft items ranging from furniture to book bindings.

Eric Mosbacher (1903–98) and **Gwenda David** (1905–2002), British translators, writers, and literary agents. The two translated Ignazio Silone's work *Fontamara* in 1934, the year they were married. In addition to continued translations, David went on to become a prominent literary agent and Mosbacher became a well-known journalist.

Sir Oswald Mosley (1896–1980), British politician, member of Parliament, leader of the British Union of Fascists.

Ion Smeaton Munro (?–?), British author. Munro wrote *Through Fascism to World Power: A History of the Revolution in Italy* (1933).

Gorham Munson (1896–1969), American author, journalist, critic, and editor. Munson first contacted Pound on January 16, 1932, on behalf of J. C. Grey, the literary editor of the *New York Sun*, soliciting a contribution for the newspaper's literary section. A correspondence developed that lasted until

1939. Graduating from Wesleyan University in 1917, Munson taught briefly at the Ridgefield School in Connecticut and the Riverdale Country Day School in New York (1917–19). He then lived in Greenwich Village where he became close to Hart Crane, Jean Toomer, and Waldo Frank. During this period Munson founded the literary journal *Secession* in collaboration with his friends Kenneth Burke and Matthew Josephson. In 1932, Munson turned his attention to economics and politics, becoming an advocate of Major C. H. Douglas' social credit theories. From 1932–41, he was American correspondent for A. R. Orage's *The New English Weekly.* In 1933, he became editor of his own social credit journal, *New Democracy,* which ran until 1936. Munson was the author of *Aladdin's Lamp* (1945), a book concerning social credit and its implications for economic reform.

Jacques Necker (1732–1804), Swiss-born banker, author, and father of the writer Madame de Staël. Born in Geneva, Jacques Necker began his career as a clerk in a Swiss bank of Isaac Vernet. By 1762, Necker was a partner in the bank, working in its Paris branch. In 1765, he was in complete control of the bank as its only director. Necker helped to finance the French government through private loans. In 1772, he retired from the bank and turned to writing on financial topics. However, he returned to public life in 1776 as director-general of finances for the French government. His policies were not a success. Necker relied on loans rather than taxes to float the financial affairs of the government, and he was dismissed from his position in 1781. He was recalled by the French government in 1788. When Necker supported the calling of the Estates General, opposition with the government again grew against him. The siege of the Bastille was triggered by the announcement of Necker's second dismissal from the government on July 14, 1789.

Jane Soames Nickerson (1900–88), British journalist and author. Soames was a *London Times* correspondent in Paris and secretary to journalist Hilaire Belloc in the 1930s. She was the author of *The English Press: Newspapers and News* (1936) and *A Short History of North Africa, From Pre-Roman Times to the Present: Libya, Tunisia, Algeria, Morocco* (1961).

Otto Ernst Niemeyer (1883–1971), British civil servant and banker. Niemeyer served in the Treasury until 1927. He then became an adviser to the Bank of England and, in 1938, its executive director. He retired as executive in 1952.

Montagu Collet Norman (1871–1950), British civil servant and banker. Norman was appointed deputy governor to the Bank of England in 1918, and then governor in 1920. He remained in this position until 1944, when he left his post due to ill health. While at the Bank of England, he grappled with Britain's World

War I debt to the United States, domestic inflation in Britain, the disruption and volatility of exchange rates, the threat of economic collapse in Central Europe, and the reparation issue. In dealing with international economic issues Norman worked closely with the League of Nations. When World War I broke out, Norman became a key planner of Britain's economic strategy during the conflict.

Amédée Ozenfant (1886–1966), French painter, critic, editor, and educator. Ozenfant was a friend and associate of the modernist architect Le Corbusier. After World War I, they initiated an avant-garde movement known as "Purism," which incorporated elements of cubist aesthetic and machine design. Ozenfant edited the journal *L'Elan* (1915–16). Later, he established and co-edited, with Le Corbusier, the Purist journal *L'Esprit nouveau* (1920–5). Ozenfant was professor at the University of Washington in Seattle (1939–53) and head of the Ozenfant School of Fine Arts in New York. His major critical work was *Art* (1928), which was translated into English by **John Rodker** as *Foundations of Modern Art* (1931).

Albert Parry (1901–92), Russian-born American freelance writer. Parry was a fellow in the department of history at the University of Chicago. Though he wrote primarily on international affairs and history, he also wrote a book entitled *Garrets and Pretenders; a History of Bohemianism in America* (1933), which Pound may have known.

John William Wright Patman (1893–1976), American politician. Patman served as a Democratic representative for Texas from 1929–76.

Brigit Patmore, neé Ethel Elizabeth Morrison-Scott (1888–1965), British author. Brigit Patmore was one of the principal members of Pound's London circle in the years before World War I. Patmore married the son of the widely known Victorian poet Coventry Patmore. Through her in-laws, she found herself in the salon of Violet Hunt, who had family connections with the Pre-Raphaelites. Hunt introduced Patmore to Ezra Pound, **Ford Madox Ford**, **W. B. Yeats**, **H. G. Wells** and others. Patmore was close to **T. S. Eliot** and his first wife Vivienne. Patmore introduced the poet, critic, and novelist Richard Aldington to his future wife, the poet H.D. However, after H.D. and Aldington's marriage ended, Patmore and Aldington began a ten-year relationship, living and traveling together through Europe. During this time, Aldington wrote his best-known novel, *Death of a Hero* (1929). Patmore herself published two novels, *This Impassioned Onlooker* (1926) and *No Tomorrow* (1929). In the winter of 1928–9, the first year of Aldington and Patmore's relationship, Pound played enthusiastic host to the couple in Rapallo, Italy. Brigit Patmore kept in touch with Pound until her death in 1965.

Micun M. Pavicevic (1879–?), Montenegran writer, editor, and diplomat.

Silvio Pellico (1788–1854), Italian writer and nationalist.

Giovanni Battista Pergolesi (1710–36), Italian composer. Pergolesi had a brief but productive life, composing in many genres of music. His best-known works today are his *Stabat Mater* (1730) and opera *La serva padrona* (1733).

Alfred Perlès (1897?–1990?), Austrian-born journalist and novelist, also went by the name of Alfred Barret. Perlès was recommended to *Globe* by his close friend, **Henry Miller**, author of *Tropic of Cancer* and *Tropic of Capricorn*. Perlès had shared a small apartment with Miller in Clichy in the early 1930s. Along with Miller, in Paris in the 1930s, Perlès was associated with Lawrence Durrell, Anais Nin, and Jack Kahane's Obelisk Press.

Helmut Petri (1907–98), German anthropologist. Petri became a member of Frobenius' Forschungsinstitut für Kulturmorphologie in 1935 and in 1938–9 he carried out field research in western Australia. At the outbreak of World War II he was inducted into the German army. After the war, he returned to the Institut and in 1953–4 led its second expedition to western Australia. In 1956, he became a professor at the University of Frankfurt and in 1958, he became director of the Instituts für Völkerkunde at the University of Köln—a position he held into the 1970s.

Francis Picabia (1879–1959), Cuban-born French painter. Before World War I, Picabia was associated with the circle of Apollinaire, Marie Laurencin, Picasso, and Léger. He also frequented Gertrude Stein's salon and was associated with Alfred Stieglitz and his circle in New York. Pound met Picabia around 1921, when Pound settled in Paris. By this time, Picabia had moved on from the cubist influences of the pre-war era and was involved with the Dada/surrealist movements and part of Tristan Tzara's and Man Ray's circles. Pound was impressed with the painter's work. When he arrived in 1939 in New York for his first US visit in decades, Pound told reporters that Picabia was "the man who ties knots in Picasso's tail" (Stock, *Life*, p. 466).

Luigi Pirandello (1867–1936), Italian dramatist and novelist. Before World War I, Pirandello was primarily a writer of prose fiction. In 1914, he published his first critically acclaimed novel, *The Late Mattia Pascal*. In 1916, he found his medium: the theater. In 1921, Pirandello wrote what would become his most-performed and best-known plays: *Six Characters in Search of an Author* and *Henry IV*. In 1934, he received the Nobel Prize for literature. Pirandello's support of Mussolini and the Fascist cause made him a controversial figure.

George Henry Lane Fox Pitt-Rivers (1890–1966), British author. Pitt-Rivers wrote on eugenics and was associated with rightist/racist political movements in Britain. During World War II, due to his pro-Hitler sympathies, Pitt-Rivers was held by the foreign secretary as a political prisoner from 1940–2. Among his books were *The Clash of Culture and the Contact of Races; an Anthropological and Psychological Study of the Laws of Racial Adaptability, with Special Reference to the Depopulation of the Pacific and the Government of Subject Races* (1927).

Antoninus Pius (born 86 CE, ruled 138–61 CE), Roman emperor. Antoninus was successor to and adopted son of the emperor Hadrian. Antoninus' rule was relatively quiet after Hadrian's long and tempestuous reign. His governing style was less intrusive and aggressive than his immediate predecessors and he was deferential to the Senate. Residing for the most part in Rome, Antoninus concerned also himself with legislative tasks and kept a careful watch on the financial affairs of the empire. Pound was much taken with Antoninus' rule and mentions him frequently in *The Cantos,* often in connection with the *Lex Rhodia de Iactu*, a code dealing with maritime law (see Cantos XLVI, LXXVIII, LXXXVII, LXXXIX, XCIV, XCVI–XCVIII, CII, CV, and CVI).

Odon Por (1883–?), Hungarian-born economist. Por was associated with A. R. Orage's circle and published a two-part article "Land Reform v. Agricultural Labourer" in the January 15 and 22, 1914 issues of *The New Age*. Later that same year he published two other pieces in *The New Age*: "Strike in Italy" (July 2, 1914) and "War and After" (September 17, 1914). Por's *Fascism* and *Guilds and Co-operatives in Italy* were translated and published in England in 1923. Beginning in 1934, Pound kept up a voluminous correspondence with Por concerning economic theory until the collapse of the Fascist regime. Given Pound's own association with *The New Age* before World War I, he was probably aware of Por much earlier than the 1930s. By the time Pound began his correspondence with him, Por had a minor position in the Italian government and many contacts within Fascist circles. Por used these contacts to help Pound and, in turn, Pound translated Por's work *Politica economico-sociale in Italia anno XVII–XVII* (1940) into English.

Niccolo Antonio Porpora (1686–1766), Italian composer and voice instructor. Franz Joseph Haydn was one of Porpora's pupils.

Arthur Pound (1884–1966), American historian, writer, and editor. The majority of Pound's published works concern the history of industrialization and invention in the United States. He served as associate editor of *The Atlantic Monthly* (1936–40). Ezra Pound's characterization of Arthur Pound as a General Motors "yes man" probably relates to his book *The Turning Wheel; The Story of General Motors through Twenty-five Years, 1908–1933* (1934).

Cuthbert W. Pound (1864–1935), associate judge, New York State Court of Appeals, August 1915–March 1932; Chief Judge March 1932–May 1934. The upstate New York associations of the Pound family lend credence to Homer's claim that Cuthbert was a relation.

Nathan Roscoe Pound (1870–1966), lawyer, author, botanist, and legal theorist. Pound is best known as an advocate of reform in the American judicial system. Born in Lincoln, Nebraska, Pound studied at Harvard Law School where he later served as dean (1916–36).

Mario Praz (1896–1982), Italian scholar, critic, and professor of Italian. Praz taught at the universities of Liverpool and Manchester (1924–34). Much of his work concerns the connection between Italian and English literature. Praz's critical writings include studies of Poe, Swinburne, Wilde, de Sade, Joyce, and T. S. Eliot.

Baron Byron Khun de Prorok (1896–1954), French archaeologist, adventurer, and writer. De Prorok was educated at the University of Geneva. As an archaeologist, he worked on excavations at Carthage from 1920–5. For most of his life de Prorok organized expeditions that had little scientific value, usually involving the sensational search for some legendary site or figure. His books include *Digging for Lost African Gods* (1926), *Mysterious Sahara* (1929), and *In Quest of Lost Worlds* (1935). Though de Prorok's archaeological achievement was negligible, he was innovative in the use of film as a means of documenting his expeditions and digs. Unfortunately, it appears that most of this film record has been lost.

Samuel Putnam (1892–1950), American author, poet, translator, and editor. Before World War II, Putnam was in France with his family as editor of the short-lived journal *The New Review*, an "international notebook for the arts" (1930–2). Pound and Richard Thoma were associate editors of the magazine. **George Antheil** and **Hilaire Hiler** were contributing editors. *The New Review* published seven books under its imprint "The New Review Publications." Putnam later translated works in French, Spanish, and Italian into English, including works of Cervantes, Pirandello, Rabelais, and de Sade. He wrote a memoir entitled *Paris Was Our Mistress: Memoirs of a Lost and Found Generation* (1947) in which Pound prominently figures.

John Quinn (1870–1924), American corporate lawyer, art collector, and patron. During Pound's 1910–11 trip to America, Pound met John Quinn through the painter John Yeats, father of William Butler Yeats. Quinn was a patron to Irish and English artists including Yeats, Augustus John, Gwen John, and George Russell. Pound struck up a very productive relationship with Quinn. Through an extensive correspondence with Quinn, Pound expanded the lawyer's patronage and he acquired the work of Wyndham Lewis, Henri Gaudier-Brzeska, William Wadsworth, and other Vorticist artists. Quinn also collected works by Picasso, Matisse, Lautrec, Henri Rousseau, and Jules Pascin, as well as works by American painters Marsden Hartley, Walt Kuhn, Arthur Davies, Maurice Prendergast, and John Sloan. Though Pound was able to enlist Quinn in supporting his circle of artist and writers, Quinn remained fiercely independent in his patronage.

Arthur Germanovich Raffalovich (1853–1921), Russian publicity agent in France for the Czarist government. After the after the Russian revolution, he published a series of books on Russia and economics. In 1931, the Librairie du Travail published his *L'Abominable vénalité de la presse, d'après les documents des archives russes.*

Marco Ramperti (1887–1964), Italian author. Ramperti was an Italian journalist and author who belonged to the Futurist and Fascist movements. He was tried after World War II for his support of the Salò Republic but was never sentenced.

Man Ray (born Emmanuel Radnitsky, 1890–1976), American painter and photographer. Man Ray is primarily known for his photography and his involvement in the Dada and surrealist movements. He was close to the French artist Marcel Duchamp.

Eugen Relgis (1895–1987), Jewish writer from Romania who later moved to Ecuador. Relgis was author of *The Principles of Humanism* (1931).

Joachim von Ribbentrop (1893–1946), Nazi official. Ribbentrop was Hitler's ambassador to Britain 1936–8. He became Hitler's foreign minister 1938–45. He was executed at Nuremberg as a war criminal.

Alexander Friedrich Ladislaus Roda Roda (1872–1945), Austrian humorist. Roda Roda contributed two articles to *Globe.*

John Rodker (1894–1955), British author, translator, and publisher. Pound probably met Rodker through the author Mary Butts in London in 1917. In 1919, Rodker succeeded Pound as London editor for *The Little Review.* That same year he founded the London-based Ovid Press. During its brief existence,

Ovid Press published work by **Wyndham Lewis, T. S. Eliot**, Pound, and others. Pound's works published by Ovid include *The Fourth Canto* (1919), *Hugh Selwyn Mauberley* (1920) and *A Draft of Cantos 17–27* (1928).

André Roosevelt (1879–1962), American explorer and world adventurer. First cousin of Theodore Roosevelt, André Roosevelt became famous for making the first films of Bali and founding the Haitian tourist industry.

William Michael Rossetti (1829–1919) British literary critic, editor of the journal *The Germ*, brother of **Dante Gabriel Rossetti** (1828–82) British painter, translator, and poet. Both were central figures in the Pre-Raphaelite movement in Victorian England.

Gioachino Rossini (1792–1868), Italian composer. Rossini began writing operas at the age of 18 and quickly achieved fame. Many of his operas are still standard repertoire. After working with opera companies across Italy and France, he stopped writing operas at age 37.

Edmondo Rossoni (1884–1965), Italian journalist, political radical, writer, and minister in the Italian Fascist government. John P. Diggins describes Rossoni's career in *Mussolini and Fascism: The View From America* (Princeton, 1972): "During the prewar years Rossoni edited the anarcho-syndicalist paper of New York, *Il Proletario*, working shoulder to shoulder with 'Big Bill' Haywood, Eugene Debs, and other stalwarts in the labor struggle. At this time he demonstrated his hatred of patriotism by spitting on the flag of Italy. But when Italy entered the war in 1915, he rushed back to his homeland. By 1918 he was organizing labor unions to 'fight Communism.' By 1925, as Minister of Corporations under Mussolini, he was telling workers that Fascism was the ultimate expression of the syndicalist-nationalist idea" (p. 87).

Mayer Amschel Rothschild (1743–1812), German financier. Mayer Amschel Rothschild was the founder of the House of Rothschild, the powerful European banking family.

Franklin Roudybush (1906–98), American diplomat and educator. Roudybush was director of the Foreign Service School for Diplomatic and Counsel Service in Washington, DC. He was also assistant editor of the magazine *World Digest*.

William Henry Denham Rouse (1863–1950), classicist, Sanskrit scholar, folklorist, and translator. Educated at Doveton College in Calcutta and Cambridge University, Rouse taught at Cheltenham College and served as headmaster at Rugby. He was instructor in Sanskrit at Cambridge University. His numerous translations include Augustine's *Confessions*, the *Argonautica*, Lucretius' *De Rerum Natura*, Ovid's *Metamorphoses*, and the works of Marcus Aurelius and Cicero. His most important and best-known translations are those of Homer's *Iliad* and *Odyssey* (1938, 1937 respectively). Pound carried on an extensive correspondence with Rouse from 1934 to 1940. The subject of this exchange was Rouse's translations of Homer (see Introduction pp. 1–35).

Jean-Jacques Rousseau (1712–78), French philosopher and writer.

Olga Rudge (1895–1996), American violinist. Originally from Youngstown, Ohio, Rudge was educated in Europe. In 1910, she was sent to the Paris Conservatoire to further her studies in the violin. From about 1915 on, Rudge performed in London and Pound probably first heard her perform in the Aeolian Hall on November 10, 1920. Pound was in the audience as "William Atheling" the music reviewer at *The New Age*, and afterward wrote admiringly of her playing.

In the mid-1920s, Pound and Rudge began a relationship that was to last to the end of Pound's life, moving from Paris to Italy when Pound and his wife relocated to Rapallo. Rudge settled in Venice, but she also maintained a home in Sant'Ambrogio, near Rapallo. In the 1930s, when Pound's wife Dorothy was in London during the summers visiting her mother Olivia and son Omar, Pound would stay with Olga in Venice. The relationship revolved, in part, around their mutual love of music. Pound encouraged Rudge's playing, providing her frequent chances to play in his Rapallo concert series in the 1930s. He also supported her research into Vivaldi's work. In 1925, Olga gave birth to Pound's daughter, Mary Rudge (later, de Rachewiltz).

Antonio de Oliveira Salazar (1889–1970), Portuguese dictator and academic. Salazar studied law at the University of Coimbra and became a professor of political economy at the same university. He became politically active in the 1920s and was part of the 1926 coup against the government. He served in the new government as minister of finance until he became prime minister in 1932. He ruled as dictator until 1968. Salazar sympathized with General Franco in the Spanish Civil War, but he was interested with maintaining ties with Britain. Portugal maintained neutrality in World War I until Allied victory was certain. Salazar then allowed Allied troops to use bases in the Azores.

Harrison Salisbury (1908–93), American journalist and author. At the time Salisbury contributed to *Globe*, he was working for United Press. In 1949, he was hired by the *New York Times*. In 1955, he won the Pulitzer Prize for his international reporting. Salisbury became editor of the *Times*' Op-Ed page in

1970, retiring in 1973. Salisbury was the author of more than twenty-nine books, including *Moscow Journal: The End of Stalin* (1961), *The 900 Days: The Siege of Leningrad* (1969), *War Between Russia and China* (1969), and *The Long March: The Untold Story* (1985).

Baron James Arthur Salter (1881–1975), British economist, diplomat, and Conservative member of Parliament 1937–50. Salter served as general secretary for the Reparations Commission (1920–2) and as director of the Economics Section of the League of Nations (1931–7).

William Saroyan (1908–81), Armenian-born American novelist, playwright, screenwriter, and short-story writer. Saroyan, only in his late twenties when contacted by *Globe*, was already well known with the publication of his short story collection *The Daring Young Man on the Flying Trapeze* (1935). During the years 1936 and 1937, he published three other books: *Inhale and Exhale*, *Three Times Three*, and *The Gay and the Melancholy Flux*.

Paolo Sarpi (1551–1623), Venetian diplomat, intellectual, and patriot. In 1606, in his capacity as official counselor to the Senate of Venice, Sarpi played a principal role in defending the city-state's independence in a dispute with Pope Paul V.

Baronet Philip Albert Gustave David Sassoon (1888–1939), British government official, member of Parliament. Sassoon was the son of Sir Edward Albert Sassoon and Aline Caroline, daughter of Baron Gustave de Rothschild, of the French branch of the Rothschild family. From 1924–9 and again from 1931–7 Sassoon served as under-secretary of state for air. From 1937 until his death, he served as First Commissioner of Works.

Gino Saviotti (1891–?), Italian editor, novelist, and translator. Saviotti edited the Genoa-based journal *L'Indice*. Pound saw *L'Indice* as an important vehicle for introducing an Italian audience to British and American modernism. For a brief time (1930–1), Pound had an editorial position with *L'Indice*. (For a overview of Pound's involvement with and contributions to *L'Indice*, see Redman, *Ezra Pound and Italian Fascism*, pp. 78–84.)

Hjalmar Horace Greeley Schacht (1877–1970), German financier and Nazi official. Schacht was appointed president of the Reichsbank in 1923. He resigned in 1930 because he opposed the continuation of Germany's reparations payments mandated under the Versailles Treaty. In 1931, Schacht became a supporter of the Nazi Party. When the Nazis came to power in 1933, Schacht was again appointed president of the Reichsbank. In 1934, Schacht was appointed minister of the economy. Conflicts within the inner circles of the Nazi government, especially with Hermann Goering, caused him to resign as minister in 1937. In 1939, Schacht resigned as president of the Reichsbank over conflicts concerning armaments expenditures. Schacht was imprisoned in a concentration camp for allegedly participating in the 1944 plot to assassinate Hitler. He is mentioned in Canto 52.

Jakob Schaffner (1875–1944), Swiss-born novelist living in Germany.

Arthur Schnitzler (1862–1931), Austrian physician, playwright, and novelist.

George Samuel Schuyler (1895–1977), African American journalist, novelist, political commentator. Schuyler was on the staff at the *Pittsburgh Courier*. His books include the satiric *Black No More: Being an Account of the Strange and Wonderful Workings of Science in the Land of the Free, A.D. 1933–1940* (1931) and *Slaves Today: A Story of Liberia* (1931). Schuyler also contributed articles on issues of race to Mencken's *American Mercury* in the late 1920s and early 1930s.

Montgomery Schuyler (1877–1955), American diplomat and scholar. Schuyler was briefly American Minister to Ecuador (1913) and later El Salvador (1921–5). He was also a scholar with interests including Sanskrit drama and lexicography, Iranian religion and literature, and the history of New York State. Schuyler was involved with the Technocracy movement and served on its National Survey of Product Capacity, which produced *The Chart of Plenty* in 1935 under the leadership of **Harold Loeb**.

William Pierce Shepard (1873–1948), American academic. Shepard was professor of Romance Languages and Literatures at Hamilton College. He taught Pound French, Spanish, Italian, and Provençal. Pound dedicated his *Spirit of Romance* to Shepard. (For information on Shepard's extensive Provençal collection maintained at Hamilton, see *The William P. Shepard Collection of Provençalia* [Clinton, NY: Hamilton College, 1971].)

Ignazio Silone (1900–78), pseudonym for Secundo Tranquilli, was an Italian writer and opponent of fascism. He lived in exile in Zurich.

Rodger L. Simons (?–?). Simons was described in the first issue of *Globe* as a "[y]oung American journalist; University of Minnesota. Was in banking business and hated it. Became science and movie editor of 'St. Paul Dispatch.' Married a Swedish girl and went to her country as correspondent for 'Chicago Daily News.' Now has a news and feature service of his own called Continental and American News Features, Inc. in Stockholm."

Wallis Warfield Simpson (1896–1986), American-born wife of Edward, Duke of Windsor. Edward abdicated the British throne on December 10, 1936, to marry the American Mrs. Simpson, who was a two-time divorcée. He married her on June 3, 1937.

Upton Sinclair (1878–1968), American novelist, politician, essayist, and playwright. Sinclair's most famous work was *The Jungle* (1906), a classic "muckracking" novel about the meat packing industry in Chicago. The novel provoked such public outrage that it caused a federal investigation and the establishment of the Pure Food and Drug Act of 1906. In 1933, after winning the Democratic nomination for governor, Sinclair published his political agenda in *I, Governor of California, and How I Ended Poverty: A True Story of the Future.* In this pamphlet, Sinclair called for a social security system for the state, large public works projects, and the establishment of government agencies to regulate industries and businesses. Though his politics did not jibe with Pound's, Pound was interested in Sinclair as another writer concerned about economic reform.

John Jermain Slocum (1914–97), American writer, scholar, and numismatist. Slocum met Pound by chance while he was canoeing on the Salzach River in Austria in 1935. Pound was attending the Salzburg music festival. Slocum was a contemporary and friend of **James Laughlin** at Harvard. After his graduation from Harvard in 1936, Slocum went to work on the staff of the *North American Review.* He got the magazine to run Pound's "The Jefferson-Adams Correspondence" (*North American Review,* CCXLIV 2 [Winter 1937/38] 314–24). Slocum hosted Pound in New York City during his 1939 visit.

George Ephraim Sokolsky (1893–1962), American newspaper editor, columnist, and author. Sokolsky wrote, lectured, and broadcasted on behalf of conservative political and economic causes. Sokolsky went to Russia to edit the only English language newspaper in Petrograd (now St. Petersburg), the *Daily News.* However, in March 1918, after the newspaper's reports about internal conflicts within the Russian revolutionary government which resulted in the downfall of Alexander Kerensky's regime, he was ordered to leave the country. Sokolsky now became an ardent advocate for American democracy and capitalism. In the 1930s, after a lengthy stay in China, Sokolsky returned to the United States. He wrote as columnist for the *New York Herald Tribune* and later for the *New York Sun.* In 1937, he began a weekly radio broadcast for the National Association of Manufacturers. Sokolsky appeared on the popular radio show *Town Meeting of the Air.*

Francesco Spinedi (1898–?), Professor of Political Economy at the University of Rome.

Aleksei Grigorievich Stakhanov (1906–77), Russian coal miner who initiated a movement to speed up industrial production in the Soviet Union under Stalin.

Dimitri Stancioff (1864–1940), Bulgarian lawyer, state minister, and ambassador. It is not clear when Pound met Stancioff. Surviving correspondence indicates that Pound was writing to Stancioff's son Ivan and his wife Anna in 1935. After her husband's death, Anna Stancioff and her son escaped from Bulgaria in the wake of the Russian invasion at the end of World War II. They immigrated to the United States and settled near Washington, DC. Ezra and Dorothy Pound kept in touch with the Stancioffs while Pound was held at St. Elizabeths.

Charles Vincent Emerson Starrett (1886–1974), Canadian-born American journalist, novelist, anthologist, bibliophile, and essayist. Starrett's short stories, serialized novels, and thrillers were published in *Collier's* and *Smart Set*. Starrett briefly edited *Poetry* magazine in the 1920s. He is best known for his mystery and detective fiction. In 1934, Starrett, Christopher Morley, Alexander Woollcott, and others formed the "Baker Street Irregulars," the famous Sherlock Holmes Club. Starrett assembled several anthologies of detective stories—one, *Fourteen Great Detective Stories,* for the Modern Library series (1928).

Alberto De Stefani (1879–1969), Italian economist. De Stefani served as finance minister in Italy during the early years of Mussolini's regime, but was forced to resign in 1925.

Cesare Sterbini (1783–1851), Italian librettist. Sterbini wrote the libretto for **Rossini**'s *Il barbiere di Siviglia.*

Jesse Isidor Straus (1872–1936), American businessman and ambassador. Straus was a chief executive with R. H. Macy & Company of New York. He served in several capacities as an economic adviser during the New York governorship of Franklin D. Roosevelt. When Roosevelt became president in 1933, Straus was appointed ambassador to France. Straus had hoped to become secretary of commerce, but Roosevelt felt that in dealing with France he needed Straus' business expertise.

Igor Stravinsky (1882–1971), Russian composer. Though Stravinsky was one of the foremost composers of the twentieth century, Pound had a limited admiration for his music. His opinion of the composer may have been shaped by his association with George Antheil. At the beginning of his career, Antheil had a tense relationship with Stravinsky and felt himself to be the rival of the older composer.

Leonard Alfred George Strong (1896–1958), London-based Anglo-Irish poet, critic, and journalist. Strong's "Kilkenny Emigrants," about Irish villagers traveling to Dublin, was published in the first issue of *Globe* (March 1937, 27–9).

Lloyd Paul Stryker (1885–1955), American lawyer. Stryker was Pound's contemporary at Hamilton College. L. P. Stryker was the son of Hamilton College President, the Reverend Melancthon Woolsey Stryker, whom Pound remembered fondly. Pound included the elder Stryker's translation of Martin Luther's hymn text "Ein Feste Burg Ist Unser Gott" in his anthology *Confucius to Cummings* (1964). L. P. Stryker was Alger Hiss' defense attorney in his first perjury trial in 1949. He was author of *Andrew Jackson: A Study in Courage* (1929). In 1945, another Hamiltonian, Elihu Root, Jr., the son of the Nobel Laureate Elihu Root, suggested that Lloyd Stryker be considered to defend Pound against treason charges.

Jesse Hilton Stuart (1906–84), American novelist, short story writer, and poet. Stuart's work dealt with rural Kentucky life. Stuart attended Vanderbilt University in 1931–2, where he studied with such teachers as Robert Penn Warren. Stuart went on to become author of over sixty volumes of prose and poetry.

Alphonsus Joseph-Mary Augustus Montague Summers (1880–1948), British writer, self-styled expert in demonology and witchcraft, and one-time Catholic priest. A notorious eccentric, Summers dressed like an eighteenth-century cleric, down to the long black cape, as he strolled London. Though his passion was primarily for the occult, he also edited Restoration-era plays. In 1926, Summers published his famous and strange *The History of Demonology and Witchcraft*. He followed it with books on witches, werewolves, and the occult. He was also an expert on the Gothic novel and published *The Gothic Quest: A History of the Gothic Novel* (1938).

Reverend Henry S. Swabey (1916–95), Anglican clergyman. Swabey was a vicar in the eastern counties of England and also served the Anglican Church in Canada. While at the University of Durham, Swabey wrote a thesis entitled "The Church of England and Usury." Swabey must have been attending the University of Durham when he began corresponding with Pound around 1935. He continued to write to the poet until 1971 on topics ranging from church history to economic reforms. He and Pound had a shared interest in social credit issues.

Hope Williams Sykes (1901–73), American novelist. Sykes, a former school teacher, lived and worked in Fort Collins, Colorado. Her best-remembered novel is *Second Hoeing* (1935). The novel depicts the lives of Volga German immigrants from the Soviet Union working as migrant workers harvesting beets on farms in northern Colorado. The book was widely praised by reformers and critics for its portrayal of child labor. The Sugar Act of 1937, which prohibited child labor and established minimum wages for field workers, was passed under the influence of Sykes' book.

André Pierre Gabriel Amédée Tardieu (1876–1945), French statesman and prime minister. Tardieu was French prime minister from 1929–30 and in 1932. He also served as right-wing member of the Chamber of Deputies from 1926–36.

Henry John Temple (Lord Palmerston, 1784–1865), British statesman and prime minister, 3rd Viscount Palmerston. Lord Palmerston was prime minister twice (1855–8, 1859–65). He played a key role in the consolidation of the British Empire and the formulation of its foreign policy in the nineteenth century.

Alfred Tennyson (1809–92), British poet. Tennyson was appointed British poet laureate in 1850 by Queen Victoria.

Dorothy Thompson (1894–1961), American international affairs journalist, newspaper columnist, and radio broadcaster. In the mid-1930s, Thompson was at the height of her career as a journalist. In March 1936, she began to write her influential column "On the Record" for the *New York Herald Tribune*.

Harold William Thompson (1891–1964) folklorist, musicologist, author, and professor. Thompson was an alumnus of Hamilton College (PhB 1912). Thompson went on to earn his MA and PhD from Harvard (1915) and taught for twenty-five years at Teacher's State College, later University of Albany (SUNY). He is known for his best-selling book *Bodies, Boots and Britches* (1939), an omnibus of upstate New York folklore and song. Thompson counted among his friends and acquaintances Pete Seeger, Count Basie, Carl Sandburg, Grant Wood, "Lead Belly" Ledbetter, and Paul Robeson. Thompson wrote an eight-page laudatory article profiling Pound for the March 1936 issue of the *Hamilton Alumni Review*. The article initiated a correspondence between Thompson and Pound. (See McWhirter, "'Dear Poet-general and Walloper': The Correspondence of Ezra Pound and Harold W. Thompson 1936–39," *Paideuma* [forthcoming]).

George Holden Tinkham (1870–1956), American politician. Tinkham was a Republican representative from Massachusetts from 1915–43. Tinkham, nicknamed "Uncle George" by Pound, corresponded with the poet from 1933–41. Of all Pound's correspondents in the American government, Tinkham was the most friendly towards Pound and a warm epistolary relationship developed. Tinkham, who was wealthy, slightly eccentric, and well-traveled, visited Pound in Italy in 1939. A conservative native of Boston, Tinkham was sympathetic to a number of Pound's hobby horses—especially his disdain for the League of Nations.

Federigo Tozzi (1883–1920), Italian short story writer and novelist. Considered one of Italy's most important early modernist writers. He was born into a peasant family in Siena and died in Rome.

Ignatius Timothy Trebitsch-Lincoln (1872 or 1879–1943), Hungarian-born spy. Trebitsch-Lincoln adopted multiple personae during his world travels. Born in Hungary to Jewish parents, he had numerous "careers" including protestant minister, Anglican priest, Buddhist abbot, member of British Parliament, personal secretary to a millionaire, and journalist. He spied for various countries, including Bulgaria, Turkey, Germany, China, and Japan. After World War I, he ended up in Italy and joined Mussolini's Black Shirts. Later he moved to China and became a Buddhist monk and took the name Chao Kung. He became an advisor to a warlord and later counseled Chiang Kai-shek. *Newsweek*, in an article on April 21, 1934, described him as "the human chameleon." He was stabbed to death by a Japanese assassin in 1943.

Mikhail Nikolayevich Tukhachvesky (1893–1937), marshal of the Soviet Armed Forces. Perhaps because Tukhachvesky was a young and popular figure in the military, Stalin moved against him during the Purges of the 1930s. Tukhachvesky and his family were executed.

Francis Tweddell (1863–1939), American pediatrician. Tweddell corresponded with Pound concerning a possible cure for tuberculosis. (For details and discussion of this correspondence, see O. Pound, "Canto 113: Tweddell, Men Against Death and Paul de Kruif," *Paideuma*, 11, pp. 173–80, and W. Flory, *The American*, pp. 96–7.)

Ubaldo Degli Uberti (1881–1945), Italian chief naval press officer. Uberti became acquainted with Pound around 1934. It is possible that they met in Rome where Uberti was based. Uberti translated a number of Pound's pieces for publication in Italy. As editor of *La marina republicana*, he published 26 lines of Pound's notorious "Italian" Canto 72 in January 1945 as well as its companion, Canto 73 in its entirety in February 1945. These two Cantos were suppressed in subsequent editions of *The Cantos* until 1985.

Notari Umberto (1878–1950), Italian writer, editor, and artist. Notari was director of the paper *L'Ambrosiano* and of the Milanese advertising agency "Le Tre I." He was associated with **Filippo Tommaso Marinetti** and the Futurist movement.

Cornelius Vanderbilt IV (1898–1974), American journalist and author. Vanderbilt was the son of magnate Cornelius Vanderbilt III and the author of *Farewell to Fifth Avenue* (1935).

Fritz-René Vanderpyl (1876–1965), Dutch-born art critic, novelist, and poet. Vanderpyl was art critic for the Paris-based *Le Petit Parisien*. Pound was already acquainted with Vanderpyl in 1920. Pound wrote Schofield Thayer that he had asked Vanderpyl to write "a set of 'medallions' of painters, Vlaminck, Derain,... etc.. He is very intimate with them all. has done for them, especially Vlaminck, more or less what I have done in London for Gaudier & Lewis" (see Sutton, *The Dial*, p. 57). Vanderpyl was friendly with Maurice de Vlaminck and most of the "Fauves," as well as Guillaume Apollinaire and others in Picasso's circle. Pound probably introduced Vanderpyl to James Joyce in 1920 and Vanderpyl joined Joyce's inner circle. Vanderpyl's works include *De Giotto a Puvis de Chavannes* (1913), *Peintres de mon époque* (1931), a study of the nineteenth-century Belgian artist *Antoine Wiertz* (1931), and a volume of poetry, *Voyages* (1920), illustrated by Vlaminck.

Giuseppe Verdi (1813–1901), Italian composer. Verdi is perhaps the most renowned of the nineteenth-century operatic composers. With the premiere of *Nabucco* (1842), his career soared. He premiered *Rigoletto* in 1851, followed by *Il Trovatore* (1853), *La Traviata* (1853), *Aïda* (1871), *La Forza del destino* (1862), and *Don Carlos* (1867).

Joseph Vogel (1904–95), American novelist and poet. Vogel graduated from Hamilton College in 1926 with the ambition of becoming a well-known writer. In 1927, he began a correspondence with Pound to cultivate him as a literary contact. Vogel and Pound shared venues in Ethel Moorehead and Ernest Walsh's *This Quarter* and Charles Henri Ford's *Blues: A Magazine of New Rhythms*. Vogel became associated with the communist left and helped to organize a small literary journal, *Dynamo*. He was contributing editor to other little magazines like *Front* and *The Morada*. Vogel published three novels: *At Madame Bonnard's* (1935), *Man's Courage* (1938), and *Straw Hat* (1940). Perhaps because of Pound's tepidness as a patron, Vogel published a dismissive letter in the *New Masses*, targeting Pound and the Paris-based journal *transition* ("Literary Graveyards," October 1929). Vogel was solicited for a contribution to *Globe* by James Dunn. (For the Vogel–Pound correspondence, see C.

McWhirter, "'The Dean of Corpses': The Correspondence of Ezra Pound and Joseph Vogel," *Paideuma* 27:2–3 [Fall/Winter 1998], 197–225.)

Horace Jeremiah Voorhis (1901–84), American politician. Voorhis was Democratic representative for California. He served in Congress from 1936 until 1946, when he lost his seat to Republican Richard Nixon. Voorhis and Pound corresponded in the 1930s discussing reforming the Federal Reserve System, the national debt, and other economic issues. (For a brief summary of the correspondence and discussion, see Surette, *Pound in Purgatory*, pp. 131–5.)

Bruno Walter, born **Bruno Schlesinger** (1876–1962), German conductor. After studying at the Stern Conservatory of Berlin as a pianist, Walter turned to conducting. He debuted in 1894 and after that went to work under the composer Gustav Mahler at the Hamburg Opera. In 1933, Walter left Germany and settled in Austria. There he became active in organizing and conducting at the Salzburg Festivals. After the Anschluss with Germany in 1939, Walter left Austria for France and then the United States. He spent the rest of his career in Los Angeles. Pound had a strong dislike of Walter's conducting and musical interpretation. Writing of a performance during the 1936 Salzburg Festival in the *Delphian Quarterly* ("Money Verses Music," January 1936), he complained: "[W]hen Bruno Walter plays Mozart one has merely the dull rage at hearing what one believes Mozart to have been, being smeared over and reduced to the level of sausage and sauerkraut" (cf. Schafer, *Music*, p. 383).

H. G. Wells (1866–1946), British journalist, fiction writer, historian, and political activist. Pound met Wells during his early days in London. Wells was an intimate of two of Pound's close friends from that period, Violet Hunt and Rebecca West. Wells' vast literary output was in large part motivated by his interest in social and economic reforms. Even his works of science fiction, a literary form he played a large role in creating, could be seen as "thought experiments" in alternative historical and social realities. He published almost 100 books, including *The Time Machine* (1895), *The Invisible Man* (1897), *War of the Worlds* (1898), *Outline of History* (1920), and *Experiment in Autobiography* (1934).

Francois de Wendel (1874–1949), French industrial magnate.

Albert Richard Wetjen (1900–48), British-born American adventure story writer. Wetjen lived in Portland, Oregon, and later in San Francisco. He was a frequent contributor to the *Saturday Evening Post* in the late 1930s, and winner of an O. Henry citation in 1927 for his story "Command" in *Sea Stories*.

Luther Whiteman (?–?), American journalist and author. Whiteman wrote for the journal *New Democracy*. He was co-author of *Glory Roads: The Psychological State of California* (1936) with Samuel L. Lewis. This book dealt with economic reform movements in California in the 1930s.

Heinrich Albert Wieschhoff (1906–61), German anthropologist. Wieschhoff belonged to Frobenius' Forschungsinstitut für Kulturmorphologie specializing in African studies. Pound's contact with Wieschhoff was through his correspondence with **Douglas Clayton Fox,** an assistant at the Institüt. Before World War II, Wieschhoff left Germany for the United States and took a position at the University of Pennsylvania. Wieschhoff was interested in early economies and published an exhibition catalogue entitled *Primitive Money* for the University of Pennsylvania Museum of Anthropology and Archaeology (1945). Interested in contemporary African politics and policies as well, Wieschhoff became acquainted with Ralph Bunche. Later, Wieschhoff became an aide to the Secretary General of the United Nations, Dag Hammerskjöld. Wieschhoff was killed in the same plane crash in the Congo that took Hammerskjöld's life.

Clive Wigram (1873–1960), private secretary to King George V from 1931 to the king's death in 1936. He was assistant private secretary to the king from 1910 to 1931.

(Cecily) Ellen Wilkinson (1891–1947), British suffragist, member of Parliament, and government minister. Wilkinson was first elected to the House of Commons for the Labour Party in 1926. In that year, she earned her moniker "Red Ellen" for her vigorous support of labor in that year's General Strike. Wilkinson co-authored a book on the labor upheaval entitled *A Workers' History of the Great Strike* (1927). In 1929, she was appointed Parliamentary secretary to the minister of health by **Ramsay MacDonald.** However, she fought with MacDonald over various policy issues, and lost her seat in the 1931 general election. In 1935, she was re-elected to Parliament. In 1936, she joined with others to publish a leftist weekly journal called *Tribune*. Wilkinson opposed the rise of Fascism and Nazism on the Continent, arguing at the 1936 Labour Party Conference that Britain should give military aid to the anti-Franco Spanish Popular Front. She traveled to Spain in 1936 with **Clement Attlee** to survey the results of German air attacks and to give encouragement to the International Brigade fighting Franco.

William Carlos Williams (1883–1963), American poet, novelist, short story writer, critic, playwright, and physician.

Sir Arnold Talbot Wilson (1884–1940), British soldier, diplomat, member of Parliament, and author. After World War II, Lieutenant Colonel Wilson was administrator of Iraq from January 10, 1919 to October 1, 1919. In 1920, he became Britain's chief political resident of the Arabian (Persian) Gulf for Bahrain, Kuwait, Oman, Qatar, and the Trucial States. Wilson was the author of a number of books on the Middle East, including *Mesopotamia, 1917–1920; a Clash of Loyalties; a Personal and Historical Record* (1931), *Persia* (1932), and a biography of Sir Richard Burton (1937).

William E. Woodward (1874–1950), American historian and journalist. Woodward sat on several advisory boards involving business affairs during the Roosevelt administration. Pound references three books: *George Washington, the Image and the Man* (1926), *Meet General Grant* (1928), and *A New American History* (1936). Pound carried on a correspondence with Woodward from 1933 to 1938.

Alexander Woollcott (1887–1943), journalist, author, humorist, and radio broadcaster. Woollcott was author of the popular *While Rome Burns* (1934). The two writers attended Hamilton College, with Pound graduating in 1905 and Woollcott graduating in 1909. The two corresponded in early 1937. (See "Serious Character to Funny Man: Ezra Pound's Brief Correspondence with Alexander Woollcott," by C. McWhirter and Ramsay Muhly, *Paideuma*, 24:1: 107–16.)

Ken Yanagisawa (1889–1953), Japanese diplomat and poet. Yanagisawa pursued his passion for French literature at Tokyo University, and in 1924 he published *An Anthology of Modern French Poetry (Gendai Furansu shishû).* Katue Kitasono, in a letter of November 7, 1936, tells Pound that he has contacted "Mr. Ken Yanagisawa who is a powerful official of the department of Foreign Affairs, and he himself an intellectual and good poet" in order to put Pound in touch with the Japanese legation in Rome. Pound writes back to Kitasono (EP to KK, January 1, 1937) asking him to thank Yanagisawa for the letter he sent to Rome upon Pound's behalf. The contact resulted in Pound's meeting with Hajime Matsumiya, a councillor of the Japanese Embassy in Rome.

William Butler Yeats (1865–1939), Irish poet and playright. Pound established a close relationship with Yeats soon after his arrival in London. It was through Olivia Shakespear, the mother of his wife Dorothy, that Pound first met Yeats in 1909. The younger poet had a significant influence upon the older. During the winter seasons of 1913–16 they lived together at Stone Cottage in Sussex (see Longenback, *Stone Cottage*, for this period). The mutual impact of this time spent working together clearly shows in both poets' work. In 1928, Yeats moved to Rapallo where he was Pound's neighbor until Yeats' death in 1939. By this time the two had become somewhat estranged over Pound's increasing eccentricity and volatility when discussing his political and economic hobby horses.

Lin Yutang (born Lin Ho-lok, 1895–1976), Chinese author, translator, and philologist. Lin Yutang was born in Amoy, Fukien Province, China. He was educated in Shanghai, in the United States at Harvard University, and at the University of Leipzig where he received his doctorate in linguistics in 1923. Pound became aware of Lin Yutang through Vincent Starrett's article on the Chinese scholar in the first issue of *Globe* ("Chinese Man of Letters," March 1937, 16–19).

Paolo Zappa (1899–1957), administrative director of the Turin-based journal *La Stampa*. Pound was enthusiastic over a run of unsigned articles that Zappa published in *La Stampa* in 1932 and which were subsequently published in book form as *I mercanti di cannoni* (1932).

Ahmed Bey Zogu (1895–1961), King Zog I of Albania 1928–39. After years of attempted coups, Zog was overthrown by Italian forces.

Béla Zsolt (1895–1949), Hungarian journalist and novelist. Before World War I, Zsolt was a leader of the Hungarian "Decadent" avant-garde movement. During World War II, he was sent as forced labor to the Ukraine. Out of his experience, Zsolt wrote one of the first Holocaust memoirs, *Nine Suitcases* (1946–7).

Louis Zukofsky (1904–1978), American poet and critic. In 1927, Zukofsky submitted "Poem Beginning 'The'" to Pound for his journal *The Exile*. Pound was taken with the long poem, as was his wife Dorothy, especially the section entitled "Third Movement: *In Cat Minor*." Pound placed the poem in the third issue of *The Exile* (1928). During the 1930s Pound included Zukofsky's poetry in his *Profile* (1932) and *Active Anthology* (1933). In 1938 Pound dedicated *Guide to Kulchur* "To Louis Zukofsky and Basil Bunting strugglers in the desert." Zukofsky was a leading member of the "Objectivist" movement in poetry. The movement appeared in force in the February 1931 issue of *Poetry*. Besides Zukofsky's poetry and his essay "Sincerity and Objectification," the issue included poetry from George Oppen, Charles Reznikoff, William Carlos Williams, Basil Bunting, Kenneth Rexroth, and Robert McAlmon. This issue of *Poetry* formed the core of Zukofsky's *An "Objectivists" Anthology* (1932), which carried a dedication to Pound. About the time Pound and Zukofsky began to correspond, Zukofsky began his long poem "*A*" (1927–78).

SELECTED BIBLIOGRAPHY

Adams, Stephen J. and Tryphonopoulos, Demetres P. (eds), *The Ezra Pound Encyclopedia*, Westport, CT: Greenwood Press, 2005.

Ahamed, Liaquat, *Lords of Finance: The Bankers that Broke the World*, New York: Penguin, 2009.

Auden, W. H. and Isherwood, Christopher, *Journey to a War*, New York: Random House, 1939.

Baldwin, Neil, *Man Ray American Artist*, New York: Clarkson N. Potter, 1988.

Bowsworth, R. J. B., *Mussolini*, New York: Bloomsbury (USA), 2002.

Brooks, Van Wyck, *Fenollosa and his Circle; with Other Essays in Biography*, New York: Dutton, 1962.

Carpenter, Humphrey, *W. H. Auden: A Biography*, Boston: Houghton Mifflin Co., 1981.

Carpenter, Humphrey, *A Serious Character: The Life of Ezra Pound*, London: Faber & Faber, 1988.

Cheadle, Mary Paterson, *Ezra Pound's Confucian Translations*, Ann Arbor: University of Michigan Press, 1997.

Conover, Anne, *Olga Rudge & Ezra Pound*, New Haven, CT: Yale University Press, 2001.

Conquest, Robert, *The Great Terror: A Reassessment*, Oxford: Oxford University Press, 1990.

Davis, Earle, *Vision Fugitive: Ezra Pound and Economics*, Lawrence, KS: University of Kansas Press, 1968.

Ellmann, Richard, *James Joyce*, Oxford: Oxford University Press, [Revised Edition] 1983.

Fenollosa, Ernest, *Epochs of Chinese and Japanese Art, an Outline History of East Asiatic Design*, London: W. Heinemann, 1912.

Flory, W., *The American Ezra Pound*, New Haven: Yale University Press, 1989.

Forde, Victoria M., *Poetry of Basil Bunting*, Hexham: Bloodaxe Books, 1991.

Gallup, Donald, *Ezra Pound: A Bibliography*, Charlottesville: University of Virginia Press, 1965.

Gilbert, Stuart, *James Joyce's Ulysses: A Study*, New York: Vintage; [2nd Revised edition] (1952).

Gordon, Lyndall, *T. S. Eliot: An Imperfect Life*, New York: Norton, 1998.

Keene, Donald, *Emperor of Japan: Meiji and His World, 1852–1912*, New York: Columbia University Press, 2002.

Kodama, Sanhide, *American Poetry and Japanese Culture*, Hamden, CT: Archon Books, 1984.

Kodama, Sanhide, *Ezra Pound and Japan, Letters and Essays*, Reading Ridge, CT: Black Swan Books, 1987.

Kurth, Peter, *American Cassandra: The Life of Dorothy Thompson*, Boston: Little, Brown and Company, 1990.

Lan, Feng, *Ezra Pound and Confucianism: Remaking Humanism in the Face of Modernity*, Toronto; Buffalo: University of Toronto Press, 2005.

Longenbach, James, *Modernist Poetics of History: Pound, Eliot, and a Sense of the Past,* Princeton, NJ: Princeton University Press, 1987.

Longenbach, James, *Stone Cottage: Pound Yeats and Modernism*, Oxford: Oxford University Press, 1988.

Makin, Peter, *Pound's Cantos*, London: Allen & Unwin, 1985.

Mencken, H. L., *Letters of H.L. Mencken*, J. Forgue (ed.), Boston: Northeastern University Press, 1981.

Moody, A. David, *Ezra Pound: Poet. A Portrait of the Man and His Work, Volume II, The Epic Years 1921–1939*, Oxford: Oxford University Press, 2014.

Nylan, Michael and Wilson, Thomas, *Lives of Confucius: Civilization's Greatest Sage through the Ages*, New York: Doubleday, 2010.

Pound, Ezra, *Pound/Joyce: The Letters of Ezra Pound to James Joyce*, Forrest Read (ed.), New York: New Directions, 1967.

Pound, Ezra, *The Chinese Written Character as a Medium for Poetry*, San Francisco: City Lights Books, 1969.

Pound, Ezra, *Guide to Kulchur*, New York: New Directions, 1970.

Pound, Ezra, *Jefferson and/or Mussolini*, New York: Liveright, 1970.

Pound, Ezra, *The Selected Letters 1907–1941*, D. D. Paige (ed.), New York: New Directions, 1971.

Pound, Ezra, *Selected Prose, 1909–1965*, William Cookson (ed.), New York: New Directions, 1973.

Pound, Ezra, *Ezra Pound and Music: The Complete Criticism*, R. Murray Schafer (ed.), New York: New Directions, 1977.

Pound, Ezra, *Ezra Pound and Dorothy Shakespear: Their Letters, 1909–1914*, A. Walton Litz and Omar Pound (eds), New York: New Directions, 1984.

Pound, Ezra, *The Cantos*, New York: New Directions, 1986.

Pound, Ezra, *Selected Letters of Ezra Pound and Louis Zukofsky*, Barry Ahearn (ed.), New York: New Directions, 1987.

Pound, Ezra, *Pound/The Little Review*, Thomas L. Scot *et al* (eds) New York: New Directions, 1988.

Pound, Ezra, *The Letters of Ezra Pound to Alice Corbin Henderson*, Ira B. Nadel (ed.), Austin: University of Texas Press, 1993.

Pound, Ezra, *Ezra Pound and Senator Bronson Cutting: A Political Correspondence, 1930–1935*, Albuquerque: University of New Mexico Press, 1995.

Pound, Ezra, *Pound, Thayer, Watson, and* The Dial: *A Story in* Letters, Walter Sutton (ed.), Gainesville, FL: University Press of Florida, 1995.

Pound, Ezra, *Machine Art and Other Writings: The Lost Thought of the Italian Years*, Maria Luisa Ardizzone (ed.), Durham and London: Duke University Press, 1996.

Pound, Ezra, *Pound/Cummings: The Correspondence of Ezra Pound and E. E. Cummings*, Barry Ahearn (ed.), Ann Arbor: University of Michigan Press, 1996.

Pound, Ezra, *Ezra and Dorothy Pound: Letters in Captivity, 1945–1946*, Omar Pound and Robert Spoo (eds), Oxford: Oxford University Press, 1998.

Pound, Ezra, *The Correspondence of Ezra Pound and Senator William Borah*, Sarah C. Holmes (ed.); foreword by Daniel Pearlman, Chicago: University of Illinois Press, 2001.

Pound, Ezra, *Poems and Translations*, Richard Sieburth (ed.), New York: Library of America, 2003.

Pound, Ezra, *The Pisan Cantos*, Richard Sieburth (ed.), New York: New Directions, 2003.

Pound, Ezra and Fenollosa, Ernest, *The Classic Noh Theatre of Japan*, New York: New Directions, 1959.

Qian, Zhaoming (ed.), *Ezra Pound & China*, Ann Arbor: University of Michigan Press, 2003.

Qian, Zhaoming (ed.), *Ezra Pound's Chinese Friends: Stories in Letters*, Oxford: Oxford University Press, 2008.

de Rachewiltz, Mary, *Ezra Pound Father and Teacher: Discretions*, New York: New Directions, 1975.

Rainey, Lawrence S., *Ezra Pound and the Monument of History: Text, History, and the Malatesta Cantos*, Chicago, IL: University of Chicago Press, 1991.

Rainey, Lawrence, *Institutions of Modernism*, New Haven: Yale University Press, 1999.

Redman, Tim, *Ezra Pound and Italian Fascism*, Cambridge: Cambridge University Press, 1991.

Roussel, David, "The Letters of Langston Hughes and Ezra Pound" *in Ezra Pound and African-American Modernism*, Michael Coyle, (ed.), Orono, ME: National Poetry Foundation, 2010.

Schwartz, Delmore, *Letters of Delmore Schwartz*, Robert Phillips (ed.), Princeton, NJ: Ontario Review Press, 1984.

Sims, R. L., *Japanese Political History Since the Meiji Restoration, 1868–2000*, London: C. Hurst, 2001.

Skidelsky, Robert, *Oswald Mosley*, 3rd edn, London: Papermac, 1990.

Skidelsky, Robert, *John Maynard Keynes* (3 vols), London: Penguin Books: 1994–2002.

Solt, John, "The Hooking of Distant Antennae: Ez Po & Kit-Kat," in *Ezra Pound and Europe*, Richard Taylor and Claus Melchior (eds), Atlanta, GA: Rodopi, 1993.

Solt, John, *Shredding the Tapestry of Meaning: The Poetry and Poetics of Kitasono Katue (1902–1978)* (Harvard East Asian Monographs 178), Cambridge, MA: Harvard University Press, 1999.

Spence, Jonathan, *The Search for Modern China,* New York: W. W. Norton, 1990.

Stock, Noel, *The Life of Ezra Pound*, New York: Pantheon Books, 1970

Surette, Leon, *Pound in Purgatory: From Economic Radicalism to Anti-Semitism*, Urbana: University of Illinois Press, 1999.

Terrell, Carroll F., *A Companion to* The Cantos *of Ezra Pound*, Berkeley, CA: University of California Press, 1993.

Tryphonopoulos, Demetres P., "Letters" in *Ezra Pound in Context*, Ira Nadel (ed.), Cambridge: Cambridge University Press, 2010.

Vose, Clement E., Gorham Munson Papers on the American Social Credit Movement and *New Democracy*, Middletown, CT: Wesleyan University Archives, 1977.

Watson, Steven, *Strange Bedfellows: The First American Avant-garde*, New York, NY: Abbeville Press, 1991.

Wilhelm, James J., *Ezra Pound: The Tragic Years, 1925-1972*, Pennsylvania: Pennsylvania State University Press, 1994.

Wilson, Edmund, *Axel's Castle: A Study in the Imaginative Literature of 1870–1930*, New York: Collier Books, 1991.

Womersley, David, "Introduction," in Edward Gibbon, *The History of the Decline and Fall of the Roman Empire* (Volume 1), David Womersley (ed.), London: Penguin Books, 1995.

Ziegler, Philip, *King Edward VIII: A Biography*, New York: Knopf, 1991.

INDEX